THE COMPLETE PRIVATE PILOT

A TEXT BOOK WITH THE WHOLE STORY ON BECOMING A PILOT

by
Robert E. Gardner

asa PUBLICATIONS / SEATTLE, WA

THE COMPLETE PRIVATE PILOT

Copyright© 1985 by ASA, Inc.

PRINTED IN THE UNITED STATES OF AMERICA

ISBN 0-940732-39-4

asa PUBLICATIONS / 6001 6TH SOUTH / SEATTLE, WA 98108

TABLE OF CONTENTS

INTRODUCTION

by Richard L. Taylor

A new aviation book — one that plows new ground, one that develops material never before considered — is pretty hard to come by. And until there are some radical changes in the types of aircraft we fly and the techniques necessary to fly them, the situation is quite likely to stay that way.

But there are always better, if not "new," ways to communicate aviation information . . . that's what Bob Gardner has accomplished with The Complete Private Pilot.

A writer embarking on the task of creating a fundamental aviation text is faced with a formidable challenge; if prospective pilots are to reap the benefits of his work, the writing must be at once very readable and very comprehensive. The Complete Private Pilot does both of those in spades, as Bob Gardner reaches into his own aeronautical experience and brings to the reader a clear exposition of the knowledge required by the budding private pilot.

It's not *all* here — you'll continue learning (we hope!) long after your initial study of regulations, weather, navigation, and so on — but The Complete Private Pilot is a great way to get started.

Your author has met the challenge well. The Complete Private Pilot is indeed readable, comprehensive, and perhaps more important than those, it's a book which will lead you to a greater *understanding* of flying's fundamentals.

I've always contended that a smart pilot is a *safe* pilot . . . you are to be commended for your choice of The Complete Private Pilot as a bedrock book in your aviation library.

PROLOGUE

ASA Publications has earned a worldwide reputation in aviation education with their test preparation books and cassette courses. That reputation for excellence is based in part on ASA's policy of going beyond test requirements into in-depth coverage of subject material. This book continues this policy by covering all of the subjects you can expect to be questioned on in the Private Pilot written examination but going beyond the test questions for a full understanding of each subject.

Aviation has a language of its own and you want to speak it fluently, so we have provided a glossary with a pronunciation guide. Terms in **bold print** in the text are listed in the glossary. Many aviation terms are pronounceable acronyms (UNICOM, VASI), and others are just initials (FAA, ETA), and you want to know which is which. Each chapter will include review questions so that you can test your understanding of the material covered in that chapter. The questions are taken from the Private Pilot Test Book, FAA-T-8080-1. The ASA Private Pilot Workbook exercises are intended to give you a further insight into the subjects.

ASA Publications has always met the needs of pilots preparing for written examinations by going beyond "test preparation" into background information, and that philosophy is continued in this book. When you have completed this book and the accompanying workbook exercises you will be ready for the FAA written examination *and* the oral examination for your Private Pilot checkride.

Good luck!

CREDITS

Original Artwork: . . . . **Dick Bringloe and Don Szymanski**

Photos Courtesy of:

Robert E. Gardner . . . . . Figures 2-10, 2-26, 3-9, 4-1, 7-8, 7-9, 7-10
7-11, 7-12, 7-13, 7-14, 7-15, 10-10

NASA . . . . Figures 2-8, 2-9, 2-36, 10-14

Rutan Aircraft Company . . . . Figure 2-24

Sigma-Tek Aircraft Instruments . . . . Figures 3-6, 4-5, 4-9, 4-12

Cessna Aircraft . . . . Figures 3-8, 3-10, 3-11, 4-17

American Avionics . . . . Figures 4-13, 4-18, 4-19, 8-5

Safe Flight . . . . Figure 4-7

Henry Geijbeek . . . . Figure 8-1

NARCO . . . . Figures 8-14, 8-15, 8-22, 9-2, 9-8

ARNAV . . . . Figure 8-24

Allied-Bendix . . . . Figure 11-30

3-M StormScope Weather Mapping System . . . . Figure 11-31

Washington State Aeronautics Commission . . . . . . Figures
16-3, 16-4, 16-5

PREFACE

Your mind is like a computer's memory bank. When you have a new experience or sensation, your mind compares it to what is in storage and either modifies what has been stored or adds the new data to the memory bank. Each flight will add new experiences and soon your mind will say, "That's not new — I've done this before!", and soon flying high above the mountains or gliding quietly into a grass strip will become a part of you. This book is planned to build your aviation knowledge in the same way.

Chapters One and Two will familiarize you with your airplane and the forces you will control to make it fly safely and efficiently. The airplane engine and the instruments you use to check its operation are discussed in Chapter Three, followed by a discussion of how flight instruments operate in Chapter Four. You must know how to safely load your airplane and predict its performance under varying conditions — Chapters Five and Six will cover those areas. The bricks and mortar of navigation is pilotage — Chapter Seven tells you how. Electronics — radio navigation and communication are the subjects of Chapters Eight and Nine. In Chapter Ten you will learn how to operate your airplane at both large airports with towers and jet traffic and small country airports where you may be the only pilot for miles around.

The mysteries of weather won't be so mysterious after you read Chapter Eleven to learn how weather information is gathered and interpreted. Chapter Twelve tells you which publications you should use to look up important information about flying in general and your trip in particular, and Chapter Thirteen warns of physiological effects of flight on your body. Chapters 14 and 15 explore regulation: the airspace system which we all must understand and the regulations we all must adhere to. Winding it all up is a VFR cross-country flight which you will plan and fly, using all of the information and knowledge you will acquire as you read the book.

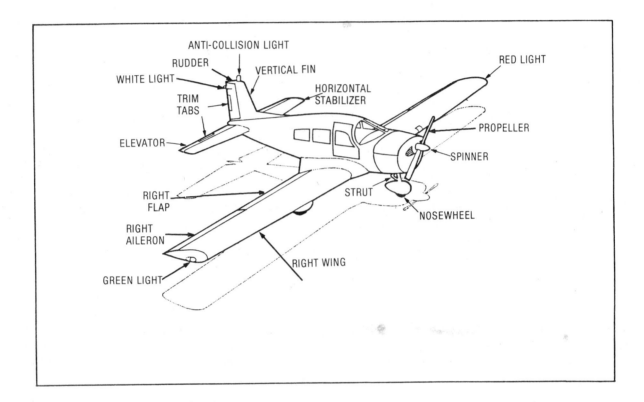

In this book we are going to assume that your training airplane is all-metal, has one engine, a fixed-pitch propeller, and a non-retractable landing gear. A stroll along the ramp of your hometown airport will show you that there are many variables, however, and you may want to compare features on other airplanes with the one you fly. Here are some things to look for:

FUSELAGE CONSTRUCTION

The fuselages of almost all of the airplanes you see will be of aluminum construction with internal strengthening members. A close look will show that on some models more attention has been paid to reducing drag caused by rivet heads and other protrusions. Looking at non-metal airplanes will take you to both the past and the future. Fabric-covered airplanes with tubing structures (wood-framed airplanes are really classics!) are lovingly restored and flown by proud owners, but no less proud are the pilots of modern composite aircraft, formed of fiberglass or similar materials which offer great strength and minimal drag.

WINGS — Almost all modern airplanes have a single wing, mounted either above or below the fuselage. Most, but not all, high wing airplanes have supporting struts. Low wing and strutless high wing airplanes are cantilevered: the internal structure is designed to support the load and there are no struts.

Wing fuel tanks are either "wet wings" with the wing structure serving as the fuel container, or are rubber bladders contained within the wing.

AILERONS — You won't find many airplanes that do not have ailerons, which are movable control surfaces at the outer trailing edge of the wings. Ailerons are used to bank the airplane. A control wheel or stick at the pilot station is moved in the direction of bank desired, and the ailerons are deflected through a system of cables, pulleys, and bellcranks or pushrods. When no control force is exerted, the ailerons are held flush with the wing surface by the airstream.

FLAPS — The hinged portions of the trailing edges of the wings near the fuselage are called flaps, and are normally used to steepen the glide angle without increasing airspeed. As you walk along the ramp you will see many different types of flaps, some that simply hinge down and others that extend down and backward. Older airplanes may not have any flaps at all.

EMPENNAGE — The horizontal stabilizer, the rudder, the vertical fin, the elevator, or any combination thereof is referred to by pilots as the airplane's empennage or "tail feathers". These surfaces allow the pilot to change the airplane's attitude in relation to the horizon by moving the nose up and down, or left and right, as seen by the pilot. There may be a fixed horizontal stabilizer with a movable elevator, or the whole horizontal assembly may be movable. Fore-and-aft movement of the control wheel or stick is transmitted by cables and pulleys to these control surfaces, and left-right movement is controlled by the rudder, which is mounted at the rear of the vertical fin. The pilot depresses the rudder pedal in the desired direction of nose movement and a cable system moves the control surface. You will see V-tails, T-tails, and straight tails, and maybe a home-built airplane with no horizontal surfaces mounted on the tail.

LANDING GEAR — The two main landing wheels and their supporting structure are designed to withstand landing loads and to support the airplane on the ground. A third, smaller wheel mounted either forward (tricycle) or aft (conventional) is for ground steering control only. Nosewheels are usually close to or a part of the engine mount and are definitely not designed to absorb landing loads. (Your instructor will devote a lot of training time to making sure that you do not land on the nose wheel!)

The shiny cylinders on nose wheels and some main landing gear are called struts. They absorb the shock of landing and are filled with air and oil, just like your car's shock absorbers. When a strut is "flat" there is no cushioning effect and vibrations are transmitted to the entire airframe. You will see some airplanes which use a spring steel assembly on the main landing gear instead of a strut.

Wheel pants, or fairings, reduce aerodynamic drag and add a knot or two to airspeed. Landing gear which retracts into the wing or fuselage adds considerably to cruise speed.

Almost all airplanes use disc brakes on the main landing gear, and you can see the discs if there are no wheel pants. Checking brake condition is considerably easier to do on airplanes than it is on cars. If the nose wheel is not steerable with the rudder pedals and swivels freely, steering is accomplished by tapping the brake lightly on the side toward the turn.

PROPELLER — The propellers you see may be either fixed or variable in pitch, or blade angle. You will probably see some amphibians with pusher-type propellers, but most are mounted up front and pull the airplane through the air. The conical spinner is not only decorative but serves to direct air into the cooling air intakes.

ENGINE — Modern airplanes have four- or six-cylinder flat opposed engines: when you open the cowling you will see that the cylinders are on opposite sides of the engine, and that the flat profile allows maximum aerodynamic streamlining of the cowling. As you walk along the ramp you may see an older airplane with a radial engine, its cylinders arranged in a "star" pattern.

LIGHTS — The lighting system on a modern airplane consists of position lights on the wingtips and tail (red on the left, green on the right, and white on the tail), an anticollision light system which may be either red or white (or both), and one or more landing lights. Many airplanes also have bright flashing strobe lights to increases the chances of being seen during both day and night flights.

The subject of **aerodynamics** deals with the forces acting on bodies in motion through the air; in fact, "aerodyne" means an aircraft deriving lift from its motion through the air. To oversimplify, an airplane flies because the pilot causes it to accelerate down the runway until its wings develop a lifting force greater than its weight, and it lands because the pilot causes the lifting force to be less than its weight. In flight, the pilot controls the magnitude and direction of lift through use of the flight controls.

To make the airplane go where you want it to go and do what you want it to do, you use the flight controls as tools and, just like any artisan, you have to know what your tools are capable of and how they are used.

As a pilot, you will be working with the forces of lift, drag, thrust, and weight. Of these, lift is the force that allows you to move in three dimensions. While it is true that *anything* can be made to "fly" if enough power is applied, an airplane features **airfoils** — shapes specifically designed to develop lift. The amount of lift generated by an airfoil is a function of the area of the lifting surface, the density of the air, the velocity of the airflow over the lifting surface, and the coefficient of lift. This is how these elements are related:

Lift = Coefficient of lift x area x velocity^2 x density/2

COEFFICIENT OF LIFT

Don't be intimidated by the words "coefficient of lift" — they apply to physical relationships that are easy to visualize. Before investigating just what coefficient of lift means, or how the other factors affect lift development, you should understand how an airfoil develops

lift. Figure 2-1 shows a fluid (illustrated as ping-pong balls) moving through a tube with a restriction in it. If 1,000 units of fluid enter one end of the tube each second, and 1,000 units leave the tube each second, and there is not enough room at the restriction for 1,000 units of fluid to pass, something clearly has to change at the restriction. That "something" is velocity — fewer units must travel at a higher velocity if 1,000 units per second are going to pass the restriction.

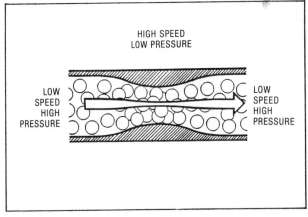

Figure 2-1. Bernoulli Tube

As the fluid moves through the tube, its total energy consists of forward movement **(kinetic energy)** and the static force it exerts against the walls of the tube. At the restriction, the energy of forward movement increases and, since total energy can neither increase nor decrease within the system, the static pressure has to decrease. A scientist named Daniel Bernoulli discovered this effect: when a fluid is accelerated the pressure it exerts is reduced. Bernoulli's Theorem accounts for most of the lift developed by an airfoil. You might consider an airfoil as a device designed to accelerate airflow.

If you are having difficulty relating tubes and fluids to airplane wings, figure 2-2 shows an airfoil with air (a fluid) flowing over it, and with pressure distribution attributable to Bernoulli indicated. Note that at points where airflow is slowest, the pressure is greatest; this is the reverse application of Bernoulli's Theorem.

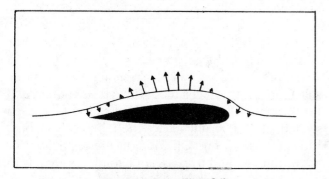

Figure 2-2. Bernoulli Airfoil

A second contributor to total lift is Newton's Third Law: for every action there is an equal and opposite reaction. As the airfoil moves through the air it pushes the air downward and, in accordance with Newton's Law, the air exerts an equal upward force. Because of differences in wing design and in operating conditions, it is impossible to say what percentage of total lift can be attributed to Bernoulli or to Newton at any time. In figure 2-3, the dashed lines represent lift due to pressure difference and the solid lines indicate lift due to Newton's Law.

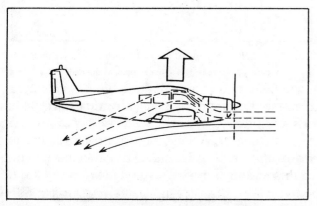

Figure 2-3. Sources of Lift

Part of the explanation of coefficient of lift has to do with the curvature, or camber, of the upper surface of the wing. A large curve, or **camber**, means greater

acceleration of the air over the upper surface. Oncoming free air is drawn upward toward the low pressure area on top of the wing, accelerates over the curvature, and flows off the trailing edge (downwash). Most general aviation airplanes change camber and increase lift by moving the trailing edge up or down with control surfaces called ailerons and flaps. Changing lift development by changing wing camber is largely the province of the designer, and is only partially under the control of the pilot. **Angle of incidence**, *which is defined as the angle at which the wing is fastened to the fuselage*, is set by the designer at 1° to 3° in relation to the longitudinal axis and is beyond the control of the pilot.

Wing design is one element of the coefficient of lift, and the other is **angle of attack** — over which the pilot has direct control. An imaginary line drawn from the leading edge of the wing to the trailing edge is called the chord line, and *the angle between the chord line and the relative wind is called the angle of attack* (figure 2-4). If relative wind is an unfamiliar term, consider this: you are sitting in a convertible at a stop light with the wind blowing on the left side of your face — the wind that you feel is the true wind. When the light changes, and the car accelerates, the wind strikes you directly in the face — that is the relative wind, caused by motion.

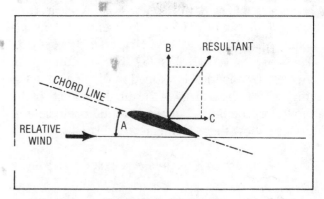

Figure 2-4. Angle of Attack

In flight, *the relative wind is parallel and opposite to the flight path*. Figure 2-5 shows this relationship in level flight, climbing, and descending. To the wing of a military jet climbing almost vertically, the relative wind is coming straight down, while to the wing of an aerobatic airplane completing a loop, the relative wind

Angle of Attack

is coming straight up. More importantly, when a pilot attempts to maintain altitude by using angle of attack alone, without adding power, the relative wind strikes the bottom of the wing as shown in the illustration. This is called mushing flight (figure 2-6) and, if the pilot does not lower the nose to decrease the angle of attack, an aerodynamic stall is imminent.

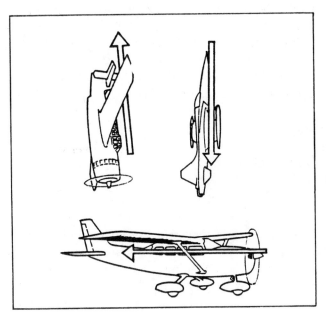

Figure 2-5. Relative Wind is Opposite to Flight Path

Figure 2-6, Mushing Flight

Lift developed by pressure difference (Bernoulli lift) depends on a smooth flow of air over the upper surface of the wing. As angle of attack is increased (figure 2-7), the air being drawn over the top surface of the wing begins to tear away from the wing surface at the trailing edge, causing loss of lift. At high angles of attack the airflow near the trailing edge of the wing even reverses and begins to flow forward! Aerodynamicists devote considerable time and effort to designing wings that maintain a layer of smoothly flowing air over the maximum area of wing surface.

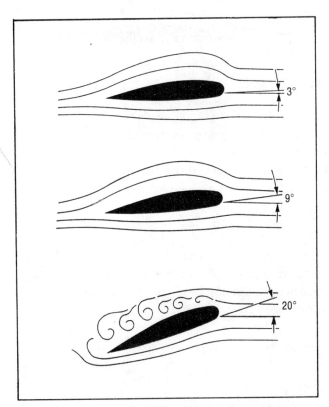

Figure 2-7. Increasing Angle of Attack to the Stall Point

A simple explanation of the aerodynamic stall is that the angle of attack can be increased until the oncoming air is unable to make the sharp turn necessary to follow the wing's surface, and begins to separate from it at the trailing edge. The separation point moves forward on the wing as the angle of attack is increased. The designer controls the progression of this process by twisting the wing slightly from the wing roots to the tips so that the inner sections of the wing lose lift first and the outer sections (where the ailerons are located), continue to develop lift until the wing is fully stalled.

The NASA photographs (figures 2-8 and 2-9) show how increasing the angle of attack causes the area of disturbed airflow to expand until total loss of lift occurs. With an angle of attack of 16°, there is still smooth airflow at the outer ends of the wings, while the inner sections are covered with disturbed airflow.

Figure 2-8. NASA Photo — 16° Angle of Attack (Modified Wing)

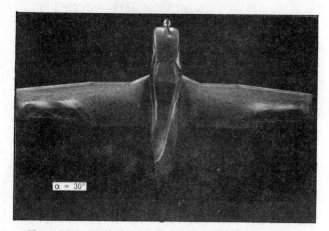

Figure 2-9. NASA Photo — 30° Angle of Attack (Modified Wing)

The airflow in the vicinity of the ailerons on this experimental airfoil remains attached to the wing surface and the "pilot" of this wind-tunnel model would retain some roll control. The same wing at an angle of attack of 30° is fully stalled, with no smooth airflow remaining on the wing surface. Notice that air flowing through the gap between the aileron and the wing provides a small area of smooth airflow over the aileron itself. A normal (unmodified) wing stalls at an angle of attack of 18°-20°.

To ensure that the wing root stalls first, some manufacturers install "stall strips" on the leading edge of the wing near the root. Some airplanes have slots in the leading edge near the wingtip which direct high pressure air from beneath the wing to the upper surface and ailerons, and thus retain controllability at high angles of attack (figure 2-10). Short takeoff and landing (STOL) airplanes usually have some type of device on the leading edge of the wing which extends only at high angles of attack and which channel airflow in the same manner as the fixed slot in the illustration. Large jet aircraft also use leading edge lift devices.

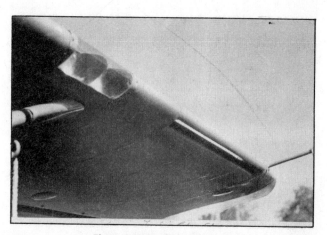

Figure 2-10. Leading Edge Slots

Figure 2-7 also shows that the lift developed by the wing increases as angle of attack increases, until the angle of attack reaches a critical value (usually 18° - 20°) beyond which the air no longer flows smoothly over the wing surface and the wing stalls. The *only* thing that stalls the wing is exceeding the critical angle of attack. In training, most of your stall practice will be at slow speeds, with the nose of the airplane above the horizon, but you must realize that *the wing can be stalled at any airspeed and in any attitude*. The lift developed by the wing must support the weight of the airplane, and the pilot controls lift by varying the angle of attack. If the weight being supported by the wing is increased, either by overloading the airplane or by adding "G" (gravity) forces while maneuvering, the angle of attack must be increased to provide the necessary lift.

There is always the danger of exceeding the critical angle of attack and stalling the wing.

VELOCITY

Velocity of airflow over the lifting surface plays a major role in lift development. The effect of airspeed is dramatically evident because lift varies as the square of the airspeed: double the airspeed and the lift quadruples; cut the airspeed in half and the lift drops to 25 percent of the former value. Your control of lift through airspeed will play a major role in your ability to fly efficiently — flying "by the numbers" insures that you always have the proper angle of attack for the condition of flight (figure 2-11).

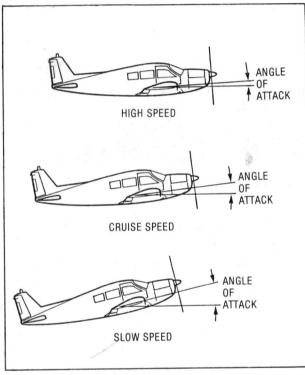

HIGH SPEED

CRUISE SPEED

SLOW SPEED

Figure 2-11. Angles of Attack Vs. Attitude and Speed

AREA

The pilot has very little control over the area of the lifting surface except when the flaps are designed to add area. The wing area of a jet airliner increases considerably as it approaches the runway, as its flaps are extended downward and backward. A wing with a large surface area is desirable at low speeds but would add unacceptable amounts of drag due to skin friction at high speeds.

AIR DENSITY

Changes in air density affect the creation of lift because it takes molecules of air flowing over the lifting surface to create lift, and as you climb there are fewer air molecules. High altitude means less lift, unless angle of attack or airspeed or both are increased. Water vapor in the air (high relative humidity) means that fewer air molecules are available for lift generation (it takes air, not water, to create lift), so high moisture content also means less lift. Air density decreased by either high altitude or high moisture content will also decrease propeller efficiency (the propeller is an airfoil), and will decrease the power output of the engine which needs air, not moisture, to burn fuel efficiently. It isn't necessary to climb to high altitudes to encounter reductions in air density, because air (a gas) expands when heated. At sea level on a hot day in July there will be fewer air molecules available to develop lift.

DRAG

Lift is the first tool you will learn to control and use. The second tool you must understand is drag. There are two types of drag for you to be concerned about: **parasite drag** and **induced drag**. Parasite drag is largely beyond the control of the pilot because it comes from such things as struts, fixed landing gear, rivet heads, antennas, and the friction of air passing along the skin of the airplane. Engine cooling drag is 20% of total parasite drag — those air inlets behind the propeller channel a tremendous volume of air over and around the engine. Parasite drag increases as the square of the speed: double the airspeed and the drag quadruples. That is what limits top speed — when all of the available horsepower is being used to overcome drag, you can't go any faster. Figure 2-12 shows how parasite and induced drag vary with airspeed and how each contributes to total drag.

Induced drag is the inevitable result of lift development. You know how Bernoulli's and Newton's effects in combination provide high pressure on the bottom of the wing and low pressure on the top — these forces are resolved at the wingtip as the high pressure air corkscrews up and around the wingtip toward the low pressure area. This meeting of high and

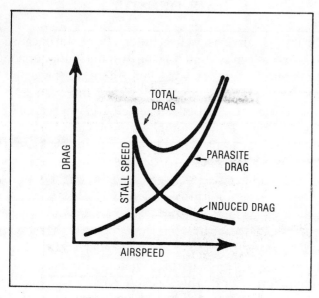

Figure 2-12. Drag and Speed Graph

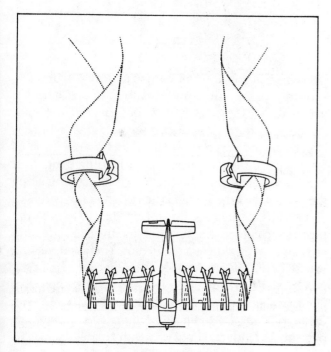

Figure 2-13. Wingtip Vortices

low pressure air, with the rotational velocity imparted to the air, creates induced drag (figure 2-13).

At large angles of attack, with great pressure differences, induced drag is a considerable force; however, as airspeed increases and angle of attack is reduced induced drag becomes less of a factor. Every time that you change the angle of attack, you change the induced drag. Induced drag varies inversely as the square of the airspeed. You will see many modern airplanes with winglets, devices which reduce induced drag by controlling the mixing of high and low pressure air at the tip of a lifting surface, and anything that reduces total drag adds to efficiency. Most recent design advances have been accomplished through drag reduction programs, because increasing performance through the addition of sheer horsepower has reached a practical limit.

THRUST

Your third tool will be the thrust developed by the propeller as it is rotated by the engine and pulls the airplane through the air. Remember, the propeller is an airfoil, and all of the relationships of velocity, air density, and angle of attack apply. During the takeoff roll, thrust is at its maximum, and total drag is at a minimum. This imbalance of forces allows the airplane to accelerate. As airflow over the wing increases, lift begins to develop, and when the recommended takeoff speed has been attained the pilot helps the process by increasing the angle of attack. The airplane then becomes airborne (accelerates upward) as lift exceeds weight. The contribution of parasite drag, which increases with speed, will cause total drag to equal total thrust, and as airspeed stabilizes lift will equal weight. *In any steady state flight condition, whether climbing, descending, or flying straight and level, the forces of lift and weight are equal and the forces of thrust and drag are equal* (figure 2-14).

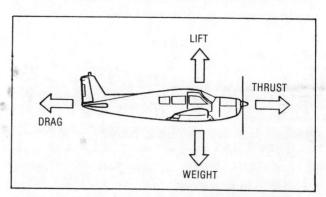

Figure 2-14. Relationship of Forces Acting on an Airplane

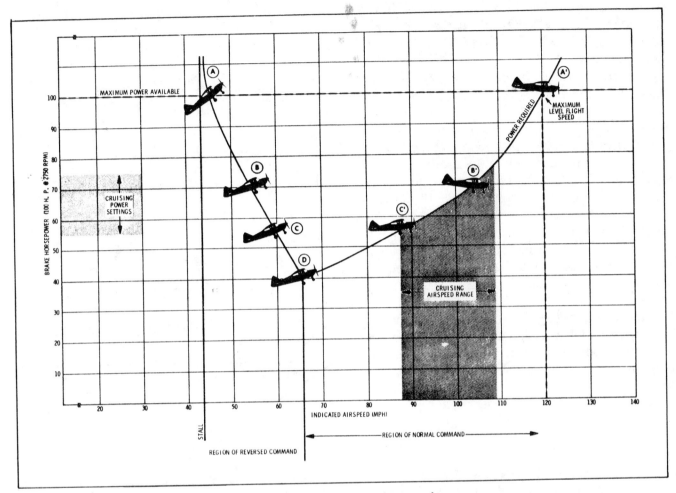

Figure 2-15. Region of Reversed Command

Adding thrust will cause the airplane to accelerate (just as reducing power will cause it to decelerate) until the thrust/drag relationship has equalized and the airplane is stable at a new airspeed. You control the airplane's flight path by adjusting its attitude in relation to the horizon, and by changing thrust with the throttle. Attitude plus power equals performance.

REGION OF REVERSED COMMAND

If you haven't heard the terms "hanging on the prop" or "behind the power curve" yet, you will hear them from your instructor when you start work on short field takeoffs and landings. Induced drag is greatest at high angles of attack, and it is possible for you to fly at such an extreme angle of attack that it takes all of the available power just to equal induced drag and maintain altitude! Figure 2-15 shows seven airplanes, with the airspeed and power being used by each. Airplane D is operating at the speed and power setting for best endurance — using the least power to maintain altitude with an airspeed of 40 miles per hour. The airplanes to the right of airplane D (A, B, and C) are operating normally: with increased power each airplane achieves a higher airspeed. Look to the left of airplane D, however. Airplane C is using 15 more horsepower than airplane D but is going slower!

Look at airplane B — using almost twice as much power as airplane D to fly 10 knots slower. Finally, look at poor airplane A. That is "hanging on the prop!" Airplane A is using every available ounce of power to maintain altitude while flying at only 47 miles per hour.

Airplanes A, B, and C are all operating in the **region of reversed command** (behind the power curve), where it takes more power to fly more slowly. That's just the reverse of the normal power and airspeed relationship, and that's where the "region of reversed command" got its name.

You can tell by looking at the illustration that the pilots of airplanes A, B, and C probably can't see over the noses of their airplanes, and that is a good warning that speed is dangerously slow (additionally, the airspeed indicator is least accurate at high angles of attack!). If the pilot of an airplane operating in the region of reversed command reduces power or suddenly retracts the flaps, the only means of regaining the lost lift is to lower the nose, and there may not be enough altitude available for that.

You, the pilot, control both lift *and* drag. If you increase drag by operating at a high angle of attack you must add thrust (power) to overcome that drag, and you only have so much power available. Keep some power in reserve — don't operate at high angles of attack which put you behind the power curve.

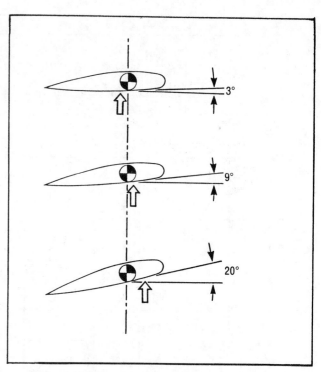

Figure 2-16. Movement of Center of Pressure with Changes in Angle of Attack

CENTER OF PRESSURE VS CENTER OF GRAVITY

All of the lift forces developed by the wing can be said to be concentrated in a single point called the **center of lift**, or the center of pressure, which you can visualize as a force pushing up on the bottom of the wing (the arrow in figure 2-16). The center of pressure moves as the angle of attack changes. When you increase the angle of attack, the center of pressure moves forward on the bottom of the wing, and it moves aft as you decrease the angle of attack. If the airplane is properly loaded, the center of pressure will always be behind the **center of gravity.** If the center of pressure moves forward of the center of gravity, the nose of the airplane will pitch uncontrollably upward. With the center of pressure aft of the center of gravity, the tendency is for the airplane to be nose heavy. The designer counteracts this by having the horizontal stabilizer at a negative angle of attack, which creates a downward pressure at the tail. Chapter 5 discusses airplane loading in more detail.

AXES OF CONTROL

You control the airplane around three axes of rotation: lateral, longitudinal, and vertical. All three pass through the center of gravity (note the CG symbols in figure 2-17. The lateral axis of your airplane extends from wingtip to wingtip, and you control the pitch (nose up-nose down) attitude of the airplane by use of the elevator control. As you apply back pressure to the control wheel (or yoke) the elevator deflects upward and the air passing over it pushes the tail down.

You have effectively increased the camber or curvature of the horizontal stabilizer/elevator, and have developed a downward force. In the cockpit, you see this as the nose rising in relation to the horizon. Relaxing the back pressure, or exerting forward pressure, will lower the nose by reducing the downward force.

The throttle also contributes to control around the lateral axis: as you add throttle, the increased air flow

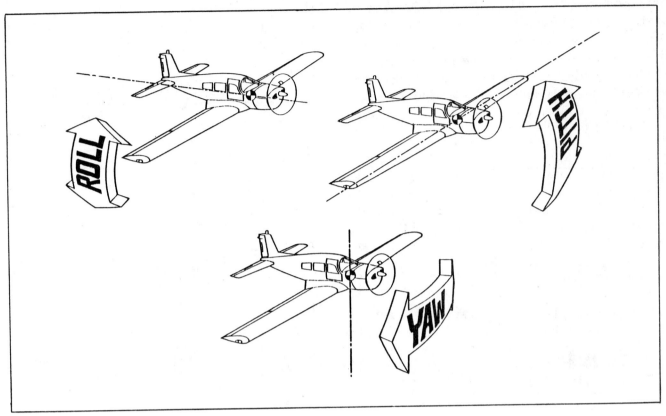

Figure 2-17. Axes of Control Around the Center of Gravity

from the propeller will push the tail down as it passes over the elevator ("blowing the tail down"). A power reduction will result in less downward pressure on the elevator, and the nose will move below the horizon (figure 2-19). This is a built-in safety factor, insuring that the angle of attack will be reduced and the airplane will maintain flying speed if power is suddenly reduced.

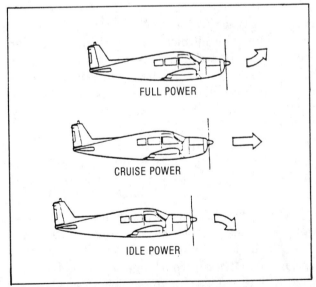

Figure 2-19. Effect of Throttle on Attitude

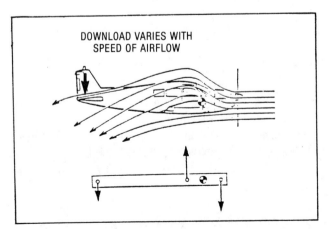

Figure 2-18. Downforce on Tail Effects Center of Gravity

You control the airplane around the longitudinal, or roll, axis (which extends from nose to tail) with the ailerons, and the resultant movement is called "banking". Deflecting an aileron downward increases both the angle of attack and the camber of that portion of the wing, and the increased lift that results raises the wing. At the same time, the aileron on the other wing is being deflected upward, decreasing both angle of attack and camber and reducing the lift of that wing. Thus one wing rises, the other lowers, and the airplane banks (figure 2-20).

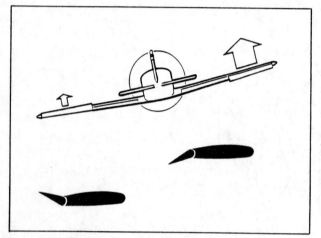

Figure 2-20. Ailerons are Used for Roll Control

When you deflect one aileron down into the windstream, the other aileron "hides" behind the curvature of the wing. The wing on the side of the down aileron is dragged backward, which slows the turn. The slowing effect of the down aileron is called adverse aileron drag, and is overcome by the rudder. Designers have overcome this imbalance in some cases by equalizing the drag caused by both ailerons.

The rudder controls the airplane around the vertical, or yaw, axis. You use the rudder to offset any force which attempts to move the nose of the airplane from side to side (like adverse aileron drag). The rudder is a movable surface attached to the rear of the vertical fin which changes the camber and angle of attack and varies the lift force being exerted on either side of the tail surfaces. Because of the long lever arm between the cockpit and the tail surfaces, a very small rudder movement is seen as a large nose movement.

In figure 2-21, a large yawing force to the right caused by a crosswind on takeoff or landing is offset by a small force applied to the rudder. Some airplanes are called

"short coupled" because the tail is so close to the cockpit that very large rudder inputs are required for directional control, especially at low speeds.

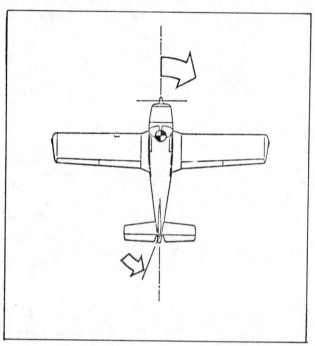

Figure 2-21. Small Rudder Deflection Offsets
Large Yawing Tendency

CONTROL EFFECTS AND STABILITY

The three axes of control pass through the center of gravity. How the designer has related the centers of lift or pressure to the center of gravity affects the stability of the airplane.

Your airplane is designed to be stable around the yaw (vertical) axis by placing the tail surfaces away from the center of gravity. If you are in straight and level flight and depress the right rudder pedal, the nose will swing to the right, but will return very quickly to the original position when pressure is released. This is called "streamlining" — if no pressure is exerted on a control surface it will align itself with the airstream. (Do this experiment without passengers on board; it's unsettling for those in the back seat!)

Stability around the longitudinal axis is provided by dihedral, the upward slant of the wings from their roots to the wingtips (figure 2-22). If the airplane is disturbed from straight and level flight by a wing being lowered, the descending wing will be at a greater angle of attack than the rising wing and the resulting increase in lift on the lowered wing will result in the wings leveling themselves. This built-in levelling effect makes small bank angles more difficult to sustain than larger bank angles. Almost all airplanes have good short-term lateral stability but poor long term lateral stability: in the absence of an autopilot don't expect hands-off, wings-level flight for long periods of time.

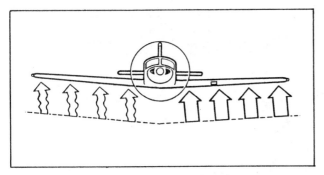

Figure 2-22. Effect of Dihedral

Stability around the lateral (pitch) axis is provided by the relationship between the center of gravity and the downward force on the horizontal stabilizer (figure 2-23). If you disturb the airplane from straight-and-level by pulling back slightly on the control yoke and then releasing it, the airplane will climb briefly until airflow over the horizontal stabilizer diminishes, and then the reduced download on the stabilizer will allow the nose to drop below the horizon. The airspeed will then increase (momentarily) and the increasing download on the horizontal stabilizer created by the added airflow will raise the nose above the horizon. These oscillations will gradually diminish in amplitude until the airplane regains level flight.

The designer provides this stability when establishing the permissible limits of center of gravity movement. For every pitch attitude there is a power setting that creates just enough download on the horizontal stabilizer for the airplane to maintain level flight; an increase in power will cause the nose to pitch up, the speed to decrease, and the airplane to climb, and a reduction in power will have the opposite effect. Airplanes with the horizontal stabilizer mounted high on the vertical fin

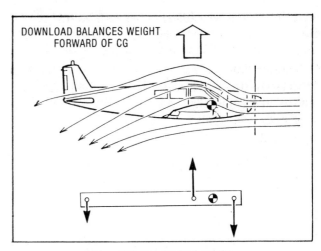

Figure 2-23. Longitudinal Stability

(T-tails) get little or no control effect from power changes because the control surface is above the propeller's discharge air (propwash). T-tailed airplanes (and all jets) must derive pitch control force solely from the relative wind.

An aerodynamic surface from the early days of flight is reappearing on modern aircraft. A canard (figure 2-24) is a lifting surface mounted forward of the center of gravity which looks like a small wing. It has a slightly

Figure 2-24. Canard

greater angle of attack than the main wing and thus will stall before the main wing. The lift developed by the canard is forward of the center of gravity, eliminating the need for a horizontal stabilizer. With the drag of the horizontal stabilizer and any elevator deflection eliminated, canards are faster and more fuel efficient than conventional airplanes.

TRIMMING CONTROL SURFACES

Control surfaces are provided with trim tabs (figure 2-25) so that the pilot can maintain a desired control position without exerting constant pressure.

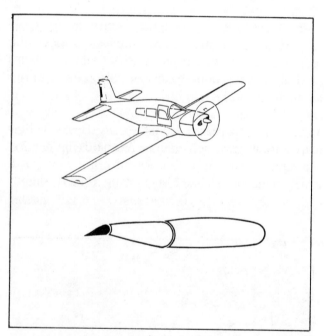

Figure 2-25. Trim Tabs

Most trimming surfaces move in the opposite direction from desired control movement: if you want the elevator to be deflected upward the trim tab is deflected downward, and it exerts a force to hold the elevator in the desired position.

As you move up into more complicated, higher-powered airplanes, you will find that trim controls for all three axes are available in the cockpit. At the basic trainer level, some trim tabs are literally metal tabs to be adjusted on the ground and then test flown to assess the effect of the change. Airplanes with movable tail

surfaces rotate the whole horizontal stabilizer/rudder assembly in reaction to trim wheel movement, and airplanes with stabilators (a movable stabilizer/elevator) move the stabilator with trim force. Three forms of elevator trim control are pictured (figure 2-26): a horizontal stabilizer with elevator and elevator trim tab, a movable horizontal stabilizer, and (on Mooneys) an entire tail surface which moves with trim input. V-tailed airplanes use ruddervators which, as their name implies, are combination control surfaces.

Figure 2-26. Three Forms of Elevator Trim Control

Trim tabs are used *only* to relieve control pressures, and are not to be used by themselves to change the airplane's attitude. When the airspeed and altitude are at the desired values, any remaining control pressures should be trimmed off.

FLAPS

Flaps are auxiliary control surfaces; that is, you do not use flaps to control the airplane around the three axes of control. *Flaps allow the pilot to descend at a steep angle without increasing airspeed*, which becomes very important during approaches to land (figures 2-27 and 2-28). *Flaps are not speed brakes* — in fact, the designer establishes maximum speeds for flap deflection to avoid structural overloads. Because flaps increase both the camber of the wing and the angle of attack by lowering the trailing edge, they allow the same amount of lift to be developed at a lower airspeed. You will experiment with this in training by maintaining altitude while extending flaps and gradually slowing the airplane.

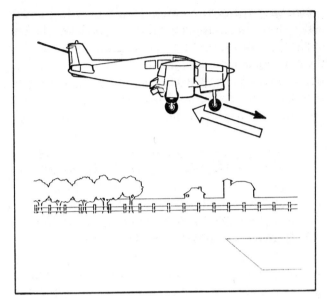

Figure 2-28. Use of Flaps Allows a Steeper Descent Angle

extension changes the location of the center of pressure on the wing and causes a pitch change. You should find out whether extending the flaps will cause your airplane to pitch nose up or nose down, and be ready to maintain a constant attitude as you apply flaps.

There are several types of flaps in general use (figure 2-29). Plain flaps are hinged portions of the trailing edge

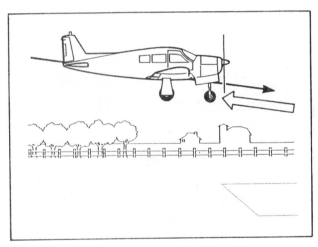

Figure 2-27. Landing Approach Without Flaps

Typically, the first increments of flap extension add more lift than drag, and so some airplanes use a takeoff flap setting of 15°-20°. Retracting the flaps when you do not have sufficient airspeed to support the airplane in the no-flaps configuration will cause loss of altitude — do not retract the flaps until you have sufficient airspeed. As you near full flap extension you get more drag than lift, and these are the approach settings. Flap

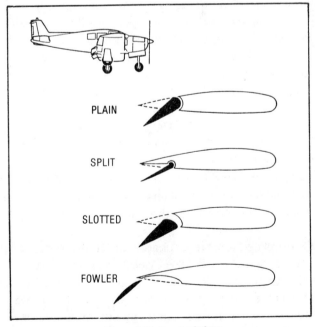

Figure 2-29. Types of Flaps

of the wing: deflecting them increases wing camber and thereby increases lift. Fowler flaps extend downward and also back, adding to wing area as well as camber. Split flaps extend downward from the trailing edge, while the upper wing surface is undisturbed.

Designers also add high lift devices to the leading edge of the wing to channel high pressure air over the upper wing surface. These leading edge flaps are also referred to as slats, and you will see them on modern airline jets as well as short-takeoff-and-landing (STOL) airplanes. Flaps can be extended electrically, hydraulically, or manually, and some leading edge devices are extended by aerodynamic pressure.

Another means of increasing descent rate without increasing airspeed is the use of spoilers. Spoilers are vertical "fences" that may be extended from the top surface of the wing to disrupt airflow, killing lift.

Spoilers have been used as flight controls on gliders for many years, and are now being used on powered airplanes.

Because the extension of flaps affects the angle of attack (by moving the chord line), or changes the wing area, flap use lowers the stall speed — with a greater angle of attack (or more area), less air has to flow over the wing to develop the same amount of lift. Figure 2-30 is a typical table of stall speed vs flap extension related to bank angle. When referring to similar tables, you should be aware that airspeed indicator accuracy suffers at high angles of attack (low airspeeds).

TORQUE

"Torque" is really the result of four factors, although the end effect is the same: a tendency to yaw to the left in airplanes with propellers and engines that rotate clockwise as seen from the pilot's seat (figure 2-31).

One major factor is discharge air from the propeller corkscrewing around the fuselage as it moves aft, and striking the left side of the vertical tail surfaces. During the takeoff roll, the force it exerts to move the tail to the right is seen by the pilot as a movement of the nose to the left.

GROSS WEIGHT 2750 LBS		ANGLE OF BANK			
		LEVEL	30°	45°	60°
POWER		GEAR AND FLAPS UP			
ON	MPH	62	67	74	88
	KTS	54	58	64	76
OFF	MPH	75	81	89	106
	KTS	65	70	77	92
		GEAR AND FLAPS DOWN			
ON	MPH	54	58	64	76
	KTS	47	50	56	66
OFF	MPH	66	71	78	93
	KTS	57	62	68	81

Figure 2-30. Stall Speed Table

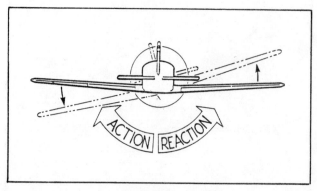

Figure 2-31. Action/Reaction

Another factor is Newton's law of equal and opposite reactions: as the engine and propeller rotate clockwise, a counterclockwise force is transmitted through the engine mounts to the airframe. The designer may increase the angle of attack of the left wing to offset this force, or mount the engine offset from the centerline to minimize the torque reaction.

A third major contributor is called P-factor, because the culprit is the propeller. As the blade on the right side of the propeller disc descends it is exerting a force on the air (downwash effect, because the propeller is an airfoil), while the blade on the left side of the disc is at a low angle of attack and is exerting little or no force. The descending blade is also moving at a higher speed relative to the air than is the ascending blade, and this increased velocity creates more lift on the right side of the propeller disc, pulling the nose of the airplane to the left.

The last factor contributing to left-turning tendency is gyroscopic precession, and this is especially noticeable in airplanes with conventional landing gear (taildraggers). The propeller is a rotating mass, just like a solid disc of metal, and if a force is applied to a rotating mass it will act as though the force had been applied 90° in the direction of rotation (figure 2-32). When the pilot of a taildragger lifts the tail during the takeoff run, the forward tilting of the propeller disc exerts a force at the right rear of the propeller disc which adds to the left-turning tendency. The illustration (figure 2-32) shows P-factor and raising of the tail combining to create a left-turning force.

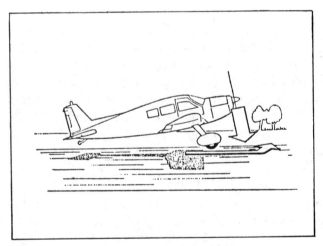

Figure 2-32. Gyroscopic Precession

As you begin the takeoff roll, power is at a maximum and airflow over the control surfaces (with the exception of propeller discharge air) is at a minimum. Discharge air and P-factor will combine to turn the airplane to the left unless you provide offsetting rudder pressure to keep the plane moving straight down the runway. As you rotate the airplane to climb attitude, P-factor increases because the angle of attack of the

blade descending on the right side of the propeller disc has increased, and you must continue to apply right rudder. A high power-low airspeed situation will always call for right rudder pressure. A common error is an attempt to offset torque effects by banking to the right rather than by use of right rudder.

Levelling off at cruise altitude, the forces of discharge air and P-factor still exist, although diminished because of reduced power, but now the airplane designer provides a corrective force. The left wing is rigged so that it develops slightly more lift at cruise speed than the right wing, offsetting the left-turning tendency. The vertical fin is also slightly offset, so that at cruise speeds the push of discharge air on the left side of the tail surfaces is corrected for. These corrections are exactly effective at only one airspeed: go faster or slower and aileron or rudder trim will be required.

DYNAMICS OF THE TURN

The lift developed by an airfoil acts perpendicular to the relative wind, and in level flight that force is vertical, with no horizontal component. If you roll into a 90° bank, all of the lifting force will act horizontally, and with no vertical lift the airplane cannot maintain altitude (figure 2-33). (The military demonstration teams do it, but they have a tremendous power-to-weight ratio, and jet fighter fuselages are designed to provide some lift).

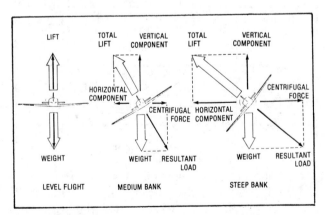

Figure 2-33. Forces During Normal Coordinated Turns

In normal flying, you will not bank more than about 55° (60° of bank is considered acrobatics), and as you bank the wings you will be varying the relationship between the vertical and horizontal components of lift. It is the horizontal component of lift that causes the airplane to turn. When a portion of the total lift developed by the wing acts horizontally, the remaining vertical component will be inadequate to support the weight of the airplane, and additional lift must be supplied by increasing the angle of attack, or the airspeed, or both to avoid loss of altitude. Increasing the angle of attack increases induced drag (remember that induced drag is is the price you pay for lift), and, unless that drag is offset with thrust, you must inevitably lose airspeed in a level turn.

As you bank more and more steeply, and increase the angle of attack to maintain altitude (without adding power), you will soon reach the critical angle of attack and the wing will stall. Figure 2-34 shows the relationship between the bank angle in degrees and the percentage increase in stall speed. Note that in a 60° bank the stall speed will increase by 40%, from 60 knots to 84 knots, for example. Figure 2-34 also shows the relationship between bank angle and load factor.

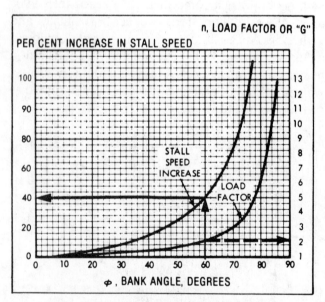

Figure 2-34. Increase in Stall Speed and Load Factor

Load factor is the ratio between the weight that the wing is being required to support and the weight of the airplane. If an airplane which weighs 2,000 pounds is banked 60°, the horizontal component of lift is 2,000 pounds and the vertical lift required to maintain

altitude is also 2,000 pounds: the wing is supporting 4,000 pounds and the load factor is 2.0. As figure 2-35 shows, the horizontal component of lift is opposed by centrifugal force and the vertical component is opposed by weight, and as the bank steepens, the resultant load and the lift required to support it increase dramatically.

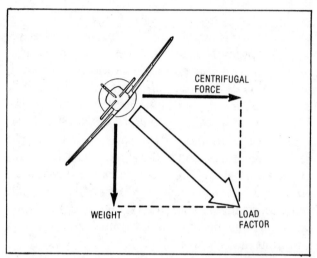

Figure 2-35. Two Forces Cause Load Factor During Turns

From what has been said so far, you would assume that the rudder plays no part in turning an airplane, since it is the horizontal component of lift that supplies the turning force. This is true to the extent that no rudder pressure is required to sustain the turn itself, but rudder pressure *is* required to roll into and out of the turn because of adverse aileron drag, and may be required to overcome "torque" forces.

The rudder controls the airplane around the yaw (or vertical) axis. As an aileron is deflected downward to initiate a bank, that down aileron creates drag which opposes the turn. Rudder pressure is required to overcome this adverse aileron drag. The amount of rudder pressure required depends on the degree of aileron deflection. When the desired bank has been established, and the ailerons are neutralized, there is no aileron drag and therefore no rudder pressure is required to offset it. Rolling back to wings level flight requires aileron deflection, and rudder must be applied to offset the resulting drag. The slip and skid, or ball, instrument reflects your skill in providing just enough rudder pressure (coordinating aileron and rudder): if you use too much rudder you will force the ball to the outside of the turn, resulting in a skid. If you use too little rudder pressure the ball will fall to the inside of the turn and the airplane will be in a slip.

As discussed earlier, airplanes with propellers that turn clockwise as seen from the pilot's seat tend to turn left unless design features or pilot action counteract that tendency. When you are established in a turn to the left, then, no rudder pressure is required. It may take slight rudder pressure to hold your airplane in a right turn, however, since these forces act to roll it back to level flight. Again, the ball tells the tale.

One of the stock production numbers at an ice skating show has a line of skaters pivoting around a center, with the central skaters marking time and the outer skaters racing madly to keep up. When you bank your airplane's wings steeply, you re-create this situation aerodynamically: the inside, or lower wing is moving quite slowly, while the top, or outside wing has to cover a greater distance in exactly the same time and so must travel considerably faster. This results in more lift being developed by the outside wing, and the plane develops an overbanking tendency which may require opposite aileron to avoid a too-steep bank. Pilots who use rudder to maintain a turn while using opposite aileron to avoid overbanking risk a cross-control stall.

STALLS AND SPINS

Increasing the angle of attack until the air no longer flows smoothly over the wing surface will result in an aerodynamic stall, as discussed earlier, and the designer's placement of the center of lift and the center of gravity make the stall self-correcting *if both wings stall simultaneously*. If one wing stalls before the other, the stalled wing will drop, the nose of the airplane will descend below the horizon and, if no corrective action is taken, a spin will result. *An airplane must be stalled before it will spin.* In a well-developed spin, the lower or inside wing remains stalled while the higher or outside wing continues to develop lift — the indicated airspeed in a spin will be quite low. Because a spin must be preceded by a stall, your flight instruction will emphasize stall recognition and recovery. Most airplanes are not approved for intentional spins, and before you or your instructor attempt an intentional spin you should check the Approved Flight Manual or Pilot's Operating Handbook. Most flight manuals include instructions on how to recover from an inadvertent spin, and you should become familiar with these instructions. An hour of dual instruction in an aerobatic airplane with a qualified instructor will erase any doubts about your ability to handle an inadvertent spin.

Figure 2-36 shows a test airplane on which NASA has installed experimental flow control devices on the

Figure 2-36. Experimental Spin Recovery Flow Control Devices

outboard sections of the wings to improve spin
recovery characteristics. Note the pilot's emergency
escape door and the drag parachute.

AERODYNAMICS
SECTION REVIEW

1. When are the four aerodynamic forces that act on an airplane in equilibrium?

    1. When the aircraft is at rest on the ground.
    2. When the aircraft is accelerating.
    3. When the aircraft is decelerating.
    4. During unaccelerated flight.

2. The purpose of the rudder on an airplane is to

    1. control the yaw.
    2. control the overbanking tendency.
    3. maintain a crab angle to correct drift.
    4. maintain the turn after the airplane is banked.

3. The term angle of attack is defined as the

    1. angle between the wing chord and the direction of the relative wind.
    2. angle between the airplane's climb angle and the horizon.
    3. angle formed by the longitudinal axis of the airplane and the chord line of the wing.
    4. specific angle at which the ratio between lift and drag is the highest.

4. As altitude increases, the indicated airspeed at which a given airplane stalls in a particular configuration will

    1. decrease as the true airspeed increases.
    2. decrease as the true airspeed decreases.
    3. remain the same as at low altitude.
    4. increase because the air density becomes less.

5. What causes an airplane (except a T-tail) to pitch nosedown when power is reduced and the controls are not adjusted?

    1. The CG shifts forward when thrust and drag are reduced.
    2. The downwash on the elevators from the propeller slipstream is reduced and elevator effectiveness is reduced.
    3. When thrust is reduced to less than weight, lift is also reduced and the wings can no longer support the weight.
    4. The upwash on the wings from the propeller slipstream is reduced and the angle of attack is reduced.

6. What effect does an increased load factor have on an airplane during an approach to a stall?

    1. The airplane will stall at a higher airspeed.
    2. The airplane will have a tendency to spin.
    3. The airplane will be more difficult to control.
    4. The airplane will have a tendency to yaw and roll as the stall is encountered.

7. What determines the longitudinal stability of an airplane?

    1. The location of the CG with respect to the center of lift.
    2. The effectiveness of the horizontal stabilizer, rudder, and rudder trim tab.
    3. The relationship of thrust and lift to weight and drag.
    4. The dihedral, angle of sweepback, and keel effect.

8. The left-turning tendency of an airplane caused by P-factor is the result of the

    1. clockwise rotation of the engine and the propeller turning the airplane counterclockwise.
    2. propeller blade descending on the right, producing more thrust than the ascending blade on the left.
    3. gyroscopic forces applied to the rotating propeller blades acting 90° in advance of the point the force was applied.
    4. spiral characteristics of the slipstream air being forced rearward by the rotating propeller.

9. The purpose of wing flaps is to

    1. enable the pilot to make steeper approaches to a landing without increasing airspeed.
    2. enable the pilot to reduce the airspeed for the approach to a landing.
    3. enlarge or control the wing area to vary the lift.
    4. create more drag in order to utilize power on the approach.

10. In what airspeed and power condition is torque effect the greatest in a single-engine airplane?

    1. Low airspeed, high power.
    2. Low airspeed, low power.
    3. High airspeed, high power.
    4. High airspeed, low power.

11. What makes an airplane turn?

    1. Centrifugal force.
    2. Rudder and aileron.
    3. Horizontal component of lift.
    4. Rudder, aileron, and elevator.

12. As you maneuver an airplane you should realize that it can be stalled

    1. only when the nose is high and the speed is low.
    2. only when the airspeed decreases to the published stalling speed.
    3. at any airspeed and in any attitude.
    4. only when the nose is too high in relation to the horizon.

13. To counteract the effect of torque in a conventional single engine propeller-driven airplane, a pilot would normally add

    1. left rudder pressure during the takeoff roll and while climbing with full power.
    2. right rudder pressure when entering a glide from level cruising flight.
    3. right rudder pressure during the takeoff roll and while climbing with full power.
    4. left rudder pressure when entering a climb from level cruising flight.

You don't have to be a mechanic to be a safe pilot, but a knowledge of how your engine works, and what the engine instruments are telling you, will make it easier to give your engine tender loving care and get long, reliable service from it.

There are many similarities between an automobile engine and an airplane engine. Both are **internal combustion engines**, both use spark plugs, and both use some type of fuel metering system related to throttle position. Many advances in modern automotive engines such as turbocharging and fuel injection are based on earlier aviation applications.

An aircraft engine is a four-cycle engine: figure 3-1 illustrates the four cycles. The fuel-air mixture is drawn into the cylinder as the piston moves downward on the intake stroke; as the piston moves upward with the valves closed, the mixture is compressed during the compression stroke. The burning of the fuel-air mixture after ignition drives the piston downward during the power stroke, and as the piston rises again with the exhaust valve open, the exhaust stroke ends the four stroke cycle. Because your aircraft engine has four or more cylinders, each igniting at a different time, there is always one piston on a power stroke, and the process is continuous.

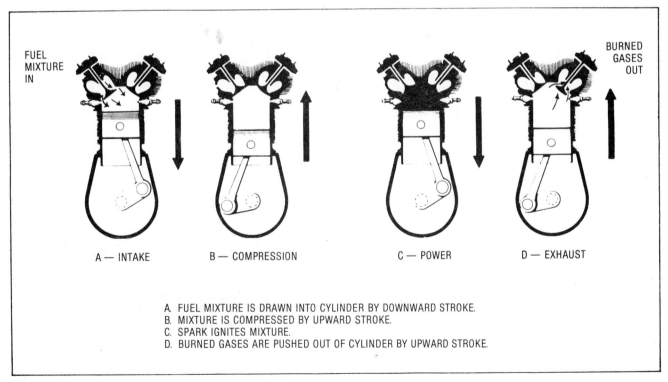

FUEL MIXTURE IN

BURNED GASES OUT

A — INTAKE   B — COMPRESSION   C — POWER   D — EXHAUST

A. FUEL MIXTURE IS DRAWN INTO CYLINDER BY DOWNWARD STROKE.
B. MIXTURE IS COMPRESSED BY UPWARD STROKE.
C. SPARK IGNITES MIXTURE.
D. BURNED GASES ARE PUSHED OUT OF CYLINDER BY UPWARD STROKE.

Figure 3-1. Four Strokes of an Aircraft Engine

IGNITION

Your airplane engine uses a **magneto** as the source of ignition. Magneto may not be a familiar term to you, but your gas lawnmower, chain saw, or outboard motor all use magnetos. A magneto is a self-contained source of electrical impulses, using the physical motion of a coil and a fixed magnetic field to develop ignition voltage. To start the engine, you provide that physical motion by pulling a cord on your lawnmower, chain saw, or outboard. The starter motor does the job in the airplane, rotating the engine until the magneto-developed spark ignites the mixture. You have probably seen older airplanes without electrical systems (and newer airplanes with starter problems) being started manually — rotating the propeller by hand ("propping") causes the magneto to generate a voltage which goes to the spark plug to ignite the fuel/air mixture. Hand-propping an airplane is a hazardous undertaking which requires an experienced and knowledgeable person both in the cockpit and at the propeller. Once an airplane engine is started, the magnetos provide continuous ignition on their own — the airplane's electric system and the starter motor have done their jobs.

Each cylinder in your airplane engine has two spark plugs, each fired by a different magneto. This has two advantages: better combustion efficiency, and safety — the engine will run on either magneto if one should develop a problem. *Magnetos are totally independent of the aircraft electrical system.*

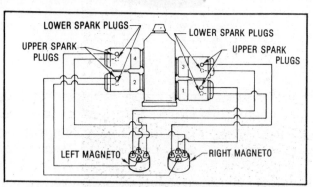

Figure 3-2. Spark Plugs and Magnetos

When you turn the ignition off, with a key or with switches, you are connecting the electrical output of the magneto to the metal block of the engine where it is shorted to electrical ground and cannot fire the spark plugs. This "shorting out" is done through a wire called a P-lead, and if a P-lead is broken its associated magneto can fire the spark plugs even with the ignition in the OFF position. For this reason, you should treat all propellers with respect — moving the propeller might cause a magneto to start the engine unexpectedly if a P-lead has broken. During the preflight check of the airplane and its systems you will run the engine on each magneto separately. As you cut the ignition sources in half you will lose some power, reflected as a drop in revolutions per minute (RPM). If no drop occurs when one magneto is shut off, that magneto probably has a broken P-lead, and the flight should be delayed until a mechanic checks it. Some authorities recommend checking for a broken P-lead just before shutting the engine down after a flight, by turning the ignition switch to its "OFF" position momentarily while at idle power; if the engine continues to run, there is probably a broken P-lead.

INDUCTION SYSTEMS

An airplane engine is a big air pump, taking in air through the induction system, mixing it with fuel, burning it, then pumping it overboard through the exhaust system. You will become familiar with two types of induction systems: **carburetor** and **fuel injection**. Figure 3-3 shows a float type carburetor similar to those in most light airplane installations.

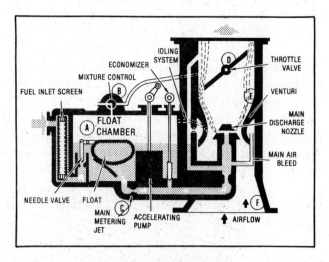

Figure 3-3. Float Type Carburetor

Carburetor type induction systems are generally less expensive than fuel injection, and are easier to adjust. However, they do not deliver an equal fuel/air mixture to each cylinder, and are prone to induction system icing.

As air flows upward through the restriction called the **venturi** its speed increases and pressure drops, (remember Bernoulli's Theorem?). The air in the float chamber is vented to the outside, so the difference between outside air and the reduced pressure in the venturi forces fuel out of the float chamber, through the main discharge nozzle, and into the airstream. The amount of airflow through the carburetor is governed by the position of the throttle valve — you control that directly from the cockpit. The amount of fuel metered into the mixture is governed by the mixture control, and you control that in the cockpit as well. When you "step on the gas" in your automobile, or add power in your airplane, you are really controlling airflow directly and fuel flow indirectly. You really increase power by stepping on the air, not the gas.

As the fuel and air mixture expands in the carburetor throat it drops in temperature by 40° to 60°F, due to both expansion of the air and evaporation of the fuel. If there is any moisture in the intake air, this sudden drop in temperature may cause the moisture to freeze on the carburetor walls and throttle valve, restricting airflow and reducing power just as surely as if you had retarded the throttle. Power loss due to carburetor ice is a possibility any time the outside air temperature is between 20°F and 70°F, with high relative humidity or visible moisture in the air.

To counter this threat, the manufacturer provides a carburetor heat control which takes heated air from a muff around the exhaust and directs it into the carburetor to melt the ice. Because the air gets its heat from the exhaust, carburetor heat must be used before the engine loses so much power that the heat from the exhaust is inadequate to do the job. This should be no problem if you keep an eye on your engine power instruments when operating in conditions where carburetor ice is possible.

As ice forms on the throttle valve and in the carburetor throat, the reduction in power will be reflected in a reduction in RPM (with a fixed-pitch propeller). Application of FULL carburetor heat will result in a momentary further loss of RPM, then as the ice melts and makes its way through the engine in the form of water the RPMs will rise again (expect a moment or two of engine roughness!). The initial reduction in power experienced when the carburetor heat (figure 3-4) is applied is due to hot air being less dense than cold air — this reduction in intake air density makes the fuel/air mixture ratio richer.

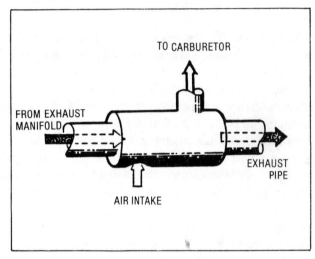

Figure 3-4. Carburetor Heat

Carburetor heat should be either full ON, which causes a slight power loss, or full OFF while you watch for symptoms of icing. Partial heat is only used when you have additional instrumentation intended specifically for the detection of carburetor ice.

FUEL INJECTION

A fuel-injected induction system delivers an equal fuel/air mixture to each cylinder and requires careful adjustment. Because there is no carburetor, there can be no carburetor ice. Fuel injection systems are installed in more powerful airplanes, and virtually all **turbocharged** engines. Fuel injection systems (figure 3-5) cannot develop carburetor ice, but induction system icing is not impossible. The intake air passes through a filter, and if that filter is clogged by wet snow or ice the air supply to the engine will be reduced and a power loss will result.

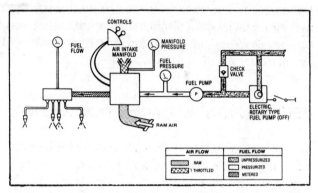

Figure 3-5. Fuel Injection System

The primary power instrument in a fuel-injected engine installation is the **manifold pressure** gauge. Induction system icing will show up as a reduction in manifold pressure, and if you suspect that a loss of power is due to icing there will always be some form of alternate air source so that the engine can breathe. When a controllable pitch (or constant speed) propeller is installed, the reduction in manifold pressure will be the only indication of induction system icing because the RPM will be held constant by a governor.

Fuel injected engines have a reputation of being hard to start when hot. This problem, when it exists, is usually caused by vapor lock, the result of fuel boiling into vapor in the fuel lines. When you shut down the engine at the completion of a flight, the flow of cooling air no longer exists, and the engine must simply radiate its heat to its surroundings. It is inevitable that the fuel lines absorb some of this heat. The manufacturer's approved flight manual will include a "hot start" procedure, and if it doesn't work you may simply have to wait until the fuel cools to a liquid state.

FUEL SYSTEMS

Some airplanes have very simple fuel systems, with the fuel flowing to the engine by gravity feed, and others have complex systems of main and auxiliary tanks with associated pumps and switches. You must understand your airplane's fuel system to be sure that fuel is available to the engine from startup to shutdown. Every year pilots make forced landings (or worse) due to fuel starvation, only to learn that fuel was available from another tank.

Follow the manufacturer's starting instructions to the letter. A cold engine will require priming, either with a plunger-type manual primer, an electric fuel pump, or in some cases, pumping the throttle. Avoid overpriming — you may flood the engine or create a fire hazard. If your manufacturer's pilot's operating handbook requires that you take off and land with the fuel selector on the main tanks, or cautions you to use the auxiliary tanks only in straight-and-level flight, observe those restrictions — there may be interruptions in fuel flow if you don't.

MIXTURE CONTROL

An airplane engine needs a mixture of approximately 15 parts of air for each part of fuel. If there is more air than 15:1 the mixture is called "lean", and when the ratio falls below 15:1 it is a "rich" mixture. There is a mixture control on your automobile carburetor or fuel injection system which is adjusted during tuneups or when you move to the mountains from the flatlands. Airplanes make altitude changes of that magnitude in a matter of minutes, and you can't pull off the road to adjust the mixture, so the manufacturer provides a mixture control in the cockpit. Your engine needs additional cooling while supplying the power demands of takeoff and initial climb, and that additional cooling is provided by burning extra fuel or using a full rich mixture. Some carburetors have an enrichment valve which provides extra fuel when the throttle is full forward.

As the airplane climbs into air of diminishing density, the volume of air passing through the carburetor does not decrease but the weight does, and that upsets the 15:1 ratio toward the rich side: weight of fuel is unchanged, weight of air is decreased. Most manufacturer's operating handbooks require that the mixture control be full rich during climbs — check your handbook. When you arrive at cruise altitude, lean the mixture as recommended by the manufacturer. If you fail to lean at cruise altitude you are wasting fuel and are not operating the engine efficiently. Retarding the mixture control until the tachometer reaches a peak will do the trick in the absence of instrumentation for precise mixture adjustment. (See the section on MIXTURE INSTRUMENTATION.)

As you descend from cruise altitude, the reverse situation occurs: the mixture control has been leaned back to reduce the amount of fuel entering the mixture and, as the airplane descends into air of increasing density, the ratio swings to the lean side, with too much air for the amount of fuel. The recommended procedure is to enrich the mixture during the descent, but if you forget, the situation will be called to your attention by roughness as the engine tries to run on too little fuel. You will probably make several small mixture adjustments during the descent prior to going to full rich as a part of the pre-landing checklist.

Any time air of reduced density is introduced into the induction system, you can expect the symptoms of a too-rich mixture. If you are flying at 9,500 feet with the mixture properly leaned, and add carburetor heat "just in case", the hot, less dense air will enrich the mixture and may cause rough running until the carburetor heat control is returned to the cold position. If you are operating at a high-altitude airport, the thin air may cause roughness during idle operation and taxiing, and the addition of carburetor heat during runup will make the roughness worse. Under those conditions, lean the mixture for the highest RPM during a full-power runup and leave it in that position for takeoff.

MIXTURE INSTRUMENTATION

Your airplane may be equipped with an **exhaust gas temperature gauge** (EGT) for precise mixture adjustment. These instruments read the highest temperature when the mixture is "just right": too much air or too much fuel and the exhaust temperature drops. There are also mixture settings to be used for best power and for best economy. Each engine manufacturer has guidelines on how the EGT instrument should be used, so before you use the EGT for mixture adjustment, familiarize yourself with the manufacturer's recommendations.

Airplanes with fuel injection systems will have a fuel flow gauge calibrated in gallons per hour or pounds per hour, and the performance tables will tell you the correct fuel flow for climb and for cruise power at different altitudes. Although these instruments are calibrated as flow meters, they actually measure fuel

pressure, and a restriction in the fuel metering system may cause an incorrect high fuel flow indication. Solid state transducers are becoming available which actually measure fuel flow very accurately.

FUEL GRADE AND CONTAMINATION

An airplane engine is designed to operate most efficiently on one grade of fuel. There are three grades of aviation gasoline in use today: Grade 80 (which is dyed red), Grade 100 Low-Lead (which is blue), and Grade 100 (which is colored green). The latter two differ only in lead content. Although many engines still in service specify Grade 80, it is being phased out by the petroleum industry. When the correct fuel for your airplane is not available, it is permissible to use a *higher* grade of fuel temporarily until the correct grade is available. If your engine specifications call for Grade 80 fuel, you can use a higher grade — but check to see if the engine manufacturer has issued special operating procedures. NEVER use fuel of a lower grade than that specified for your engine. *An easy memory aid is this: as you step up in fuel grade, the number of letters in the color of the dye increases: red, blue, green.*

If the wrong grade of aviation gasoline has been pumped into your tanks (or, even worse, jet fuel), it will take only a few minutes of operation for destructive forces to be generated. It is always good practice to supervise the fueling of your airplane.

NOTE: Many airplane engines have received Supplemental Type Certificates (STCs) authorizing the use of automotive fuel. Make no assumptions: do not use automobile gas unless you are *sure* it is approved for your engine.

FAA tests indicate that engines using automobile fuel are more prone to induction system icing.

In addition to being sure that the fuel being pumped into your tanks is the correct grade, you must also guard against fuel contamination. The most common contaminant is water: airplane engines refuse to burn water, and your engine will let you know there is water in the fuel by running rough or stopping entirely. A common source of water in the tank is condensation. If you leave the fuel tanks partially full overnight, the cooling temperatures will cause the fuel to contract, drawing moist air into the tanks. This moisture will condense on the cold walls of the tank and sink to the bottom because water is heavier than gasoline.

One of your preflight duties is to drain fuel samples from low points in the fuel system; if any water shows up in the sample, continue to drain until no further contamination is apparent. The fuel pickup for the engine is at the low point in the tank, and water should show up there first, but it is possible for water to pool in the tank and not move toward the low point until the airplane moves. If the airplane has been parked in one place for an extended period, rock the wings vigorously and drain the sumps again after giving any trapped water time to move toward the low point of the fuel system. If the airplane has been parked on a slope, water may collect in the tank on the downhill side — drain the sumps with the airplane on a level surface.

You can practically eliminate condensation by being sure that the airplane's tanks are full at the end of each day's flying. While you are checking for water in the fuel, look for dirt or any other foreign matter which might cause a problem in the carburetor or fuel injectors. The fuel passes through many filters by the time it reaches your tanks from the refinery, and the odds against having a contaminant pumped into your tanks are high, but a moment's inattention during the fueling process can lead to disaster.

Any discussion of fuel contamination must address the question of running a tank dry. Never run a fuel tank dry, because you *may* introduce contaminants into the engine that would normally just float around in the bottom of the tank. A secondary consideration, especially true with fuel injection, is introducing air into the fuel lines when the tank runs dry. Fuel injected engines may be difficult to re-start, even when you have switched to a full tank. Both electric and engine-driven fuel pumps work best with fluid, not with air, and it may take a few moments before the pumps are re-primed to deliver fuel to the engine. *Do not run a fuel tank dry.*

DETONATION AND PRE-IGNITION

When driving your automobile, any unusual noise usually gets your attention. If you notice a pinging or knocking sound when adding power, you know that you may have to make a shop visit to have the timing checked. In flight, you can't hear the engine pinging, and must be sure to avoid conditions which might lead to **detonation**. Detonation occurs when the fuel/air mixture explodes instead of burning evenly. This develops stresses that can destroy the engine in a very short time. Factors which lead to detonation are fuel of too low a grade, high operating temperature, or a mixture which is too lean. To avoid detonation, you must use the specified fuel grade (or a higher grade), avoid operation with too lean a mixture, and keep a watchful eye on engine temperatures.

Pre-ignition occurs when a "hot spot" within the cylinder causes the fuel/air mixture to ignite prematurely, and is usually caused by deposits on the spark plugs or valves. It usually has the same causes as detonation, and can be prevented in the same way. Your reaction, when detonation or pre-ignition are suspected, must be directed toward cooling the engine. A richer mixture, a lower power setting, or a higher airspeed will help cool the engine and reduce any tendency toward detonation.

ENGINE INSTRUMENTATION

An airplane *must* have at least an oil temperature gauge and an oil pressure gauge, but may have additional instruments to give you a better picture of what is going on inside the cowling. A major consideration is avoiding overheating, and the engine manufacturer uses several methods to accomplish this. Aircraft engines are air-cooled, and during pre-flight you will see the cooling fins on the cylinders. The excess fuel in a rich mixture is used as a cooling agent during takeoff and climb, while oil serves as a coolant at all times. The oil which circulates through and around the engine as a lubricant picks up heat as it travels. It passes through an oil cooler, where the heat is given up to the air, and the oil is cooled for another trip around. The oil temperature gauge will reflect how well the oil is able to perform this cooling task. If you have allowed the oil level to fall below recommended levels, the amount available may not be able to do the job adequately, and high oil temperature will result.

The oil pressure gauge is an indication of how well the oil is lubricating the engine. High oil temperature AND low oil pressure would indicate a *major* problem and usually calls for a landing at the nearest airport. The **cylinder head temperature gauge**, when installed, is an excellent indicator of potentially damaging overheating. When the CHT (figure 3-6) starts rising toward the red line, enriching the mixture, reducing power, increasing airspeed, or opening the cowl flaps (if installed) will all contribute to temperature reduction. Excessively high temperatures will cause power loss, detonation, increased oil consumption, and possible internal engine damage.

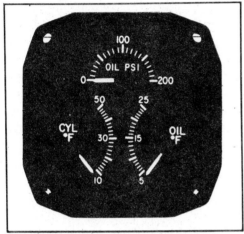

Figure 3-6. Cylinder Head Temperature Gauge

ELECTRICAL SYSTEM

The airplane's electrical system consists of a battery and a generator or alternator with associated voltage regulators, current limiters or other protective devices. The primary function of the battery is to provide power to the starter motor — after the engine starts, the magnetos provide ignition, and the generator or alternator takes on the task of powering the radios, instruments, lights, electrical landing gear or flaps, and recharging the battery. Individual circuits are protected by circuit breakers or fuses.

Most modern airplanes use alternators rather than generators. Early electrical systems used generators (first wind-driven, then geared to the engine), because in their simplest form generators were self-energized

with permanent magnets. They were large and heavy in relation to their output. The electrical output of an engine-driven generator is a function of engine speed, and generators became unable to handle the electrical demands of modern airplanes at taxiing and idle speeds. Airplane manufacturers switched to alternators because alternators are smaller and lighter for a given output and because the output voltage of an alternator is not dependent on engine speed. In combination with a voltage regulator, an alternator can provide a constant output voltage from idle RPM to full throttle.

Unlike a generator, however, an alternator requires current flow through its field windings in order to produce electricity, and this current must come from the battery. If the airplane battery is totally discharged, no current is available for the alternator field coils and the alternator is inoperative. Starting the airplane with an external power source or even by hand-propping will get the airplane back in the air, but the battery cannot be recharged by the alternator. A new or recharged battery is the only answer.

Alternator failure (which can be as simple as a broken or slipping drive belt) means that the battery must supply all required power until it is completely discharged, which may occur in a disconcertingly short time. Most airplanes with alternators have split electrical master switches (figure 3-7) which allow the pilot to disconnect the alternator field coils from the battery after all non-essential electrical loads have been reduced. This will extend battery life for a few precious minutes.

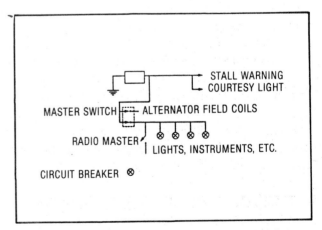

Figure 3-7. Alternator with Split Electrical Master Switches

You will find an **ammeter** on your instrument panel with a zero center and + and – indications, or a **loadmeter** which reads from zero to some value such as 75 amperes and reflects the actual electrical load on the system. With the zero center ammeter, a reading on the minus side indicates that the alternator is not providing enough electricity to recharge the battery. With a loadmeter, a reading of zero indicates that there is no alternator output. During the preflight runup, turn on the landing light or pitot heat momentarily to see if the ammeter reflects a change in the electrical load. If system failure is indicated or suspected in flight, turn off unnecessary electrical equipment to reduce the load on the battery. A clue: almost all fuel gauges are electric, and if both fuel gauges begin to sink toward empty you may be out of electricity instead of gas.

On the ground, when you turn on the airplane's master switch, listen for the click of the solenoid being operated by battery current, and for the electric gyro instruments to begin spinning. The absence of these audible clues means a dead battery. Learn what your airplane has for an electrical supply and what the normal and abnormal indications are. You may find that a re-set function (or a second voltage regulator) has been provided so that you can overcome momentary electrical failure. In any case, an electrical failure will not affect engine operation.

VACUUM SYSTEM

Certain flight instruments are powered by vacuum, just as windshield wipers on older cars were vacuum operated (figure 3-8). The vacuum pump is mounted on the rear of the engine, together with other engine-driven accessories such as fuel pumps and magnetos.

There is a vacuum indicator on the instrument panel so that you can keep tabs on the health of the vacuum system. Vacuum pump drive shafts are designed to shear (like an outboard motor shear pin) if internal mechanical failure occurs.

FIXED PITCH PROPELLERS

A fixed pitch propeller is a compromise between performance and speed. A propeller with a very flat blade angle (pitch) is called a climb prop. It takes very

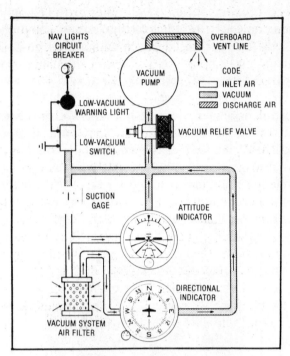

Figure 3-8. Vacuum System

small bites of the air as it pulls itself and the airplane forward. The engine is able to develop takeoff power very quickly — you will notice in the specifications for your airplane a statement such as "150 horsepower at 2700 RPM" — and you will get good takeoff performance. When that flat pitch propeller which revved up to 2,700 RPM very rapidly at sea level gets to 10,000 feet, however, taking small bites of thin air won't give you much cruise airspeed. If high speed at cruise altitude is what you want, you need a propeller with a greater blade angle, which will take bigger bites of the thin air and improve cruise speed. When taking off and climbing with a cruise propeller, however, you will be amazed at how much runway you will leave behind before that propeller — now taking big bites of dense air — gets up to 2,700 RPM. You have sacrificed takeoff and climb performance for cruise speed. Any fixed-pitch propeller is, therefore, a performance compromise.

CONTROLLABLE PITCH (CONSTANT SPEED) PROPELLERS

The solution is a propeller that has a flat pitch (high RPM) for takeoff, and a coarse pitch (low RPM) for cruise: a **controllable pitch propeller** or constant speed propeller. These two names are used almost interchangeably. Although a controllable pitch propeller was at one time a ground-adjustable propeller, today's installations use a governor to change blade angle and thus maintain constant RPM.

You will have two power instruments with a constant speed propeller installation: the **tachometer**, and a **manifold pressure gauge** which is now your primary power instrument (figure 3-9). The manifold pressure gauge reacts directly to throttle movement. For takeoff, the propeller control (linked to the governor to control RPM) is set full forward for high RPM. After the engine/propeller team have done their work and gotten you into the air in a hurry, you set climb power by first retarding the throttle, and then retarding the propeller control. During the climb, because barometric pressure decreases 1' per 1,000' of altitude, you must adjust the throttle setting to maintain climb power.

Figure 3-9. Tachometer and Manifold Pressure Gauge

At cruise altitude, set cruise power according to the manufacturer's cruise chart for that altitude. As you retard the prop control at altitude, the governor will

increase the blade angle to take bigger bites of the air (low RPM): the characteristics of a a cruise prop. Once you have set the propeller control to the desired RPM, the governor will change blade angle as required to maintain that RPM. If you have to add power to climb, or to increase airspeed, always advance the propeller control before the throttle; this will ensure that dangerously high pressures are not developed in the cylinders. Most pre-landing checklists include a reminder to move the propeller control to the high RPM position, to position it properly in case of an aborted landing. With the prop control full forward, you have completed the first half of the "increase power" procedure.

TURBOCHARGING

We have discussed how the decrease in air density with altitude causes the manifold pressure to drop, requiring more throttle to maintain climb power. A turbocharger (figure 3-10) allows sea level manifold pressure to be maintained to much higher altitudes by compressing air and packing it into the intake manifold. A turbine wheel is spun by exhaust gas, and a compressor on the same shaft compresses outside air and directs it into the induction system.

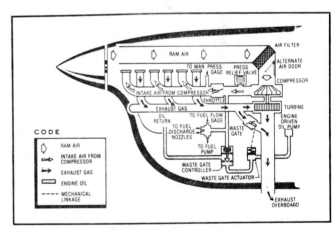

Figure 3-10. Turbocharging System

A "waste gate" controls the amount of exhaust that passes over the turbine. When no turbocharging is needed or desired, the waste gate is fully open and the exhaust gases bypass the turbine.

As manifold pressure drops off, and "boosting" is

required, the waste gate is adjusted so that more of the exhaust gases pass through the turbine. When the waste gate is fully closed, all of the exhaust passes through the turbine before being discharged to the atmosphere, and further climb will cause manifold pressure to decrease. When full boost from the turbocharger is being used, and further climb will result in reduced power, the engine has reached its critical altitude.

Some turbocharger installations require that you control the manifold pressure manually, while others use automatic controllers. Where manual control is provided, the pilot must be sure that the waste gate is fully open prior to takeoff, except at high altitude airports where additional power may be required. Applying the full exhaust force to the turbine at a low altitude airport by having the waste gate closed will cause destructive pressures (overboosting). Automatic controllers adjust the waste gate position in accordance with power demands, and the possibility of overboosting is eliminated. Many turbocharger installations have a fixed orifice through which a minimum amount of exhaust gas always passes, bypassing the waste gate. This limits the maximum available power but reduces the possibility of overboosting.

Turbocharging allows you to get above most of the weather, but it has its drawbacks. The discharge air from the compressor to the induction system is very hot, and hot air is less dense than cool air. This raises the possibility of having to run an overly rich mixture to keep temperatures down. Many turbocharger installations include an intercooler, a heat exchanger which cools the air coming from the compressor before it enters the intake manifold.

Pilots of turbocharged airplanes must be very temperature conscious, keeping in mind that high temperatures can lead to preignition or detonation. They must also guard against sudden power reductions which will shock-cool the red-hot turbocharger. Turbocharger installations may have additional engine instrumentation, such as a **Compressor Discharge Temperature gauge** (CDT), so that the pilot can get maximum utilization from the turbocharger without developing damaging internal engine temperatures.

PRESSURIZATION

A turbocharged airplane can take a pilot to altitudes where there is insufficient oxygen to sustain life, and a supplemental oxygen supply is mandatory to take full advantage of turbocharging unless the airplane is pressurized. Pressurization allows the pilot and passengers to enjoy near-sea level pressure in the cabin at flight altitudes above 10,000 feet, and cabin pressures in the order of 8,000 feet at altitudes up to 40,000 feet.

A pressurized airplane is very tightly sealed, and is much stronger structurally than an unpressurized airplane. As you walk around the ramp, you can identify pressurized airplanes by their rounded windows and doors. The pressurization system (figure 3-11) takes compressed air (called "bleed air") from the turbocharger and, in effect, "inflates" the cabin to maintain a comfortable cabin pressure for passengers. Bleed air is also used for cabin heating and de-icing functions on jet aircraft.

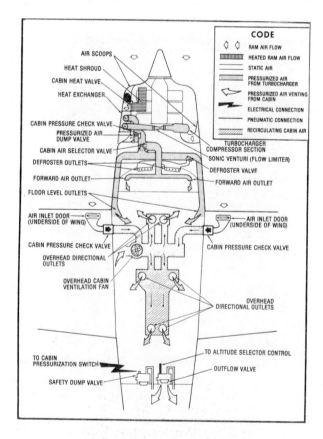

Figure 3-11. Pressurization System

Every pressurized airplane has a maximum allowable differential between the pressure in the cabin and the outside atmosphere. This maximum is based on structural considerations, because it is possible to have *too much* cabin pressure. A pressurization controller operates an "outflow valve", which allows air to leak out of the cabin at a controlled rate to maintain a pressure differential well below the maximum allowable. The outflow valve is backed up by a safety valve that will release pressure before the maximum differential is reached. Air constantly leaks out of the cabin of a pressurized airplane through the outflow valve, and only a large opening such as a failed window would lower the cabin pressure enough to require that the occupants use an emergency oxygen system.

The operation of the pressurization system varies with different types and models of airplanes, and you should study the operation of any system thoroughly before using it. One of your major concerns should be that the pressurization system activate and deactivate without discomfort for yourself and your passengers. Pressurization "bumps", when the occupants feel sudden pressure changes in their ears, are usually caused by incorrect use of the pressurization controls.

AIRCRAFT ENGINES
AND INSTRUMENTS
SECTION REVIEW

1. What action can a pilot take to aid in cooling an engine that is overheating during a climb?

    1. Lean the mixture to best power condition.
    2. Increase RPM and reduce climb speed.
    3. Reduce rate of climb and increase airspeed.
    4. Increase RPM and climb speed.

2. How is engine operation controlled on an engine equipped with a constant-speed propeller?

    1. The throttle controls power output as registered on the manifold pressure gauge and the propeller control regulates engine RPM.
    2. The throttle controls power output as registered on the manifold pressure gauge and the propeller control regulates a constant blade angle.
    3. The throttle controls engine RPM as registered on the tachometer and the mixture control regulates the power output.
    4. The throttle controls engine RPM as registered on the tachometer and the propeller control regulates the power output.

3. Is it necessary to preflight an aircraft that was hangared the night before in ready-to-fly condition?

    1. No, if the aircraft has not been handled since hangaring.
    2. Yes, because fuel contamination from condensation is possible.
    3. Yes, because the oil level should always be checked.
    4. No, if the same person who hangared the aircraft will act as pilot in command.

4. The presence of carburetor ice, in an airplane equipped with a fixed-pitch propeller can be verified by applying carburetor heat and noting

    1. an increase in RPM and then a gradual decrease in RPM.
    2. a decrease in RPM and then a constant RPM indication.
    3. an immediate increase in RPM with no further change in RPM.
    4. a decrease in RPM and then a gradual increase in RPM.

5. The uncontrolled firing of the fuel/air charge in advance of normal spark ignition is known as

    1. combustion.
    2. pre-ignition.
    3. atomizing.
    4. detonation.

6. If the engine oil temperature and cylinder head temperature gauges have exceeded their normal operating range, the pilot may have been

    1. operating with the mixture set too rich.
    2. operating with higher-than-normal oil pressure.
    3. using fuel that has a higher-than-specified fuel rating.
    4. operating with too much power and with the mixture set too lean.

7. If an engine continues to run after the ignition switch is turned to the OFF position, the probable cause may be

    1. the mixture is too lean and this causes the engine to diesel.
    2. the voltage regulator points are sticking closed.
    3. a broken magneto ground wire.
    4. fouled spark plugs.

8. Detonation occurs in a reciprocating aircraft engine when

    1. the spark plugs are fouled or shorted out and the wiring is defective.
    2. hot spots in the combustion chamber ignite the fuel/air mixture in advance of normal ignition.
    3. there is too rich a fuel/air mixture.
    4. the unburned charge in the cylinders explodes instead of burning evenly.

9. For internal cooling, reciprocating aircraft engines are especially dependent on

    1. a properly functioning thermostat.
    2. air flowing over the exhaust manifold.
    3. the circulation of lubricating oil.
    4. a lean fuel/air mixture.

10. If the grade of fuel used in an aircraft engine is lower than specified for the engine, it will most likely cause

    1. a mixture of fuel and air that is not uniform in all cylinders.
    2. lower cylinder head temperatures.
    3. an increase in power which could overstress internal engine components.
    4. detonation.

1-3; 2-1; 3-2; 4-4; 5-2; 6-4; 7-3; 8-4; 9-3; 10-4.

ANSWERS for AIRCRAFT ENGINES AND INSTRUMENTS SECTION:

Figure 4-1. Flight Instruments

PITOT-STATIC INSTRUMENTS

The **pitot-static system** consists of a pitot (pressure-sensing) tube, a static (zero pressure) source and related plumbing and filters (figure 4-1). The pitot-static instruments are the **airspeed indicator**, the **altimeter**, and the **vertical speed indicator**; they measure changes in air pressure caused by the airplane's vertical and horizontal movements in the atmosphere.

The airspeed indicator requires input from both the pitot (pressure) and static (unchanging) sources. Air from the static port fills the airspeed instrument case, while air from the pitot tube is led to a diaphragm. As airspeed changes, the pressure exerted on the diaphragm also changes and the movement of the diaphragm in response to these changes is transmitted to the indicator needle. The designer tries to locate the pitot tube so that it registers pressure in free air and is not affected by local airflow around the supporting structure. The airspeed indicator is the only instrument which uses air pressure from the pitot tube.

The static port is located where the airplane's motion through the air will create no pressure at all: on the side of the fuselage or on the back of the pitot tube. The airspeed indicator is calibrated to read the difference in pressure between impact air and still air — both inputs are required. If either the pitot tube or the static

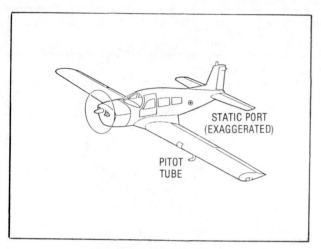

Figure 4-2. Pitot-Static Sources

port (figure 4-3) is blocked, the system will be useless, much like trying to get electricity from only one side of an electrical outlet.

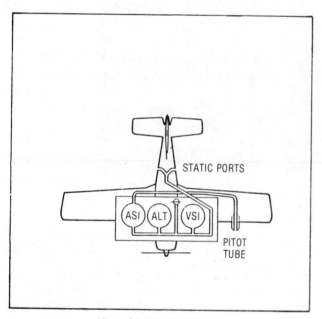

Figure 4-3. Pitot-Static System

Blockage of the static system would disable the airspeed indicator, the altimeter, and the vertical speed indicator.

At the start of the takeoff roll, there is no difference in pressure between the pitot and static inputs, and the airspeed indicator reads zero. As the airplane accelerates, the pressure in the pitot tube increases and that

pressure is transmitted to the airspeed indicator needle. The designer cannot completely isolate the pitot and static inputs from the effects of airflow around the wing or fuselage, so an airspeed correction table is provided (figure 4-4). The needle on the airspeed indicator reads indicated airspeed (IAS); when corrected for installation or position error, it becomes calibrated (CAS). Note in figure 4-4 that the greatest difference between indicated and calibrated airspeed occurs at low speeds which require high angles of attack, and that as the angle of attack is reduced and speed increases, the difference between IAS and CAS becomes negligible. The colored arcs on the airspeed indicator are usually based on calibrated airspeed; other operating speeds may be based on indicated airspeed. Check the operator's handbook to be sure.

FLAPS UP	IAS	60	80	100	120	140	160	180	—
	CAS	68	83	101	119	139	158	177	—
FLAPS DOWN 20°-40°	IAS	50	59	60	70	80	90	100	110
	CAS	57	60	66	74	83	92	102	111

Figure 4-4. Airspeed Correction Table

It takes a pressure of about 34 pounds per square foot on the pitot side of the airspeed indicator's diaphragm to make the airspeed needle register 100 knots at sea level. As the airplane climbs to altitude, the air becomes less dense. The airplane will have to move much faster through the less dense air at altitude in order to develop a pressure of 34 psf in the pitot tube, so the *true* airspeed will be faster than 100 knots when the airspeed indicator shows 100 knots. Your flight computer will allow you to make accurate calculations of true airspeed using IAS, pressure altitude, and temperature, but a good rule of thumb is that *true airspeed increases by 2% per 1,000' of altitude.* At sea level, under standard conditions, indicated and true airspeed will be equal; at 10,000' MSL, an indicated 100 knots means a true airspeed of 120 knots. Your airplane may have an airspeed indicator similar to figure 4-5, which allows you to enter pressure altitude and temperature and read true airspeed directly.

Figure 4-5. Airspeed Indicator

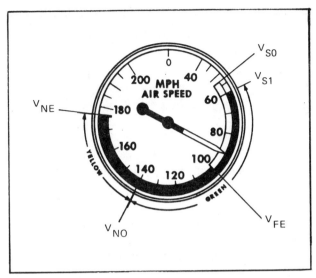

Figure 4-6. Airspeed Indicator Markings

You will use true airspeed in flight planning, but most airspeeds that you will use in actual flight are indicated airspeeds. You will always use the same indicated airspeeds, regardless of altitude. For example, if you are taking your flight training at a sea level airport and find that 70 knots indicated is the correct final approach speed, you will use 70 knots indicated airspeed on final when you fly to an airport at 5,000' above sea level. Your *true* airspeed will be 77 knots (2% times 5 = 10%, 1.1 times 70 = 77). Because the airplane approaching the airport at 5,000' is moving faster through the air in order to have an indicated airspeed of 70 knots, its groundspeed will be higher and landing roll will be longer. A pilot who adds a few knots "just in case" while on final approach at a high altitude airport may have difficulty getting stopped on the available runway. Flying at the manufacturer's recommended airspeed will have predictable results.

AIRSPEED INDICATOR MARKINGS

The airspeed indicator has colored arcs to alert you to limiting airspeeds, and you should be aware of their significance (figure 4-6). Most markings are based on calibrated airspeed. Check your airplane's Approved Flight Manual.

WHITE ARC — The low-speed end indicates the power-off stall speed in the landing configuration (V_{so}), and the high-speed end indicates the maximum allowable speed with flaps fully extended (V_{fe}).

GREEN ARC — The low-speed end indicates the power-off stall speed in a specified configuration, usually gear and flaps ups (V_{s1}), and the high-speed end indicates maximum structural cruising speed (V_{no}) which should be exceeded only in smooth air.

YELLOW ARC — The caution range: pilots should avoid operating at airspeeds in the caution range except when in smooth air.

RED LINE — This is the never-exceed speed (V_{ne}). Destructive aerodynamic forces may result from flight at or above the red line.

SPEEDS NOT MARKED ON THE AIRSPEED INDICATOR

Every airplane has a design maneuvering speed (V_a), which is the optimum speed in turbulence at maximum gross weight. *Maneuvering speed is reduced as weight is reduced.* Flight at maneuvering speed ensures that the airplane will stall before damaging aerodynamic loads are imposed on the wing structure.

Best angle of climb speed (V_x) is that speed which gives the most altitude in a given distance. You should fly at V_x to clear obstructions. Because flight at V_x requires a steep pitch attitude, engine cooling airflow and visibility are reduced. Climb at V_x only as long as necessary to clear the obstruction, then accelerate to V_y.

Best rate of climb speed (V_y) will produce the greatest gain in altitude in a given time, better visibility over the nose, and better engine cooling. If getting to altitude quickly is your goal, use V_y.

The manufacturer may designate other speeds, which you will find in the Pilot's Operating Handbook and possibly placarded on the instrument panel. Landing gear extension and retraction speeds, and speeds for partial flap extension will be found in the operating handbook and not on the airspeed indicator.

ANGLE OF ATTACK INDICATORS

The airspeed indicator can be considered a form of angle of attack indicator, since indicated airspeed is dependent on angle of attack in addition to power setting. Several manufacturers provide actual angle of attack indicators, however, which are calibrated to measure the actual angle between the chord line and the relative wind and provide you with angle of attack information by some form of "safe-unsafe" instrument reading (figure 4-7). One such instrument compares air pressure changes both vertically and horizontally and measures sink rate. In every case, you need only keep the instrument's needle in the "safe" area and no interpretation is required.

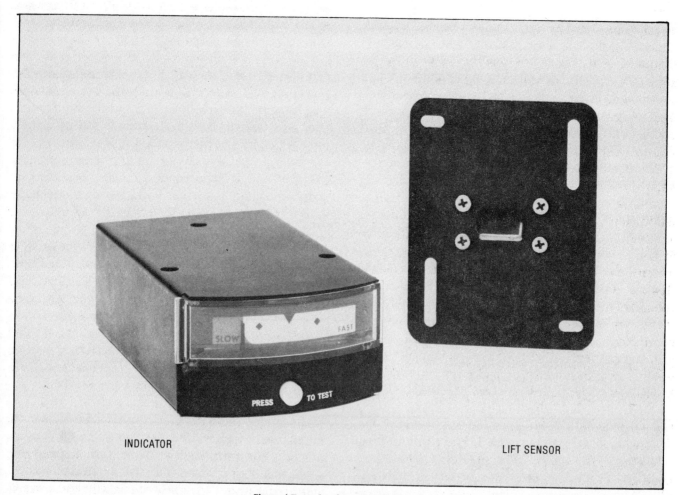

INDICATOR   LIFT SENSOR

Figure 4-7. Angle of Attack Indicator

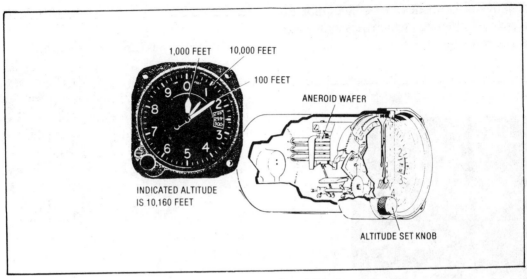

Figure 4-8. Altimeter / Indicated Altitudes

ALTIMETER

Aircraft altimeters are aneroid (dry) barometers calibrated to read in feet above sea level. The altimeter gets its input from the static port, which is unaffected by the airplane's movement through the air. An aneroid barometer contains several sealed wafers with a partial internal vacuum, so as the airplane moves vertically and the outside pressure changes, the wafers expand and contract much like an accordion. This expansion and contraction is transmitted through a linkage to the altimeter needles (figure 4-8).

Barometers provide a means of weighing the earth's atmosphere at a specific location. At a Flight Service Station or National Weather Service office, an actual mercury barometer may be used, and on a standard day the weight of the atmosphere will support a column of mercury (Hg) 29.92 inches high at sea level. Inches of mercury are the units of measure for barometric pressure and altimeter settings. The equivalent metric measure is 1013.2 millibars and, since our weather is transmitted internationally, the Weather Service uses both inches and millibars in its reports.

Up to 18,000', altitude is measured above sea level, and sea level pressure may vary from 28.50' to 30.50' Hg (these are extremes). Your altimeter has an adjustment knob and an altimeter setting window (figure 4-8), so that you can enter the sea level barometric pressure

(altimeter setting) at your location as received from a nearby Flight Service Station or air traffic control facility. The altimeter will, when properly set, read altitude above mean sea level (MSL). As you increase the numbers in the altimeter setting window, the hands on the altimeter also show an increase: each .01 increase in the window is equal to 10 feet of altitude, each .1 is 100 feet, etc.

Above 18,000' (and after you get your instrument rating, since all operations above that altitude must be under instrument flight rules), you will set the window to 29.92' Hg and you will be reading your altitude above the standard datum plane. By international agreement, a standard day at sea level is defined as having a barometric pressure of 29.92 (with the temperature 15°C or 59°F), and by setting your altimeter to 29.92 it will read altitude above that standard level. Below 18,000', having the correct altimeter setting will keep you out of the trees, while above 18,000' (where there are no trees or mountains), the common altimeter setting of 29.92 provides altitude separation for IFR flights. There are several altitude terms with which you should become familiar:

INDICATED ALTITUDE is simply what the hands on the altimeter point to. The long hand reads hundreds of feet (the calibrations are 20'), the next largest hand reads thousands of feet, and the third indicator reads in tens of thousands. The three-needle altimeter is easily misread, and many new airplanes are being equipped with a drum-pointer altimeter which has only one needle and a counter (figure 4-9).

Figure 4-9. Drum-Pointer Altimeter

Refer to figure 4-10.

Altimeter A's smallest (10,000') needle is just past one, the second largest (1,000') needle is between zero and one, and the largest (100') needle is on the five:

One..................	10,000
+ No.................	1,000
+....................	500
	10,500

Altimeter B reads 9,500' — is that the answer you would get?

ABSOLUTE ALTITUDE is your actual height above the surface as read by a radar altimeter.

PRESSURE ALTITUDE is what the hands of the altimeter indicate when the altimeter setting window is set to 29.92' Hg. You will use pressure altitude in computations of density altitude, true airspeed, and true altitude.

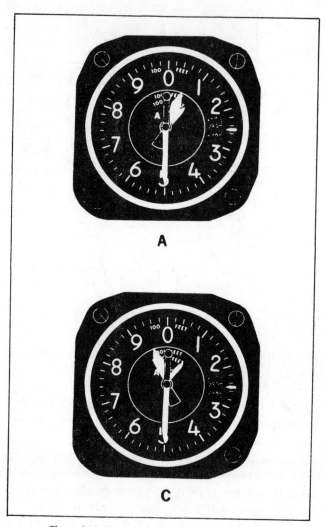

Figure 4-10. Three-Needle Instrument Indicators

DENSITY ALTITUDE is a critically important altitude; however, you can't read it on your altimeter but must calculate it, using pressure altitude and temperature. Density altitude is performance altitude — the airplane and engine perform as though they are at a different altitude than their true altitude. All performance charts are based on density altitude, and this book will deal with it in detail in Chapter Six.

TRUE ALTITUDE is your height above sea level. When you set your altimeter setting window to the local altimeter setting, the altimeter should read field elevation (above sea level). If it doesn't, record the instrument error. Differences of over 75' indicate that the instrument needs overhaul or replacement. (Before you take any drastic steps, be sure that your airplane is

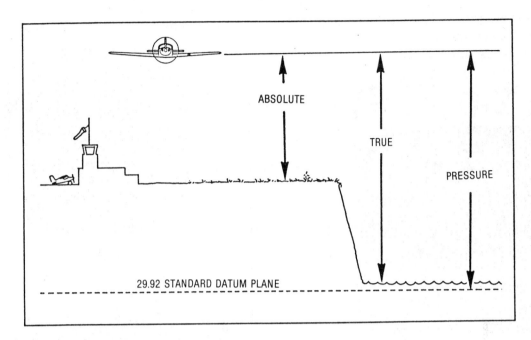

Figure 4-11. Altitude Definitions

not simply located at a point below the published field elevation.) The illustration (figure 4-11) shows an airplane with its altitude above the ground (absolute altitude), above sea level (true altitude), and above the standard datum plane of 29.92' (pressure altitude).

Any obstruction to the static port or static lines will make the altimeter unusable, so some aircraft have alternate static sources vented inside the cockpit. When using the alternate static source, there will be slight errors in the altimeter and airspeed indications. The pressure inside the cockpit is lower than the outside pressure — with the alternate static source selected, the altimeter will read slightly high, the airspeed indicator will read high, and the vertical speed indicator will read correctly after momentarily indicating a climb.

EFFECTS OF TEMPERATURE AND PRESSURE ON ALTIMETER INDICATIONS

When you fly into an area of lower barometric pressure (while maintaining a constant altimeter setting) your true altitude will be lower than your indicated altitude,

and that can be dangerous. Avoid this by frequently checking with ground stations to keep the altimeter set to an altimeter setting received from a station within 100 miles. If you fly into an area of colder temperatures, where air density is increased, indicated altitude will again be higher than true altitude.

"From High to Low, Look Out Below"

applies to both pressure and temperature. You have no means of adjusting for temperature changes, so remember that pressure levels rise on warm days and descend on cold days, and if you are flying a constant pressure level (altimeter setting), you may be dangerously low on a cold day.

VERTICAL SPEED INDICATOR

The vertical speed indicator (figure 4-12) is a static-pressure instrument which reflects rate of climb or descent by detecting rate of change in air pressure. Its internal construction is similar to that of the altimeter, but the aneroid wafer in the vertical speed indicator has a very small leak which allows its internal pressure to stabilize when altitude is not changing. During changes, there is a pressure differential between the air

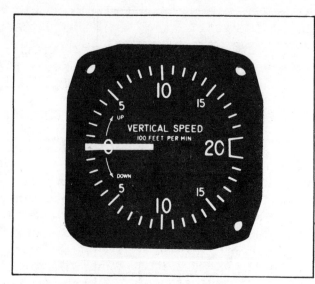

Figure 4-12. Vertical Speed Indicator

TURN AND SLIP INDICATOR

Your airplane may have either a turn needle or a turn coordinator, but in either case a ball instrument will be included. Both the turn needle and the turn coordinator (figure 4-13) indicate the rate of turn of the aircraft: when the turn needle is deflected one needle-width, or when the turn coordinator's airplane wing is on the index, the airplane is turning at the rate of 3° per second, and a complete circle will take 2 minutes. The turn and slip indicator shows rotation around the yaw axis (the ball), and around the roll axis (the miniature airplane or the needle).

in the wafer and the air surrounding it, and the instrument indicates the change in this differential as climb or descent rate in feet per minute. The needle will lag actual changes in altitude until the rate of change stabilizes. However, if your instrument is marked "IVSI", this lag has been eliminated and it is an Instantaneous Vertical Speed Indicator. The VSI is not a required instrument for either VFR or IFR flight, but you won't find many airplanes without one. If the static port is clogged or frozen the VSI will be unusable — select the alternate static source if one is available.

GYROSCOPIC INSTRUMENTS

The attitude indicator, the turn indicator, and the directional gyro or heading indicator operate on the principle of gyroscopic rigidity in space. A spinning body, such as a bicycle wheel, will maintain its position in space as long as a rotational force is applied — riding your bike "no hands" is an example of this. Precession, or turning, occurs when any external force is applied to the spinning body, which will react as though the force has been applied at a point 90° away in the direction of rotation. You lean your bicycle to the right, and the turning force is as though pressure has been applied to the left front of the wheel — 90° in the direction of rotation. Actually turning the wheel to the right may cause the bicycle to topple over to the right, again the result of gyroscopic precession.

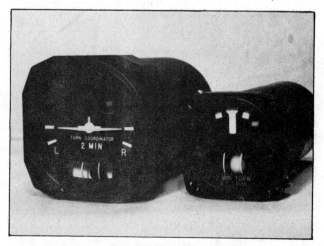

Figure 4-13. Turn and Slip Indicator

Unlike the turn needle, the turn coordinator is designed so that it reflects *roll* rate as well as *turn* rate. Neither instrument indicates bank angle. Bank angle, turn rate, and airspeed are interrelated, as shown in figure 4-14. For a given bank angle, the rate of turn increases as the airspeed decreases. Consider a light trainer and a jet, both banked 20°: the trainer would complete a 360° turn in a much shorter time than the jet and with a much smaller radius. If both airplanes maintained a 3° per second turn rate, they would both complete the circle at the same time — but the jet would be at an extreme bank angle. The bank angle for a 3° per second turn is approximately 15 percent of the true airspeed, so the trainer at 80 knots would bank 12°, while the jet at 400 knots would have to bank 60°.

The ball indicates the *quality* of the turn, with respect to rudder-aileron coordination. The force that causes

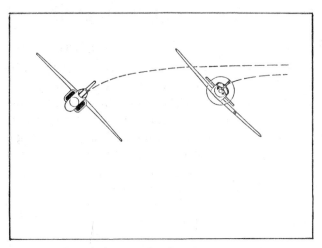

Figure 4-14. Rate and Radius of Turn vs. Speed

an airplane to turn is the horizontal component of lift (figure 4-15), which is opposed by centrifugal force. If the rate of turn is too great for the angle of bank,

Table 4-1. Constant Bank and Airspeed Table

CONSTANT BANK

Airspeed	Rate	Radius	Load Factor
Increases	Decreases	Increases	Same
Decreases	Increases	Decreases	Same

CONSTANT AIRSPEED

Angle of Bank	Rate	Radius	Load Factor
Increases	Increases	Decreases	Increases
Decreases	Decreases	Increases	Decreases

centrifugal force is greater than the horizontal component of lift, and the ball rolls toward the outside of the turn. This is termed a "skidding" turn, and either a steeper bank angle (increasing horizontal component) or less rudder pressure on the inside of the turn (reduced centrifugal force) will return the ball to the center. The reverse situation has the ball falling to the inside of the turn in a "slip", caused by too little centrifugal force and too much horizontal component.

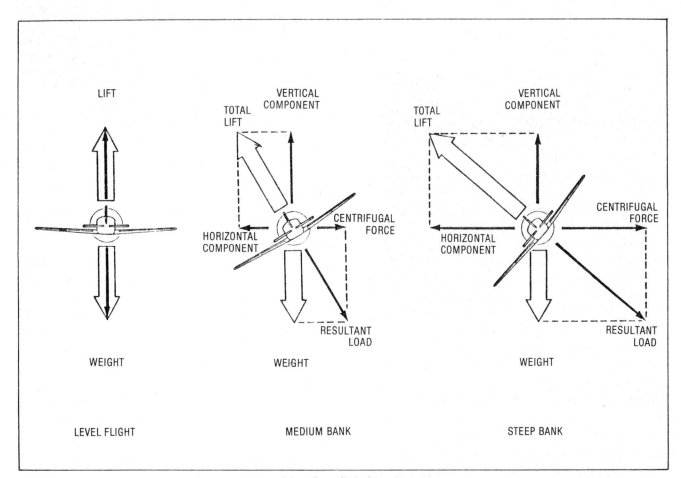

Figure 4-15. Forces During Normal Coordinated Turns

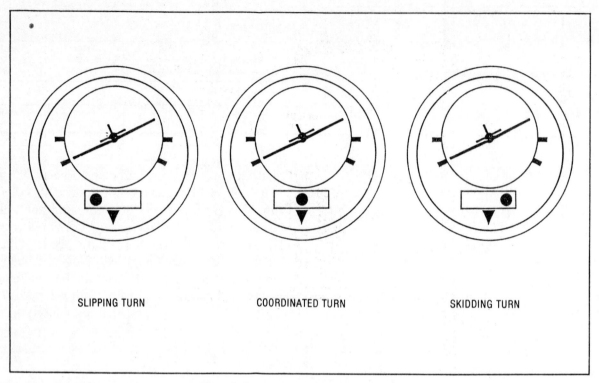

SLIPPING TURN   COORDINATED TURN   SKIDDING TURN

Figure 4-16. Interpreting the Ball Instrument

Less bank angle or more inside rudder will return the ball to the center (figure 4-16). A rule of thumb is to *"step on the ball"* — apply pressure to the rudder pedal on the side of the instrument that the ball is on.

Turn needles or turn coordinators are almost always electrically driven, but you may find a turn needle driven by vacuum from an engine-driven vacuum pump or a **venturi**. Be sure that you know what makes your turn indicator operate.

In most trainer-type airplanes, the gyro instruments (attitude and heading indicator) are vacuum operated. An engine-driven vacuum pump draws air into the instrument case and as the air passes over turbine wheels it imparts a rotational force (figure 4-17). When the gyroscope rotors are up to speed they become fixed in the plane of rotation, and the airplane moves around them. The instrument presentations are so designed that the pilot has an accurate representation of airplane attitude and heading. Not all gyro installations are entirely vacuum operated — you may find that your heading indicator is electric and the attitude indicator is vacuum, or both may be electrically operated. Check the power source for each instrument in your airplane so that you can better deal with failures.

ATTITUDE INDICATOR

The gyroscope and its linkage cause the horizon disc (figure 4-18) to move in both pitch and roll behind the miniature airplane. If you compare the movement of the horizon line in the attitude indicator with the movement of the natural horizon, you will see that the instrument instantly and accurately reflects changes in the pitch and roll attitude of the airplane. It is this instantaneous representation that makes the attitude indicator the most valuable instrument on the panel when reference to the natural horizon is lost. The bank angle markings at the top of the instrument are 10°, 20°, 30°, 45° (the dot), 60° and 90°. For control of pitch attitude —nose up or nose down — keeping the miniature airplane's wings near the horizon line is the thing to do if you are caught unexpectedly in poor visibility, or while flying at night with a poorly defined horizon.

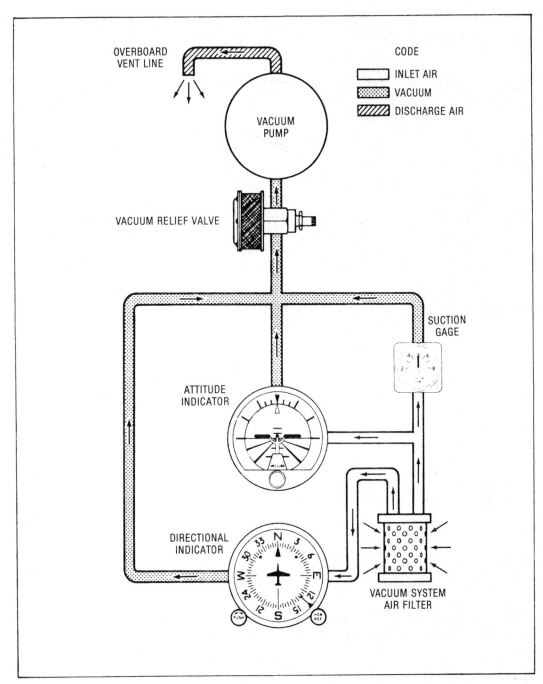

Figure 4-17. Vacuum Operated Gyro Instruments

As part of your flight training, your instructor will have you control the airplane solely by reference to the flight instruments, and you will be expected to demonstrate your ability to maneuver the airplane by instruments on your private pilot checkride.

Figure 4-18. Attitude Indicator

HEADING INDICATOR

You shouldn't always trust your heading indicator (directional gyro) (figure 4-19) to tell you which way

Figure 4-19. Heading Indicator

you are heading. The heading indicator is not a very smart instrument: it only repeats the heading that has been set into it. For that reason, it has an adjustment knob, and must be set to correspond to the magnetic compass (or to the runway heading) before it can be used for navigation.

If you fail to set the heading indicator properly before takeoff, and do not notice that it disagrees with the **magnetic compass**, you can be many miles off course in a very short time.

Because the gyro's rotor spins at a velocity of about 18,000 RPM, its bearings must have a minimum of friction. As the bearings wear, or as dirt and contaminants (such as tobacco tar) collect at these critical points, the gyro will begin to slowly precess (drift) away from the heading you have set. You should check the heading indicator against the magnetic compass at least every 15 minutes, and more often if the instrument is showing signs of age such as grinding noises or rapid precession. Reset the heading indicator to the magnetic compass only when the airplane is in straight and level, unaccelerated flight. The magnetic compass develops errors during banks, climbs, and descents, and you do not want to set these errors into your heading indicator.

MAGNETIC COMPASS

The only instrument in your airplane that does not depend on some source of external power is the magnetic compass (figure 4-20). All of your navigational procedures are based on magnetic information. Unfortunately, the magnetic compass is subject to more errors than any other instrument.

The magnetic compass consists of a card floating in a liquid, pivoted on a needle point, and having affixed to it small permanent magnets that align themselves (and therefore the card) with the earth's magnetic field. The card is marked so that you see an N on the compass when the magnets are being attracted to the magnetic North Pole. The magnetic compass is subject to several errors: oscillation error, acceleration error, and **northerly turning error**. Because of the single-point suspension, the compass card swings in even the

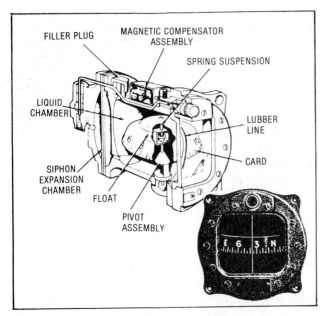

Figure 4-20. Magnetic Compass

heading, the compass will indicate a turn to the north, while deceleration on an east or west heading will cause the compass to indicate a turn to the south.

Use this memory aid: **A N D S** — *Accelerate North, Decelerate South.* (See figure 4-21.)

It is because of northerly turning error and acceleration error that you must set the heading indicator to agree with the magnetic compass *only* in straight and level, unaccelerated flight.

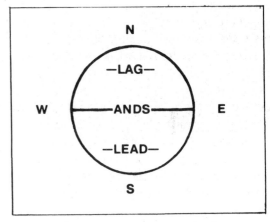

Figure 4-21. Compass Errors

slightest turbulence, and you must average its swings to approximate a constant heading. If your compass does *not* swing when the air gets rough, check to be sure that the fluid hasn't leaked out!

Northerly turning error is caused by the fact that the lines of force of the earth's magnetic field are parallel to the earth's surface at the Equator, but bend downward toward the surface as latitude increases and are essentially vertical at the magnetic poles. This force, which pulls the ends of the compass magnets downward, is called "magnetic dip": when the airplane banks and the compass card tilts, the compass magnets, affected by dip, introduce a compass error. When you turn from a generally northerly heading, the compass will momentarily turn in the opposite direction, slow to a stop, and then follow the progress of the turn — but *lagging* the actual heading change. The amount of lag diminishes as the heading approaches east or west. Conversely, when you turn from a southerly heading the compass jumps out ahead of the turn, and *leads* the heading change, with the amount of lead again diminishing as east or west is approached. The amount of lead or lag which is attributable to northerly turning error is approximately equal to the airplane's latitude.

Acceleration error is evident on headings of east or west. If the airplane is accelerated, without changing

Magnetic deviation is an error which affects the accuracy of the magnetic compass but is caused by external forces. The magnetic influence of ferrous (steel) engine parts and electrical wiring cause deviation; Chapter Seven discusses the effect of deviation on navigation.

If you must rely solely on your magnetic compass for navigation, the most effective way to change heading is the timed turn. Note the magnetic compass heading, determine how many degrees you want to turn, and turn at 3° per second (using the index on the turn coordinator or turn needle) for the appropriate number of seconds. If you complete the turn within 5° or 10° of your target heading you are within acceptable limits.

VERTICAL CARD MAGNETIC COMPASSES

You may find an airplane with a vertical card magnetic compass. These relatively new devices contain no liquid, and have little or no oscillation error. Acceleration error and Northerly Turning Error are present, but are quickly damped by internal electrical currents. They are considerably more expensive (but easier to use) than liquid-filled compasses.

SLAVED GYRO SYSTEMS

If your airplane has a horizontal situation indicator (HSI) as a heading indicator, it may derive its directional information from a remote magnetic compass (or flux detector) mounted in the tail or wingtip, away from electrical influences. The weak electrical signals from the remote magnetic flux detector are amplified before being transmitted to the heading indicator, which then rotates or "slaves" into agreement with the directional information from the remote source. The system includes compensating devices to minimize or eliminate any deviation error. The exact location of the amplifier and compensating devices varies between manufacturers, and the location of the magnetic flux detector is determined by the installer. Figure 4-22 illustrates a possible installation with optional flux detector locations.

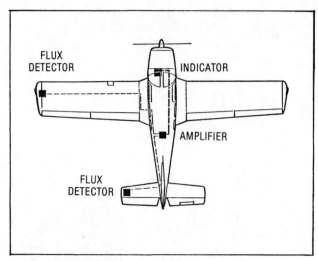

Figure 4-22. Slaved Gyro System

In most installations, a "slaving switch" is provided so that you can rapidly adjust the heading indicator card to agree with the liquid-filled magnetic compass during the preflight checks, and in some installations you can select "free gyro" and adjust the heading indicator just as you do with simpler systems.

FLIGHT INSTRUMENT
REVIEW SECTION

1. The turn coordinator provides an indication of

    1. the movement of the airplane about the yaw and roll axes.
    2. the angle of bank to but not exceeding 30°.
    3. attitude of the airplane with reference to the longitudinal axis.
    4. motion of the airplane about the lateral and vertical axes.

2. To receive accurate indications during flight from a heading indicator the instrument must be

    1. set prior to flight on a known heading.
    2. calibrated on a compass rose at regular intervals.
    3. adequately powered so that it seeks the proper direction.
    4. periodically realigned with the magnetic compass as the gyro precesses.

3. In the Northern Hemisphere, a magnetic compass will normally indicate a turn toward the north if

    1. a right turn is entered from an east heading.
    2. a left turn is entered from a west heading.
    3. an aircraft is decelerated while on an east or west heading.
    4. an aircraft is accelerated while on an east or west heading.

4. Deviation in a magnetic compass is caused by

    1. presence of flaws in the permanent magnets of the compass.
    2. the difference in the location between true north and magnetic north.
    3. magnetic ore deposits in the Earth distorting the lines of magnetic force.
    4. magnetic fields within the airplane distorting the lines of magnetic force.

5. In the Northern Hemisphere, a magnetic compass will normally indicate initially a turn toward the east if

    1. an aircraft is decelerated while on a south heading.
    2. an aircraft is accelerated while on a north heading.
    3. a right turn is entered from a north heading.
    4. a left turn is entered from a north heading.

6. How do variations in temperature affect the altimeter?

    1. Pressure levels are raised on warm days and the indicated altitude is lower than true altitude.
    2. Higher temperatures expand the pressure levels and the indicated altitude is higher than true altitude.

3. Lower temperatures lower the pressure levels and the indicated altitude is lower than the true altitude.

4. Indicated altitude varies directly with temperature.

7. If it is necessary to set the altimeter from 29.15 to 29.85, what change is made on the indicated altitude?

1. 70-foot increase.
2. 700-foot increase.
3. 700-foot decrease.
4. 70-foot decrease.

8. The pitot system provides impact pressure for only the

1. airspeed indicator, altimeter, and vertical speed indicator.
2. altimeter and vertical speed indicator.
3. vertical speed indicator.
4. airspeed indicator.

9. What is an important airspeed limitation that is not color coded on airspeed indicators?

1. Never-exceed speed.
2. Maximum structural cruising speed.
3. Maneuvering speed.
4. Maximum flaps-extended speed.

10. Refer to the airspeed indicator. Which of the color coded markings on the airspeed indicator identifies the never-exceed speed?

1. Lower A/S limit of the yellow arc.
2. Upper A/S limit of the white arc.
3. Upper A/S limit of the green arc.
4. The red radial line.

11. Refer to the airspeed indicator. Which of the color coded markings identifies the power-off stalling speed with wing flaps and landing gear in the landing position?

1. Upper A/S limit of the green arc.
2. Upper A/S limit of the white arc.
3. Lower A/S limit of the green arc.
4. Lower A/S limit of the white arc.

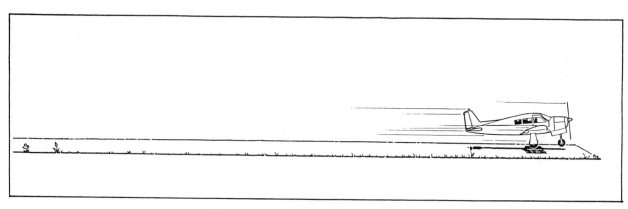

Figure 5-1. One Possible Result of Overloading

It would be nice to have an airplane in which we could fill all of the seats and all of the baggage area, fuel up to capacity, and take off safely without worrying about loading, but that is seldom (if ever) possible. The manufacturer dictates a maximum gross weight figure based on several factors including structural strength of the landing gear, power loading (weight per horsepower), wing loading (weight per square foot of wing area), strength of the wing structure, etc. *Overloading an airplane can have serious consequences!*. (See figure 5-1.)

Airplanes are assigned to categories depending on the amount of weight the wing structure can sustain, and those categories dictate how the airplane can be used. The requirements are based on "G's" — one G is 1 x the force of gravity (or the weight of the airplane). A *Normal* category airplane can have a load of 3.8 Gs imposed on its wing, a *Utility* category airplane is stressed for 4.4 Gs, and an airplane in the *Aerobatic* category is designed to withstand a load of 6 Gs. Aerobatic airplanes usually have G meters installed to record how many Gs the airplane experienced during

an aerobatic maneuver, (some sadder but wiser pilots have said that a G meter gives you information you really don't want to know!). Many airplanes are certificated in both the Normal and Utility categories, but are then limited in gross weight, in weight distribution, or in authorized maneuvers.

If you overload an airplane, the wing will have to be flown at a greater than normal angle of attack to develop enough lift to support the extra weight — this increases the stall speed, decreases the cruise speed, and limits the angle you can bank before reaching the critical angle of attack. Carrying more than the design maximum weight also means longer takeoff runs. If you combine overweight with a soft runway surface or a high density altitude, you are asking for trouble.

Loads applied to the wing during maneuvering can overstress the airplane's structure. Figure 5-2 shows the relationship between bank angle and load factor, and you can see that for a normal category airplane 3.8G will be reached at about a 75° bank angle and for an airplane certificated in the Utility category a bank of about 77° will bring the load factor to 4.4G. If the wing is designed for a wings level load of 2,000 pounds and you load the airplane to 2,500 pounds, in a 60° bank you will be adding an additional 1,000 pounds to the load on the wing.

A one-time overload may not cause problems, but repeatedly overstressing components may cause them to fail many flight hours later, while performing normal maneuvers.

Some airplanes are additionally limited to a "zero fuel" weight, which usually shows up as a placard saying "All weight in excess of 3,500 pounds must be in the form of fuel," or something similar. The designer establishes this limitation to insure that not all of the weight is concentrated in the fuselage, where an overload can exert a damaging bending force on the wing structure.

Center of gravity (CG) location relates directly to longitudinal stability. You will recall from Chapter Two that the airplane is maneuvered around three axes which pass through the center of gravity, and that all lift forces are concentrated at the center of pressure on the wing. The designer knows how the center of pressure will move as angle of attack changes, and limits the allowable movement of the center of gravity so that a properly loaded airplane will always be controllable.

Figure 5-3 shows how airflow over the horizontal stabilizer creates a downward pressure (download) which offsets the nose-down tendency caused by the center of pressure being aft of the center of gravity. As

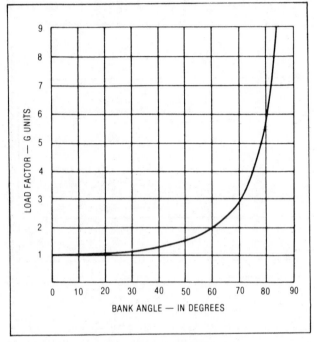

Figure 5-2. Load Factor Chart

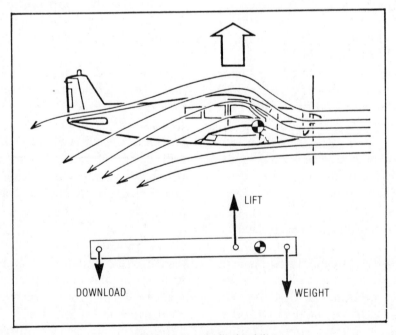

Figure 5-3. Longitudinal Stability

angle of attack is increased, the center of pressure moves forward; at the same time, airflow over the horizontal stabilizer is diminishing, reducing the downward pressure.

At the critical angle of attack, the center of pressure is so close to the center of gravity, and the elevator has so little downward pressure, that the nose pitches down and the airplane reduces the angle of attack. This natural tendency to reduce the angle of attack and avoid stalling is a built-in safety factor available *only* when the airplane is loaded within design limits.

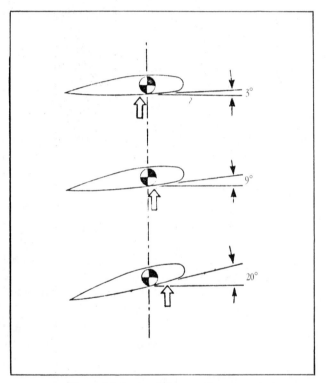

Figure 5-4. Center of Pressure Movement

If the airplane is loaded so that the center of gravity is forward of the designed forward limit, a greater than normal downward pressure on the horizontal stabilizer will be required, and the up elevator necessary to balance the weight up front will add drag. The wing will have to be flown at a greater angle of attack to develop enough lift to support the weight of the airplane *and* the download on the tail, which will slow the airplane and increase the stall speed. During the landing flare, the elevator may not have enough travel available to prevent landing on the nosewheel, especially if power

has been reduced and airflow over the tail surfaces diminished. On a takeoff attempt with a forward center of gravity, additional speed (and runway) will be required before the heavy nose can be rotated to climb attitude.

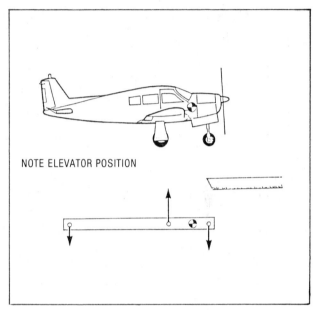

NOTE ELEVATOR POSITION

Figure 5-5. Forward CG Loading

Loading the airplane so that the center of gravity is at the aft limit has *some* advantages: less download on the horizontal stabilizer is required, so there is less drag and the airplane can fly at a smaller angle of attack. These factors pay off in cruise speed and fuel economy. Load the airplane so that the CG falls outside of the design limits, however, and you have a tiger by the tail.

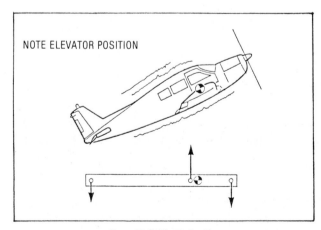

NOTE ELEVATOR POSITION

Figure 5-6. Aft CG Loading

Stall speed will be lower, but if a stall does occur recovery will be difficult, if not impossible. In cruise flight, the elevator control forces will be so light that you might inadvertently overstress the airplane, and during the landing flare you may have difficulty maintaining the proper attitude.

It is worthwhile to compute weight and center of gravity location for several typical loadings: for example, full fuel and a single pilot; full fuel, a 170 pound pilot and three 170 pound passengers; or half filled tanks, two persons on board and maximum authorized baggage. These calculations will provide benchmarks so that an unusual loading situation will be recognized, and a weight and balance calculated for that special situation.

Another effect of loading an airplane so that the center of gravity falls outside the aft limits of the envelope relates to rudder authority. You know that the rudder rotates the airplane around the vertical (yaw) axis, and that the vertical axis passes through the center of gravity. Let's design an imaginary airplane with the rudder 12 feet from the center of gravity location with the airplane properly loaded. On a day with a gusty crosswind it might take full rudder deflection to keep the airplane pointing straight down the runway during the takeoff roll. Now, let's reload that airplane so that the center of gravity moves aft 12 inches, so that the distance from the rudder to the CG is only 11 feet. With the lever arm reduced by 1 foot, full rudder pressure may not be adequate to handle the crosswind! You will hear some airplanes referred to as "short coupled" — this means that the distance from the CG to the rudder is short even when the airplane is properly loaded, and it takes quick and assertive rudder use to maintain directional control on takeoff.

Improper (or unbalanced) distribution of weight outside of the fuselage can also have undesirable effects. In a typical single-engine airplane, if one wing tank is full and the other is empty, you will need aileron pressure to hold the wings level. The aileron drag will cause a yaw which must be overcome with rudder. The total effect is a reduction in speed and in fuel economy.

Twin-engine airplanes with baggage compartments in the wings offer ample opportunity for misloading and creating lateral imbalance.

WEIGHT AND BALANCE CALCULATIONS

One document which must be in the airplane at all times is the manufacturer's data required to compute the weight and center of gravity location under different loading conditions. You will find this information in the Approved Flight Manual (not the Owner's Handbook) for older airplanes, and in the Pilot's Operating Handbook for newer airplanes. The airplane's empty weight and center of gravity position have been furnished by the manufacturer and serve as a starting point. If equipment has been added or removed since the airplane was built, an FAA Form 337 will have been prepared by the mechanic who performed the work. This updates the empty weight and center of gravity location, and that form will be with the weight and balance data (also check the airframe maintenance log).

The empty weight of the airplane includes unusable fuel and optional equipment; full oil *may* be included — check the data for your airplane. Gasoline weighs 6 pounds per gallon and oil weighs 7.5 pounds per *gallon*, not per quart. Typically, engine oil capacity is given in quarts — it's easy to include the weight of the oil at 7.5 pounds per quart and really mess up the calculations!

The balance portion of the weight and balance problem introduces two new terms: **arm** and **moment**. The easiest way to visualize these terms is to go back to your childhood teeter-totter. Assume that it was 12 feet long, pivoted in the center, and that you weighed 50 pounds. When you sat on one end of the teeter-totter the arm (distance from the pivot point to your seat) was 6 feet, making the moment (your weight times the arm) 300 foot-pounds. A 50-pound friend sitting on the other end of the board an equal distance from the center would balance the teeter-totter. Without a 50-pound friend, though, to have any fun at all you needed a 100 pound playmate on the other end of the board 3 feet from the pivot point, or maybe a 75 pound friend 4 feet from the pivot point. To balance, in other words, there had to be a moment of 300 foot-pounds on each side of the pivot. The airplane manufacturer provides data on distance (arm) from a datum point which you can multiply times the weight of fuel, baggage, or passengers to derive the moment. The manufacturer may provide moments for various weights without requiring the intermediate step of providing the distance (arm). You may have to inter- polate between given weights if your passengers, baggage, or fuel load do not exactly match the tabu- lated values.

Figure 5-7 shows a graphic method of presenting the weight and balance information and determining the position of the center of gravity, and figures 5-8 and 5-9 show a tabular method. To avoid large, confusing numbers, moments are presented as moment/1000. With the tabular method, the CG position is deter- mined by dividing the total moments by the total weight. As weights are shifted around within the airplane by moving baggage from forward compart- ments to aft compartments, by moving passengers, or even by extending and retracting the landing gear, the center of gravity follows the weight — if the weight moves aft so does the CG.

Use figure 5-7:

Calculate the CG and determine the plotted position on the CG moment envelope chart.

	Weight	Mom/1000
Empty weight	1,350	51.5
Pilot and front passenger	380	—
Fuel 48 gal	288	—
Oil 8 qts.	15	–0.2

1.   CG 38.9, out of limits forward.
2.   CG 39.9, utility category.
3.   CG 38.9, normal category.
4.   CG 39.9, normal category.

From the loading graph, find the moment/1000 for pilot and front seat passenger weight of 380 lb: 14.0. Find the moment/1000 for 288 lbs of fuel: 13.8. Total weight = 2,033 lbs, total moment/1000 = 79.1. Center of gravity = total moment ÷ total weight = 79,100 ÷ 2,033 = 38.9. Plot on the center of gravity moment envelope a weight of 2,033 lbs and a moment of 79.1; the plotted point falls in the normal category area.

Use figures 5-8 and 5-9:

Upon landing, the front passenger (180 lb) departs the airplane. A rear passenger (204 lb) moves to the front passenger position. What effect does this have on the CG if the airplane weighed 2,690 lb and the moment/ 100 was 2,260 just prior to the passenger transfer?

1.   The weight changes but the CG is not affected.
2.   The CG moves forward approximately 0.1".
3.   The CG moves forward approximately 2.4".
4.   The CG moves forward approximately 3.0".

Compute the CG before the passenger movement:

CG = total moment ÷ total weight = 226,000 ÷ 2,690 = 84.01"

$$2,690 \qquad 226,000 = 84.01"$$

Front passenger departs: –180 lbs   –15,300

$$2,510 \qquad 210,700 \text{ total moment}$$

Compute moment for 204 lb passenger in both rear and front seats:

204 x 121	= 24,684 moment
	before moving.
204 x 85	= 17,340 moment
	after moving.

7344 reduction

210,700 – 7,344 after passenger moves forward = 203,356 moment.

CG = total moment ÷ total weight

203,356 ÷ 2,510 = 81.02 or 3" forward.

Remember, the CG moves with the weight!

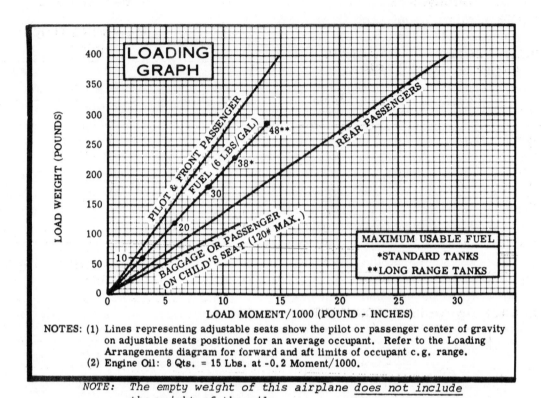

NOTES: (1) Lines representing adjustable seats show the pilot or passenger center of gravity on adjustable seats positioned for an average occupant. Refer to the Loading Arrangements diagram for forward and aft limits of occupant c.g. range.
(2) Engine Oil: 8 Qts. = 15 Lbs. at -0.2 Moment/1000.

NOTE: The empty weight of this airplane does not include the weight of the oil.

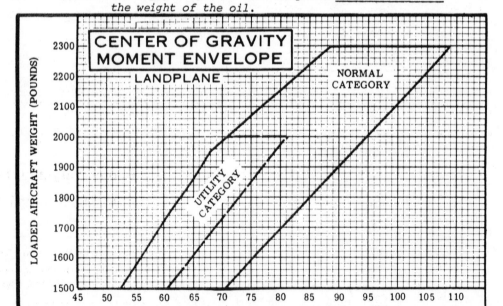

Figure 5-7. Loading Graphs

OCCUPANTS

FRONT SEATS ARM 85 / REAR SEATS ARM 121

Weight	Moment 100	Weight	Moment 100
120	102	120	145
130	110	130	157
140	119	140	169
150	128	150	182
160	136	160	194
170	144	170	206
180	153	180	218
190	162	190	230
200	170	200	242

BAGGAGE OR 5TH SEAT OCCUPANT ARM 140

Weight	Moment 100
10	14
20	28
30	42
40	56
50	70
60	84
70	98
80	112
90	126
100	140
110	154
120	168
130	182
140	196
150	210
160	224
170	238
180	252
190	266
200	280
210	294
220	308
230	322
240	336
250	350
260	364
270	378

USABLE FUEL

MAIN WING TANKS ARM 75

Gallons	Weight	Moment 100
5	30	22
10	60	45
15	90	68
20	120	90
25	150	112
30	180	135
35	210	158
40	240	180
44	264	198

AUXILIARY WING TANKS ARM 94

Gallons	Weight	Moment 100
5	30	28
10	60	56
15	90	85
19	114	107

*OIL

Quarts	Weight	Moment 100
10	19	5

*Included in Basic Empty Weight

Empty Weight - 2015

MOM/100 - 1554

MOMENT LIMITS vs WEIGHT

Moment limits are based on the following weight and center of gravity limit data (landing gear down).

WEIGHT CONDITION	FORWARD CG LIMIT	AFT CG LIMIT
2950 lb (take-off or landing)	82.1	84.7
2525 lb.	77.5	85.7
2475 lb. or less	77.0	85.7

Figure 5-8. Tabular Method

Weight	Minimum Moment 100	Maximum Moment 100	Weight	Minimum Moment 100	Maximum Moment 100
2100	1617	1800	2600	2037	2224
2110	1625	1808	2610	2048	2232
2120	1632	1817	2620	2058	2239
2130	1640	1825	2630	2069	2247
2140	1648	1834	2640	2080	2255
2150	1656	1843	2650	2090	2263
2160	1663	1851	2660	2101	2271
2170	1671	1860	2670	2112	2279
2180	1679	1868	2680	2123	2287
2190	1686	1877	2690	2133	2295
2200	1694	1885	2700	2144	2303
2210	1702	1894	2710	2155	2311
2220	1709	1903	2720	2166	2319
2230	1717	1911	2730	2177	2326
2240	1725	1920	2740	2188	2334
2250	1733	1928	2750	2199	2342
2260	1740	1937	2760	2210	2350
2270	1748	1945	2770	2221	2358
2280	1756	1954	2780	2232	2366
2290	1763	1963	2790	2243	2374
2300	1771	1971			
2310	1779	1980	2800	2254	2381
2320	1786	1988	2810	2265	2389
2330	1794	1997	2820	2276	2397
2340	1802	2005	2830	2287	2405
2350	1810	2014	2840	2298	2413
2360	1817	2023	2850	2309	2421
2370	1825	2031	2860	2320	2428
2380	1833	2040	2870	2332	2436
2390	1840	2048	2880	2343	2444
			2890	2354	2452
2400	1848	2057	2900	2365	2460
2410	1856	2065	2910	2377	2468
2420	1863	2074	2920	2388	2475
2430	1871	2083	2930	2399	2483
2440	1879	2091	2940	2411	2491
2450	1887	2100	2950	2422	2499
2460	1894	2108			
2470	1902	2117			
2480	1911	2125			
2490	1921	2134			
2500	1932	2143			
2510	1942	2151			
2520	1953	2160			
2530	1963	2168			
2540	1974	2176			
2550	1984	2184			
2560	1995	2192			
2570	2005	2200			
2580	2016	2208			
2590	2026	2216			

Figure 5-9. Moment Limits vs. Weight

WEIGHT AND BALANCE
REVIEW SECTION

Use figure Q5-1 for review problems 1 through 3.

1. Determine the CG moment/1000 with the following data:

	WEIGHT/lb	Moment/1000
Empty weight	1,350	51.5
Pilot and front passenger	340	—
Fuel (std. tanks)	Capacity	—
Oil	8 Qts	−0.2

   1. 38.7 lb./in.
   2. 69.9 lb./in.
   3. 74.9 lb./in.
   4. 77.0 lb./in.

2. What is the maximum amount of fuel that may be aboard the airplane on takeoff if it is loaded as follows?

	Weight/lb.	Moment/1000
Empty weight	1,350	51.5
Pilot and front passenger	340	—
Rear passengers	310	—
Baggage	45	—
Oil 8 qts.	15	—

   1. 24 gal.
   2. 34 gal.
   3. 40 gal.
   4. 46 gal.

3. What is the maximum amount of baggage that may be loaded aboard the airplane for the CG to remain within the loading envelope?

	Weight/lb.	Moment/1000
Empty weight	1,350	51.5
Pilot and front passenger	250	—
Rear passengers	400	—
Baggage	—	—
Fuel 30 gal.	—	—
Oil 8 qts.	15	−0.2

   1. 120 lb.
   2. 105 lb.
   3. 90 lb.
   4. 75 lb.

4. Calculate the CG and determine the plotted position on the CG moment envelope chart.

	Weight/lb.	Moment/1000
Empty weight	1,350	51.5
Pilot and front passenger	380	—
Fuel 48 gal.	288	—
Oil 8 qts.	15	−0.2

   1. CG 38.9, out of limits forward
   2. CG 39.9, utility category
   3. CG 38.9, normal category
   4. CG 39.9, normal category

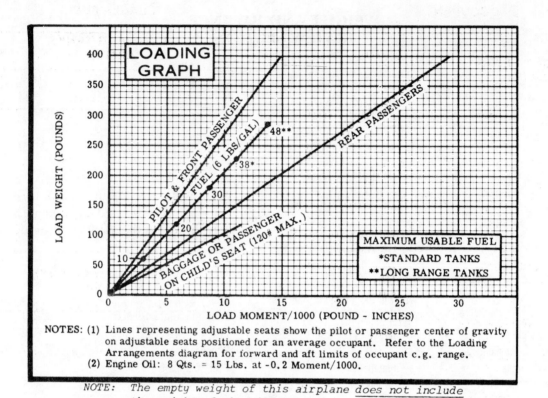

NOTES: (1) Lines representing adjustable seats show the pilot or passenger center of gravity
            on adjustable seats positioned for an average occupant. Refer to the Loading
            Arrangements diagram for forward and aft limits of occupant c.g. range.
       (2) Engine Oil: 8 Qts. = 15 Lbs. at -0.2 Moment/1000.

*NOTE: The empty weight of this airplane <u>does not include</u>
          the weight of the oil.*

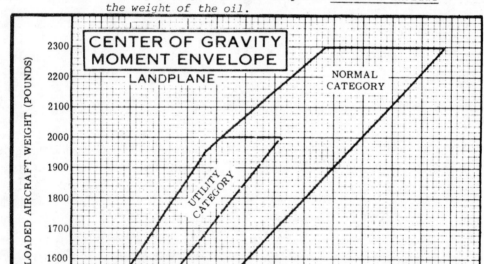

Figure Q5-1.

OCCUPANTS

FRONT SEATS ARM 85 / REAR SEATS ARM 121

Weight	Moment/100	Weight	Moment/100
120	102	120	145
130	110	130	157
140	119	140	169
150	128	150	182
160	136	160	194
170	144	170	206
180	153	180	218
190	162	190	230
200	170	200	242

BAGGAGE OR 5TH SEAT OCCUPANT ARM 140

Weight	Moment/100
10	14
20	28
30	42
40	56
50	70
60	84
70	98
80	112
90	126
100	140
110	154
120	168
130	182
140	196
150	210
160	224
170	238
180	252
190	266
200	280
210	294
220	308
230	322
240	336
250	350
260	364
270	378

USABLE FUEL

MAIN WING TANKS ARM 75

Gallons	Weight	Moment/100
5	30	22
10	60	45
15	90	68
20	120	90
25	150	112
30	180	135
35	210	158
40	240	180
44	264	198

AUXILIARY WING TANKS ARM 94

Gallons	Weight	Moment/100
5	30	28
10	60	56
15	90	85
19	114	107

*OIL

Quarts	Weight	Moment/100
10	19	5

*Included in Basic Empty Weight

Empty Weight - 2015
MOM/100 - 1554

MOMENT LIMITS vs WEIGHT

Moment limits are based on the following weight and center of gravity limit data (landing gear down).

WEIGHT CONDITION	FORWARD CG LIMIT	AFT CG LIMIT
2950 lb (take-off or landing)	82.1	84.7
2525 lb.	77.5	85.7
2475 lb. or less	77.0	85.7

Figure Q5-2.

Weight	Minimum Moment 100	Maximum Moment 100		Weight	Minimum Moment 100	Maximum Moment 100
2100	1617	1800		2600	2037	2224
2110	1625	1808		2610	2048	2232
2120	1632	1817		2620	2058	2239
2130	1640	1825		2630	2069	2247
2140	1648	1834		2640	2080	2255
2150	1656	1843		2650	2090	2263
2160	1663	1851		2660	2101	2271
2170	1671	1860		2670	2112	2279
2180	1679	1868		2680	2123	2287
2190	1686	1877		2690	2133	2295
2200	1694	1885		2700	2144	2303
2210	1702	1894		2710	2155	2311
2220	1709	1903		2720	2166	2319
2230	1717	1911		2730	2177	2326
2240	1725	1920		2740	2188	2334
2250	1733	1928		2750	2199	2342
2260	1740	1937		2760	2210	2350
2270	1748	1945		2770	2221	2358
2280	1756	1954		2780	2232	2366
2290	1763	1963		2790	2243	2374
2300	1771	1971				
2310	1779	1980		2800	2254	2381
2320	1786	1988		2810	2265	2389
2330	1794	1997		2820	2276	2397
2340	1802	2005		2830	2287	2405
2350	1810	2014		2840	2298	2413
2360	1817	2023		2850	2309	2421
2370	1825	2031		2860	2320	2428
2380	1833	2040		2870	2332	2436
2390	1840	2048		2880	2343	2444
				2890	2354	2452
2400	1848	2057		2900	2365	2460
2410	1856	2065		2910	2377	2468
2420	1863	2074		2920	2388	2475
2430	1871	2083		2930	2399	2483
2440	1879	2091		2940	2411	2491
2450	1887	2100		2950	2422	2499
2460	1894	2108				
2470	1902	2117				
2480	1911	2125				
2490	1921	2134				
2500	1932	2143				
2510	1942	2151				
2520	1953	2160				
2530	1963	2168				
2540	1974	2176				
2550	1984	2184				
2560	1995	2192				
2570	2005	2200				
2580	2016	2208				
2590	2026	2216				

Figure Q5-3.

Use figures Q5-2 and Q5-3 for review problems 5 through 7:

5. Determine if the airplane weight and balance is within limits.

Front seat occupants . . . . 340 lb.
Rear seat occupants . . . . 295 lb.
Fuel . . . . 44 gal.
Baggage . . . . 56 lb.

1. Within limits.
2. 20 lb. overweight, CG within limits.
3. Weight within limits, CG out of limits forward.
4. 39 lb. overweight, CG out of limits forward.

5. Which action can adjust the airplane's weight to maximum gross weight and the CG within limits for takeoff?

Front seat occupants . . . . 425 lb.
Rear seat occupants . . . . 300 lb.
Fuel, main tanks . . . . 44 gal.

1. Drain 12 gal. of fuel.
2. Drain 9 gal. of fuel.
3. Transfer 12 gal. of fuel from the main tanks to the auxiliary tanks.
4. Transfer 19 gal. of fuel from the main tanks to the auxiliary tanks.

7. What effect does a 35-gal. fuel burn have on the weight and balance if the airplane weighed 2,890 lb. and the MOM/1000 was 2,452 at takeoff?

1. Weight is reduced by 210 lb. and the CG is unaffected.
2. Weight is reduced to 2,680 lb. and the CG moves forward.
3. Weight is reduced to 2,855 lb. and the CG moves aft.
4. Weight is reduced by 210 lb. and the CG is aft of limits.

Airplanes are manufactured and fly all over the world, and pilots everywhere rely on consistent performance in accordance with their airplane's Operating Handbook. Would you expect an airplane manufacturer to provide a different handbook to a Peruvian mountain pilot than is provided to a miner in Death Valley?

Obviously, the operating conditions vary widely in altitude and temperature. It is not necessary, and the reason lies in the term "International Standard Atmosphere (ISA)". At airplane manufacturing sites, engineering test flights go on in rain and in sunshine, in summer and in winter. All of the airspeeds, rates of climb, fuel burns, and takeoff and landing distances determined by test pilots are reduced to what they would be on a standard day at sea level.

By internationally accepted standards, a standard day has a barometric pressure of 29.92' Hg and a temperature of 15°C (59°F), and the standard atmospheric temperature lapse rate (decrease in temperature with increasing altitude) is assumed to be 2°C per 1000' of altitude above sea level — the International Standard Atmosphere.

Engineers take the information from the test flights, reduce it to its equivalent under standard conditions, and furnish the pilot with charts and graphs to predict airplane performance under widely varying pressure and temperature conditions.

DENSITY ALTITUDE

The basis for predicting performance is density altitude — pressure altitude corrected for non-standard temperature. Your responsibilities as a pilot will include calculating the effect that existing or forecast weather conditions will have on your takeoff and climb performance from a departure airport. You must also consider the true airspeed and fuel consumption rate at your chosen cruise altitude, and compare the predicted landing distance to the amount of runway available at the destination airport (and any enroute airports you might have to use in an emergency). You will have to compute the density altitude for the different airports, consult your airplane's performance charts, and get the numbers for the expected conditions.

In the discussion of the factors that produce lift, you learned that the density of the air has a direct effect on the amount of lift developed at a given airspeed or angle of attack, and you learned that high altitude, high temperature, and high humidity separately or in combination have the worst effect on performance. All of the charts, tables, computers, etc., that will be used in the calculation of density altitude performance take into account only pressure altitude and temperature — no provision is made for the effects of humidity on performance (figure 6-1). A conservative approach is to add 1,000' to any density altitude you arrive at by use

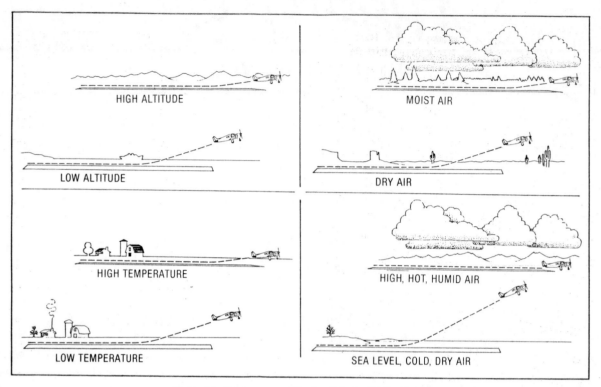

Figure 6-1. Circumstances Affecting Length of Takeoff Run

of pressure altitude and temperature and then calculate the performance figures based on that altitude.

The quickest way to determine pressure altitude when you are in the airplane is to note the setting in the **Kollsman window** (the little window you use for entering altimeter setting), then set it to 29.92; the altimeter will indicate pressure altitude. (Return the altimeter setting to its previous setting before you forget it!) If you are determining density altitude for a distant airport and have gotten its temperature and altimeter setting from the hourly weather sequence reports, determine the difference between 29.92 and the reported altimeter setting and apply the difference to the field elevation:

Altimeter setting . . . 30.20   Field elevation 2,348
             −29.92   −280
           ─────   ─────
        .28 = 280'   Pressure altitude = 2,068

(1.00" = 1,000', .1" = 100', .01" = 10')

To be sure that you apply the pressure difference correctly, ask yourself which way the altimeter needles will move as the altimeter setting is changed from 30.20 to 29.92. In the example, they will move counterclockwise, and the pressure difference must be subtracted from the field elevation to derive pressure altitude at that airport.

Figure 6-2 will be found in your Private Pilot Question Book and provides pressure difference factors for you to apply: determine the pressure altitude by applying the pressure difference factor from the columns on the right to the field elevation. Find the temperature on the bottom scale, draw a vertical line from the temperature to the pressure altitude (slanting) line, then draw a horizontal line to the left margin to read density altitude.

Another method is to use the slide rule side of your flight computer by setting the pressure altitude (29.92 reading of the altimeter) in the window opposite the temperature and read density altitude at the index. You can use the reading of your airplane's outside air temperature (OAT) gauge without correction.

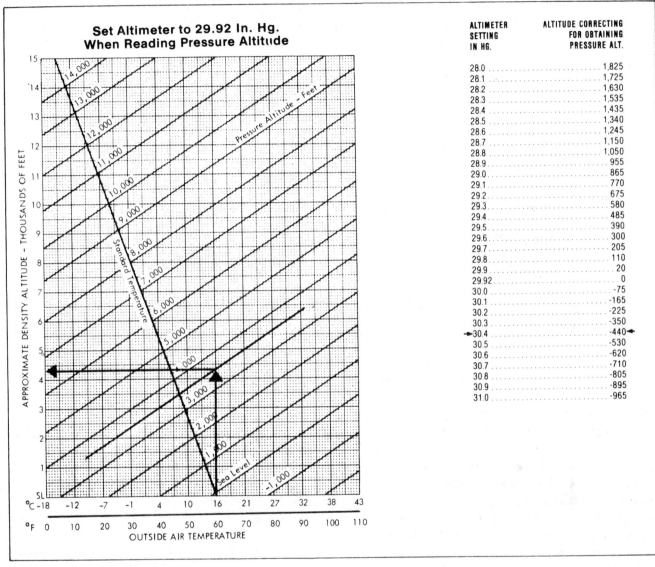

Figure 6-2. Pressure Altitude and Density Chart

Pressure altitude, density altitude, and true altitude are all equal at sea level on a standard day, a condition which does not often occur. Pressure altitude is equal to density altitude only when the temperature is standard for that pressure altitude. If the air mass is warmer than standard, density altitude will be higher than pressure altitude and, if the air mass is colder than standard, density altitude will be lower than pressure altitude. You will read performance figures for turbo-

props and jets given as "ISA + 10°" or "ISA - 5°". These figures show performance at temperatures differing from the International Standard Atmosphere.

Because true altitude is the actual altitude above mean sea level, when you are on the ground your altimeter should read the published airport elevation when you set the altimeter to the current local altimeter setting.

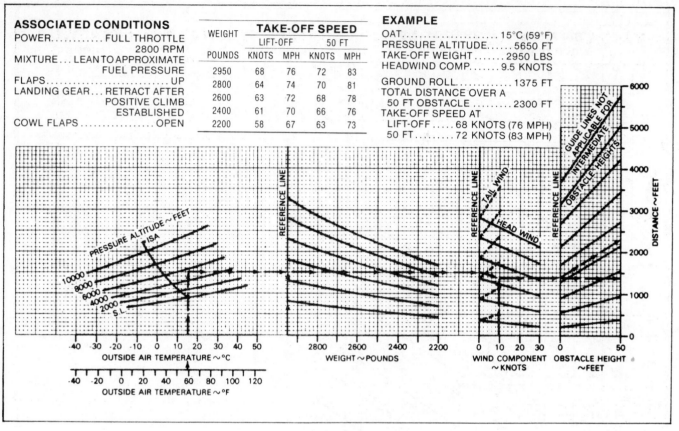

ASSOCIATED CONDITIONS

POWER............FULL THROTTLE
                       2800 RPM
MIXTURE...LEAN TO APPROXIMATE
                  FUEL PRESSURE
FLAPS.............................UP
LANDING GEAR...RETRACT AFTER
                  POSITIVE CLIMB
                     ESTABLISHED
COWL FLAPS................OPEN

WEIGHT	TAKE-OFF SPEED			
	LIFT-OFF		50 FT	
POUNDS	KNOTS	MPH	KNOTS	MPH
2950	68	76	72	83
2800	64	74	70	81
2600	63	72	68	78
2400	61	70	66	76
2200	58	67	63	73

EXAMPLE

OAT.......................15°C (59°F)
PRESSURE ALTITUDE......5650 FT
TAKE-OFF WEIGHT........2950 LBS
HEADWIND COMP........9.5 KNOTS

GROUND ROLL.............1375 FT
TOTAL DISTANCE OVER A
  50 FT OBSTACLE.........2300 FT
TAKE-OFF SPEED AT
  LIFT-OFF.....68 KNOTS (76 MPH)
  50 FT........72 KNOTS (83 MPH)

Figure 6-3. Take-Off Distance

TAKEOFF AND CLIMB PERFORMANCE

Figure 6-3 is a takeoff performance chart. Note the line marked "ISA" which represents the standard temperature for each altitude shown. Also note how an increase in either temperature, pressure altitude, or weight will adversely affect takeoff distance.

Follow the example problem through to see how the takeoff distance was derived. Now try this one:

OAT...........................Standard
Pressure altitude...............4,000 ft.
Takeoff weight.................2,800 lb.
Headwind component...........20 kts.

Determine total distance to clear a 50 foot obstacle.

1. 1250 ft.
2. 1500 ft.
3. 1750 ft.
4. 1900 ft.

Figure 6-4 is another table used to predict takeoff performance. It may be necessary to interpolate one or more of the values given. Be conservative; if your answer falls between two values, select the longer takeoff distance. Read the notes and be sure that you are duplicating the conditions under which the engineers arrived at the figures, remembering that factory pilots used a new airplane in top condition. Add a "fudge factor" for the effects of time on the airframe and engine. Factory performance figures assume normal pilot techniques —you do not have to be super-pilot.

TAKE-OFF DISTANCE FROM HARD SURFACE RUNWAY WITH FLAPS UP

GROSS WEIGHT POUNDS	IAS AT 50 MPH	HEAD WIND KNOTS	AT SEA LEVEL & 59°		AT 2500 FT. & 50°F		AT 5000 FT & 41°F		AT 7500 FT. & 32°F	
			GROUND RUN	TOTAL TO CLEAR 50 FT OBS	GROUND RUN	TOTAL TO CLEAR 50 FT OBS	GROUND RUN	TOTAL TO CLEAR 50 FT OBS	GROUND RUN	TOTAL TO CLEAR 50 FT OBS
2300	68	0	865	1525	1040	1910	1255	2480	1565	3855
		10	615	1170	750	1485	920	1955	1160	3110
		20	405	850	505	1100	630	1480	810	2425
2000	63	0	630	1095	755	1325	905	1625	1120	2155
		10	435	820	530	1005	645	1250	810	1685
		20	275	580	340	720	425	910	595	1255
1700	58	0	435	780	520	920	625	1095	765	1370
		10	290	570	355	680	430	820	535	1040
		20	175	385	215	470	270	575	345	745

NOTES: 1. Increase distance 10% for each 25°F above standard temperature for particular altitude.
2. For operation on a dry, grass runway, increase distances (both "ground run" and "total to clear 50 ft. obstacle") by 7% of the "total to clear 50 ft. obstacle" figure.

Figure 6-4. Take-Off Data

Gross weight. . . . . 1,700 lbs.
OAT . . . . 66°F
Pressure altitude . . . . 5,000 ft.
Wind (headwind) . . . . 20 kts.

Distance to clear a 50' obstacle?

1.   575 ft.
2.   633 ft.
3.   518 ft.
4.   930 ft.

The manufacturer's takeoff performance tables or the operating procedures section of the approved flight manual will contain a recommended takeoff speed. This speed must be attained before you rotate the airplane to climb attitude — you can't force the airplane to lift off or climb at a slower speed. A good rule to follow is this: you should have accelerated to 75% of takeoff speed in the first half of the available runway. If the airplane has not reached that speed by the midway point you should stop, taxi back, and do some performance calculations.

MAXIMUM RATE-OF-CLIMB DATA

| GROSS WEIGHT POUNDS | AT SEA LEVEL & 50°F | | | AT 5000 FT. & 41°F | | | AT 10,000 FT. & 23°F | | | AT 15,000 FT. & 5°F | | |
	IAS MPH	RATE OF CLIMB FT/MIN	GAL. OF FUEL USED	IAS MPH	RATE OF CLIMB FT/MIN	FROM S.L. FUEL USED	IAS MPH	RATE OF CLIMB FT/MIN	FROM S.L. FUEL USED	IAS MPH	RATE OF CLIMB FT/MIN	FROM S.L. FUEL USED
2300	82	645	1.0	81	435	2.6	79	230	4.8	78	22	11.5
2000	79	840	1.0	79	610	2.2	76	380	3.6	75	155	6.3
1700	77	1085	1.0	76	825	1.9	73	570	2.9	72	315	4.4

NOTES: 1. Flaps up, full throttle, mixture leaned for smooth operation above 3,000 ft.

2. Fuel used includes warm up and take-off allowance.

3. For hot weather, decrease rate of climb 20 ft. min. for each 10°F above standard day temperature for particular altitude.

Figure 6-5. Maximum Rate-of-Climb Data

CLIMB PERFORMANCE

Figure 6-5 is used to predict rate of climb and fuel used during climb. Note how climb performance drops off with altitude, how indicated airspeed for maximum rate of climb decreases with altitude, and how much fuel is used during climb.

Pressure altitude. . . . . sea level
Temperature . . . . 89°F
Gross weight. . . . . 2,000 lbs.
Indicated airspeed . . . . 79 MPH

After climbing for five minutes your altimeter would read approximately:

1.   4,100 ft.
2.   4,000 ft.
3.   3,900 ft.
4.   4,260 ft.

Apply the following conditions to the above chart.

Pressure altitude.. . . . . 5,000'
Temperature. 61° F
Gross weight. . . . . 2,000 lbs.
Indicated airspeed. . . . . 79 MPH

Assume you have climbed at a constant rate for 3 minutes. What would be the approximate gain in altitude?

1.   1,810 ft.
2.   1,790 ft.
3.   1,710 ft.
4.   1,830 ft.

takeoff, and will accelerate to V_y as soon as the obstacles are cleared. Both forward visibility and engine cooling are adversely affected by the nose-high

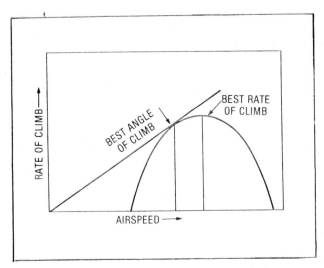

Figure 6-6. Relationship Between Airspeed and Climb Rate

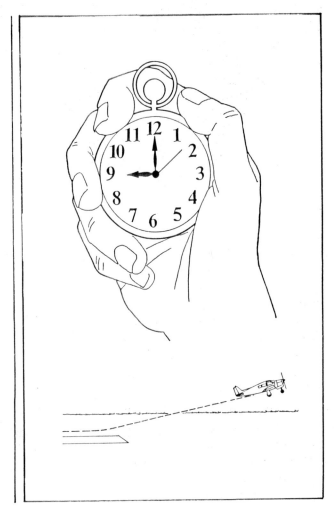

Figure 6-8. Best Rate of Climb Speed

Figure 6-7. Best Angle of Climb Speed

BEST ANGLE AND
BEST RATE OF CLIMB SPEEDS

Figure 6-6 plots the relationship between airspeed and climb rate in feet per minute for a typical light airplane. A line from the origin of the graph is tangent to the curve at the best angle of climb speed and the apex of the curve is the best rate of climb speed.

The best angle of climb speed (V_x) is safely above the stall and slightly slower than the best rate of climb speed (V_y). You will use V_x for clearing obstacles after

attitude at the best angle of climb speed (figures 6-7 and 6-8).

It has nothing to do with design climb speeds, but it is a fact that you will gain more altitude per unit of distance when climbing into the wind than when climbing downwind. You are climbing x number of feet per minute and spending more minutes while climbing into the wind. If you climb at 60 knots into a 60 knot wind you will go straight up!

CRUISE POWER SETTINGS
75% MAXIMUM CONTINUOUS POWER (OR FULL THROTTLE)
2800 LBS

PRESS ALT.	ISA-20°3C (–36°F)								STANDARD DAY (ISA)								ISA+20°C (+36°F)							
	IOAT		ENGINE SPEED	MAN. PRESS	FUEL FLOW PER ENGINE		TAS		IOAT		ENGINE SPEED	MAN. PRESS	FUEL FLOW PER ENGINE		TAS		IOAT		ENGINE SPEED	MAN. PRESS	FUEL FLOW PER ENGINE		TAS	
FEET	°F	°C	RPM	IN HG	PSI	GPH	KTS	MPH	°F	°C	RPM	IN HG	PSI	GPH	KTS	MPH	°F	°C	RPM	IN HG	PSI	GPH	KTS	MPH
SL	27	-3	2450	23.1	8.2	13.6	156	180	63	17	2450	23.8	8.2	13.6	159	183	99	37	2450	24.4	8.2	13.6	162	186
2000	19	-7	2450	22.8	8.2	13.6	158	182	55	13	2450	23.5	8.2	13.6	162	186	93	34	2450	24.2	8.2	13.6	165	190
4000	12	-11	2450	22.6	8.2	13.6	161	185	50	10	2450	23.3	8.2	13.6	165	190	86	30	2450	23.9	8.2	13.6	168	193
6000	7	-14	2450	22.3	8.2	13.6	164	189	43	6	2450	23.0	8.2	13.6	167	192	79	26	2450	23.4	8.0	13.4	170	195
8000	0	-18	2450	21.8	8.0	13.3	166	191	36	2	2450	21.8	7.6	12.8	167	192	72	22	2450	21.8	7.2	12.3	168	193
10000	-8	-22	2450	20.3	7.2	12.3	164	189	28	-2	2450	20.3	6.8	11.8	165	190	64	18	2450	20.3	6.5	11.4	166	191
12000	-15	-26	2450	18.8	6.4	11.3	162	185	21	-6	2450	18.8	6.2	10.9	163	188	57	14	2450	18.8	5.9	10.6	163	186
14000	-22	-30	2450	17.4	5.9	10.5	169	183	14	-10	2450	17.4	5.6	10.1	160	184	50	10	2450	17.4	5.3	9.8	160	184
16000	-29	-34	2450	16.1	5.3	9.7	156	180	7	-14	2450	16.1	6.1	9.4	156	180	43	6	2450	16.1	4.9	9.1	155	178

NOTES: 1. Full throttle manifold pressure settings are approximate.
2. Shaded area represents operation with full throttle.

Figure 6-9. Cruise Chart

CRUISE PERFORMANCE

Figure 6-9 is a cruise chart for a typical single engine airplane with a controllable pitch propeller.

This is the 75% power chart for this airplane; its approved flight manual will contain similar charts for 65%, 55% and possibly 45%. True airspeed and fuel consumption figures are given for standard conditions, and conditions much colder and warmer than standard. You must check the winds and temperatures forecast for your desired cruise altitude to estimate time enroute and fuel burn.

What is the expected fuel consumption for a 1,000 mile flight under these conditions?

Pressure altitude . . . . 8,000 ft.
Temperature . . . . –18°C
Manifold pressure . . . . 21.8" Hg
Wind . . . . Calm

1.   41.9 gal.
2.   69.6 gal.
3.   71.4 gal.
4.   73.8 gal.

If the manufacturer of your airplane provides a maximum rate of climb chart your figures can be further refined. Remember that for day VFR you must land with a 30 minute fuel reserve, and that 45 minutes in reserve is required for night VFR. In planning your flight, don't look for the altitude and power setting that will give maximum speed if the fuel consumption will force a fuel stop enroute. A slower speed that makes the fuel stop unnecessary will pay off in the long run because of the time lost on the ground and the fuel burned in climbing back to cruise altitude.

DESCENT PLANNING

The most efficient way to descend is to maintain cruise speed while descending at a comfortable rate, and in VFR conditions you are in complete command of where and when to start down. Add 1000' to the destination airport's field elevation for pattern altitude, and subtract that figure from your cruise altitude to determine how much altitude must be lost. Divide that figure by 300 and you will have the number of miles from your destination to begin your descent at 300 feet per mile.

LANDING DISTANCE

Your pre-flight planning must include familiarizing yourself with the runway length and condition at the destination airport. Be sure to ask the briefer what surface winds are forecast (if your destination has a weather observer) in order to anticipate which runway will be in use. Figures 6-10 and 6-11 show two different types of landing distance charts, and you will notice again that altitude and temperature (density altitude) have a definite effect on landing performance. Notice the speeds recommended by the manufacturer: they provide a safe margin above the stall and should be adhered to.

LANDING DISTANCE
FLAPS LOWERED TO 40° — POWER OFF / HARD SURFACE RUNWAY — ZERO WIND

GROSS WEIGHT LBS.	APPROACH SPEED IAS, MPH	AT SEA LEVEL & 59°F		AT 2500 FT. & 50°F		AT 5000 FT. & 41°F		AT 7500 FT. & 32°F	
		GROUND ROLL	TOTAL TO CLEAR 50 FT. OBS	GROUND ROLL	TOTAL TO CLEAR 50 FT. OBS	GROUND ROLL	TOTAL TO CLEAR 50 FT. OBS	GROUND ROLL	TOTAL TO CLEAR 50 FT. OBS
1600	60	445	1075	470	1135	495	1195	520	1255

NOTES:
1. Decrease the distances shown by 10% for each 4 knots of headwind.
2. Increase the distance by 10% for each 60°F temperature increase above standard.
3. For operation on a dry, grass runway, increase distances (both "ground roll" and "total to clear 50 ft. obstacle") by 20% of the "total to clear 50 ft. obstacle" figure.

Figure 6-10. Landing Distance Chart

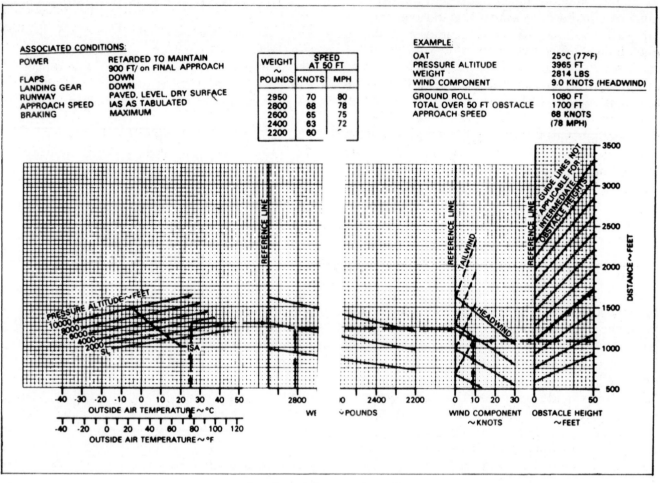

Figure 6-11. Landing Distance Graph

Additional airspeed means more energy that must be dissipated and more runway left behind before the wing can no longer support the aircraft and the wheels touch down.

Use figure 6-10:

Determine the total landing distance required to clear a 50' obstacle.

    Pressure altitude . . . . 7,500 ft.
    Headwind. . . . . 8 kts.
    Temperature . . . . Std.
    Runway surface . . . . dry grass

    1.   1,004 ft.
    2.   1,255 ft.

    3.   1,506 ft.
    4.   1,757 ft.

Use figure 6-11:

What is the approximate landing roll?

    OAT . . . . 90°F
    Pressure altitude . . . . 4,000 ft.
    Weight . . . . 2,800 lbs.
    Tailwind component. . . . . 5 kts.

    1.   1,200 ft.
    2.   1,575 ft.
    3.   1,725 ft.
    4.   1,950 ft.

GROUND EFFECT

When induced drag was discussed in Chapter Two, it was associated with low speeds and high angles of attack — typically takeoff and landing conditions. When the wing is less than one-half the wingspan above the ground, induced drag is reduced by the interaction between the ground and the wingtip vortices and downwash. If you can get the wing within 3 feet of the ground, induced drag is reduced by 48%. This reduction in drag is called ground effect.

All airplanes experience **ground effect**, but it is more noticeable in low wing airplanes. The reduction in induced drag causes "float" if excess airspeed is used on final, and downwash from the wing bouncing off of the surface reduces elevator effectiveness, causing the nose to pitch down slightly. On takeoff, ground effect will enable the airplane to lift off at a speed below normal stall speed. If the pilot stays in ground effect, and accelerates before climbing, this is a useful soft field or high altitude technique. If the pilot attempts to climb out of ground effect before gaining at least best angle of climb speed (V_x), the airplane may sink back to the surface.

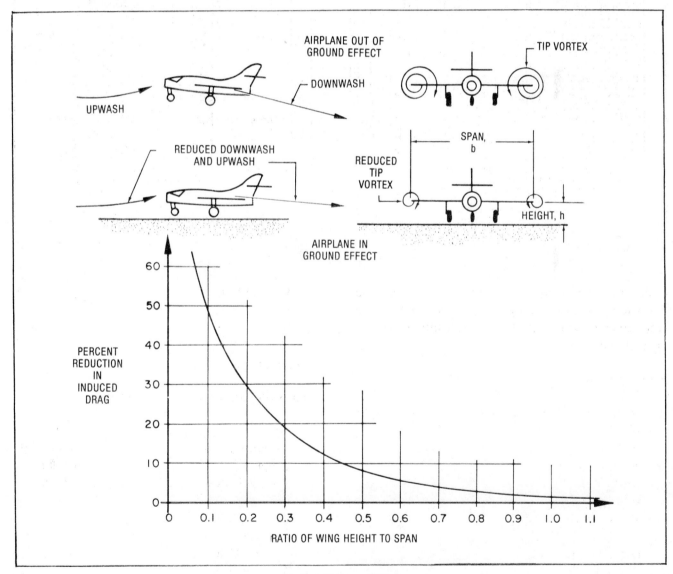

Figure 6-12. Ground Effect

PERFORMANCE
REVIEW SECTION

1. After takeoff, which airspeed would permit the pilot to gain the most altitude in a given period of time?

   1. Cruising climb speed.
   2. Best rate-of-climb speed.
   3. Best angle-of-climb speed.
   4. Minimum control speed.

2. What effect does high density altitude have on aircraft performance?

   1. It increases engine performance.
   2. It reduces an aircraft's climb performance.
   3. It will decrease the runway length required for takeoff.
   4. It increases lift because the light air exerts less force on the airfoils.

3. How can pressure altitude be determined?

   1. Set the field elevation in the altimeter setting window and read the indicated altitude.
   2. Set the altimeter to the field elevation and read the value in the altimeter setting window.
   3. Set the altimeter to zero and read the value in the altimeter setting window.
   4. Set 29.92 in the altimeter setting window and read the indicated altitude.

LANDING DISTANCE

FLAPS LOWERED TO 40° — POWER OFF / HARD SURFACE RUNWAY — ZERO WIND

GROSS WEIGHT LBS.	APPROACH SPEED IAS, MPH	AT SEA LEVEL & 59°F		AT 2500 FT. & 50°F		AT 5000 FT. & 41°F		AT 7500 FT. & 32°F	
		GROUND ROLL	TOTAL TO CLEAR 50 FT. OBS	GROUND ROLL	TOTAL TO CLEAR 50 FT. OBS	GROUND ROLL	TOTAL TO CLEAR 50 FT. OBS	GROUND ROLL	TOTAL TO CLEAR 50 FT. OBS
1600	60	445	1075	470	1135	495	1195	520	1255

NOTES: 1. Decrease the distances shown by 10% for each 4 knots of headwind.

2. Increase the distance by 10% for each 60°F temperature increase above standard.

3. For operation on a dry, grass runway, increase distances (both "ground roll" and "total to clear 50 ft. obstacle") by 20% of the "total to clear 50 ft. obstacle" figure.

Figure Q6-1.

4. Determine the approximate fuel flow at 75% maximum continuous power at 6,500 feet with a temperature 36° higher than standard. (See figure Q6-1.)

   1. 12.4 gal/hr.
   2. 12.7 gal/hr.
   3. 13.1 gal/hr.
   4. 13.7 gal/hr.

5. What effect does higher density altitude have on propeller efficiency?

   1. Increased efficiency due to less friction on the propeller blades.
   2. Reduced efficiency because the propeller exerts less force than at lower density altitudes.
   3. Reduced efficiency due to the increased force of the thinner air on the propeller.
   4. Increased efficiency because the propeller exerts less force on the thinner air.

6. An airplane is usually affected by ground effect at what height above the surface?

   1. Between 100 and 200 ft. above the surface in calm wind conditions.

2. Less than half of the airplane's wingspan above the surface.
   3. Twice the length of the airplane's wingspan above the surface.
   4. Three or four times the airplane's wingspan.

7. Which adverse effect must a pilot be aware of as a result of the phenomenon of ground effect during takeoff?

   1. Difficulty in getting airborne even though airspeed is sufficient for normal takeoff.
   2. Becoming airborne before reaching recommended takeoff speed.
   3. Settling back to the surface immediately after becoming airborne.
   4. Difficulty in climbing the first 20 feet after takeoff.

8. Of the following conditions, which would be most critical when taxiing a nosewheel equipped high-wing airplane?

   1. Direct headwind.
   2. Direct crosswind.
   3. Quartering tailwind.
   4. Quartering headwind.

9. If you plan to land at an airport where the elevation is 7,500 feet, the indicated approach airspeed should be

    1. higher than that used for a sea level airport, and some power should be used until touchdown.
    2. the same as that used at a sea level airport.
    3. lower than that used at a sea level airport.
    4. higher than that used at a sea level airport.

10. As altitude increases, the indicated airspeed at which a given airplane stalls in a particular configuration will

    1. decrease as the true airspeed decreases.
    2. decrease as the true airspeed increases.
    3. remain the same as at low altitude.
    4. increase because the air density becomes less.

11. Of what practical value is pressure altitude?

    1. A pilot should use it to check the accuracy of the altimeter during standard conditions.

    2. To use on all aircraft performance charts since the charts are based on pressure altitude.
    3. To use for obstacle clearance at higher altitudes where accurate altimeter settings are not available.
    4. To use for computer solutions to determine density altitude, true altitude, true airspeed, etc.

12. Determine the approximate ground roll distance for takeoff under the following conditions? (See figure Q6-1.)

    OAT . . . . 90°F
    Pressure altitude . . . . 2,000 ft.
    Takeoff weight . . . . 2,500 lb.
    Wind . . . . 20 kts.

    1. 650 ft.
    2. 800 ft.
    3. 1,000 ft.
    4. 1,250 ft.

VFR pilots *navigate* by a system of *pilotage*; that is, they lay out a course on an aeronautical chart and direct the flight of their aircraft along that course by reference to the terrain. Pilots *plan* their flights by dead reckoning. That statement deserves some explanation: in the days of sail, mariners kept track of their position as accurately as they could by estimating their speed and the effects of wind and current and, having a "deduced reckoning" of where they had travelled since their last known position, they logged the result as "ded. reckoning". The airplane pilot of today lays out a course line, allows for wind and magnetic errors, derives a heading and a groundspeed, and estimates a time of arrival at the destination. That is dead reckoning — the planning phase. Unlike the sailor, the VFR pilot can maintain a visual track over the ground and pass over charted reference points. That is pilotage. From the early days, pilot has meant navigator.

AERONAUTICAL CHARTS

You will use three types of charts as a VFR pilot. The World Aeronautical Chart (WAC) is printed on a scale of 1:1,000,000, or approximately 16 statute miles to the inch. The contiguous (48) United States are covered by just 11 WAC charts. Because each chart covers such a large area, WACs are usually used by pilots of relatively fast airplanes for long cross-country flights. They are not as detailed as sectional charts, they do not include all airports, and boundaries of controlled airspace are not shown. WAC charts are revised annually.

Sectional charts are used for most VFR local and medium-range cross-country navigation. With a scale of 1:500,000, or approximately 8 statute miles to the inch, it takes 34 charts to cover the continental U. S., 16 to cover Alaska, and 1 for the Hawaiian Islands. Sectionals are excellent for visual navigation: they show roads, freeways, railroads, power lines, lakes, rivers, terrain contours and populated areas. Military airfields, public, private and emergency airports are also shown. An excerpt from the Seattle Sectional Chart is included with this book and will be used in the flight planning, airspace, and regulations sections. Sectional charts are revised every six months.

Terminal Control Area (TCA) Charts, with a scale of 4 miles to the inch, are published for those areas that have TCAs. Because VFR pilots must always know where they are in relation to the boundaries of the Terminal Control Area, TCA charts are highly detailed and include VFR reporting points for easy reference. Revised TCA charts are issued every six months.

GEOGRAPHICAL COORDINATES

The sailor who "dead reckons" a voyage across untracked waters needs to be familiar with latitude and longitude — you do not. You will use latitude-longitude coordinates with some advanced radio navigation systems but lat-long coordinates do not play a part in practical VFR flying. You will be using the lat-long lines on your WAC or sectional chart, however, so a brief explanation is in order.

Figure 7-1 shows **parallels** of latitude marching upward from the Equator (0° latitude) to the Poles (90° North or South latitude). If you slice a globe along lines of latitude, the slices get progressively smaller toward the poles, so distance measurements along latitude lines are useless.

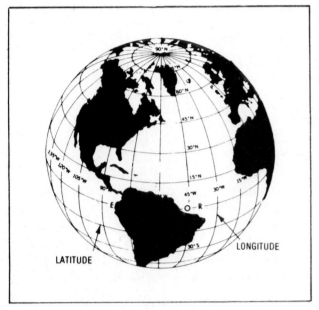

Figure 7-1. Meridians and Parallels

Lines of longitude are called **meridians**, and divide the earth from pole to pole, the 0° meridian passing through Greenwich, England. Meridians are numbered eastward across Europe and Asia and westward across the Atlantic Ocean and the Americas until the 180° meridian is reached in mid-Pacific. The continental United States lies roughly between 70° and 125° West longitude and between 26° and 49° North latitude. Meridians are **Great Circles**: if you slice a globe along meridians, all of the slices will be the same size. All meridians are the same length: 10,600 nautical miles from Pole to Pole, 60 nautical miles per degree.

Each degree is further divided into 60 minutes, and this makes it possible to measure distance accurately: one minute of latitude equals one **nautical mile** when measured along a line of longitude toward either pole.

As you look at your aeronautical chart, lines of longitude and latitude are at right angles. As you look at a globe, however, lines of longitude converge toward the poles. Because there is some unavoidable distortion of scale between the bottom and the top of an aeronautical chart, you should make course measurements as close as possible to the mid-latitude portion of the chart.

On the excerpt of the Seattle sectional chart, find the Easton State airport near the right center. Count up 15 minutes from the latitude line marked 47° to find the latitude of Easton State. Count left 11 minutes from the longitude line marked 121° to find the longitude of Easton State. Its geographic position is 47° 15' 15' north, 121°11'15' west. You don't need to be any more accurate than the nearest minute in order to locate an airport using latitude and longitude. The geographic position of all airports is found in the Airport/Facility Directory (A/FD).

TIME

The measurement of time is an integral part of air navigation. Before leaving the discussion of longitude and the 0° meridian, the subject of time zones and time conversions should be covered. The only rational way to have flight times and weather information apply across the country and around the world is to have a single time reference. That reference is the time at Greenwich, England (on the 0° line of longitude), or Greenwich Mean Time. Each 15° of longitude east or west of Greenwich marks a one hour time difference. Figure 7-2 shows the time differences across the United States with a legend for time conversion to and from Greenwich Mean Time (GMT) or **ZULU time**.

ZULU is the phonetic identifier for the letter Z; in the 24 hour clock system GMT is shown as 0800Z, 2200Z, etc. You should become familiar with time zone conversions for your area of operations. Here are two time conversion problems to illustrate:

An aircraft departs an airport in the central standard time zone at 0930 CST for a 2-hour flight to an airport located in the mountain standard time zone. What should the landing time be?

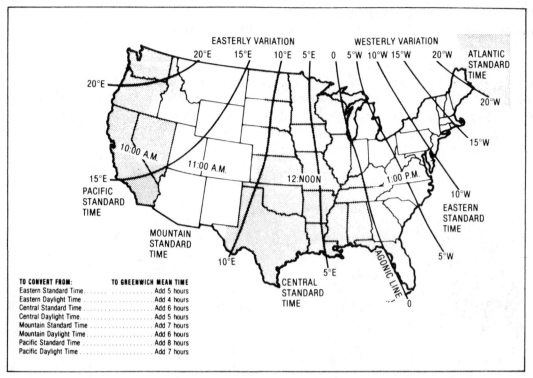

Figure 7-2. Magnetic Variation Chart / Time Conversion Table

1. 0930 MST.
2. 1030 MST.
3. 1130 MST.
4. 1230 MST.

There are two ways of approaching this problem. First, according to the time difference chart, at the departure time of 0930 CST it is 0830 MST, and a 2 hour flight should land at 1030 MST. The second method is to add 2 hours to 0930 CST to get the CST landing time at the destination (forget to set your watch back?). Subtract the one hour time difference to get 1030 MST.

An aircraft departs an airport in the pacific standard time zone at 1030 PST for a 4-hour flight to an airport located in the central time zone. At what Greenwich mean time should the landing be?

1. 2030Z.
2. 2130Z.
3. 2230Z.
4. 2330Z.

What is GMT at departure? The chart says that to convert PST to GMT you must add 8 hours, so takeoff time is 1830Z. Arrival time after a 4-hour flight will be 2230Z.

Flight Service Station personnel and air traffic controllers use ZULU time, and will be reluctant to do time conversions for you. (Of course, you can buy a watch with dual time zones!) If you are planning a departure for 1800 local time and there is a forecast for thunderstorms after 2100Z at your destination, you will have to know time conversion to be able to relate that to your estimated time of arrival. As a new pilot, you will probably stay within one time zone or possibly travel between two time zones. Just remember that, for example, you live in the "plus 5" time zone (plus 6 in the summer), and conversions will come easily to you.

STATUTE AND NAUTICAL MILE SCALES

Navigators on the sea or in the air find the use of nautical miles for distance measurement convenient because a nautical mile is 6000 feet (really 6080, but that complicates things) and is also one minute of latitude. When you counted up 15 minutes to locate the latitude of Easton State airport, you counted up 15 nautical miles. You will find mileage scales for both nautical and **statute miles** on aeronautical charts and plotters. In studying the Federal Aviation Regulations you will find that the FAA mixes statute and nautical measurements indiscriminately. Airspeed indicators are calibrated in **knots** (nautical miles per hour) only, or in knots and MPH — you will find a conversion scale on your flight computer. *Winds are always given in knots*, so you must be sure that you are dealing with like units when flight planning.

MAGNETIC COMPASS ERRORS

For flight planning purposes you must recognize that although the lines of latitude and longitude on charts are neatly perpendicular and relate to the **True North Pole** there is nothing in your airplane that relates to True North. The magnetic compass indicates the direction to the magnetic North Pole, which is in northern Canada (figure 7-3).

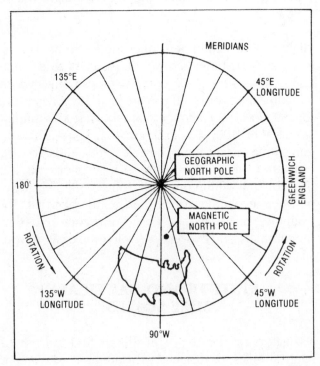

Figure 7-3. Magnetic & True North Poles

You must take the **variation** between true north and magnetic north into account when flight planning.

Figure 7-4 shows **isogonic lines**, or lines of equal magnetic variation, across the continent. Along the line which passes through Chicago and Key West, a pilot looking toward the North Star or the True North Pole will also be looking toward the magnetic North Pole, and there will be no variation. That line of zero variation is called the **agonic line**.

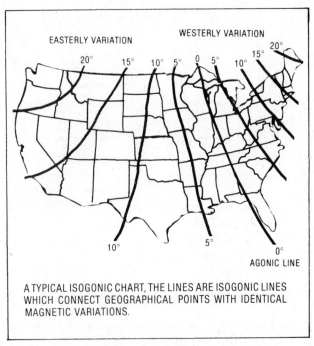

Figure 7-4. Isogonic Lines

East or West of that line, the angle between true and magnetic north increases. A pilot in Los Angeles who measures a course line on an aeronautical chart in relation to the longitude lines (or true north) must subtract 14° from that true course to get a magnetic course *("East is least")*, while a pilot in Philadelphia will add 10° *("West is best")*.

A course, whether identified as true or magnetic, is only a line on a chart linking departure point and destination. For flight planning purposes, you must allow for magnetic influences in the airplane itself and for the effect of wind drift. Because your airplane has some iron and steel components which are affected by the earth's magnetic field, and because it contains

FOR (MH)	0	30	60	90	120	150	180	210	240	270	300	330
STEER (CH)	2	28	56	88	120	152	183	212	240	268	298	328

Figure 7-5. Compass Correction Card

wiring which creates a magnetic field within the airplane itself, the airplane's magnetic compass develops an error called **deviation** which varies with aircraft heading. Looking back at figure 7-4 it is apparent that the heading of the airplane has nothing to do with magnetic variation — a pilot in Seattle must apply a 22° Easterly variation regardless of the direction of flight. Because magnetic deviation is unique to each airplane and is dependent on heading, a compass correction card (figure 7-5) must be prepared by accurately lining up the airplane on known magnetic headings, checking the magnetic compass reading, and recording the deviation error for each heading. Small adjustment magnets are provided so that the error can be minimized.

This compass correction table is originally made at the factory but should be re-checked by a mechanic whenever cockpit equipment installations are made. When a pilot has applied variation and deviation to a measured true course, the result is the compass course:

TRUE ± VARIATION = MAGNETIC ± DEVIATION = COMPASS.

Variation is shown on navigational charts to the nearest one-half degree. You will find that rounding off to the nearest whole degree will speed up your calculations without affecting accuracy. If you make long flights over water or featureless terrain, deviation and compass course will be very important to you, and an accurate compass correction card may be a lifesaver. Pilots who fly by reference to the surface (pilotage) will make little use of compass **heading** except to adjust their gyroscopic heading indicators.

Any difference between an airplane's planned **course** and its **track** over the ground is caused by wind drift — the difference between an airplane's course and its **heading** is caused by **wind drift** correction. Always compute the **wind correction angle** first, and then apply variation and deviation, as National Weather Service winds aloft forecasts are always referenced to True North.

CORRECTING FOR WIND DRIFT

Figure 7-6 shows the effect of wind drift on an airplane's flight path if no corrective action is taken.

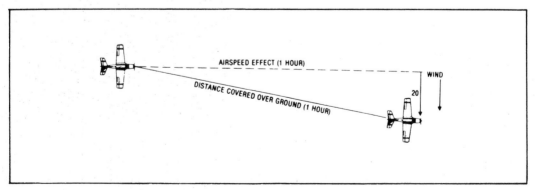

Figure 7-6. The Effect of Wind

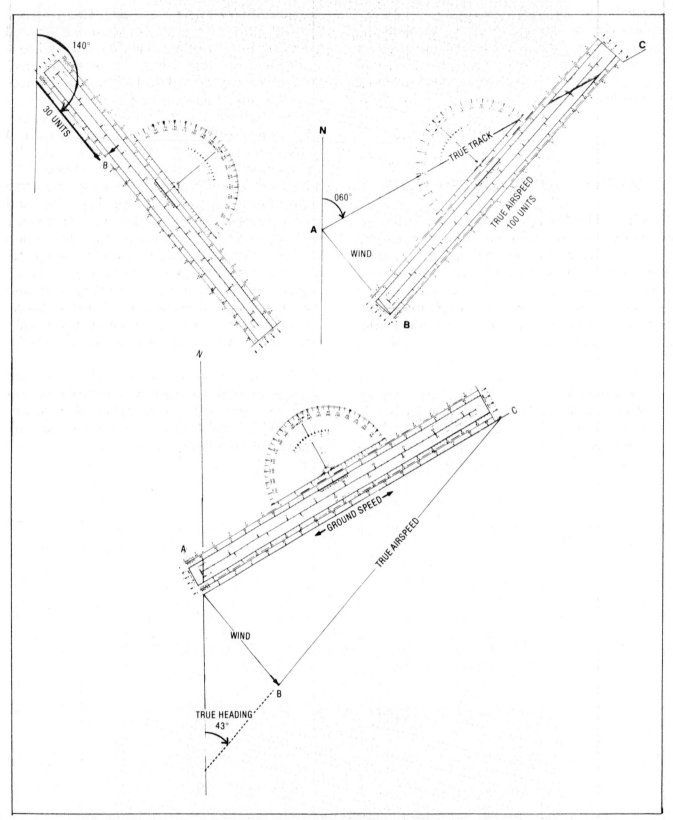

Figure 7-7. Wind Triangle

The wind correction angle necessary to offset the wind drift will allow the airplane's track over the ground to agree with the planned course. Determining wind correction angle with a known wind direction, wind velocity, true course and true airspeed is a trigonometry problem.

SOLVING THE WIND TRIANGLE

The **wind triangle** consists of four known values and two unknowns. You know the angle between true north and your course (true course), and the angle between true north and the wind direction; you also know your true airspeed and the wind velocity. With these values, you can construct a triangle to solve for the unknowns: groundspeed and true heading. Refer to figure 7-7.

Wind direction . . . . 320° true
Wind velocity . . . . 30 knots
True course . . . . 060°
True airspeed . . . . 100 knots

The vertical line represents true north. Line A-B represents the true wind, and is drawn downwind — a wind from 320° "blows" the line to 140°. The length of line A-B represents the wind velocity in convenient units. Using a protractor, draw a line of indefinite length from point A so that the angle represents the true course as measured on your chart. A line with a length representing the true airspeed (100 knots) is drawn from point B to intersect the true course line at point C. The distance from point A to point C is the groundspeed, (103 knots) and the angle that line B-C makes with the true north line (043°) is the true heading. The wind correction angle (17°) is the difference between the true course and the true heading. Magnetic variation must be applied to convert true heading to magnetic heading, and deviation applied to that to get compass heading. Very few pilots draw wind triangles, because the triangle can be solved mechanically and electronically much more quickly, but it's a great way to really teach yourself the fundamentals of aerial navigation.

Winds aloft forecasts are only available for selected altitudes: 3,000', 6,000', 9,000', etc. In most cases you will have to interpolate for your planned cruise altitude. Keep in mind that these are *forecasts*, and don't expect extreme accuracy.

USING THE SLIDE-TYPE COMPUTER

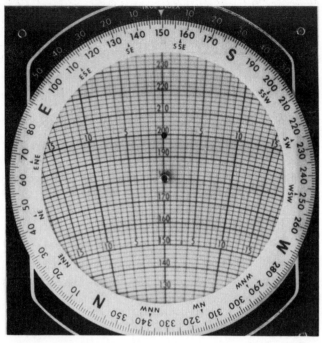

Figure 7-8.

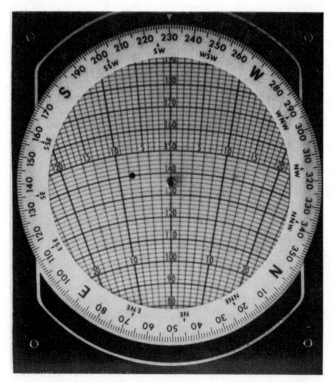

Figure 7-9.

True course . . . . 230°
True airspeed . . . . 140 MPH
Wind. . . . . 150° at 17 knots

(Convert wind or airspeed so that both are in the same units. 17 knots = 19.6 MPH)

Orient the rotatable disk so that the true wind direction (150°) is at the true index. From the center, count *up* the number of units representing wind velocity (19.6) (figure 7-8). Rotate the disk so that the true course (230°) is aligned with the true index; note that the wind dot is now in the correct relationship to the course. Move the slide until the wind dot falls on the speed arc representing the true airspeed (140) (figure 7-9). You have solved the wind triangle: the ground-speed (135 mph) is read directly under the center grommet and the wind correction angle (8° left) is read under the wind dot. A left wind correction angle is subtracted from the true course and a right wind correction angle is added to the true course to get true heading.

USING THE CIRCULAR COMPUTER

Use Figure 7-10:

True course . . . . 115°
True airspeed . . . . 90 kts
Wind. . . . . 240° at 38 kts

Make a wind dot where the wind direction line crosses the wind velocity arc. Rotate the disk with the wind dot to align the true course with the true index; rotate the outer disk to align the true airspeed with the true index. The position of the wind dot now shows you the number of knots of crosswind component and head-wind/tailwind component. Find the number of knots of crosswind component on the outer scale; opposite it you will read the wind correction angle. If the cross-wind component is more than 10% of the true airspeed use the larger of the two angles. Apply the head-wind/tailwind component to the true airspeed to get groundspeed. If the wind correction angle exceeds 5° read the "effective true airspeed" to the left of the true index.

ELECTRONIC FLIGHT COMPUTERS

Hand-held electronic flight computers are available which are self-prompting and read out answers directly. A limited list of their functions includes wind problems, time-speed-distance problems, conversions, and true airspeed/density altitude problems. Because they lead you through each problem with requests for data, no instruction for their use is necessary.

At least one electronic calculator offers a form of area navigation (Chapter 8) by reading out course and distance between two points defined by their distance and bearing from a navigational aid.

Time-speed-distance problems can be solved with a simple four-function pocket calculator, and you will learn how in this chapter. Without a table of trigonometric functions, a four-function calculator cannot do wind triangle solutions.

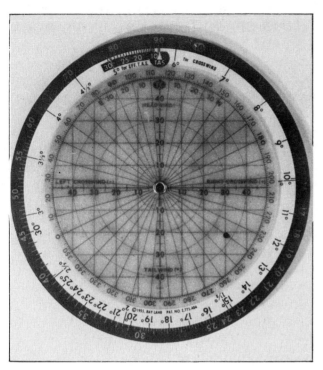

Figure 7-10. Plotting and Finding Groundspeed and Wind Correction Angle

Right crosswind component = 31 kts.
Tailwind component = 21 knots
Wind correction angle is greater than 10°:

Opposite 20° on "Effective True Airspeed" scale read 84.5 knots. Add 21 knot tailwind to TAS to get groundspeed of 105.5.

ACCURACY

Before relying too heavily on the results of wind problems, you must consider that the data you are working with is not precise. The National Weather Service wind direction forecasts are in 10° increments and can be off as much as 45° (for wind velocities forecast to be less than 25 knots) before a corrected forecast is issued. You can calculate headings to one-half of one degree but you cannot fly that accurately. Also, most pilots understand and accept deviation error in the magnetic compass but ignore it until their heading indicator fails. It is for these reasons that you must follow your progress over the ground visually.

PERSONAL COMPUTERS

A pilot with a computer at home or office can buy any one of a myriad of programs designed to make flight planning quick, easy, and accurate. These programs vary from the inexpensive, which read out only heading, groundspeed, and time enroute, to the very costly programs which not only provide flight planning information for several airplanes (so you can decide which one is most cost-efficient for the trip) but what kind of fuel and food service is available at the destination. The best computer programs (regardless of cost) are those which print out a flight log for you to take along.

Subscribers to data banks such as The Source and CompuServe have access to flight planning and weather information through their personal computers.

GROUNDSPEED VS AIRSPEED

When you drive your automobile for one hour at 60 miles per hour, you can be fairly certain that you will travel 60 miles during that hour. In flight, whether or not one hour at 60 miles per hour will actually cover 60 miles will be determined by the wind. If you somehow manage to get airborne under control and are flying into a 60 MPH headwind with an airspeed of 60 MPH, you aren't going to make it out of sight of the airport: your speed over the ground will be zero. This is an extreme example, although pilots in the Plains states have a fund of stories about airplanes "flying" in strong winds that prove that it can happen. You need to develop an understanding of the airspeed/ground-speed relationship on a more normal basis.

First, forget the comparison with the automobile and standardize all speed measurements in knots: the National Weather Service provides wind velocity information in knots and confusion will result if you mix units of measurement. The General Aviation Manufac-turer's Association has standardized on knots for airspeed indicators. The same flight computer solution that you used to determine wind correction angle gave you a groundspeed figure. You entered true airspeed and true wind direction and velocity and the computer read out groundspeed. You determine true airspeed by reference to cruise performance charts (Chapter Six) or by applying the 2% per 1,000' rule to your indicated airspeed (Chapter Four).

No matter how you arrived at the groundspeed figure, you must use it in combination with the measured distance to the destination to determine time enroute.

It is important to make frequent groundspeed checks while enroute to ensure that your actual groundspeed agrees with your planned groundspeed. Remember, the winds you used in flight planning were *forecast* winds. In planning your flight, you must be sure that upon arrival at your destination you have at least 30 minutes fuel left on board in the daytime and 45 minutes reserve fuel at night. Learn to think in terms of *time in your tanks* instead of distance. The Owner's Manual may say that you have a range of 450 miles, but if you are using 10 gallons per hour and have 35 gallons on board you will only stay airborne for 3½ hours no matter how far you have managed to fly.

RATE PROBLEMS: TIME-SPEED-DISTANCE, FUEL BURN

Rate problems are solved on the slide rule side of your flight computer: the inner, rotatable disk represents time, and the outer, fixed disk represents miles or gallons. The numbers on both disks must be interpreted with common sense, because you must provide the decimal points. For instance, 30 on the computer might be .3 for one problem and 300 for another. As you try some sample problems, you will see how common sense is applied. The arrow at the 60 on the rotatable disk is the speed or rate arrow (some instructors call it the speedometer needle), and you will use it for all calculations of miles per hour, knots, or gallons per hour: read it as "something per hour". The computer lets you mechanically solve for any single unknown in these equations:

$$\text{Distance} = \text{speed} \times \text{time}$$

$$\text{Gallons} = \text{fuel burn rate} \times \text{time}$$

The computer presents the information in this form, with time on the inner, rotatable disc:

Speed or GPH		Distance or Gallons
60	=	Time

If you determine that the distance between two checkpoints is 23 nautical miles, and your elapsed time between the checkpoints is 14.3 minutes (14 minutes and 18 seconds), set 14.3 on the inner time scale opposite 23 on the outer distance scale and read 96 opposite the speed arrow: your groundspeed is 96 knots. It couldn't very well be 9.6 or 960 knots, could it? Finding 14.3 and 23 in this problem isn't too difficult because numbers between 1 and 99 are read directly.

In preflight planning you find that the distance to your destination is 248 NM and you learn from doing a wind problem that your predicted groundspeed is 114 knots. Put the speed arrow opposite 114 (now the 10 on the outside scale is read as 100, the 11 as 110, etc.) and find 248 on the outside scale. It is between 24 and

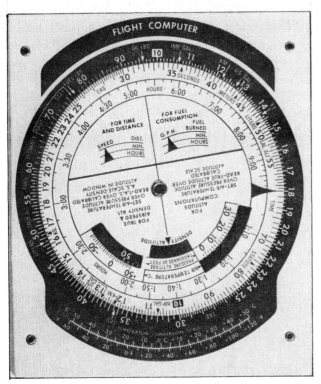

Figure 7-11. 180/60 X 30 = 90

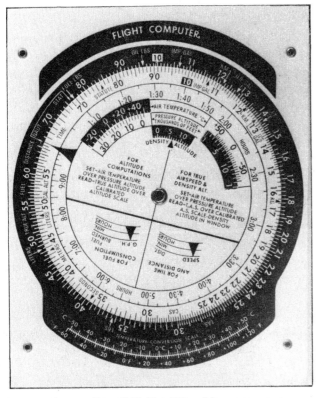

Figure 7-12. 11 ÷ 100 = 6.6

25, now read as 240 and 250. On the inner, rotatable (time) disk opposite 248, read the estimated time enroute as 130 minutes or 2:10. When elapsed time is the unknown, be careful not to confuse minutes with tenths of hours.

The cruise charts tell you that your fuel consumption rate will be 8.2 gallons per hour — how much fuel will you burn on the 248 mile trip? Place the rate arrow opposite 8.2 (between 80 and 90) and find 2:10 on the inside, time scale. Across from 2:10 (or 130) you will find 17.7 on the outside scale which now represents gallons. Make sense? Just over 2 hours at 8 gallons an hour has to be just over 16 gallons, doesn't it? Always check computer problems "in your head" to make sure that you are in the ballpark.

Time-speed distance and fuel problems can be worked out using a typical four-function calculator by cross-multiplying and then dividing. Try the three problems above with your pocket calculator. First, remember that the speed/rate arrow represents 60 and is always at the lower left. Time is always at the lower right. Here is the first problem you did with the slide rule type computer set up for a four-function calculator:

$$\frac{96}{60} \; :: \; \frac{23}{?}$$ Multiply two knowns diagonally across (60 x 23) and divide by the third known factor, 96.

14.375 minutes may be more accuracy than you want or need (don't forget that 14.4 minutes is 14 minutes and 24 seconds!).

This is the second problem above:

$$\frac{114}{60} \; :: \; \frac{248}{?} \; = \; 60 \times 248 \div 114 = 130.526$$

The third problem you did with the slide rule computer was a fuel problem. Set it up on your pocket calculator:

$$\frac{8.2}{60} \; :: \; \frac{?}{130} \; = \; 8.2 \times 130 \div 60 = 17.766$$

Just set the problem up on your calculator as you would on the flight computer, cross-multiply and divide.

Don't throw your flight computer away — you need it for density altitude, true altitude, and true airspeed problems, plus conversions.

MISCELLANEOUS SOLUTIONS

Around the edge of your flight computer you will find arrows with "naut" and "stat" for mileage conversion, and TAS for airspeed calculations. On the rotatable disk there are windows for calculations requiring input of pressure altitude and temperature. Some computers have a window for true altitude, others only provide for density altitude and airspeed calculations.

For mileage conversions, place the known value under the appropriate arrow, NAUT or STAT, and find the converted value under the other arrow. Statute miles = knots x 1.15 and knots x .87 = statute miles (figure 7-13).

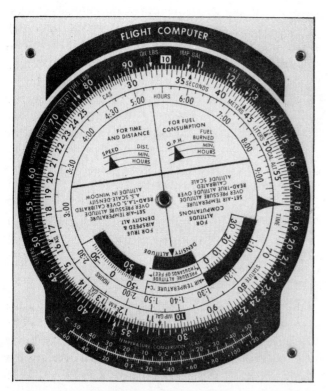

Figure 7-13. 220 Naut. = 254 Stat.

Density altitude and airspeed problems use the same window (figure 7-14). You need to know the air temperature and pressure altitude to compute density

altitude. True airspeed calculations require air temperature, pressure altitude, and indicated airspeed. Convert temperature to Centigrade (C°) if it is in Fahrenheit (F°), and place the temperature opposite the pressure altitude in the window marked FOR AIRSPEED AND DENSITY ALTITUDE.

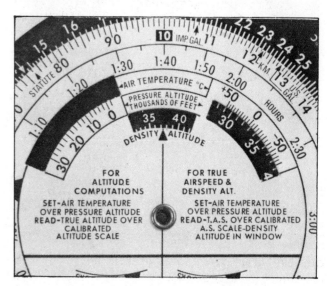

Figure 7-14. Density Altitude & True Airspeed

The markings are very small and extreme accuracy is difficult to achieve. When you have the temperature and pressure altitude properly set you will find the density altitude in the window marked for it. Opposite the indicated airspeed on the rotatable scale, you will find true airspeed on the outside scale. Figure 7-15 shows a solution for a temperature of –10° and a pressure altitude of 7,500'.

The density altitude window indicates 6,300'. If your indicated airspeed is 120 knots and you want to know true airspeed, don't move anything — just look opposite 120 on the inner scale and read 131.5 on the outer scale.

Do as many calculations as possible before takeoff — have distances between checkpoints written down and have an easy-to-use timer available. Your time for in-flight calculations will be limited, and thorough preflight preparation will make them easier.

Use common sense. Question wind correction angles of 30°-40° or more and headwind/tailwind compo-

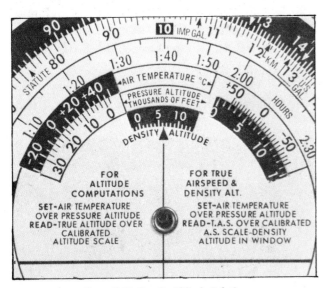

Figure 7-15. Density Altitude Solution

nents that seem out of line. Use groundspeed check-points that are 10 miles or more apart so that a small timing error will not have a major effect on your calculations, and choose checkpoints that allow accurate timing: roads, railroads, or shorelines make better checkpoints than city limits or tops of hills.

Always orient a chart to your direction of flight, and learn to read charts upside down, so that visual checkpoints appear in correct relationship to the nose of your airplane. Finally, if you draw a line on your chart from departure point to destination, follow the line with your finger, and fly your airplane over every visual feature (road, drive-in theater, lake, etc.) along that line, you can't possibly get lost.

CHART READING.

In other chapters you will learn how to look at your aeronautical chart to determine radio frequencies and airspace designations. To fly by pilotage you must be able to quickly and accurately identify ground reference points visually. Refer to the Seattle sectional chart excerpt and the chart legend at the back of the book.

The importance of knowing the height of terrain and obstructions is obvious. Notice that in each rectangle formed by lines of latitude and longitude there is a large blue number with an adjacent smaller number. This represents the height above mean sea level of the highest terrain *or* man-made obstruction within that rectangle in thousands and hundreds of feet. 8^3, for instance, means that the highest obstruction is 8,300 feet above sea level. The heights of specific terrain features is indicated by a dot and the measured altitude. Man-made obstructions such as radio and television towers have two numbers adjacent to them. The top number (in bold italics) is the height of the top of the obstruction above mean sea level, and is the most meaningful number to you in choosing an altitude in that area. The number in parentheses is the actual height of the structure. Towers which are more than 1,000 feet in height (which usually require supporting guy wires that are virtually invisible) have a special symbol as shown in the chart legend.

Freeways, highways, and railroads are excellent references. Notice that major freeways are identified with their route numbers — Interstate 90 crosses the chart from Seattle to the lower right corner. You can often orient yourself by noticing an interchange or an obvious jog in a road, or by the relationship between a road and some other physical feature. Because they are centered in large right-of-way areas, power lines are just as useful as roads — you can see the cleared right-of-way much further than you can see the power lines themselves.

Drive-in theaters and racetracks make good orientation points. Be wary of lakes — in a dry year the lake you are looking for might not be the same shape as indicated on the chart (or may not exist at all!).

Changes in elevation are depicted with contour lines. On the sectional chart excerpt you can see how tightly packed the contour lines are in the Cascade Mountains. Notice the interval between contour lines. The lines are every 500 feet on sectionals and every 1,000 feet on WAC charts.

PILOT NAVIGATION
SECTION REVIEW

1. What is the true course from Cedar Rapids (airport a in the illustration) to Fairfield (airport e)? The magnetic variation is 5° E.

   1. 013°.
   2. 193°.
   3. 198°.
   4. 188°.

2. While flying from Cedar Rapids to Fairfield, you cross Interstate 80 at 1015 and the highway west of Wellman at 1022. What is your estimated time of arrival at Fairfield if your groundspeed remains constant?

   1. 1028.
   2. 1035.
   3. 1040.
   4. 1020.

3. Your airplane uses 8.6 gallons of fuel per hour. You plan a 250 mile flight at an average groundspeed of 115 knots. What is the minimum fuel required for the trip (allow a 30 minute reserve)?

   1. 18.7 gallons.
   2. 23.0 gallons.
   3. 15.6 gallons.
   4. 26.1 gallons.

4. Your groundspeed between Cedar Rapids and Fairfield is 111 knots. At an average fuel consumption rate of 7.2 gallons per hour, how much fuel will you use enroute?

   1. almost 3.4 gallons.
   2. at least 5 gallons.
   3. 2.5 gallons.
   4. 4.2 gallons.

5. Your true course is 270°, your true airspeed is 110 knots, the wind is from 330° at 18 knots, and the magnetic variation is 6° W. What is your groundspeed and magnetic heading?

   1. 119 knots; 278°.
   2. 100 knots; 264°.
   3. 101 knots; 284°.
   4. 119 knots; 272°.

6. Upon refueling at your destination after a 345 nautical mile flight you take 32 gallons of fuel (tanks were full on departure). During the flight, your groundspeed averaged 136 knots. What was the fuel consumption rate for this flight?

   1. 11.0 gallons per hour.
   2. 14.0 gallons per hour.
   3. 15.4 gallons per hour.
   4. 12.6 gallons per hour.

Figure 7Q-1. Excerpt from Chicago Sectional Aeronautical Chart

Refer to the Seattle sectional chart excerpt for questions 7 and 8.

7. What kind of lighting is available at the Cashmere-Dryden airport (47° 30' 45'N 120° 29' 15'W)?

   1. Runway lighting on request.
   2. Rotating beacon only.
   3. Pilot-controlled runway lighting.
   4. Runway lights are on dusk-to-dawn.

8. How tall is the antenna for radio station KPQ, 8 miles northwest of the Wenatchee airport (47° 23' 56' N 120° 12' 20' W)?

   1. 560 feet.
   2. 943 feet.
   3. 313 feet.
   4. 630 feet.

Figure 8-1. VOR Signal Transmitter

As a VFR pilot, you will probably use radio aids to navigation only as a backup to pilotage, rather than as a primary method of navigation. If, however, there is a radio airway going the same way you are, many flight planning problems will be minimized (if not eliminated) by using it.

The FAA has established the VHF omni-directional range (VOR) system as the primary means of electronic navigation in federally controlled airspace, and you will find that most airplanes have at least one VOR receiver. The VOR system operates in the Very High Frequency range (108.0 MHz to 117.95 MHz), just above the FM broadcast band and below that band of frequencies designated for aircraft radio communication. VHF radio waves are subject to line-of-sight

limitations (figure 8-2) and you may find that at low altitudes you will be unable to receive a usable VOR signal.

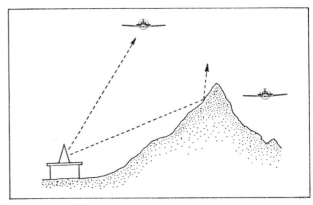

Figure 8-2. Line-of-Sight Limitations

VOR's are classified as high altitude, low altitude, and terminal VOR's. You should consult the Airport/Facility Directory to learn which class any VOR you propose to use falls into. It also lists altitudes and/or radials where the signal is unusable.

Altitude (Feet)	Line of Sight (Statute Miles)
500	30
1,000	45
2,000	65
3,000	80
5,000	100
7,000	120
10,000	140
15,000	175

Figure 8-3. Line-of-Sight Ranges

Your aeronautical chart shows three symbols for VORs: VOR, VORTAC, and VOR-DME (figure 8-4). There is no difference between these three types of stations as far as your cockpit course guidance indication is concerned. VORTAC and VOR-DME will be discussed under DISTANCE MEASURING EQUIPMENT in this chapter. All three types of transmitters broadcast a three-letter identifier in Morse Code, so that you can be sure that you have tuned the correct station and that the station is transmitting a usable signal. The FAA removes the identifier from the signal of any station undergoing maintenance or adjustment.

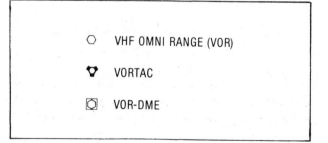

○	VHF OMNI RANGE (VOR)
▼	VORTAC
▣	VOR-DME

Figure 8-4. VOR Symbols

The VOR ground station transmits a signal which is identifiable as 360 radials or lines of position to your airborne receiver-indicator, and these radials are oriented in relation to magnetic north. This not only eliminates consideration of magnetic variation from your flight planning calculations, but gives you a quick chart reference to magnetic directions. Selected radials are printed in blue on the navigational charts and identified as Victor (VOR) airways. Because the VOR airways are labeled with their magnetic direction, you can "eyeball" a course without precise measurement.

The VOR indicator in your cockpit provides the answers to three questions: (1) "Where is the station from me?", (2) "Where am I in relation to the station?", and (3) "In which direction must I fly to intercept the course to my destination?"

To answer these questions, the VOR uses three elements: (1) a Course Deviation Indicator (CDI), or needle, which tells you where you are in relation to a selected radial, (2) an Omni Bearing Selector (OBS), which you use to select radials, and (3) a TO-FROM (or ambiguity) indicator (figure 8-5).

Figure 8-5. VOR Indicator

When the OBS is rotated to center the CDI needle, the TO-FROM indicator will tell you where you are from the station and where the station is from you, simultaneously. In figure 8-6 the pilot has rotated the OBS and the needle has centered with 265° selected; the TO-FROM indicator shows FROM, so the VOR is telling the

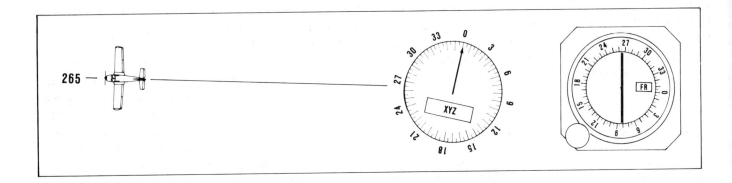

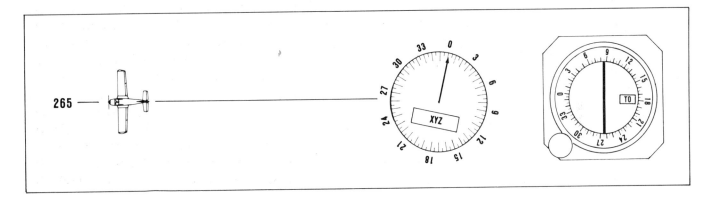

Figure 8-6. Two Indications for Same Location

pilot, "You are 265° FROM, or west of XYZ VOR, so the course TO XYZ must be 085°. Which way do you want to go?" Rotating the OBS to 085° causes the TO-FROM indicator to change to TO, although the airplane has not changed heading. *Because the VOR receiver tells the pilot the airplane's position in relation to the station, the heading of the airplane is not important.* To illustrate, in figure 8-7 both cars are on North Main Street and both airplanes are located on the 360° radial — the fact that they are heading in different directions does not alter that. Changing the heading of the airplanes would not relocate them to the 180° radial, and turning the cars would not relocate them to South Main Street.

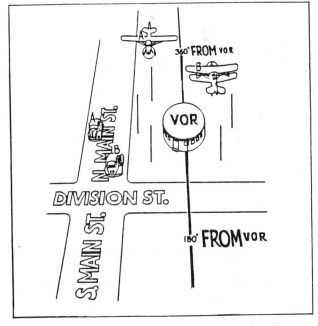

Figure 8-7. TO/FROM Indication is Independent of Heading

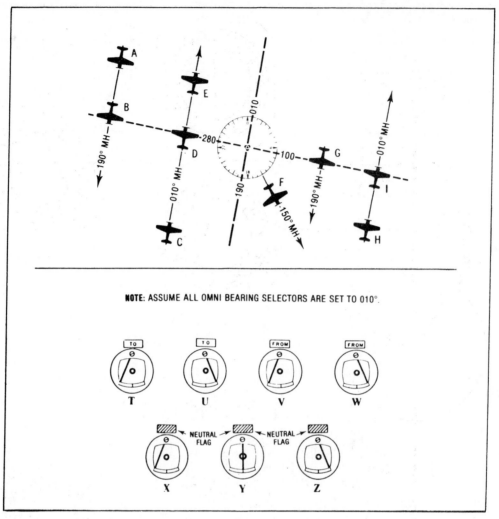

NOTE: ASSUME ALL OMNI BEARING SELECTORS ARE SET TO 010°.

Figure 8-8. Relationship of TO-FROM Indicator to Selected Radial

Figure 8-8 shows how the TO-FROM indicator is related to the VOR radial selected, and it also illustrates that heading has no effect on omni indications. All of the pilots in the illustration have selected the 010° radial with their omni bearing selectors: airplanes A and E both have indication W, while airplanes C, F, and H have indications U, T, and T respectively. Prove this to yourself by mentally turning all of the airplanes in the illustration to a heading of 010° to agree with the OBS — those south of the station will indicate TO, those north of the station will indicate FROM, and the CDI needle in each airplane shows the direction each must turn to intercept the 010° radial.

When you select an omni bearing (radial), you draw an electronic dividing line between the TO and FROM areas, and you can see the result of that division in the illustration. Airplanes B, D, G, and I are neither TO nor FROM, and their VOR indicators will show a neutral or OFF flag. You will also see an OFF flag when the transmitted signal is too weak for navigational use because of distance or low altitude.

Refer to the Seattle sectional chart excerpt. Notice that each VOR station has a magnetic compass rose centered on it, and that each has a blue box adjacent to it with the frequency and Morse Code identifier. For convenience, all VOR, VORTAC and VOR-DME stations are called VORs in this text. A pilot on a cross-country flight enroute from over the Seattle VOR to the Paine VOR would have the VOR receiver tuned to 116.8 MHz and the CDI needle centered with the OBS set to 340°.

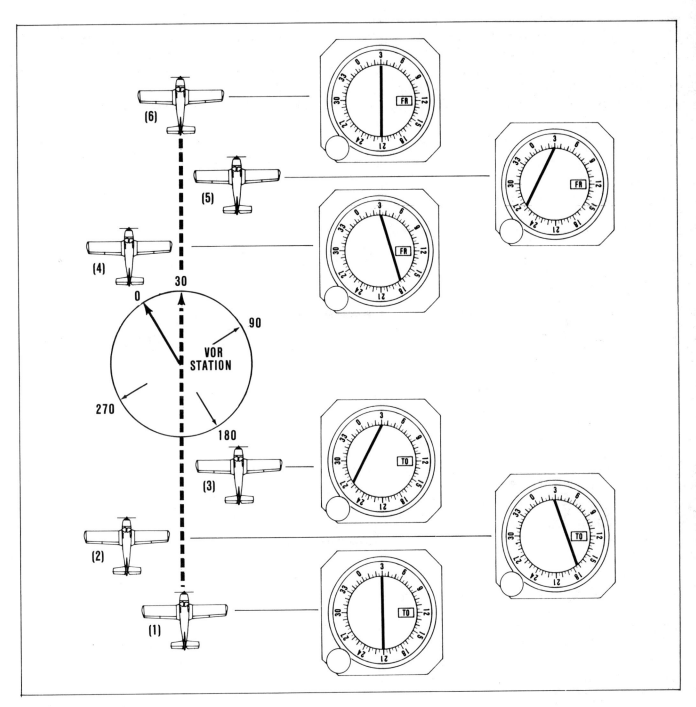

Figure 8-9. Always Fly Toward the Needle

The TO-FROM indicator would show FROM, because the airplane is north of Seattle. Half-way to Paine VOR, the receiver is tuned to 114.2 MHz and the TO-FROM changes to TO because the airplane is south of Paine — the CDI remains centered. Passing over Paine, still northbound, the indicator changes to FROM, and the pilot selects the next VOR along the way when in range. If a wind from the west drifts the airplane off course, the CDI will move off center toward the wind (left), and the pilot must select a heading into the wind which will cause the needle to move back to the center. Retain a small wind drift correction that will keep the needle centered. This is how you will navigate along VOR airways, always flying FROM the VOR behind you and then TO the VOR ahead of you, with the omni bearing differing from your heading by only the amount of wind drift correction. As long as the radial you have selected and the heading of the aircraft agree within ±40° you will always change heading toward the needle to center it.

You don't have to fly on Victor airways — you can make your own. Draw a line from the Paine VOR southwest to the Bremerton National Airport — the bearing is about 190° from Paine to Bremerton. If you are flying north from a position over the Port Orchard airport (southeast of Bremerton National), and want to intercept the direct course between Bremerton and Paine, select 010° (the reciprocal of 190°) with your omni bearing selector. The TO-FROM will read TO because Paine is generally north of you, and the CDI needle will deflect to the left. It is telling you, "select a heading to the left of 010° to go TO Paine". You decide to turn to 340°, 30° to the left of 010° (you "take a 30° cut"). As you intercept the radial, the needle moves into the center, and you turn to 010° plus or minus a wind correction.

Could you find the Port Orchard airport if you were a stranger to the Pacific Northwest? Draw a line from the Seattle VOR to Port Orchard to determine which radial of the Seattle VOR the Port Orchard airport is on, and draw another line from the Paine VOR to Port Orchard to identify the radial of the Paine VOR that crosses Port Orchard. Fly outbound on the Seattle 246° radial with the #1 radio's OBS on 246°, and the #2 radio tuned to Paine with its OBS on 184°. The needle on your #2 omni head will be deflected to the right as you fly across Puget Sound, and it will center when you are over Port Orchard.

Centering the OBS needles of two VOR indicators is a good method of locating yourself if you become disoriented. Be sure both TO-FROM flags read FROM, because you want to determine your position FROM both stations. If you are not sure whether or not you have crossed a selected radial, use this rule: if the needle is on the same side as the station, you're not there yet.

In the example above, as you fly west across Puget Sound toward Port Orchard the Paine Field VOR is to your right and the CDI needle is deflected to the right; it will center over the Port Orchard airport and deflect to the left if you go too far.

VOR needle sensitivity is a function of distance from the transmitting station. At a distance of 60 miles from the transmitter, one degree of needle deflection equals one nautical mile on the ground. The scale of your course deviation indicator is 20° wide (10° each side of center), so at a distance of 60 miles a half-scale needle deflection means that you are 5 miles off course. When you are 12 miles from the station, the same half-scale deflection means that you are only 1 mile off course. The illustration (figure 8-10) shows the distance represented by half-scale deflection at various distances from the VOR transmitter.

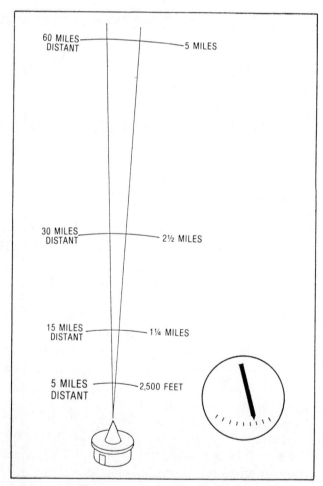

Figure 8-10. VOR Signal Spread Vs. Distance

**VOR RECEIVER CHECK
WASHINGTON**

VOR RECEIVER CHECK POINTS

Facility Name (Arpt Name)	Freq/Ident	Type Check Pt. Gnd. AB/ALT	Azimuth from Fac. Mag.	Dist. from Fac. N.M.	Check Point Description
Ellensburg (Bowers Field)	117.9/ELN	A/2300	255	3.5	Over W end of rwy 07-25.
Olympia (Olympia)	113.4/OLM	G	347		On ramp in front of admin building.
Paine (Snohomish Co. (Paine Fld)) . . .	114.2/PAE	G	022	0.4	On twy H east of rwy 11 threshold.
Seattle	116.8/SEA	A/2000	194	27	Over Nisqually River/I-5 bridge.
	116.8/SEA	A/1500	202	11.5	Over smelter stack.
	116.8/SEA	A/2500	307	19.5	Over NW end of bridge of state hwy 305.
Seattle (Crest Airpark)	116.8/SEA	A/200	106	10.3	Over centerline on apch end runway 33.

VOR TEST FACILITIES (VOT)

Facility Name (Airport Name)	Freq.	Type VOT Facility	Remarks
Seattle (Boeing Field King County Intl)	108.6	G	
Spokane Intl	109.6	G	

Figure 8-11. VOR Receiver Checkpoints (from A/FD)

The VOR airways (the blue lines on the sectional chart) are checked regularly by the FAA for accuracy. When you fly a radial of your own choosing, there may be slight inaccuracies between your "needle centered" position on the radial and your visual position in relation to ground reference points.

When the radial is considered to be totally unusable by the FAA it is listed in the Airport/Facility Directory. This is a good reason for you to check your position visually and use the VOR only as a backup for VFR flight.

Your VOR receiver-indicator should be checked for accuracy at least every 30 days, even if you only use it as a backup to pilotage. The FAA has designated VOR checkpoints on the ground at many airports, and has also designated airborne checkpoints that can be overflown and the VOR indication checked. The Airport/Facility Directory is the place to look for information on VOR checkpoints (figure 8-11). At some large airports (listed in the A/FD) a special VOR test transmitter called a VOT is installed. The VOT transmitter is designed to send a single 360° radial, so that you get a signal indicating that you are north of the station regardless of your actual location. When the VOT's frequency is selected the needle should center within 4° of 180° TO or 360° FROM.

In many cases the transmitted VOR signal is interrupted or distorted by the terrain or similar conditions, making it inaccurate and unusable at some altitudes, or in certain directions, or both. The listing for the VOR station in the Airport/Facility Directory will list any such restrictions (figure 8-12). You may also notice irregularities in the needle indication that are caused by the propeller interfering with the received signal at certain RPM settings — changing RPM will solve this problem.

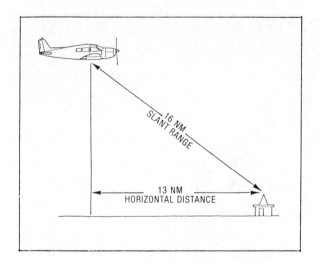

Figure 8-13. Slant Range Considerations

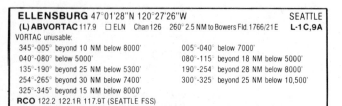

ELLENSBURG

Figure 8-12. Restrictions to VOR Signals (from A/FD)

DISTANCE MEASURING EQUIPMENT

Many airplanes are equipped with **DME** which reads the distance from the transmitting station in nautical miles. Although the DME transmitter and receiver use Ultra High Frequencies (UHF), this is of no concern to the pilot. Just tuning the DME to the frequency of the associated VOR does the trick. Range information from the DME is slant range from the ground up to the airplane, not horizontal range on the ground. If you are 6,000' above the transmitting station, the DME readout will not go below 1.0 nautical mile; accuracy suffers when close to the station because of slant range considerations (figure 8-13).

Distance information can be received from either VORTACs or VOR-DMEs — there is no practical difference to the user. The UHF range of frequencies is even more sensitive to line-of-sight limitations than the VHF range is — you may receive an adequate VOR signal when unable to receive the associated DME because of intervening terrain. In addition to distance information, some DME indicators also read out groundspeed and time to the station. Figure 8-14 shows a typical modern DME with its readouts.

Figure 8-14. Typical DME

AUTOMATIC DIRECTION FINDER

The Automatic Direction Finder (ADF) receiver in your airplane (figure 8-15) receives transmissions in the Low and Medium Frequency ranges, generally from 190 KHz to 1750 KHz. In the range from 190 KHz to 550 KHz it is used with non-directional beacons (**NDB**s) operated by the FAA or Coast Guard.

The ADF receiver will have a function switch with several positions. In the ANT or REC position it will provide no direction-finding capability, but will have good audio clarity for positive identification of the navigation station (or for listening to music, news, and sports). The TEST position will electronically deflect the ADF needle so that you can be sure that it is working, and that the signal from the navigation station is adequate for navigation.

Figure 8-15. Automatic Direction Finder (ADF)

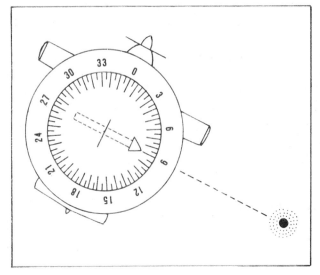

Figure 8-16. Relative Bearing

When the switch is in the ADF position, the indicator needle will point directly to the transmitting station. In contrast to the VOR, when the airplane heading changes, the ADF needle moves. You read the angle between the needle and the nose of the airplane as a bearing *relative* to the nose. What you really want to know is the *magnetic* bearing to or from the transmitting station, because all of your navigation is based on magnetic north. It is possible to compute **magnetic bearing** when **relative bearing** and magnetic heading are known.

Magnetic heading (MH): course you are steering.

Relative bearing (RB): angle between the nose of the airplane and the ADF needle, measured *clockwise*.

Magnetic bearing to the station = MH + RB

$$035° + 225° = 260°\text{ to the station}$$
(figure 8-17)

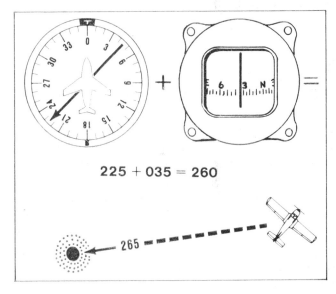

225 + 035 = 260

265

Figure 8-17. Bearing TO Station

Most light airplanes with ADF receivers have a rotatable card on the indicator. The card can be set to agree with the magnetic heading on the heading indicator to eliminate the mathematics.

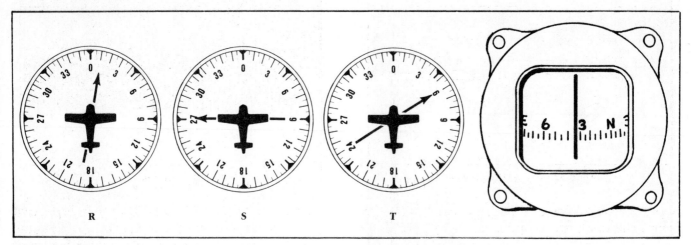

Figure 8-18. Magnetic Compass with ADF Indicators

In the illustration (figure 8-18) the magnetic heading is 035°. Can you match the ADF indicators with the correct magnetic bearing to the station?

R	1.	095°
S	2.	045°
T	3.	305°

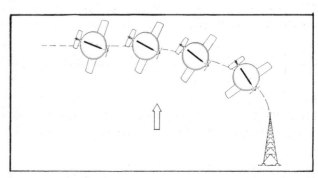

Figure 8-19. Homing — No Wind Correction

USING YOUR
AUTOMATIC DIRECTION FINDER

If your airplane is equipped with an Automatic Direction Finder receiver you can use it to "home" directly to a low frequency radio station such as an FAA radiobeacon or a standard broadcast station. "Homing" means that you turn your airplane so that the ADF indicator needle points directly ahead (0° relative) and continue to turn the airplane as required to keep the needle in that position. The drawback of homing is that if there is any wind your airplane will follow a curved track arcing downwind from the straight-line track to the station. This is not only inefficient and time consuming, but you might be drifted close to terrain or obstacles at night (figure 8-19).

The frequencies and antenna locations of broadcast stations are printed in blue on sectional charts. Broadcast stations are required to identify themselves only every 30 minutes, so you might be homing for quite a while on the wrong station!

To follow a straight track to a radio station using the ADF, you must establish a wind correction angle which will exactly offset wind drift. The first step in tracking is to place the needle at the 0° relative position by turning the airplane, just as in homing. As the wind blows the airplane downwind, the needle will move into the wind; when the needle has moved 5°, turn into the wind twice that amount (10°). This will make your heading 5° on the windward side of the direct course, with the ADF needle deflected 5° away from the wind.

If the needle moves back toward the nose (into the wind), the wind drift correction is too small — add another 5°.

If the needle moves away from the wind, the correction is too great and should be cut in half. This fine-tuning will continue until you pass over the radio antenna (figure 8-20).

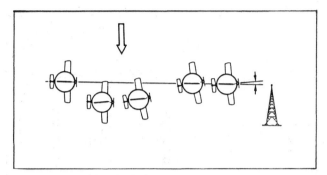

Figure 8-20. Tracking — Correcting for Wind

Figure 8-22. Electronic RMI

Another practical use of the ADF is establishing off-course checkpoints while on a VFR flight. If there is a low frequency station on either side of your course line, you can get an approximate position fix by noting when the ADF needle points directly off your wingtip toward the station (figure 8-21).

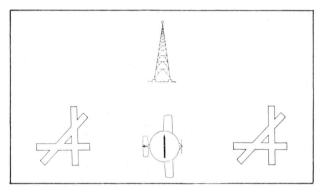

Figure 8-21. Approximate Position Fix Using ADF

RADIO MAGNETIC INDICATOR

Figure 8-22 shows a type of electronic **RMI** (Radio Magnetic Indicator) available in modern VOR receivers from many manufacturers. By selecting the frequency of the VOR station and TO or FROM, you get a direct digital readout of the radial on which you are located. This feature is also valuable in identifying radials which cross your course line and form intersections — just watch the digital numbers click by until the desired radial shows up.

A radio magnetic indicator (RMI) combines an ADF needle, one or more VOR needles, and a compass card driven by the directional gyro or similar source of magnetic information. With an RMI, the needle selected (ADF or VOR) indicates the magnetic bearing to the station continuously, without pilot input. When reading an RMI, the arrow head represents the bearing TO the station, and the tail represents bearing FROM the station. You can use the RMI to determine your bearing from the transmitting station in the same way that you use the ADF's rotatable card, except that with an RMI the card is rotated for you by a gyro. Look at the four RMI indicators below:

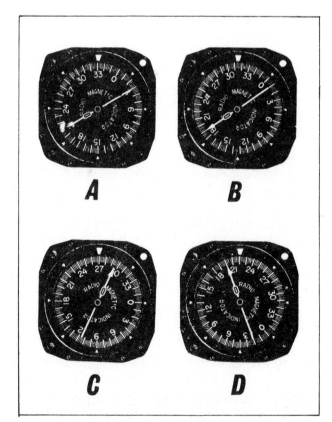

Figure 8-23. RMI Indicators

1. Indicator A shows that the airplane is 030° magnetic from the station, heading 330°. A left turn to 210° would take you to the station.

2. Indicator B shows the airplane crossing the 010° bearing from the station on a heading of 315°. To intercept the 180° bearing to the station you would turn left to any heading between 190° and 280°.

3. Indicator C shows an airplane tracking to a station with a left crosswind from 245°. The pilot has turned left (into the wind), and the needle has moved to the right of the nose.

4. Indicator D shows an airplane tracking to a station with a right crosswind from 240°. The magnetic bearing to the station is 200°.

AREA NAVIGATION

Area navigation, or RNAV, provides a means of straight-line navigation using VORTACs (or VOR-DMEs) without dog-legging from station to station. The equipment allows you to establish navigational fixes called "waypoints" along the straight line course which can be identified by the DME distance and VOR radial from the VORTAC. Steering to the waypoint is accomplished by the same left-right CDI needle used in VOR navigation, and distance to the waypoint is read out simultaneously. The RNAV equipment electronically "relocates" all of the enroute VORTACs so that they define the straight-line track. Several waypoints can be preset, and the pilot selects them in sequence as the flight progresses.

An example, using the Seattle sectional chart excerpt in the back of the book, would be an RNAV route between the Olympia airport (in the lower left corner) and Harvey Field, just east of Paine Field at the top of the chart.

The first enroute waypoint would be the Seattle 273° radial at 7.3 nautical miles, and the second would be Harvey Field, using the Paine Field 064° radial at 7.8 nautical miles. These points define a straight line course between Olympia and Harvey Field. Using

RNAV, you would have a continuous distance readout from Harvey Field. RNAV and Loran-C (below) give you the capability of accurately navigating to airports not served by any navigational aid.

LORAN-C

The Loran-C system overcomes the major drawback of the VOR system (line-of-sight reception limitation) by using a frequency of 100 KHz, in the Very Low Frequency range. Radio waves in this range can be received 1,000 to 1,200 nautical miles from the transmitting station, and they are unaffected by terrain. Best (and most consistent) accuracy is achieved within 700 nautical miles of the transmitting stations and in a position equidistant from them.

A Loran-C chain consists of a master station and two or more secondary stations, all transmitting on 100 KHz — there is no need for the pilot to tune the Loran-C receiver. The receiver is able to distinguish between different chains because each chain has a specific "group repetition rate", the rate at which each station in the chain sends out pulsed transmissions, and it is by group repetition rate that the pilot selects the chain for the area of operation. For example, when the pilot selects group repetition rate 9940, the Loran-C receiver locks on to stations in Washington, California, and Nevada and provides navigational coverage along the entire West Coast. Loran-C receivers are "user friendly" because no tuning is required and chain selection is virtually automatic.

In the airplane, the receiver determines the difference in time between the reception of the master's pulse and the pulse from each secondary station. These time differences are measured in tenths of millionths of a second. When lines of equal time difference between reception of the master pulse and that from each secondary station are plotted, they form curved lines called hyperbolas around the stations (figure 8-25); Loran-C is called a hyperbolic means of navigation.

Each secondary station in a Loran-C chain waits until a pulse is received from the master station, adds a "coding delay", and then transmits a pulse of its own.

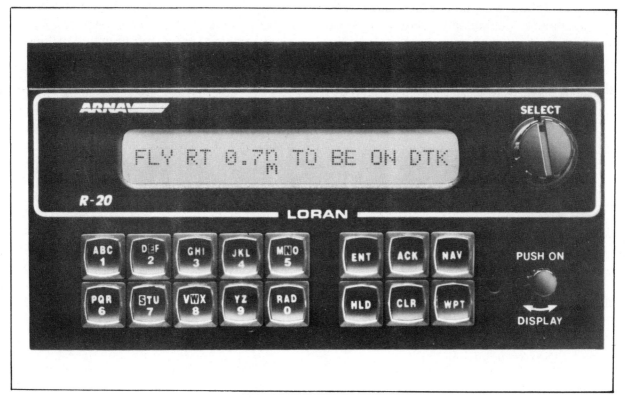

Figure 8-24. Loran C

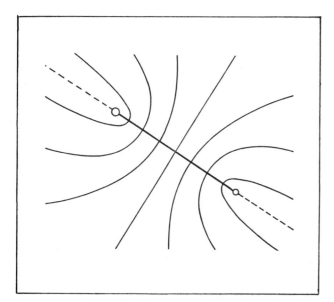

Figure 8-25. Hyperbolas Around a Station

In figure 8-26, the receiver in the airplane has received a pulse from the master station (M) and one secondary (X), and the receiver has determined that the airplane is located along a line of position between M and X.

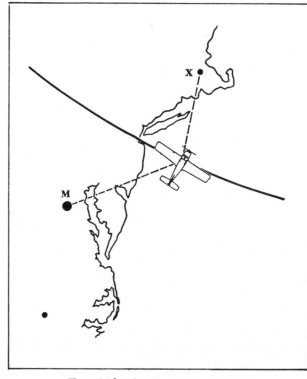

Figure 8-26. Pulses from Stations M and X

Figure 8-27 shows the reception of the M signal and that from station Y, determining a line of position which crosses the M-X line and positively fixes the airplane's position. Most Loran-C receivers will use more than two secondaries for position fixing and, if one secondary signal is weak, will automatically reject it.

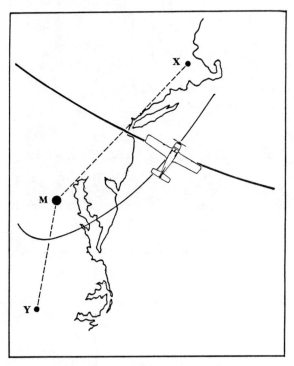

Figure 8-27. Reception of M and Y Signals

The reception, calculation, and display of position information is continuous. How the position information is displayed and used varies between equipment manufacturers, but several features are commonly available, including:

WAYPOINT DESIGNATION: A pilot can designate a remote airport, a navigational aid, an airway intersection, a favorite fishing hole, or any similar location as a "waypoint", and the Loran-C will indicate bearing and distance to the waypoint, the airplane's groundspeed, and the estimated time to the waypoint. All Loran-C equipment provides for waypoint designation using latitude and longitude. Other means such as radials from two VOR stations, or a VOR radial and DME

distance are available from some manufacturers. A very useful feature is a "present position" input which allows a pilot to enter a position into the equipment's memory for future use — this might be the "best airport restaurant" waypoint.

TRACK: The Loran-C indicator will display the *desired* track over the ground, the *actual* track over the ground, and any off-track error in both miles and degrees.

PARALLEL OFFSET: If there is a thunderstorm or terminal control area on the direct track to your destination, the Loran-C provides for offsetting your flight path several miles parallel to the direct track so that you can avoid the storm or TCA while still receiving accurate course guidance.

LAT-LONG: the airplane's position in latitude and longitude can be displayed to an accuracy of tenths of minutes (a tenth of a minute of latitude is 600 feet).

The accuracy of Loran-C position-fixing is affected by station geometry; that is, the angle formed by lines drawn between the master station and each secondary. Loran-C is most inaccurate "behind" a transmitting station, along the baseline extension. Almost all Loran-C equipment warns the pilot if accuracy is being affected by inadequate signal strength or poor station geometry.

There is presently (1985) a "mid-continent gap" in Loran-C signal coverage (figure 8-28). Because Loran-C's popularity began with marine users, the east, west, and gulf coasts and the Great Lakes region are fully covered. New stations have been proposed which will eliminate the mid-continent gap in the late 1980s.

Loran-C technology is expanding rapidly, and more features are sure to be offered in the future. Presently, some manufacturers offer the ability to "name" waypoints such as runway thresholds (BFI13), small airports (MONRO), or even a friend's house (BILLS), and navigate directly to those points. A recent advance is

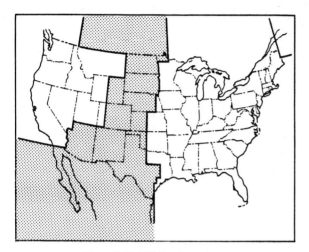

Figure 8-28. Mid-Continent Gap

the availability of terrain information along a planned route, making the pilot aware of potential conflicts. Some manufacturers have pre-programmed all VOR stations in the continental United States into their Loran-C equipment, and the pilot need only enter the 3-letter identifier of the VOR to get all of the navigational information listed above. No other navigation system presently available to general aviation allows a pilot in Chicago to push a few buttons and get a course and distance to Bangor, Maine.

RADIO NAVIGATION
SECTION REVIEW

1. Which pilot action is most likely to eliminate large fluctuations on the VOR course deviation indicator during flight?

   1. Recycle the ON-OFF switch.
   2. Recycle the frequency selector.
   3. Disconnect the microphone.
   4. Change the engine RPM.

2. How can a pilot determine when a particular VOR is unreliable?

   1. A recorded voice stating "VOR shutdown for maintenance."
   2. A continuous series of dashes replacing the coded identification.
   3. An absence of the coded identification.
   4. A coded W added to the identification.

3. You want to track inbound on the 050° radial of a VOR station. The recommended procedure is to set the course selector to

   1. 050° and make heading corrections toward the Course Deviation Indicator (CDI needle).
   2. 230° and make heading corrections away from the Course Deviation Indicator (CDI needle).
   3. 050° and make heading corrections away from the Course Deviation Indicator (CDI needle).
   4. 230° and make heading corrections toward the Course Deviation Indicator (CDI needle).

4. Your magnetic heading is 300° and the ADF needle is pointing to a station bearing 085° relative to the nose of the airplane. The magnetic bearing to the station is

   1. 385°.
   2. 025°.
   3. 215°.
   4. 205°.

5. After selecting the frequency of a VOR station, you rotate the omni-bearing selector (OBS) until the needle centers. The OBS reads 120° and the TO-FROM indicator shows TO. The airplane heading is 270°.

   1. You are southeast of the station.
   2. You are northwest of the station.
   3. You are west of the station.
   4. You are northeast of the station.

Refer to the Seattle sectional chart excerpt for question 6.

6. You are flying from Seattle to Wenatchee on the V-120 airway, with your VOR receiver tuned to 116.8 MHz and the omnibearing selector on 069°. Directly over the north end of Kachess Lake you notice that the course deviation indicator needle is

    1. deflected to the right of center. You should change heading to the left to center the needle.
    2. deflected to the left of center. You should change heading to the left to center the needle.
    3. deflected to the right of center. You should change heading to the right to center the needle.
    4. not centered. You should rotate the omnibearing selector until the TO-FROM indicator changes to TO and the needle centers.

7. Approaching Wenatchee you decide to use your Automatic Direction Finder as a backup means of radio navigation. You should

    1. tune the receiver to 1041 KHz.
    2. tune the receiver to 110.0 MHz.
    3. tune the receiver to 560 KHz.
    4. tune the receiver to 943 KHz.

8. You are over the city of Wenatchee and the airport is straight ahead. The needle on your ADF indicator (tuned in accordance with question 7) is pointing

    1. 000° relative.
    2. 090° relative.
    3. 180° relative.
    4. 240° relative.

When you listen to an AM radio at night, and tune down toward the lower end of the dial, you can pick up stations hundreds and even thousands of miles away. Low frequencies can be received at long distances even in the daytime, because they are not weakened or attenuated as they travel through the air and over the ground as much as higher frequencies are; however, atmospheric interference, or static, is a problem with low frequency transmissions. To avoid having critical aeronautical communications affected by static, frequencies in the Very High Frequency (VHF) range are used in aircraft radios. Radio transmissions in the VHF band are limited to line-of-sight (figure 9-1) and that

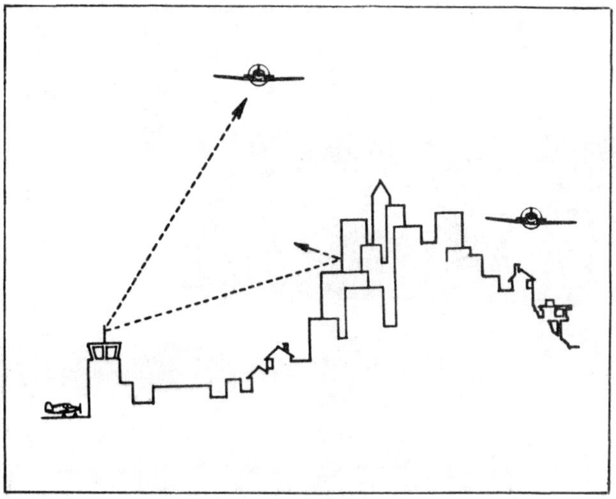

Figure 9-1. Line-of-Sight Limitations

makes altitude an important factor — as you gain altitude the range of VHF is greatly increased.

The FAA has assigned those frequencies between 118.0 MHz (Megahertz — millions of cycles per second) and 136.0 MHz for radio communication. The table below shows how they are allocated. Most modern aircraft radios are capable of transmitting and receiving on at least 360 frequencies, or channels, and 720 channels will soon be needed. The FAA spaces assignments 50 KHz (thousands of cycles per second) apart (134.0, 134.05), although there are some assignments spaced only 25 KHz apart (126.225, 126.275) which require 720 channel capability. By 1986, the FAA will have 25 KHz spacing in use at all altitudes. If you are assigned a frequency which your radio cannot tune, just ask for an alternate frequency.

This is an all-inclusive list of frequency assignments, emphasizing those that you will probably be using most.

VOICE COMMUNICATION FREQUENCIES

118.0 to 121.4 MHz — Air Traffic Control
121.5 MHz — Emergency Frequency, ELT signals
121.6 to 121.9 MHz — Airport Ground Control
121.95 MHz — Flight Schools

121.975 MHz — Private Aircraft Advisory (FSS)

122.0 MHz — FSS Enroute Flight Advisory Service ("Flight Watch")

122.025 to 122.075 MHz — FSS

122.1 MHz — FSS receive only with VOR or FSS simplex

122.125 to 122.175 MHz — FSS

122.2 MHz FSS Common Enroute Simplex

122.225 to 122.675 MHz — FSS

122.7 MHz — Unicom, uncontrolled airports

122.725 MHz — Unicom, private airports not open to public

122.75 MHz — Unicom, air-to-air, private airports not open to public

122.775 MHz — Future Unicom or Multicom

122.8 MHz — Unicom, uncontrolled airports

122.825 MHz — Future Unicom or Multicom

122.85 MHz — Multicom

122.875 MHz — Future Unicom or Multicom

122.9 MHz — Multicom, airports with no tower, FSS or Unicom

122.925 MHz — Multicom, Natural Resources

122.95 MHz — Unicom, controlled airports

122.975 MHz — Unicom, high altitude

123.0 MHz — Unicom, uncontrolled airports

123.025 MHz — Future Unicom or Multicom

123.05 and 123.075 MHz Unicom, heliports

123.1 MHz — Search and Rescue, temporary control towers

123.15 to 123.575 MHz — Flight Test

123.6 to 123.65 MHz — FSS or Air Traffic Control

123.675 to 128.8 MHz — Air Traffic Control

128.825 to 132.0 MHz — Aeronautical Enroute (ARINC)

132.05 to 135.95 MHz — Air Traffic Control

Figure 9-2 shows a typical modern aircraft radio with digital display of an active and a standby frequency, a popular feature in today's communication radios.

Figure 9-2. Typical VHF Communications Transceiver

When you select the proper communication frequency, you will transmit and receive on that frequency. Modern radios have crystal-controlled frequency selection and require no tuning. While you have the push-to-talk switch on your microphone depressed, your receiver is blocked and you cannot hear any other transmissions — each party to the communication must finish transmitting before a reply can be received. This is called **simplexing**, and most of your radio communication will be simplex. Talking on one frequency and listening on another, as you do on the telephone, is called **duplexing**, and you will be using duplex in some communications with **Flight Service Stations (FSS)** (figure 9-3).

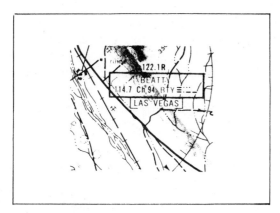

Figure 9-3. Duplex Communications

The table above gave general frequency assignments, but you need to know how to contact a specific tower, **UNICOM**, or Flight Service Station. The **Airport/Facility Directory (A/FD)** lists all of the radio frequencies available at any airport and also includes a listing of all Air Route Traffic Control Center frequencies — you will be using them for enroute radar services. A ready reference for most frequencies is your sectional aeronautical chart. Refer to the Seattle sectional chart and the sectional chart legend. Airports with control towers have a blue airport symbol, and very close to the symbol you will find a data block with "CT" such as that adjacent to the Seattle-Tacoma Airport where "CT 119.9" is the control tower frequency. If there is an asterisk (*) following the frequency, the tower does not operate continuously. If the chart says NFCT adjacent to the airport symbol it is a non-Federal control tower, operated by a private entity.

The letters **ATIS** mean Automatic Terminal Information Service, and when you listen to the ATIS frequency listed in the airport data block you receive a continuous taped broadcast of non-control information such as ceiling and visibility, altimeter setting, wind, runway in use, etc. If the ceiling is above 5,000' and the visibility is greater than 5 miles, that information might not be mentioned in the broadcast. Each time the ATIS is revised the phonetic designator is changed, and you should include in your initial call the fact that you have listened to the ATIS: "Portland Ground Control, Cessna 1234X on the ramp with information ALFA, taxi to 10R." The UNICOM (privately operated Aeronautical Advisory Service) frequency is listed at the end of the data block. Sectional charts also include a tabulation of all control tower and ATIS frequencies in the margin (figure 9-4).

Figure 9-4. Tower and ATIS Frequencies

Figure 9-5 shows how Flight Service Station frequencies are presented. Note that some frequencies are not listed directly: the heavy line box means that 121.5 and 122.2 are available (but not shown). The triangles in the upper corners mean that 122.0 is available for Enroute Flight Advisory Service (**Flight Watch**), and that frequency is not separately listed. All other frequencies are listed above the box. If a frequency which is normally standard such as 121.5 or 122.2 is not available, it will be listed above the box with a strike-through: ~~122.2~~. The notation "122.1R" means that the FSS can receive, but cannot transmit on that frequency, and this is your indication that duplex communication is required. The FSS will listen on 122.1 and transmit on the VOR navigational aid frequency.

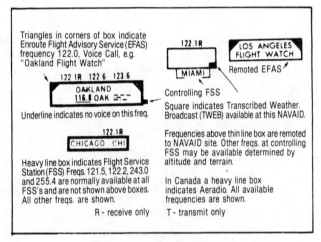

Figure 9-5. Communication Boxes

When you call a Flight Service Station on 122.1 you must advise them which navigational aid you are listening to: "Wichita Falls Radio, Ercoupe 345X, listening on the Duncan VOR". A thin blue line box indicates that the Flight Service Station has only those frequencies that are printed outside the box. Where an FSS has a remote control capability, you will see a box with LRCO (Limited Remote Communication Outlet), or a **navaid** frequency box with the name of the controlling FSS beneath the box (figure 9-6).

RADIO PROCEDURE

The Airman's Information Manual (AIM) section on correct phraseology, the phonetic alphabet, and pronunciation of numbers is included as an appendix to

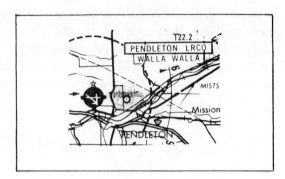

Figure 9-6. LRCO

this book. The appendix also contains the Pilot/Controller Glossary from the AIM which explains terms used in communication with air traffic controllers. You should become familiar with the contents of both. You will learn a lot just by listening on aircraft frequencies to hear how other pilots communicate with each other and with ground personnel. A visit to a Flight Service Station, control tower, or a radar facility will convince you that everyone on the ground is prepared to help you have a safe flight and that having "mike fright" will just keep you from taking advantage of the many services available.

Always listen before transmitting, so that you do not interfere with a communication in progress, and listen to what is being said — in many cases you may hear information that makes your call unnecessary. If your airplane's radio installation provides a switch so that you can transmit on either radio, be sure that you are using the correct radio before you transmit — this is a common mistake and you will hear it happen to the most grizzled old airline captains. Always begin your transmission with the name of the station that you are calling: "Logan Tower", "Orlando Ground" Dallas Radio", "Podunk UNICOM", followed by your own identification (in full, if it is the initial contact): "Twin Cessna 2345X".

It is not necessary to wait for an acknowledgement that communication has been established if you are reasonably certain that your transmission has been received: "Seattle Tower, Piper 2345X6 miles north with BRAVO, landing". Be as brief as practicable without omitting necessary information, and always give your position when requesting a clearance from Air Traffic Control. Remember this sequence: WHO you are calling, WHO you are, WHERE you are, and WHAT your intentions are.

An airplane cockpit is a noisy place, and your microphone is designed to filter out engine noise if you use it properly. Hold the microphone close to your lips and speak directly into it. Holding the microphone away from your lips will allow engine noise to mask your transmission.

RADIO USE AT UNCONTROLLED AIRPORTS

Unless an airport has an operating control tower or an active control zone, you do not even need to have a radio to use that airport. For safety's sake, however, you should have a radio — but do not expect all other airplanes in the area to have radios. Many airports have no radio facility; when operating in the vicinity of a non-radio airport use the Common Traffic Advisory Frequency (**CTAF**) listed in the Airport/Facility Directory. In most cases this will be the multicom frequency 122.9 MHz, because you will be broadcasting your position and intentions in the blind (no specific addressee): "Podunk Traffic, Mooney 2345X 10 miles north, landing". Don't use 122.9 MHz as an airborne "party line" to talk to your friends in flight — 122.75 MHz may be used for that purpose.

At airports with a UNICOM (Aeronautical Advisory Service), the UNICOM frequency will be the CTAF. Don't be surprised if you attempt to call UNICOM and get no reply — this is a non-governmental service provided by the local operator and those busy people may not hear your call. UNICOM frequencies are shared by many uncontrolled airports, and some may be so close together that pilots at different airports will interfere with one another. To avoid confusion, always begin your transmission with the name of the airport at which you are operating: "Podunk traffic, Grumman 2345X left downwind runway 16, touch and go". UNICOM is used for many purposes and is quite informal, but you should not let this informality change your normal good communication habits.

Some uncontrolled airports have Flight Service Stations on the field, and 123.6 MHz should be used for airport advisory service. Call the FSS for the active runway when departing, and be sure to call about 15 miles out when arriving to get the local weather, runway in use, and any reported traffic in the pattern. Use other FSS frequencies for in-flight filing of flight plans and requests for other services. Where Enroute Flight Advisory Service (Flight Watch) is available on 122.0 MHz (0600 to 2200 local time), use that frequency to request weather reports and forecasts (122.0 MHz is used *only* for weather information).

COMMUNICATION AT CONTROLLED AIRPORTS

A controlled airport is one with an *operating* control tower. You are required to establish communication with the tower, and to receive a clearance to operate within the airport traffic area (5 miles radius from the center of the airport, from field elevation up to but not including 3,000' AGL), whether you are arriving, departing, or just passing through. If you are departing, you must first receive taxi instructions from the ground controller, who directs all activity on the ramps and taxiways. With few exceptions, ground control operates on 121.6, 121.7, 121.8, or 121.9 MHz. Controllers will frequently shorten this by eliminating the 121: "Contact ground point seven leaving the runway". The ground controller will give you clearance to the active runway, and that clearance authorizes you to use all taxiways and cross all runways enroute to the runup area. Figure 9-7 illustrates a situation where an airplane cleared from the ramp to runway 9 would be cleared to taxi across the approach end of runway 36L and 36R enroute. If you are in any doubt about taxiing across a runway, stop and clarify the situation with the controller.

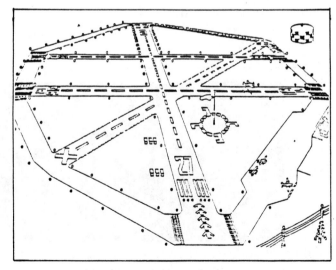

Figure 9-7. Taxiing to the Active Runway

If you are at a strange airport, ask for progressive taxi instructions and the controller will guide you.

When you are ready for takeoff, contact the tower controller for takeoff clearance. The tower (or "local") controller is responsible for all aircraft in the airport traffic area and on the active runway — don't taxi onto the runway without a clearance. You must maintain communication with the tower controllers while within their airspace (the airport traffic area). When you are 5 miles out you have departed the airport traffic area and are on your own (or you may request radar services).

On arrival, before you enter the airport traffic area you should listen to the ATIS (if there is one) and advise the tower controller on initial contact that you have the ATIS information. Where there is no ATIS, listen on the tower frequency and note the instructions given to other pilots. Once you are sure of the runway in use, wind, and altimeter setting you can say: "Miami Tower, Baron 2345X 10 miles west with the numbers." After landing, do not change to ground control until advised to do so by the tower. Some controlled airports have UNICOM, but because you will be getting all of your weather information and clearances from the tower, your use of UNICOM at a controlled airport will be limited to such things as calling for fuel, ordering rental cars, etc.

TRANSPONDER

Although the **transponder** has no microphone or speaker, it is a means of communication with ground radar facilities. Interrogation signals transmitted from the ground are received by your transponder, (figure 9-8) and it replies with a coded signal which the controller can read on the radar scope. Each time the transponder reply light flickers, it has responded to an interrogation. In congested areas the transponder will be replying to interrogation from several radars, while in remote areas it may receive only an occasional interrogation.

Always set the four numbers on your transponder to 1200 when flying VFR. Otherwise, enter a specific code as directed by a radar controller while receiving radar services. Be careful when setting your transponder — some codes have special meanings. Code 7700, for instance, is the emergency transponder code, used only to alert ground personnel that you are in distress. Code 7500 is the hijacking code, and code 7600 is used by instrument pilots in case of communications failure. Code 0000 belongs to the military.

Push your transponder's IDENT button only when told to do so by the controller. This feature causes your radar return to intensify on the controller's scope for exact identification, and when pushed it will stay activated for about 20 seconds. IDENTing when not directed to do so might result in a mis-identification by the controller. When the transponder function switch is ON, you are in Mode A (indicating your position) only, and with the function switch in the ALT (Mode C) position, the transponder will also transmit altitude information to the ground (if an encoding altimeter is installed in the airplane).

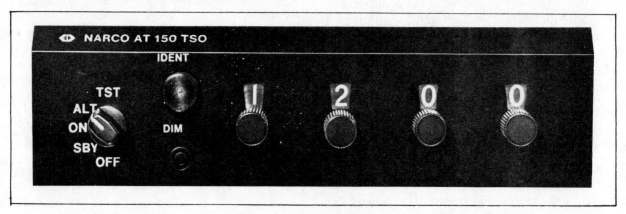

Figure 9-8. Typical Transponder

A transponder with Mode A capability is required in all Terminal Control Areas (TCA). A transponder with Mode C (altitude reporting) capability is required only in Group I TCAs and when operating in controlled airspace above 12,500' MSL. You can request a waiver of these requirements if you give ATC one hour's notice.

Almost all radar facilities require a transponder return for tracking. At those facilities with the most modern equipment, the controller does not see an actual target generated by your airplane but a computer generated target based on your transponder. That is the reason why you will occasionally see airplanes visually which have not been called to your attention by the controller — if they don't have a transponder (or if their transponder is off) — they don't show up on the radar.

RADAR SERVICES FOR VFR PILOTS

There are two types of radar service available to you as a VFR pilot: radar traffic advisory service (**flight following**) and terminal radar service. Terminal Radar Service is presently provided as Basic, Stage II, and Stage III. Almost all radar services to VFR aircraft (except Stage III) are provided on a workload permitting basis — if the controller says, "unable" to your request, you will have to get along without radar assistance.

Basic terminal radar service consists of traffic advisories and limited vectoring. This is an excellent way to fly more safely through a congested terminal area or to get to a strange airport. The radar controller will do everything possible for you, but keeping on the right side of the Federal Aviation Regulations is your responsibility. A heading which would take you into cloud or provide anything less than the required separation from clouds must be refused, and the controller advised of the reason: "Tomahawk 45X won't be able to maintain VFR on that heading." You are also required to see and avoid other aircraft. The radar is only an aid.

The controller will give you traffic information using the clock in relation to your direction of movement.

Each number on the clock represents 30°, and in no-wind conditions traffic at 2 o'clock would be 60° to the right of the nose. If you have established a 30° correction into a wind from the left, traffic reported at 2 o'clock would be directly off your right wing (figure 9-9).

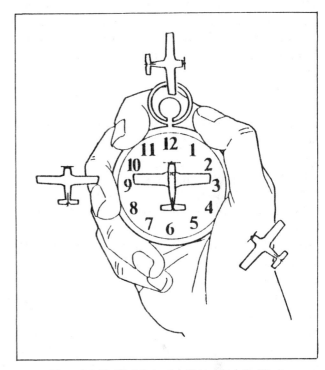

Figure 9-9. Traffic Information Using Clock Positions

Stage II radar service provides radar traffic advisories and sequencing for participating VFR aircraft; pilots will be sequenced behind other traffic. It is available on a workload permitting basis, and if the controller is too busy to provide radar service the response will be "unable".

Stage III service is provided in Terminal Radar Service Areas (**TRSAs**), which are outlined in magenta on your sectional chart (with their vertical limits), and identified in the Airport/Facility Directory. Participation is voluntary but recommended. This service is *not* limited to "workload permitting", but is available at all times. You will be separated from all IFR and all participating VFR traffic, but you must remember that not all VFR pilots participate by requesting radar service, and you may see airplanes that the radar controller has not called out to you as traffic. Generally, radar only sees those airplanes with transponders, although the capability to pick up targets by radar reflection alone can be selected. Again, the responsibility to remain clear of traffic and in VFR conditions rests with you.

You will find the frequencies for terminal radar service in the A/FD, listed under the airport served by the radar facility. In some cases the ATIS advises VFR pilots to contact Approach Control and gives the frequency. This is also true upon departure from an airport with Stage III service — the ATIS may tell you to call on a certain frequency for a clearance before calling the ground controller for taxi instructions. In either situation, if you do not desire radar services you need only advise the controller "no radar", or "Negative Stage III", and you will be on your own — then you will be one of those non-participating aircraft that everyone else is looking out for.

Radar Traffic Advisory Service provides only traffic advice, and that is what you will get if you "request radar flight following". If you are being provided with radar service after departure, the radar controller will "hand you off" to the next controller (with a frequency change), and that controller will in turn pass you along. If you are enroute and want radar service, call the nearest FSS. They will give you the correct frequency for your present location. Radar controllers will always tell you when radar service is terminated instead of just "dropping" you. You should return the favor by always advising the radar controller when you no longer desire radar service — don't just change frequencies.

Airport Radar Service Areas (**ARSAs**) are replacing Terminal Radar Service Areas; they differ in that pilot participation is mandatory. No equipment other than a radio transmitter and receiver is required to operate in an ARSA. Frequencies are listed in the Airport/Facility Directory and are shown on aeronautical charts.

VHF/DF (DIRECTION FINDING)

VHF/DF is used to aid lost or disoriented pilots. However, this subject is discussed under Radio Communications because all you need to get VHF Direction Finder service is a transmitter and a receiver. Many Flight Service Stations (listed in the A/FD) can take bearings on your radio transmissions and, after a series of bearings, give you headings to steer to a nearby airport. This is not nearly as quick or as accurate as radar, but if you are lost and have no transponder it is an excellent service. FSS specialists like to practice VHF/DF steers (in fact, each specialist must give a minimum number of "steers" to remain qualified), so don't hesitate to ask for one on some nice VFR day when you are not lost or disoriented.

EMERGENCY COMMUNICATIONS

The International Calling and Distress frequency for VHF is 121.5 MHz. *Memorize this frequency.* If you are not already in communication with some FAA facility and you become lost, disoriented, or have any kind of emergency, do not hesitate to tune to 121.5 and call, "MAYDAY, MAYDAY, MAYDAY STINSON 2345X calling any station!" You will get many answers — respond to the loudest one. Do not be reluctant to call for help for fear of embarrassment — the longer you delay in confessing your predicament, the less fuel you will have to carry out the instructions of an assisting agency. In an emergency, you should also set your transponder to 7700 — this sets off bells and buzzers at radar facilities and will help the controllers pinpoint your position even if you are too busy with the situation at hand to call anyone on the radio.

EMERGENCY LOCATOR TRANSMITTER

With very limited exceptions, every airplane must carry an emergency locator transmitter (**ELT**) which automatically transmits when it is turned on by a pilot in distress or by impact forces. ELTs transmit on both the VHF and UHF distress frequencies: 121.5 MHz and 243.0 MHz (used by the military). To be sure that your ELT will operate in an emergency, you are allowed to turn it on *briefly* during the first five minutes of each hour (while monitoring 121.5 on your communications receiver). Because ELTs have been activated by hard landings, many pilots monitor 121.5 MHz briefly before shutting down their engines, just to be sure that no signal is being transmitted. False ELT signals must be tracked down by search-and-rescue forces and verified as being false, so pilots must take every precaution against error. The battery in your ELT must be replaced when one-half of its useful life has expired, (or if your brief tests have accumulated one hour of transmitting time), and the service technician will mark that date on the side of the transmitter case.

RADIO COMMUNICATIONS
SECTION REVIEW

Refer to the Seattle sectional chart excerpt.

1. Which service is provided for aircraft operating within the Tacoma Terminal Radar Service Area?

    1. Priority for participating aircraft for the purpose of vectors, sequencing, landing, and takeoff.
    2. Separation between all participating VFR and IFR traffic.
    3. Radar vectoring and separation between all aircraft.
    4. Radar vectoring and sequencing of all traffic to all of the airports within the TRSA.

2. What UNICOM frequency, if any, is indicated for Seattle-Tacoma International Airport?

    1. None is listed.
    2. 119.9 MHz.
    3. 116.8 MHz.
    4. 122.95 MHz.

3. What is the frequency for transcribed weather broadcasts in the Ellensburg area? (east edge of chart excerpt).

    1. 122.8 MHz.
    2. 117.9 MHz.
    3. 122.2 MHz.
    4. 122.1/117.9 MHz.

4. Approaching the Wenatchee Airport (east edge of chart excerpt), which frequency would you use to obtain an airport advisory of traffic in the pattern and runway in use?

    1. 122.3 MHz.
    2. 111.0 MHz.
    3. 123.6 MHz.
    4. 122.1/111.0 MHz.

5. What is the procedure for an approach and landing at the Auburn Municipal Airport just southeast of Seattle-Tacoma Airport?

    1. Obtain a clearance from Seattle-Tacoma tower on 119.9 MHz 10 miles from Auburn.
    2. Remain below 3,000' MSL and receive an airport advisory on 122.8 MHz.
    3. Request a clearance from Seattle Approach Control on 122.0 MHz.
    4. Remain below 3,000' MSL and advise Seattle Flight Watch of your intentions.

6. Operational tests of the ELT (emergency locator transmitter) should be made only

    1. during the first 5 min. of an hour.
    2. during the annual inspection.
    3. after one-half the shelf life of the battery.
    4. upon replacing the battery.

7. When are non-rechargeable batteries of an ELT to be replaced?

    1. Every 24 mo.
    2. When 50 percent of their useful life expires or they were in use for a cumulative period of one hour.
    3. At the time of each 100 hr. or annual inspection.
    4. Annually.

8. To use VHF/DF facilities for assistance in locating an aircraft's position, the aircraft must have

    1. a VHF transmitter and receiver.
    2. an IFF transponder.
    3. a VOR receiver and DME.
    4. an ELT.

9. When making routine transponder code changes, pilots should avoid inadvertent selection of which codes?

    1. 3100, 7600, 7700.
    2. 7500, 7600, 7700.
    3. 7000, 7600, 7700.
    4. 4000, 7600, 7700.

10. When landing at an airport that does not have a tower, FSS, or UNICOM, broadcast your intentions in the blind on

    1. 123.0 MHz.
    2. 123.6 MHz.
    3. 121.5 MHz.
    4. 122.9 MHz.

11. Below FL180, enroute weather advisories should be obtained from an FSS on

    1. 122.1 MHz.
    2. 122.0 MHz.
    3. 123.6 MHz.
    4. 122.4 MHz.

12. ATIS is the continuous broadcast of recorded information

    1. alerting pilots of radar-identified aircraft when their aircraft is in dangerous proximity to terrain or an obstruction.
    2. concerning nonessential information to relieve frequency congestion.
    3. concerning noncontrol information in selected high-activity terminal areas.
    4. concerning sky conditions limited to ceilings below 1,000 ft. and visibilities less than 3 mi.

GENERAL

At any airport, you will have to be able to identify the runway in use, taxi safely, be aware of wake turbulence hazards, deal with the line crew, know who (if anyone) controls your actions, interpret lights and markings, etc. This chapter will discuss general airport operations and then differentiate between controlled and uncontrolled airports.

As your flying experience expands to include more airports, you will find some features that they all have in common. For instance, all runways are numbered according to their directions in relation to magnetic north, to the closest 10°. A runway laid out 138° from magnetic north would be numbered 14: rounded off to 140° and the zero dropped. The opposite end of the runway would be numbered 32 (the reciprocal) (figure 10-1). Some large airports have parallel runways which are identified as left, right, or center: runway 27R, runway 6L, etc.

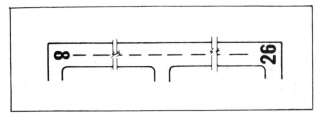

Figure 10-1. Runway Numbering

You will normally take off and land into the wind, and the wind indicator tells the direction the wind is blowing from. Every airport should have some form of wind indicator or landing direction indicator. Figure 10-2 shows several types of landing direction indicators: the tetrahedron, the windsock, and the wind tee. All of the indicators in the illustration indicate a wind from the east.

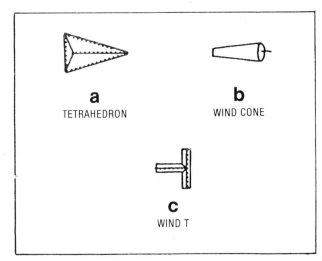

Figure 10-2. Wind Indicators

At some airports, the tetrahedron or wind tee may be tied down to show the favored runway, and will not accurately reflect wind conditions. Always observe what other pilots in the pattern are doing and conform

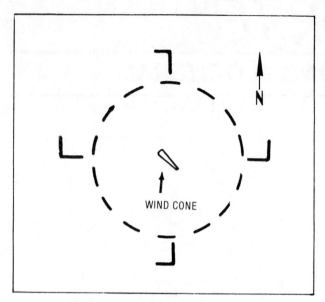

Figure 10-3. Landing Strip and Pattern Indicators

with the pattern in use. Figure 10-3 shows landing strip indicators and landing pattern indicators — the landing strip indicators parallel the runways and the

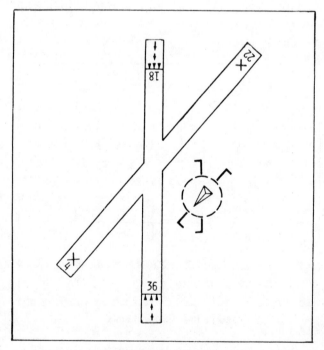

Figure 10-4. Pattern Markings

landing pattern indicators show the direction that traffic flows to and from the runways. Your pattern should conform with the traffic flow indicated for the runway in use.

Frequently, terrain or the presence of a congested area dictate the use of a right hand pattern. Figure 10-5 shows pattern indicators which keep traffic from overflying the area northwest of the water tank. Where

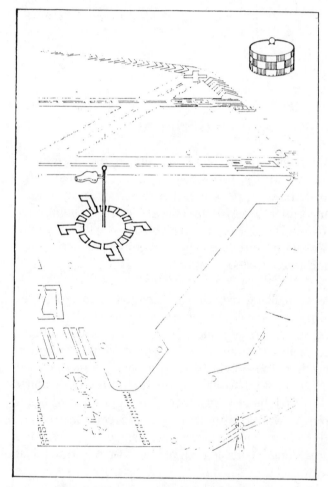

Figure 10-5. Tower and Traffic Pattern Indicators

there are no pattern indicators, the FARs require that all turns in the pattern be made to the left. When you fly over a strange airport and do not see a pattern indicator, you are safe in assuming a left-hand pattern.

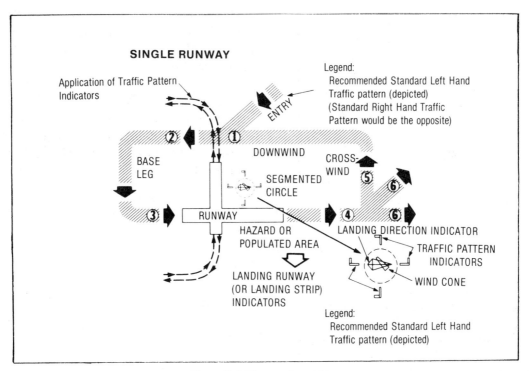

Figure 10-6. Diagram from AIM

Figure 10-6 shows the FAA recommended standard left hand traffic pattern with arrival and departure procedures. If the airport has an *FAA required* traffic pattern, you must use that pattern (few airports have such patterns. FAR Part 93 lists them).

CAUTION:

If you see another airplane in the pattern or taxiing for takeoff, plan your pattern to conform to that airplane's actions. Even if one of you is wrong, it's better than meeting head-on.

Adjacent to every airport symbol on an aeronautical chart there is a data block with the airport name, its elevation above sea level, the length of the longest runway *in hundreds of feet*, and information on lighting and radio services available. All of the information can be deciphered by use of the sectional chart legend, but you should be able to get the essential information at a glance.

For example, look at the data block for Seattle-Tacoma International Airport on the sectional chart excerpt.

The airport is 429 feet above sea level, the longest runway is 11,900 feet long, and runway lighting is available from sunset to sunrise. Radio frequencies for the control tower, Automatic Terminal Information Service, and Aeronautical Advisory Service (UNICOM) are also listed.

On the sectional chart you will notice many airports without runway symbols: these airports have unpaved runways or paved runways less than 1500' in length. Airport symbols with little protrusions around their edges indicate that services (usually fuel) are available. You will also find airports with no radio service and airports without lighting. You should never be surprised by what you find at the end of a flight — you should know all about your destination airport before you take off. Charts and the Airport/Facility Directory are the government's means of providing airport information; there are also several private publishers of booklets with VFR airport information.

Airports can be divided into two categories: controlled (tower in operation) and uncontrolled. On the sectional chart excerpt, you will see that airport symbols printed in blue are those airports with towers, and those printed in magenta have no towers. When the tower is not in operation, the airports with blue symbols become uncontrolled airports. Part-time towers are indicated by an asterisk next to the control tower frequency. Check the data blocks for the Tacoma Industrial and Olympia airports as examples of part-time towers. The Airport/Facility Directory also contains information on hours of operation.

Where runway markings are provided, you will find centerline marking, a threshold marking where the landing surface begins, and a "hold line" which separates the active runway from the taxiway. Runways used for instrument approaches have additional markings. If there are obstacles in the approach path, the threshold may be displaced; arrows will lead to the displaced threshold. Note that in the illustration (figure 10-7) the threshold of runway 27 has been displaced because of the power lines. Any paved area which *appears* to be usable, but which is not usable for normal operations, is marked with yellow chevrons. Such areas may be used as overruns at the end of a runway. In figure 10-7, the taxiway beyond the threshold of runway 18R is marked as unusable.

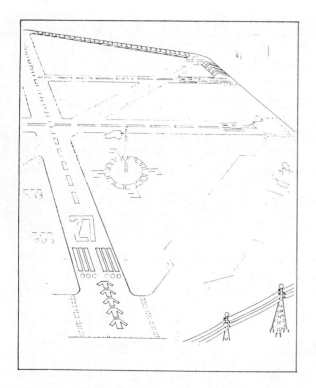

Figure 10-7. Displaced Threshold

For night operations, taxiways are marked with **omni-directional** blue lights and the active runway is marked with omnidirectional white lights. Green lights mark the threshold, and red lights alert you to the end of the landing surface — these are directional lights, showing green in one direction and red in the other. Hazards, such as the water tank in figure 10-6, are marked with red lights.

At many airports the lighting is controlled by the pilot, who transmits on a specified frequency (usually the Common Traffic Advisory Frequency), and keys the microphone briefly to turn on the lights. At most airports with pilot-controlled lighting the pilot can control the intensity of the lighting by varying the number of "clicks" of the microphone button. The lights turn off automatically after 15 minutes. On aeronautical charts, airports with pilot controlled lighting are identified by a circled letter "L", and the frequency to use is given. Details on the keying code are found in the Airport/Facility Directory.

Rotating beacons are installed at all controlled airports and many uncontrolled airports, and as they rotate the pilot sees a white flash followed by a green flash. Military airports are identified at night by two white flashes between each green flash. When the rotating beacon is lighted in the daytime, it means that the weather is below the minimums required for visual flight. You should check the actual weather and not rely on the light, however, since many rotating beacons are turned on by timers or photoelectric cells.

VASI

Visual Approach Slope Indicators (**VASI**) are installed at both controlled and uncontrolled airports, and provide a visual means for the pilot to maintain a constant glide angle (usually 3 degrees) on final approach. Information on the type of VASI and the glide path angle can be found in the Airport/Facility Directory listing for the desired airport. A VASI installation defines the approach slope by providing light boxes adjacent to the runway — each box contains a light source and filters so arranged that when the pilot is on the desired glide path the box closest to the threshold (downwind) will show a white light, and the box furthest from the threshold (upwind) will show a red light. To the pilot on the correct glide path this appears as red over white: "red over white is right". Two white lights indicate a position too high on the glide path: "white over white, you're high as a kite". If a pilot is below the desired glide path both light boxes will show a red light: "red over red — you're dead" (a little morbid, but it rhymes and conveys a strong warning). Where a Visual Approach Slope Indicator is provided, you are required to use it by flying on or above the visual glide path until descent is required for landing. Figure 10-8 shows a two-bar VASI.

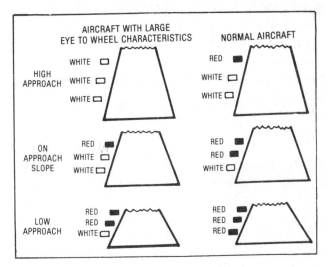

Figure 10-9. Three Bar VASI

Providing the pilot with accurate descent path information is so important that some small airports have a visual aid consisting of painted boards installed beside the runway 50-100 feet apart. The pilot aligns the boards visually to stay on the glide path. This is called a "POMOLA", for Poor Man's Optical Landing Aid (figure 10-10).

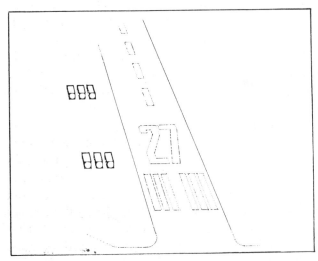

Figure 10-8. Two Bar VASI

The eyes of the pilot of a long-bodied jet are about 50 feet above the surface when the landing gear touches down, so three sets of VASI boxes (figure 10-9) are provided on runways where such jets operate. The two sets of boxes closest to the threshold define the glide path for light aircraft and the two furthest define the glide path for the jets.

The FAA has approved use of other types of visual approach aids, such as a single-source amber-green-red indicator. This VASI shows a green light when you are on the glide path, an amber light when you are high, and a red light when you are dangerously low. Other approved lighting systems include a single line of lights which show red or white depending on your position on the glide path.

Figure 10-10. POMOLA

TAXIING

Strong gusty winds can make taxiing a chore, and mishandling the controls might result in loss of control.

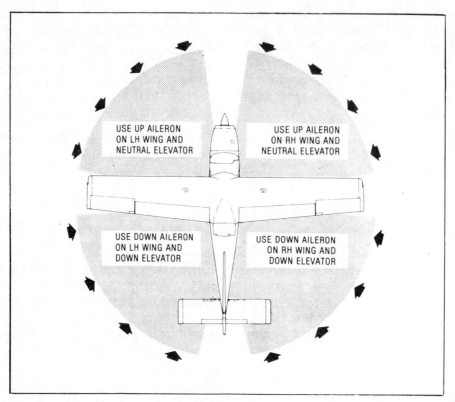

USE UP AILERON
ON LH WING AND
NEUTRAL ELEVATOR

USE UP AILERON
ON RH WING AND
NEUTRAL ELEVATOR

USE DOWN AILERON
ON LH WING AND
DOWN ELEVATOR

USE DOWN AILERON
ON RH WING AND
DOWN ELEVATOR

Figure 10-11. Taxiing Diagram

You must understand how to use the controls so that the wind cannot get beneath the wing or tail surfaces and cause you to drag a wingtip or have the propeller strike the ground.

When the wind is coming from a direction in front of the airplane, from wingtip to wingtip, hold the ailerons as though you are banking into the wind. The up-aileron on the windward side will depress the wing as the wind strikes it — the down-aileron on the opposite wing will create enough lift to oppose any overturning tendency. The elevator should be in a neutral position unless you are flying a taildragger, in which case full back elevator control will pin the tailwheel to the ground for steering control.

A quartering tailwind is most hazardous for a tricycle gear airplane, because a gust can lift the wing and tail and upset the airplane. To counter this tendency, when the wind is coming from any direction behind the airplane the ailerons should be held away from the wind, and the elevator held in neutral or slightly forward (well forward in a taildragger). The down-

aileron will now be on the windward side, and the wind from behind the wing will hold it down. Figure 10-11 illustrates this.

CROSSWIND OPERATIONS

Although airport designers try to align runways with the prevailing winds, there is always the possibility that the wind may not be blowing directly down the runway you intend to use. The manufacturer of your airplane has designated a maximum allowable crosswind component for your airplane, and you will find it either placarded in the cockpit or in the Pilot's Operating Handbook. It is called "maximum *demonstrated* crosswind component" if the factory test pilot demonstrated that the airplane was controllable with a crosswind component at the published figure. You offset the crosswind component by using ailerons to control sideways drift and rudder to keep the longitudinal axis (and the airplane's direction of motion) aligned with the runway. When the crosswind component exceeds the published maximum, these aerodynamic controls won't be able to overcome the sideways drift and the tendency of the airplane to yaw or weathercock into the wind. You will "run out of rudder".

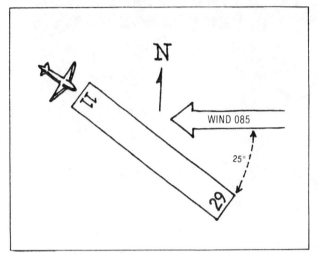

Figure 10-12. Crosswind Component

The difference between airplanes with conventional landing gear ("taildraggers") and those with tricycle landing gear becomes most obvious in crosswind takeoffs and landings. The center of gravity of a taildragger is behind the landing gear, and if a swerve begins (due to a crosswind or misuse of the rudders and/or brakes), the airplane will want to "swap ends". Quick and proper use of the rudders and/or brakes will stop this tendency. Taildragger pilots are justly proud of their abilities, and will tell you that a landing in a taildragger is not complete until the airplane is safely tied down.

The center of gravity of a tricycle gear airplane is forward of the landing gear, and upon landing the tendency is for the airplane to continue moving in the direction that it was moving at touchdown. It is your job as the pilot to be sure that at the moment of touchdown the airplane's motion is straight down the runway and that the longitudinal axis of the airplane is also aligned with the runway. If the airplane is pointed across the runway at touchdown, that is the direction it will go until you get on the rudders and straighten it out. If it is drifting sideways at touchdown due to inadequate crosswind correction, the landing gear will be subjected to side loads it was not designed to handle.

There are several techniques for crosswind takeoffs and landings and they all have one common thread: *the airplane must be pointing and moving parallel to the runway heading at liftoff or touchdown.* Some tricycle-gear airplanes have free-swivelling nose gear which aligns itself with the direction of travel as soon as it touches the runway, while on other airplanes the nose gear reacts to rudder input. If your trainer is one of the latter, any rudder input at touchdown may result in a swerve.

The crosswind diagram (figure 10-13) is one method of determining crosswind component.

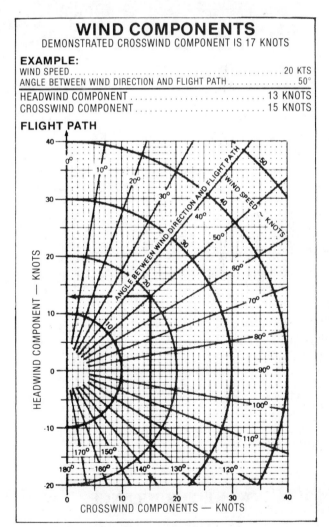

Figure 10-13. Crosswind Diagram

Find the angle between the reported wind direction and the runway heading, and follow the line repre-

Figure 10-14. Wingtip Vortices (NASA Photo)

senting that angle to its intersection with the arc representing the reported wind velocity. A line drawn downward from the point of intersection to the bottom scale will give you the crosswind component, and a horizontal line will give the headwind component.

> Reported wind . . . . 270 at 20 knots.
> Runway in use. . . . . runway 30.
> Wind angle . . . . 30 degrees.
> Crosswind component. . . . . 10 knots.
> Headwind component. . . . . 17 knots.

If you don't have a diagram available, use these thumb rules to compute crosswind component: for wind angles of less than 20 degrees, ignore the crosswind component; for wind angles of 20-40 degrees multiply the reported wind velocity by .5, for angles of 40-60 degrees multiply by .7, and for angles of 60 degrees or more, consider the full wind velocity to be the crosswind component.

WAKE TURBULENCE

An important consideration for pilots at any airport is the avoidance of wake turbulence. Every airplane leaves behind it two twin tornadoes corkscrewing aft from the wingtips. As the high pressure air below the wing tries to travel around the wingtip to the low pressure area on the top surface and the airplane moves forward, the circulation is clockwise from the left wingtip and counterclockwise from the right wingtip as seen from behind. In the NASA photograph (figure 10-14), the airplane has flown between two smoke generators and the vortices are clearly seen. Because these wingtip vortices are a product of lift development, they are strongest and most hazardous behind airplanes that are heavy, slow, and with landing gear and flaps retracted: a takeoff situation. Second most hazardous is the heavy, slow airplane in the landing configuration.

Any lifting surface creates tip vortices. How severely they affect an airplane that encounters them depends on the relative weights and wingspans. A very light airplane encountering a vortex from a heavy jet may be thrown out of control, while a medium jet in the same position might experience only momentary turbulence. Research has shown that the wingtip vortices descend 900 to 1,000' behind the generating airplane and then slowly dissipate. Crossing behind a heavy airplane and encountering both vortices can create destructive forces. An airplane with a wingspan smaller than the vortex can be rolled at a rate faster than its pilot can control (figure 10-15).

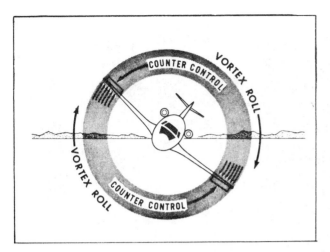

Figure 10-15. Airplane with Wingspan Smaller than Vortex

When preparing to take off, if a heavy airplane is landing you should note the point at which it touched down — *vortices are only generated when the wings are developing lift.* You should plan your takeoff roll so that you lift off beyond the point at which the heavy airplane touched down. If you are preparing to take off and a heavy airplane has just departed, you should wait at least 3 minutes for its wake turbulence to dissipate (at controlled airports the tower controller will probably delay your takeoff clearance). You can avoid its wake turbulence by lifting off at a point on the runway before its liftoff point and then climbing to windward

above the heavy airplane's flight path. (Light airplanes *can* climb more steeply than a jet's flight path for a short distance). You should be aware that wake vortices drift downwind and wait a few moments longer if you suspect they will drift into your path.

If you are landing behind an airplane which is generating hazardous wingtip vortices, note its touchdown point and overfly its landing roll so that you land beyond its touchdown point (figure 10-16). Heavy jets use up a lot more runway than you need. When landing after a heavy jet has just taken off, land on the runway numbers. Its vortices do not begin until it rotates for takeoff and begins generating lift.

Operating at an airport with crossing runways requires special care. Avoid being airborne when crossing a runway where a heavy airplane has just taken off or landed, and land short of the intersection if possible. *Remember that the heavy airplane creates vortices only when creating lift.*

LINE SIGNALS

An aspect of airport operations which is the same at both controlled and uncontrolled airports is the set of standardized hand and arm signals used by line

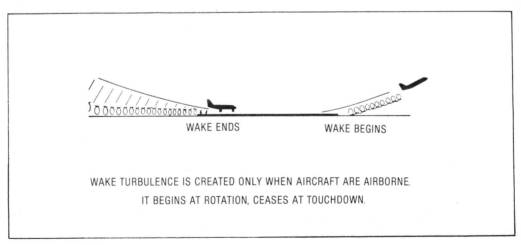

WAKE ENDS   WAKE BEGINS

WAKE TURBULENCE IS CREATED ONLY WHEN AIRCRAFT ARE AIRBORNE.
IT BEGINS AT ROTATION, CEASES AT TOUCHDOWN.

Figure 10-16. Touchdown — Rotation

Figure 10-17. Hand Signals

personnel to direct ground operations. Figure 10-17 is self explanatory. When no line personnel are available to guide you, it is usually more prudent to shut down the airplane and push it into a parking space than to attempt to gauge clearances visually.

Miscalculations are sure to be expensive.

AIRPORT OPERATIONS
UNCONTROLLED AIRPORTS

Unless you learn to fly at a tower-controlled airport, and never venture far away from the comforting sound of a controller's voice, you will spend most of your flying time at uncontrolled airports. There are approximately 12,600 airports and only about 400 have towers. Some

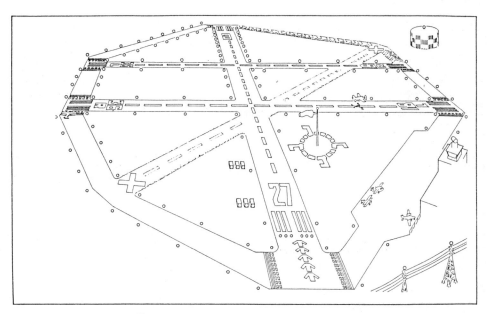

Figure 10-18. Airport Panoramic View

uncontrolled airports are served by on-field Flight Service Stations, some have UNICOM, and some have no radio facility at all. Your airplane does not have to be radio-equipped to operate at these airports. Remember, even an airport with a tower becomes uncontrolled when the last controller locks the door and goes home. Figure 10-18 shows a control tower *and* traffic pattern indicators around the windsock. When the tower is closed at night, only one of the parallel runways will be lighted, and the traffic pattern indicators will dictate traffic flow.

In preparing to depart an uncontrolled airport, it is your responsibility to be sure that VFR conditions exist and are expected to continue or improve during your flight. You must also check the wind direction and velocity and the runway in use, and taxi safely to the runup area.

If there is a Flight Service Station on the field, its personnel can provide you with weather, runway, and known traffic information. Flight Service Station briefers are trained specialists, with access to National Weather Service information on local, enroute, and destination weather conditions. FSS personnel are not air traffic controllers — they cannot give you clearance to taxi or to take off or land. UNICOM (Aeronautical Advisory Service) is even less formal, because the radio station is not operated by the government but by a private business as a service to the flying public. The operator has many other duties, and

may not always be able to answer your call. Information on runway in use received from an FSS or UNICOM is advisory only — at an uncontrolled airport *you* decide which runway to use (but be ready to defend your decision if you decide not to go with the flow!). If you are unable to communicate with UNICOM, or if the FSS is closed, the Airman's Information Manual suggests that you broadcast in the blind (no specific addressee: "Podunk traffic, Chieftain 4125 GOLF departing runway 16 at Podunk.") on the Common Traffic Advisory Frequency for that airport.

You will occasionally find runways at uncontrolled airports marked off with a large X at each end or in the center. An X-ed off *runway* is closed (see figure 10-19),

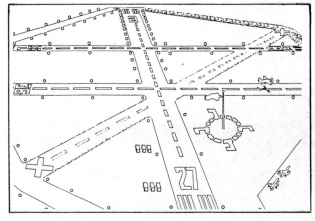

Figure 10-19. Closed Runway

and an X in the center of an airport indicates that the *airport* is closed. Some runways have displaced thresholds (figure 10-20), usually because of obstructions in the approach path, and you must land beyond the displaced threshold markings. You can taxi on or begin your takeoff run from that area of the runway between the end of the paved surface and the displaced threshold unless chevron markings indicate that it is unusable.

Figure 10-20. Displaced Threshold

Figure 10-18 includes a closed runway, an unusable taxiway, displaced thresholds, and parallel runway markings.

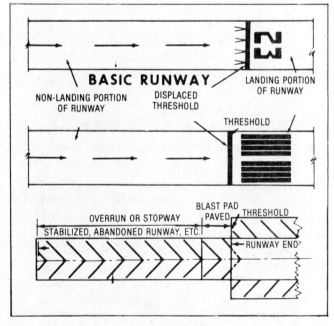

Figure 10-21. Runway Markings

When approaching an uncontrolled airport to land, you should begin planning your pattern entry about 10 miles out. Every airport has a Common Traffic Advisory Frequency, even though there may be no radio facility on the airport. Where there is a UNICOM, listen briefly to learn which runway other pilots are using so that you can plan your entry. The presence of a Flight Service Station on the airport creates an Airport Advisory Area, and you should call on 123.6 MHz when 10 miles out for an airport advisory.

Because no clearance is required to enter the traffic pattern and land at an uncontrolled airport, it is not required that you maintain continuous radio contact with the ground station. The AIM does recommend that you announce your position and intentions when 10 miles out and when on downwind, base, and final so that other pilots in the area can coordinate their movements with yours. Also, because the CTAF may be shared by several airports, your transmissions should include the name of the airport at which you intend to land. "Podunk Traffic, Duke 2345X on left downwind for runway 23." Keep your transmissions brief and to the point so that others may use the frequency.

AIRPORT OPERATIONS CONTROLLED AIRPORTS

A controlled airport is one with an operating control tower. Control towers are commissioned at airports because the volume of traffic demands a high degree of coordination, so when you operate into or depart from a controlled airport you should expect your movements to be controlled by the tower. You can ask the **tower controller** for a runway other than the active, and if safety and traffic permits, you may get it. With that exception, there is no opportunity for a pilot to make his or her own decision on where to taxi or which runway to use.

At many controlled airports there is an Automatic Terminal Information Service (ATIS) which continuously broadcasts non-control information on existing weather conditions, runway in use, and applicable Notices to Airmen. Non-control means that the ATIS gives you the information necessary to plan your arrival but you still need a clearance from the tower to operate

Table 10-1. Light Gun Signals

Color and Type of Signal	On the Ground	In Flight
STEADY GREEN	Cleared for takeoff	Cleared to land
FLASHING GREEN	Cleared to taxi	Return for landing (to be followed by steady green at proper time)
STEADY RED	Stop	Give way to other aircraft and continue circling
FLASHING RED	Taxi clear of landing area (runway) in use	Airport unsafe — do not land
FLASHING WHITE	Return to starting point on airport	
ALTERNATING RED & GREEN	General Warning Signal — Exercise Extreme Caution	

in the airport traffic area. Your first action, whether arriving or departing, should be to monitor the ATIS broadcast. Each ATIS tape is identified with a letter of the phonetic alphabet (see the Appendix). When contacting ground control, the tower controller, or an approach control facility, you should state in your initial contact that you have the ATIS information: "Bay Approach, Comanche 587 Sierra, 10 miles southeast with DELTA." Federal Aviation Regulations Part 91 requires that you establish communications with an air traffic control tower before entering the airport traffic area, but if your radio fails in flight (or if you have no radio and have made prior arrangements with the tower) you can still enter the pattern and receive clearance to land through light gun signals (Table 10-1).

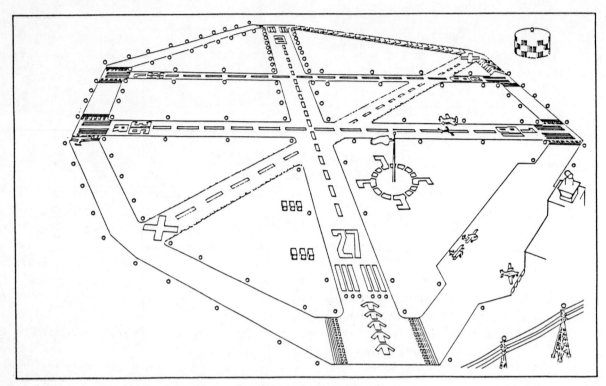

Figure 10-22. Airport Diagram

When the **ground controller** clears you to the active runway, that clearance authorizes you to cross any intersecting runways on the way to the runup area, but does not include clearance onto the active runway. In figure 10-22, a pilot cleared to runway 9 would have a clearance to taxi across the thresholds of runways 36R and 36L unless directed to hold short.

The ground controller's area of responsibility ends at the yellow hold lines, and the tower controller "owns" the runway and the airport traffic area. After landing, remain on the tower controller's frequency until directed to contact ground control.

CONTROLLED AIRPORTS VS CONTROL ZONES

It is easy to confuse a controlled airport with a control zone, because in many instances a controlled airport is located *within* a control zone. Whether or not you can operate in a control zone depends on the weather conditions in the zone — when the ceiling is more

than 1000' and the visibility is more than 3 miles, you can enter and leave without a clearance. A controlled airport has an airport traffic area, however, and it imposes a communications requirement — you must receive a clearance from the tower to take off, land, or operate within the airport traffic area. There is no symbol or marking on a chart to indicate the boundaries of an airport traffic area — only the control tower frequency and the blue airport symbol alert you to its existence.

There are many airports that have control zones but no control tower, and therefore they have no airport traffic area (note Bremerton National Airport on the Sectional chart). There are very few tower controlled airports without an instrument approach and an associated control zone, however.

When an airport has a control zone, the lighting of its rotating beacon during daylight hours is intended to indicate that the control zone is below basic VFR weather minimums, but in many cases these beacons are controlled by automatic devices and your decision on IFR vs VFR should not depend on the beacon alone.

AIRPORT OPERATIONS
SECTION REVIEW

1. An air traffic control clearance provides

   1. authorization for flight in uncontrolled airspace.
   2. priority over all other traffic.
   3. adequate separation from all traffic.
   4. authorization to proceed under specified traffic conditions in controlled airspace.

2. A flashing green air traffic control signal directed to an aircraft on the surface is a signal that the pilot

   1. is cleared to taxi.
   2. should exercise extreme caution.
   3. should taxi clear of the runway in use.
   4. should stop taxiing.

3. Which is the correct traffic pattern departure to use at a noncontrolled airport?

   1. Depart in any direction consistent with safety, after crossing the airport boundary.
   2. Make all turns to the left.
   3. Comply with any FAA traffic pattern established for the airport.
   4. Depart as arranged with other pilots using the airport.

4. If instructed by ground control to taxi to runway 9, the pilot may proceed

   1. via taxiways and across runways to, but not onto, runway 9.
   2. to the next intersecting runway where further clearance is required.
   3. via taxiways and across runways to runway 9, where an immediate takeoff may be made.
   4. via any route at the pilot's discretion onto runway 9 and hold until cleared for takeoff.

5. Prior to entering an airport advisory area, a pilot

   1. must obtain a clearance from air traffic control.
   2. should monitor ATIS for weather and traffic advisories.
   3. should contact approach control for vectors to the traffic pattern.
   4. should contact the local FSS for airport and traffic advisories.

6. The numbers 9 and 27 on a runway indicate that the runway is oriented approximately

   1. 090° and 270° magnetic.
   2. 009° and 027° true.
   3. 090° and 270° true.
   4. 009° and 027° magnetic.

7. An airport's rotating beacon operated during the daylight hours indicates

   1. that there are obstructions on the airport.
   2. that weather in the control zone is below basic VFR weather minimums.
   3. parachute jumping is in progress.
   4. the airport is temporarily closed.

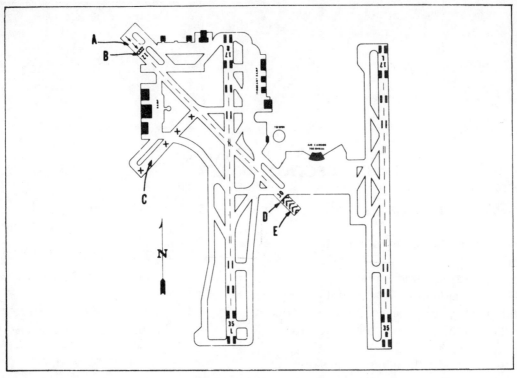

Figure Q10-1. Airport Diagram

8. Airport taxiways are identified at night by

    1. alternating red and green edge lights.
    2. amber omnidirectional edge lights.
    3. white directional edge lights.
    4. blue omnidirectional edge lights.

9. A below glide slope indication from a tri-color VASI is

    1. a pink light signal.
    2. a green light signal.
    3. an amber light signal.
    4. a red light signal.

10. How is a runway recognized as being closed?

    1. The letter C is painted in red after the runway number.
    2. Red lights are placed at the approach end of the runway.
    3. Yellow chevrons are painted on the runway beyond the threshold.
    4. X is displayed on the runway.

11. According to the diagram in figure Q10-1,

    1. takeoffs and landings are permissible at position C since this is a short takeoff and landing runway.
    2. the takeoff and landing portion of runway 12 begins at position B.
    3. Runway 30 is equipped at position E with emergency arresting gear to provide a means of stopping military aircraft.
    4. takeoffs may be started at position A on runway 12, and the landing portion of this runway begins at position B.

12. That portion of the runway identified by the letter A in figure Q10-1

    1. may be used for taxiing but should not be used for takeoffs or landings.
    2. may be used for taxiing or takeoffs but not for landings.
    3. may be used for taxiing, takeoffs, and landings.
    4. may not be used except in an emergency.

13. Wingtip vortices, the dangerous turbulence that might be encountered behind a large aircraft, are created only when that aircraft is

 1. operating at high airspeeds.
 2. heavily loaded.
 3. developing lift.
 4. using high power settings.

14. How should the controls be held while taxiing a tricycle-gear equipped airplane into a left quartering headwind?

 1. Left aileron up, neutral elevator.
 2. Left aileron down, neutral elevator.
 3. Left aileron up, down elevator.
 4. Left aileron down, down elevator.

15. VFR approaches to land at night should be made

 1. at a higher airspeed.
 2. low and shallow.
 3. with a steep descent.
 4. the same as during daytime.

16. Wingtip vortices created by large aircraft tend to

 1. sink below the aircraft generating the turbulence.
 2. rise into the takeoff pattern.

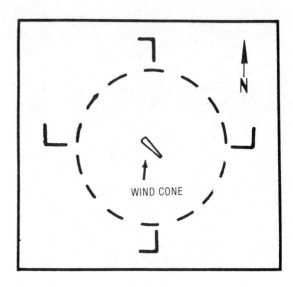

Figure Q10-2

 3. rise into the takeoff or landing path of a crossing runway.
 4. accumulate at the beginning of the takeoff roll.

17. The segmented circle shown in figure Q10-2 indicates that the airport traffic is

 1. left-hand for Rwy 17 and right-hand for Rwy 35.
 2. right-hand for Rwy 9 and left-hand for Rwy 27.
 3. right-hand for Rwy 35 and right-hand for Rwy 9.
 4. left-hand for Rwy 35 and right-hand for Rwy 17.

18. Which runway and traffic pattern should be used as indicated by the wind cone in the segment circle depicted in figure Q10-2?

1. Right-hand traffic on Rwy 35.
2. Right-hand traffic on Rwy 17.
3. Left-hand traffic on Rwy 35 or right-hand traffic on Rwy 27.
4. Left-hand traffic on Rwy 27 or Rwy 35.

19. When approaching to land on a runway served by a VASI, the pilot shall

1. intercept and remain on the glideslope until touchdown only if the aircraft is operating on an instrument flight plan.

2. maintain an altitude that captures the glideslope at least 2 mi. downwind from the runway threshold.
3. maintain an altitude at or above the glideslope.
4. remain on the glideslope and land between the light bars.

20. Airport taxiways are identified at night by

1. alternate red and green edge lights.
2. amber omnidirectional edge lights.
3. white directional edge lights.
4. blue omnidirectional edge lights.

ANSWERS for AIRPORT OPERATIONS REVIEW:

1-4; 2-1; 3-3; 4-1; 5-4; 6-1; 7-2; 8-4; 9-4; 10-4; 11-4; 12-2; 13-3; 14-1; 15-4; 16-1; 17-4; 18-3;
19-3; 20-4.

As a pilot limited to flight under Visual Flight Rules, your primary interest in weather and weather changes should be "How will that weather condition affect visibility for departure, enroute, and at my destination?". Your second area of concern will be clouds, because you must maintain separation from clouds at all times. You need to know whether clouds might form where none now exist, or if scattered clouds might merge into an impenetrable overcast. You will want to avoid thunderstorms and other severe weather for safety reasons. Flying is fun, but fighting the weather is not. Every pilot should be a student of the weather, and as the hours in your flight log accumulate you should develop a weather "sense" to keep the fun in flying.

The primary source of all weather changes is the sun. It heats the surface of the earth at varying rates, depending not only on cloud cover and the angle at which the sun's rays strike the earth but on the type of surface being heated. For instance, land changes temperature far more rapidly than water, deserts and barren areas change temperature more rapidly than forested areas, and cloud cover affects the rate at which any surface gains and loses heat. Heated air rises and, being less dense than cool air, creates low pressure areas. When the rising air has cooled, it descends and creates areas of high pressure. Air heated at the Equator rises, cools, and moves toward the North and South Poles. Meteorologists have identified three loops of rising and

descending air, as illustrated, with a net flow toward the poles at high altitude (figure 11-1). The relatively

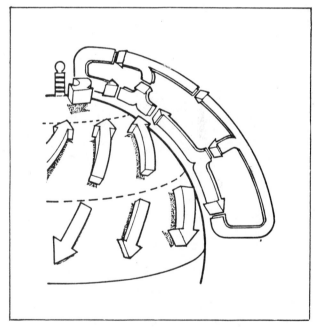

Figure 11-1. 3-Cell Circulation Pattern and Prevailing Winds

weak cell over the mid-latitudes (including the United States) flows south-to-north. The moisture content of an air mass depends on its temperature and affects its density, and it is these variations in pressure, density, temperature, and moisture content that define air masses and weather systems. The earth, of course, rotates beneath these weather systems and their effects are felt many miles distant from where the sun's heat began the process. If the earth did not rotate, air descending from the Poles would flow directly south to the Equator, to be heated again to repeat the cycle.

Because of the earth's rotation, a phenomenon known as *Coriolis Force* deflects the moving air, so that in the latitudes of the United States the prevailing upper level winds are westerly. This causes weather systems to move across the country from west to east.

Air rising in a low pressure area draws air from outside the low into the center, and the general circulation pattern is counterclockwise. An extreme example of this is the tornado or cyclone which, as it rotates, draws air, houses, trees, and other debris into its center and up, depositing them many miles away.

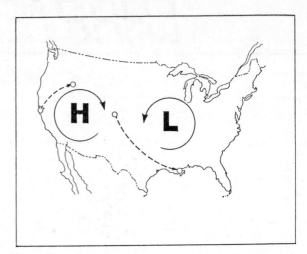

Figure 11-3. Taking Advantage of Pressure Systems

they define pressure patterns. Where the isobars are tightly packed, pressure is changing rapidly, and strong winds should be expected. Isobars which are widely spaced indicate less force to drive the wind. As the air from high pressure areas rushes to fill in the low pressure areas, you would expect the wind to blow downhill; that is, directly outward from the center of a high to the center of a low.

The air tries to do exactly that, and the driving force is called the *gradient* force. Coriolis Force deflects the wind, so that in fact the direction of air motion crosses the isobars at an angle (figure 11-5).

On the surface analysis chart, you will see wind arrows that do not seem to agree with any rule, because of the effects of local conditions or surface friction. Mountain ranges, passes, valleys — all have local influence on the direction of air movement up to about 2,000' above ground level.

As a general rule, winds above 2,000' *AGL* come from a direction several degrees clockwise from the surface wind: with a surface wind of 180°, the wind at 2,000' MSL might be from 220° and the wind at 4,000' AGL from 240°.

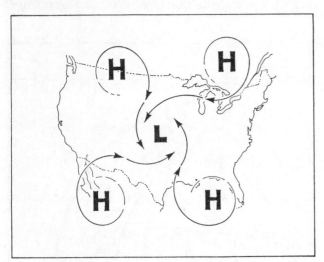

Figure 11-2. Circulation Around Pressure Centers

Air descending in a high pressure system circulates clockwise, and as the air reaches the surface it travels away from the center. Pilots on long cross-country trips can take advantage of these circulation patterns to get favorable winds (figure 11-3).

On a surface weather analysis chart (figure 11-4), you can see high and low pressure areas. These are defined by meteorologists who take barometric pressure readings at airports and National Weather Service offices across the country and plot their findings on a chart. By connecting the points of equal pressure (called *isobars*)

To understand and anticipate weather changes, you must be aware of pressure systems and their movement. To know what might happen with cloud formations and obstructions to visibility you must consider the moisture content of the air. All air contains

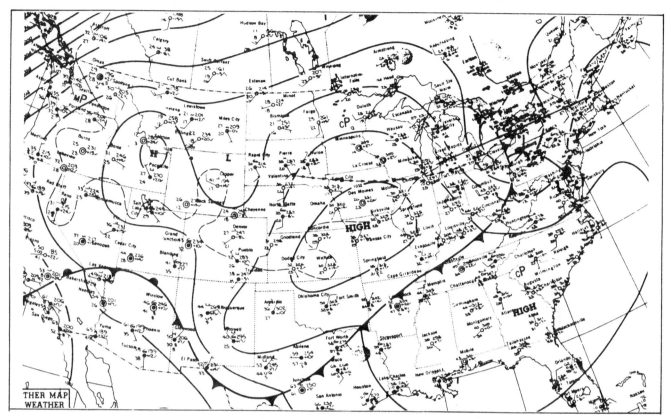

Figure 11-4. Surface Weather Map

moisture in the form of water vapor; *the amount of water a given volume of air can hold is dependent on the temperature of the air*. As a volume of air is heated the amount of moisture it can hold *in invisible form* increases: a temperature increase of 20°F doubles the

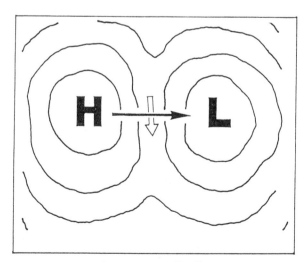

Figure 11-5. Coriolis Effect

air's capacity to hold moisture. Conversely, cooling the air reduces the amount of water vapor that can be hidden from sight, and when the air contains 100% of the moisture it can hold invisibly it becomes visible in the form of clouds, fog, or precipitation. The moisture condenses into droplets which can be seen, and which restrict your ability to see.

The temperature at which the air becomes saturated with moisture and can contain no more without that moisture getting you wet is called the **dewpoint**. You have heard the television weather person report "The temperature is 65°, the dewpoint is 48°." — under those conditions, if the air suddenly cools 17° it will be saturated and any further cooling or addition of moisture to the air will result in fog or rain. What the weather reporter calls **relative humidity** is simply how close the air is to being saturated. The illustration (figure 11-6) uses a cup of liquid (representing the atmosphere) at different temperatures to show how the percentage of moisture content increases from 50% to 100%. A good example of high relative humidity is a hot July day when the air is full of moisture but there isn't a cloud in the sky. You feel uncomfortable, because perspiration on your body can not evaporate into air already full of moisture.

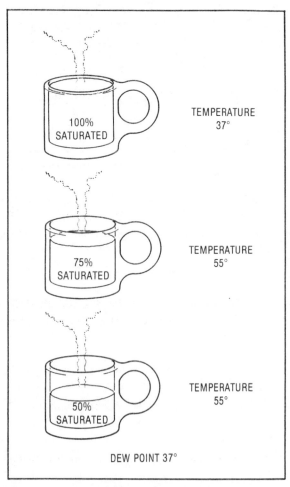

Figure 11-6. Temperature vs. Saturation

The measure of relative humidity is the spread between temperature and dewpoint. If that spread is reported to be less than 5°F, you should investigate further to determine the potential for a reduction in visibility. Is the sun rising, or setting? The answer can help you predict the temperature trend and whether the temperature/dewpoint spread will increase or decrease. Is the wind blowing from over water, or from over land? Moisture can be added to the air by evaporation from rain or bodies of water. Moisture being added to the air can tip the balance toward saturation. If your investigation shows the potential for a decrease in the difference between temperature and dewpoint for any

reason, you must consider the possibility that you will not be able to complete the trip under visual conditions.

Knowledge of the temperature/dewpoint relationship is valuable in estimating the height of cloud bases. When rising air currents are evidenced by the formation of cumulus clouds, the air is cooling at the rate of approximately 4.4°F per 1,000'. For example, if the temperature at the surface is 78°F and the dewpoint is 52°F, the difference is 16° ÷ 4.4 x 1,000 = 3,600' above the surface. This is where you would expect cloud bases to be under the conditions stated. For height of cloud bases above sea level, you must add the elevation of the station at which the observations were made.

FRONTS

A weather *front* exists where air masses with different properties meet. The terms warm and cold are relative: 30°F air is warmer than 10°F air, but that "warm" air doesn't call for bathing suits. Cold air is more dense than warm air, so where two dissimilar masses meet, the cold air stays near the surface. Figure 11-7 shows a cold front: cold air advancing from west to east and displacing warm air. Because the cold air is dense and relatively heavy, it moves rapidly across the surface, pushing the warm air up.

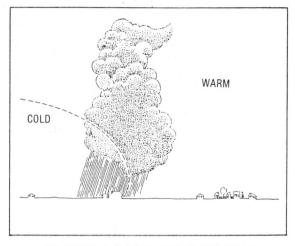

Figure 11-7. Cross-Section of Typical Cold Front

Friction slows the cold air movement at the surface, so that the front is quite vertical in cross-section and the band of frontal weather is narrow. Cold fronts can move as fast as 30 knots. Your awareness of this rapid movement, together with facts you already know about temperature and dewpoint, will allow you to make the following generalizations about cold front weather:

Visibility: Good behind the front. Warm air and pollutants rise rapidly because warm air is less dense than cold air.

Flight conditions: Bumpy, as thermal currents rise.

Precipitation: Showery in the frontal area as the warm air is forced aloft and its moisture condenses. The ability of the air to hold moisture decreases as the air cools, and as the moisture contained in each column of rising air condenses into water droplets, showers result.

Cloud type: Cumulus, due to air being raised *rapidly* to the condensation level. Cumulus clouds are a sign of unstable air; the rising air columns are warmer than the surrounding air and continue to rise under their own power.

Icing possibility: Clear ice. Cumulus clouds develop large water droplets which freeze into clear sheets of ice when they strike an airplane.

A warm front exists when a warm air mass overtakes a slow moving cold air mass; the lighter warm air cannot displace the heavier cold air, and the warm air is forced to rise as it moves forward (figure 11-8). This slow upward movement, combined with the slow forward movement characteristic of warm fronts, allows the warm air to cool slowly and, as it reaches the condensation level, stratiform clouds develop. While cold frontal conditions exist over a very short distance, warm fronts slope upward for many miles, and warm frontal weather may be extensive.

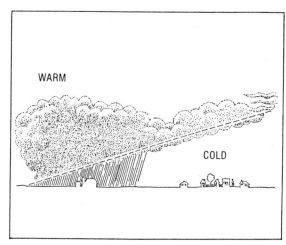

Figure 11-8. Cross-Section of Typical Warm Front

You may encounter warm front clouds 50 to 100 miles from where the front is depicted on the surface analysis chart. These are the characteristics of warm frontal weather:

Visibility: Poor; pollutants trapped by warm air aloft. Air warmed at the surface can only rise until it reaches air at its own temperature.

Flight conditions: Smooth, no thermal activity.

Precipitation: Drizzle or continuous rain as moist air is *slowly* raised to the condensation level.

Cloud type: Stratus or layered, the result of slow cooling.

Icing possibility: Rime ice; small water droplets which freeze instantaneously upon contacting an airplane and form a rough, milky coating.

Occasionally, a fast moving cold front will overtake a warm front (figure 11-9) and lift the warm air away from the surface. This is called an *occlusion*, and occluded frontal weather contains the worst features of both warm and cold fronts: turbulent flying conditions, showers and/or continuous precipitation, poor visibility in precipitation, and broad geographic extent of frontal weather conditions.

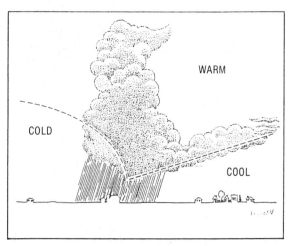

Figure 11-9. Occluded Fronts

Air masses can maintain their warm/cold identity and yet not exert any displacement force. When this happens, the front becomes stationary, and the associated weather covers a large geographic area. In your planning, what you see is probably what you will get during the flight.

When you look at a weather map which shows frontal positions, cold fronts will be marked in blue, warm fronts in red, occluded fronts will be purple, and stationary fronts will alternate red and blue. You can identify fronts on black-and-white charts because the cold front symbols look like icicles and warm front symbols appear as blisters (figure 11-10).

Occluded fronts show both icicles and blisters on the side of the front in the direction of movement, and stationary fronts show the symbols on opposite sides of the frontal line, indicating opposing forces.

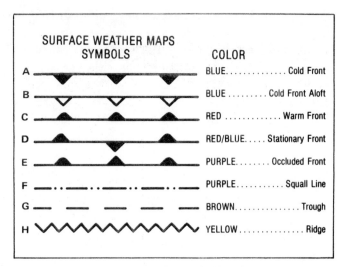

Figure 11-10. Surface Analysis Symbols

STABILITY

You need a general understanding of air mass stability in order to anticipate weather changes which might affect your flight. The amount of moisture in the air influences the rate at which the air cools with increasing altitude. The standard "lapse rate", or rate at which cooling takes place, is 2°C per 1,000' of altitude. An air mass which cools more rapidly than 2°/1,000' is considered to be unstable. Any situation that has cool or cold air overlying warm air is a potentially unstable situation because the warm air, being lighter, will rise and will cool more slowly than the surrounding air. The column of rising air then has the impetus to continue to rise; this is the basis on which thunderstorms develop.

An air mass with warm air overlying cold air is stable, because the heavy cold air cannot rise to displace the lighter warm air. *When the temperature rises abruptly with altitude, a temperature inversion exists* — this condition is marked by poor visibility because warm polluted air cannot rise above the inversion level. This is the familiar smog or haze layer, and it usually takes the passage of a major system to clean it out. The possibility of turbulence always exists at the top of an inversion layer.

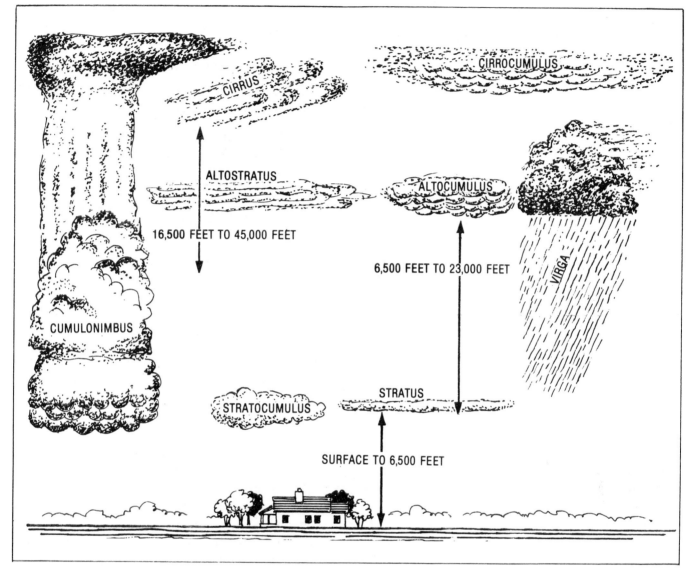

Figure 11-11. Typical Cloud Formations

CLOUD FAMILIES

What you have learned about air movement and the relationship of temperature to moisture content leads right into the study of cloud formation, and by "reading" the clouds you will be able to anticipate the effects of weather changes on your flight.

Meteorologists divide clouds into four families: high clouds, middle clouds, low clouds, and clouds with extensive vertical development. The latter group signals the presence of strong columns of rising air (called convective air currents) which at the very least mean a rough ride, and may herald the onset of precipitation or a developing thunderstorm (figure 11-11).

Nice fluffy looking clouds marking the tops of columns of rising air are called cumulus clouds, because they are in a building or accumulating stage as the air rises to the condensation level —you can expect a bumpy ride beneath them and a smooth ride above (figure 11-12). Stratocumulus clouds are in the low family, altocumulus in the middle altitudes, and cirrocumulus is the word for fluffy clouds at high altitudes. Cumulus

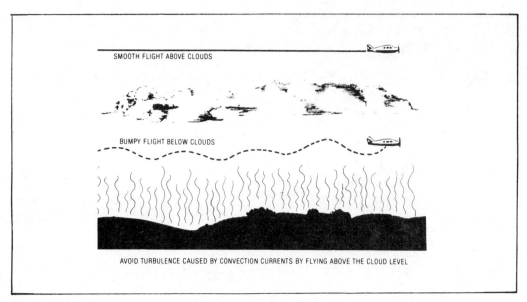

Figure 11-12. Thermal Turbulence

clouds are a sign of instability in the air mass because stable air has no tendency to move vertically.

Stratus or layered clouds indicate a stable air mass; they have little vertical development — fog is defined as a stratus cloud at the surface. A stratus cloud deck may make the day dark and gloomy, but the smooth ride will make up for it. Altostratus clouds are found in the mid-altitudes and cirrostratus are very high thin layers of ice crystals. Cloud names can be combinations: stratocumulus is a good example. Clouds with "nimbo" or "nimbus" in their names indicate the presence of precipitation. "Virga" is the name for moisture that falls from a cloud but evaporates before reaching the surface. It is a visible indication of a downdraft and possible wind shear. Do not fly beneath or through virga.

THUNDERSTORMS

Thunderstorms deserve special treatment, and they even have a special cloud name: cumulonimbus, abbreviated as CB or CU. When you hear pilots on the radio talking about "towering cues to the northwest" or "several CBs to the east" they aren't talking about pool halls or CB radio but about clouds indicating threatening weather. Three elements must be present for thunderstorm development: warm air, moisture,

and an unstable airmass. With all three present, it takes very little to begin the process: the sun heating a parking lot or a plowed field, wind blowing up a mountain slope — these are typical of the things that can start a column of rising air.

Storms begun by the sun heating the surface are called air mass thunderstorms. They are usually localized and you can fly around them. When warm, moist air moves up a mountain and a storm develops, it is called an orographic thunderstorm. A rapidly moving cold front forcing warm unstable air to rise can result in the most hazardous of thunderstorms, the squall line thunderstorm. It is not unusual, especially in the midwest, for squall lines to develop well in advance of a cold front. As you can see, the only variable is the force which starts the lifting process — after that, the storm grows on its own.

Figure 11-13 shows the life cycle of a thunderstorm, beginning with the cumulus or building stage as the warm moist air rises. The instability of the air allows this process to feed on itself as the air column, even though cooling with altitude, is warmer than the surrounding air. The moisture in the air condenses into water droplets, adding more heat to the rising air. The droplets do not fall out of the cloud initially, but are carried to higher altitudes as they grow even larger through collision with other droplets in the turbulent

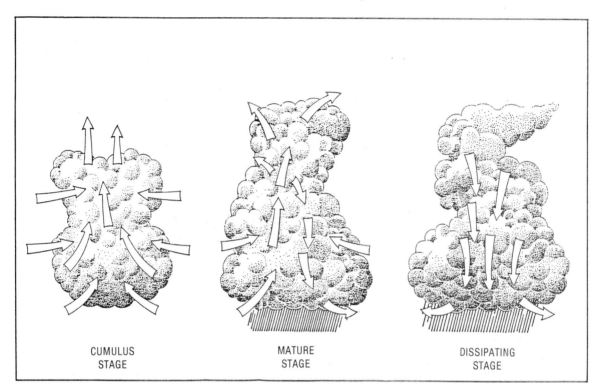

Figure 11-13. Life Cycle of a Thunderstorm

air. These growing water droplets can even freeze into hail at the top of the cloud and be blown downwind to create a hazard to aircraft well outside the cloud mass.

A thunderstorm has reached maturity when the water droplets are big enough to overcome the upward air currents and precipitation reaches the ground (figure 11-14). The falling rain creates downdrafts in opposition to the updrafts which began the whole process. This updraft/downdraft combination within a short distance makes penetrating a thunderstorm hazardous to the structural integrity of *any* size aircraft.

The downdrafts soon overpower the updrafts and the storm cell dissipates into heavy rain. The process just described is continuous as long as the conditions of warm, moist air, instability, and lifting force are present, and as far as the pilot is concerned the birth and death of individual cells is not apparent. The rapid vertical movement of air up and down in close proximity develops electrical charges, and lightning from cloud to cloud or from cloud to ground is a part of all thunderstorm activity.

The external appearance of cumulus clouds should never be used as an indicator of what might be found

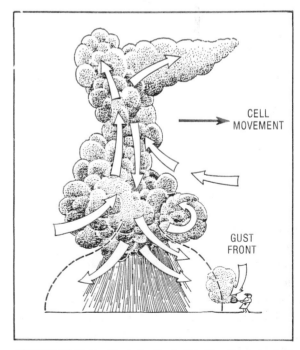

Figure 11-14. Mature Stage of a Steady State Thunderstorm Cell

inside. Gleaming white, puffy, clouds with all the outward menace of a pile of marshmallows might contain destructive forces, while a threatening grey-black area might contain only heavy rain and a few bumps. As a VFR pilot you must not fly into *any* cloud, but a knowledge of thunderstorms may save you from encountering hail in clear air downwind from a cumulonimbus cloud, or from being punished by turbulence as you fly through conflicting air currents beneath one. Severe turbulence should be expected up to 20 miles from a severe thunderstorm, and up to 10 miles from lesser storms. Thunderstorm clouds may be embedded in a continuous layer of other clouds, creating an unseen hazard for the pilot attempting to fly visually in marginal conditions. Pilots may also experience gusty winds and turbulence near the surface many miles from the actual location of a thunderstorm cell as the downdrafts strike the ground and move outward.

"Microbursts" have recently been identified as small shafts of descending air associated with thunderstorms. Because of their small diameter, microbursts are not easily detected by weather instruments, making it even more important that pilots stay away from areas where thunderstorms are existing or forecast.

WIND SHEAR

Wind shear is defined as a change in direction or speed of air movement, either horizontal or vertical, that takes place within a short distance. It can be the result of mechanical forces such as turbulence around buildings adjacent to the runway, or may be encountered when flying into the wind on the lee (downwind) side of a mountain ridge (figures 11-15 and 11-16). Wind shear is most frequently related to weather phenomena such as thunderstorms. A rapid wind shift from a headwind to a tailwind can cause an unexpected loss of altitude and airspeed, and, if a storm cell is within 15 miles of the airport, you should delay your takeoff to avoid such a shift.

You are already aware of the vertical shear forces present when an aircraft enters a mature thunderstorm and encounters updrafts and downdrafts in

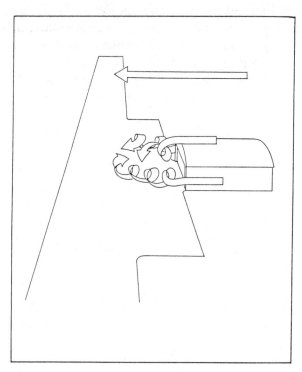

Figure 11-15. Turbulence Near Buildings

rapid succession — a pilot attempting to fight these forces could quickly exceed the load limit on the aircraft structure. The pilot's only recourse is to keep the wings level, maintain attitude (not altitude), and go along for the ride until clear of the cell. Other types of wind shear encounters will require that you keep the aircraft under control but should not endanger its safety. An example is flying through a front: the wind always shifts as you fly through a front, and this is a

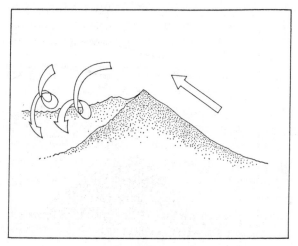

Figure 11-16. Turbulence in Mountains

form of wind shear. If you are departing an airport which is under the influence of a temperature inversion, with little or no air movement near the surface, you may be surprised by wind shear turbulence as you climb through the inversion layer if the winds 2,000' to 4,000' above the surface are at least 25 knots.

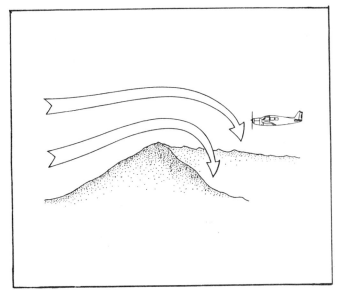

Figure 11-17. Turbulence

The gust front associated with thunderstorm-generated downdrafts can create wind shear hazards 15 to 25 miles from the storm itself, and unless its presence is revealed by blowing dust there will be no warning. Winds aloft blowing at 50 knots or more can create severe turbulence downwind from mountain ranges (figure 11-17).

If there is sufficient moisture in the air for cloud formation, a lens-shaped cloud will form which remains stationary in relation to the ground. This "standing lenticular" (called an altocumulus standing lenticular or ACSL) is a signpost warning of turbulence (figure 11-18). In your flight planning, be sure to check into the possibility of thunderstorm activity on or near your route and of strong winds aloft if you will be flying in mountainous terrain —wind shear and turbulence are uncomfortable at best.

FOG

Fog is probably the most deceptive hazard to safe flight that a VFR pilot has to consider in flight planning. Fog can form or dissipate virtually instantaneously, and it can form under conditions that appear to be ideal for flight. Still, with your knowledge of the movement of air masses and of the temperature/dewpoint relationship, you can guard against unpleasant surprises.

Radiation fog catches many pilots off guard. Calm winds and clear skies would seem to be the answers to a pilot's prayers, but when these conditions occur, and the temperature/dewpoint spread is small, radiation fog is a good possibility. The clear skies allow the land

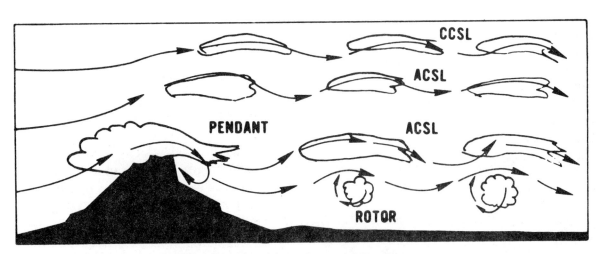

Figure 11-18. "Standing" or "Mountain" Wave Pattern

to radiate heat, cooling the air near the surface to the dewpoint and causing fog to form (figure 11-19). This is a night or early morning phenomenon, and a few hours of sunlight will raise the air temperature above the dewpoint, "burning off" the fog. From cruise altitude, a thin ground fog layer (ground fog is a type of radiation fog) may seem fairly harmless to a pilot who can see runways and buildings as though through a veil.

Figure 11-19. Radiation (Ground) Fog

On a landing approach, however, what looked thin from altitude obscures everything, because the pilot is now looking at the fog layer horizontally. When ground fog is predicted (or any time the T/DP spread is less than 3°), include a fog-free alternate airport in your planning.

Advection fog results when moist air moves, and to anticipate it you must consider where the moist air is coming from and what it is moving toward. Typically, the moist air is moving from over water to over colder land; the moist air condenses into fog when cooled by the land (figure 11-20). The process can be reversed when warm moist air from land moves over cold water.

Your key for planning purposes is knowing the wind direction, surface temperatures, and dewpoints, and whether the wind is coming from over land or water. What is the relative humidity at a reporting station upwind from you? Because advection fog is created by moving air, wind will not blow it away, and it will not

burn off as readily as radiation fog; advection fog can be persistent and can form at any time.

Upslope fog's name gives away its origin. As moist, stable air is moved toward higher terrain, it cools to its dewpoint and condenses as fog. While flying you will see it first in valleys, filling them and obscuring as much of the high ground as the moisture content of the air allows and lasting as long as the upward force exists. Contrast this with the upward movement of moist *unstable* air which can lead to thunderstorm formation.

We don't stop flying just because it's raining, but what starts out as a simple rainy day flight can end up quite differently. When rain falls into cool, almost saturated air, the moisture it adds can result in what is called precipitation-induced fog and lower visibilities well below the minimums required for flight. Occluded fronts, warm fronts, slow moving cold fronts and stationary fronts all have the ingredients necessary for the onset of precipitation-induced fog. When any of these conditions are forecast for your time or route of flight (or if you encounter precipitation), you must consider the possibility of reduced visibility due to fog.

CONDENSATION NUCLEI

In industrial areas, or anywhere that pollutants might be found in the air, fog will form more readily and dissipate more slowly. When the water vapor has something to condense on, such as a pollutant particle, fog will be more persistent than when such nuclei are not present.

SOURCES OF WEATHER INFORMATION

The Federal Aviation Regulations require that a pilot planning a flight not in the vicinity of an airport become familiar with weather reports and forecasts for the route of flight. Advances in computer technology are rapidly changing the means by which pilots can acquire this information. The opportunity for a face-to-face briefing with a Flight Service Station specialist may not exist much longer in many locations, as Flight Service Stations are consolidated, and self-briefing by

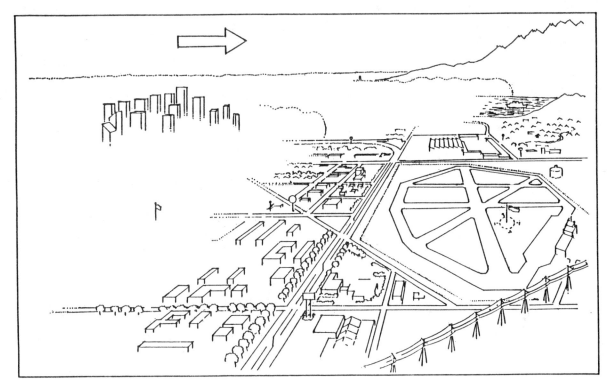

Figure 11-20. Advection Fog

computer becomes more common. The weather data made available by the National Weather Service will not change as much as will the means of delivery. Many pilots who own personal computers subscribe to weather and flight planning services and contact the Flight Service Station only to file their flight plans. These private services either have their own meteorologists or use National Weather Service data, and are able to provide computer-generated weather maps and printouts of weather reports and forecasts. With pilot input of airplane type, departure point, and destination, these services can provide a flight log complete with times enroute and fuel consumption at the most favorable altitude.

The ideal briefing is "in person" at the FSS, where you can look at the reports, forecasts, and charts from the NWS, and ask questions of the briefer before filing your flight plan. Next best is a telephone briefing by an FSS specialist who refers to the weather data to help you plan your flight; however, you must know the right questions to ask in this situation. The Airman's Information Manual and the Airport/ Facility Directory contain telephone numbers for pilot weather briefings

that are not available to the public for general weather information, and when you call you should *identify yourself as a pilot*. The briefer will need to know your destination and planned route of flight, and the type of airplane you will be flying.

You can also listen to Transcribed Weather Broadcasts (*TWEBs*) on selected radio navigational aids (VORs and NDBs) for weather updates. In flight, the Enroute Flight Advisory Service (*EFAS*), or Flight Watch, can be contacted on 122.0 MHz between 0600 and 2200 local time for direct contact with a weather briefer. If you have a radio in your airplane you will always have access to up-to-date weather information and must not rely solely on a pre-takeoff briefing.

The weather information during the morning news on national network television gives a broad overview of national weather, but the best televised source of aviation weather is AM WEATHER, broadcast early in the morning on public television. This program, designed specifically for pilots, includes information on turbulence, winds aloft, icing, tops of buildups, location of pressure systems and fronts, etc.

Time-lapse satellite photographs show movement of fronts and cloud masses across the continent, and color weather charts graphically illustrate the location of weather systems and hazardous weather.

The National Oceanographic and Atmospheric Administration (NOAA) broadcasts weather continuously on UHF frequencies in the 162 MHz range. These frequencies cannot be tuned by your aircraft radio. Radios designed specifically for receiving these broadcasts are available at electronics stores.

The FAA is currently evaluating a Voice Response System which will enable pilots to call a centrally located computer and get weather information by using a touch-tone telephone. By entering the identifiers of departure, enroute, and destination airports, the caller can receive current and forecast weather from a computer-generated voice. The computer prompts the caller to enter the planned cruise altitude, and provides winds aloft data for that altitude and altitudes 4,000' above and below it. This program is expected to spread nationwide after the evaluation period.

Pilot reports (*PIREPs*) provide the most current information for any given route. Pilots are encouraged to contact Flight Watch and report the actual conditions they are encountering. These PIREPs will be passed on to pilots inquiring about flying the same route and will provide better information about those areas between weather reporting stations.

WEATHER REPORTS

Every reporting weather station issues an hourly sequence report (*SA*) which includes cloud cover and visibility, wind direction and velocity, barometric pressure and altimeter setting, and remarks, and may include applicable Notices to Airmen. Figure 11-21 is the key to interpreting hourly sequences. Note: this key will not be available to you on your FAA written examination, so learn to read and understand the information without the key.

Figure 11-22 contains hourly sequences for five widely separated stations: Wink, TX (INK), Boise, ID (BOI),

KEY TO AVIATION WEATHER REPORTS . . . .

NOAA/PA 73029

LOCATION IDENTIFIER AND TYPE OF REPORT*	SKY AND CEILING	VISIBILITY WEATHER AND OBSTRUCTION TO VISION	SEA-LEVEL PRESSURE	TEMPERATURE AND DEW POINT	WIND	ALTIMETER SETTING	RUNWAY VISUAL RANGE	CODED PIREPS
MKC	15SCT M25OVC	1R-K	132	/58/56	/ 18Ø7	/993/	RØ4LVR2ØV4Ø	/UA OVC 55

SKY AND CEILING

Sky cover contractions are in ascending order. Figures preceding contractions are heights in hundreds of feet above station. Sky cover contractions are:

CLR Clear: Less than Ø.1 sky cover.
SCT Scattered: Ø.1 to Ø.5 sky cover.
BKN Broken: Ø.6 to Ø.9 sky cover.
OVC Overcast: More than Ø.9 sky cover.
 – Thin (When prefixed to the above symbols.)
–X Partial obscuration: Ø.1 to less than 1.Ø sky hidden by precipitation or obstruction to vision (bases at surface).
 X Obscuration: 1.Ø sky hidden by precipitation or obstruction to vision (bases at surface).

Letter preceding height of layer identifies ceiling layer and indicates how ceiling height was obtained. Thus:

E	Estimated height	V	Immediately following numerical value, indicates a variable ceiling.
M	Measured		
W	Indefinite		

VISIBILITY

Reported in statute miles and fractions. (V=Variable)

WEATHER AND OBSTRUCTION TO VISION SYMBOLS

A	Hail	IC	Ice Crystals	S	Snow
BD	Blowing dust	IF	Ice fog	SG	Snow grains
BN	Blowing sand	IP	Ice pellets	SP	Snow pellets
BS	Blowing snow	IPW	Ice pellet showers	SW	Snow showers
D	Dust	K	Smoke	T	Thunderstorms
F	Fog	L	Drizzle	T	Severe thunderstorm
GF	Ground fog	R	Rain	ZL	Freezing drizzle
H	Haze	RW	Rain showers	ZR	Freezing rain

Precipitation intensities are indicated thus: – –Very Light; – Light; (no sign) Moderate; · Heavy

WIND

Direction in tens of degrees from true north, speed in knots. 0000 indicates calm. G indicates gusty. Peak speed of gusts follows G or Q when gusts or squall are reported. The contraction WSHFT followed by GMT time group in remarks indicates windshift and its time of occurrence. (Knots X 1.15=statute mi/hr.)

EXAMPLES: 3627=360 Degrees, 27 knots; 3627G4Ø=360 Degrees, 27 knots Peak speed in gusts 40 knots.

ALTIMETER SETTING

The first figure of the actual altimeter setting is always omitted from the report.

RUNWAY VISUAL RANGE (RVR)

RVR is reported from some stations. Extreme values during 10 minutes prior to observation are given in hundreds of feet. Runway identification precedes RVR report.

CODED PIREPS

Pilot reports of clouds not visible from ground are coded with ASL height data preceding and/or following sky cover contraction to indicate cloud bases and/or tops, respectively. UA precedes all PIREPS.

DECODED REPORT

Kansas City: Record observation, 1500 feet scattered clouds, measured ceiling 2500 feet overcast, visibility 1 mile, light rain, smoke, sea-level pressure 1013.2 millibars, temperature 58°F, dewpoint 56°F, wind 180°, 7 knots, altimeter setting 29.93 inches. Runway Ø4 left, visual range 2000 feet variable to 4000 feet. Pilot reports top of overcast 5500 feet.

*TYPE OF REPORT

The omission of type-of-report data identifies a scheduled record observation for the hour specified in the sequence heading. An out-of-sequence, special observation is identified by the letters "SP" following station identification and a 24-hour clock time group, e.g., "PIT SP Ø715—X M10VC." A special report indicates a significant change in one or more elements.

U.S. DEPARTMENT OF COMMERCE– NATIONAL OCEANIC AND ATMOSPHERIC ADMINISTRATION – NATIONAL WEATHER SERVICE – REVISED JULY 1975

Figure 11-21. Key to Aviation Weather Reports

```
INK SA 1854 CLR 15 106/77/63/1112G18/000
BOI SA 1854 150 SCT 30 181/62/42/1304/015
LAX SA 1852 7 SCT 250 SCT 6HK 129/60/59/2504/991
MDW RS 1856 -X M7 OVC 11/2R+F 990/63/61/3205/980/RF2 RB12
JFK RS 1853 W5 X 1/2F 180/68/64/1804/006/R04RVR22V30 TWR VSBY 1/4
```

Figure 11-22. Hourly Sequences for Selected Stations

Los Angeles, CA (LAX), Chicago, IL (MDW), and New York, NY (JFK).

Each report begins with the three-letter identifier for the airport where the observation was made. INK, BOI, and LAX are record observations (SA), while MDW and JFK are making both a record and a special observation (RS). The four numbers following the type of observation are the time of observation using Greenwich Mean Time (Zulu time).

To operate legally under Visual Flight Rules you must know what the reported ceiling is, and the next data group gives you that information. Ceilings may be measured (lowest cloud report prefixed with M), by an instrument called a ceilometer which bounces a light off of the cloud base, estimated (prefix E) by an observer, or reported by an aircraft (prefix A). To constitute a ceiling, the lowest cloud layer must be reported as broken (BKN) or overcast (OVC); a layer of scattered clouds (SCT) or a thin layer (-SCT, -BKN, -OVC) does not constitute a ceiling but may restrict your flying when cloud clearance requirements are considered.

Cloud heights are measured above the ground and are reported in hundreds of feet, so INK, BOI, and LAX do not have legal ceilings. MDW's ceiling of 700' overcast would keep you on the ground, and JFK is reporting "ceiling indefinite 500', sky obscured". That means that the observer estimates that he or she can see 500 feet up into the clouds but cannot see the horizon in any direction. That report would make even an instrument pilot think twice. The cloud layers are reported in order of height, with the highest layer last: at LAX two layers are reported, one at 700' and one at 25,000'. Because ceiling is reported as height above ground level, you must add the field elevation to the

ceiling report to learn the height of the clouds above sea level.

After the sky and cloud report, the prevailing visibility is shown and any obstructions to visibility are identified. INK and BOI are reporting visibilities of 15 and 30 miles respectively, LAX has 6 miles in haze and smoke, MDW is reporting 1½ miles (watch those fractions!) in heavy rain and fog, and JFK has ½ mile visibility in fog (in the Remarks section, the JFK tower reports only ¼ mile visibility at its location).

Separated from the visibility report by a space is a series of five data blocks: the first is sea level pressure in millibars, a metric measure of pressure used on weather charts. The next two numbers are the temperature and dewpoint in Fahrenheit; note the T/DP spread at INK and BOI, where it is clear, and the spreads at the three reporting stations with restricted visibility. Next, the wind is reported as a four-digit group — the first two digits indicate wind direction in relation to true north in tens of degrees, and the last two digits indicate wind velocity in knots. At INK the wind is from 110° at 11 knots, gusting to 18 — the other four stations are reporting only 4 or 5 knots. The last three digit group is the altimeter setting. Standard sea level pressure is 29.92' Hg, so the first digit of the altimeter setting is either a 2 or a 3 and is omitted. You supply whichever brings the altimeter setting closest to 30.00. INK is interpreted as 30.00', BOI 30.15', LAX 29.91, etc. Everything after the altimeter setting is "remarks". You must always look for them because they may explain or expand upon information in the body of the report. At MDW, for instance, the body of the report says the prevailing visibility is 1½ miles, and the remarks say that the rain and fog obscure only 2/10 of the horizon.

Note that the time of the report at MDW is 1856, and there is a remark noting that the rain began at 1812. At JFK the visibility report is expanded for instrument pilots — it tells them that for runway 4R the visual range is 2,200 feet, variable to 3,000 feet. You can worry about that when you are instrument rated — with an indefinite ceiling and ½ mile of visibility you will not be flying at JFK under VFR! A full explanation of the criteria used in these reports is contained in AVIATION WEATHER SERVICES, (Advisory Circular 00-45B).

An important part of your flight planning is to look at or ask for the most recent hourly sequence report for your destination airport and several enroute airports, so that you can see whether the weather is good enough for VFR operations at your destination. You also should be sure that you can make an enroute stop if you have to. Check the previous hour's sequences (if they are available) to see what weather trends you can detect. Is the T/DP spread increasing, or decreasing? Pressure rising, or falling (check the altimeter setting)? Cloud layers rising or lowering? Wind picking up? Shifting? What runway will probably be in use at the destination? Any Notices to Airmen? Remember, you are required to be informed about anything that can affect the safety of your flight.

TERMINAL FORECASTS

Terminal forecasts (*FTs*) are prepared three times daily for selected reporting stations, predicting conditions for a 5 mile area surrounding the airport. Each forecast is valid for 24 hours and contains a categorical outlook for the final 6 hours of the period. Figure 11-23 contains terminal forecasts for several stations, all of them in Oklahoma.

The date-time-group 011447 indicates a transmission time on the teletype circuit of 1447Z on the first day of the month; the date-time-groups in the body of the forecast (all 011515) mean something quite different: the valid period is from 1500Z on the first day of the month until 1500Z on the second day. In reading FTs you will find that the abbreviations VFR, MVFR, IFR, and LIFR define weather conditions differently than FAR Part 91 does: VFR means a ceiling higher than 3,000' AGL and visibility greater than 5 miles; MVFR indicates a forecast ceiling between 1,000 and 3,000 feet and/or visibility forecast to be 3 to 5 miles. IFR in the categorical outlook for the final six hours of the FT means a ceiling of less than 1,000 feet and/or visibility less than 3 miles, agreeing with the Part 91 definition, while LIFR (low IFR) will be mentioned when ceilings are expected

```
OK FT 011447

GAG FT 011515 100 SCT 250 SCT 2610. 16Z 60 SCT C100 BKN 3315G22 CHC C50
  BKN 5TRW. 01Z 250 SCT 3515G25. 09Z VFR WIND..

HBR FT 011515 C120 BKN 250 BKN 3010. 17Z 100 SCT C250 BKN 3215G25 CHC C30
  BKN 3TRW. 00Z 250 SCT 3515G25. 09Z VFR WIND..

MLC FT 011515 C20 BKN 1815 BKN OCNL SCT. 20Z C30 BKN 1815G22 CHC C20 BKN
  1TRW. 03Z C30 BKN 2015 CHC C7 X 1/2TRW+G40. 09Z MVFR CIG TRW..

OKC FT 011515 C12 BKN 140 BKN 1815G28 LWR BKN V SCT. 18Z C30 BKN 250 BKN
  2315G25 LWR BKN OCNL SCT CHC C7 X 1/2TRW+G40. 21Z CFP 100 SCT C250
  BKN 3315G25 CHC C30 BKN 5TRW-. 02Z 100 SCT 250 SCT 3515G25. 09Z VFR
  WIND..

PNC FT 011515 C100 BKN 250 BKN 1810. 16Z CFP 20 SCT C100 BKN 3115 SCT V
  BKN. 00Z 250 SCT 3515G25.  09Z VFR WIND..

TUL FT 011515 C20 BKN 1915G22. 19Z C30 BKN 1815G25 CHC 3TRW. 23Z CFP C100
  BKN 250 BKN 3215G25 CHC C30 BKN 5TRW. 09Z VFR WIND..
```

Figure 11-23. Terminal Forecast

to be below 500 feet and the visibility is expected to be less than 1 mile. You want to see at least MVFR if your flight is to take place within the 18 to 24 hour outlook period.

Because they are issued every 8 hours, you should keep checking the terminal forecasts right up to departure time. If forecast ceilings and/or visibilities are dropping with each new FT, investigate further. You can also check hourly sequences against terminal forecasts to see if the actual weather is better or worse than forecast. When reading an FT, note that visibility is only given if it is expected to be less than 6 miles, and wind is only mentioned if forecast to be greater than 10 knots. You will be familiar with the abbreviations used from using the key in figure 11-21.

Note in the FT for OKC that at 1800Z in addition to strong winds there is a chance of a ceiling of 700' with sky obscured and visibility of ½ mile in heavy thundershowers. At 2100Z the ceiling is forecast to rise to 10000' scattered with visibility greater than 10 miles. CFP, then, means "cold front passage". In the outlook section, when MVFR, IFR, or LIFR are noted the reason

will be given, as in CIG TRW (ceiling and thundershowers) at MLC. When WIND is noted in the categorical outlook, expect winds in excess of 25 knots, and look for "LLWS" as a low level wind shear warning in the categorical outlook section.

AREA FORECAST (FA)

The Area Forecast is your only direct source of information on expected turbulence, icing, and heights of cloud tops. It contains a synopsis of the weather to help you evaluate the potential for change. It also includes forecasts of potentially hazardous weather as "flight precautions". Area forecasts are issued three times daily and are amended as required. The "Significant Clouds and Weather" portion is valid for 12 hours and contains an additional 6 hour outlook. Figure 11-24 is an "old format" area forecast as presented in the Private Pilot Written Test Book (FAA 8080-1). Note that quite a large area is involved: New Mexico, Oklahoma, Texas, and coastal waters. Do not expect an area forecast to be as specific as a terminal forecast.

```
FA 011240
DFW FA 011240
VALID 011300Z-020700Z
OTLK 020700Z-021900Z

NM OK TX AND CSTL WTRS...

HGTS MSL UNLESS NOTES...

TSTMS IMPLY PSBL SVR OR GTR TURBC.. SVR ICG.. AND LOW-LVL WIND SHEAR...

FLT PRCTN... SWRN TX W PECOS RVR AND NM... OCNL MDT TURBC BLO 150 WITH STG UDDFS VCNTY MTNS.

S CNTRL TX SERN TX... PATCHY CIGS AOB 010 AND VSBY BLO 3 MI IPVG AFT 15Z.

TX AND OK ALG AND WITHIN 100 MI OF CDFNT... OCNL MDT TURBC BLO 100 AND W OF FNT LLWS.

SYNS... CDFNT VCNTY ICT-LBB-HOB LN SWWD WL MOV EWD TO ABT FYV-BIG BEND LN BY 07Z.

SIGCLD AND WX...
NM AND PTN OF W TX W OF INK-BIG BEND LN...
GENLY 150-200 SCT LCLY BKN WITH LWR 80-120 SCT NERN NM SPRDG OVR AREA AFTN AND CLRG AFDK. PATCHY 40-50 SCT NERN NM AFDK.
OTLK... VFR.

OK AND TX W OF ICT-CDS-INK LN...
CIG 100-150 BKN TOPS LYRS 300. OTLK... VFR CIG ABV 100.
OK AND TX E OF ICT-CDS LN...
CIG 12-25 BKN V SCT 60 120 BKN V SCT TOPS LYRS 300 WITH CIG LCLY LWR OVR ERN OK LCLY CIG 10-14 OVC. CIG GRDLY LFTG TO 20-30 BKN V SCT 80
BY NOON WITH SCT TSTMS LCLY LWRG CONDS BLO CIG 10 X 2TRW TOPS 400.
CONDS WL LFT ABT 50-100 MI BHD CDFNT TO CIG 100 BKN. OTLK... MVFR CIG TRW BCMG VFR 100 MI W OF CDFNT.

CSTL WTRS...
GENLY 25 SCT. WDLY SCT SHWRS DVLPG AFT 18Z. OTLK... VFR BCMG MVFR TRW BY MID MRNG.

ICG AND FRZLVL... NONE OF CONSEQUENCE OUTSIDE SHWRS AND TSTMS. FRZLVL 090 NRN NM SPLG TO 145 SRN TX.

TURBC... SWRN TX W PECOS RVR AND NM ...OCNL MDT TURBC BLO 120 WITH STG UDDFS VCNTY MTNS. OCNL MDT TURBC WITHIN 100 MI OF FNT
BLO 100.

THIS FA ISSUANCE INCORPORATES THE FOLLOWING AIRMETS STILL IN EFFECT... NONE.
```

Figure 11-24. Area Forecast

You will use the area forecast to fill in the gaps between reporting stations. Learning to decipher the abbreviations used in area forecasts is a study in itself — the Flight Service Station briefer will help you with them. AVIATION WEATHER SERVICES (AC 00-45B) contains a list of commonly used abbreviations.

Because the area covered by an area forecast is so extensive, cloud heights are almost always given in feet above sea level, and you must be aware of terrain heights along your route to evaluate the effect of forecast clouds on your flight. Where "ceiling" (abbreviated as CIG) is used in an area forecast, the cloud height given is above ground level. The section headed "ICG AND FRZLVL" is your best source of forecast icing conditions.

"Thunderstorms imply possible severe or greater turbulence, severe icing, and low level wind shear" — this warning, near the top of the area forecast, applies to Oklahoma and Texas east of an ICT-CDS (Wichita-Childress) line and in the outlook for the coastal waters. Taken as a whole, this forecast warns of strong updrafts and downdrafts near the mountains, icing in thundershowers, and moderate turbulence, with improving weather behind the front. You can see the positions of fronts and pressure systems on a surface weather analysis chart (figure 11-25), keeping in mind that the information is several hours old by the time you see it.

This is an area forecast using the NEW format inaugurated in late 1984:

SFOH FA 101940
HAZARDS VALID UNTIL 110800
WA OR CA

SAN FRANCISCO HAZARDS
SFOH

FLT PRCTNS...TURBC...WA OR CA
        ...MTN OBSCN...WA OR CA
        ...IFR...WA OR CA
        ...ICG...WA OR CA

TSTMS IMPLY PSBL SVR OR GTR TURBC SVR ICG AND LLWS.
NON MSL HGTS NOTED BY MSL OR CIG

THIS FA ISSUANCE INCORPORATES THE FOLLOWING AIRMETS STILL IN EFFECT..NONE

SFOS FA 101940
SYNOPSIS VALID UNTIL 111400

SAN FRANCISCO SYNOPSIS
SFOS

AT 20Z FNTL BNDRY WRN PRNS WA OR AND NRN CA WILL CONT MOVG EWD DURG PD. STG UPR LVL TROF OVER PAC APCHG CSTL SXNS OF WA OR. WEAK LOW PRES AREA OVER NRN BAJA AND EXTRM SRN CA MOVG SLOLY EWD.

SFOI FA 101940
ICING AND FREEZING LEVEL VALID UNTIL 110800

SAN FRANCISCO ICING
SFOI

WA OR CA
FROM YXC TO LWS TO RBL TO FOT TO TOU TO YXC
OCNL MDT RIM ICGICIP FRZLVL TO ARND 160. CONDS MOVG EWD AND CONTG THRU 0800Z.

FRZLVL 050-060 ALG THE CSTS OF WA AND NWRN OR SLPG 145 SRN CA.

SFOT FA 101940
TURBC VALID UNTIL 110800

WA OR CA
FROM YDC TO LKV TO RBL TO FOT TO TOU TO YDC.
OCNL MDT TURBC BLO 120 DUE TO STG SLY LOW AND MID LVL WIND FLO. CONDS CONTG THRU 08Z.

CA
FROM 100NW RNO TO BTY TO FAT TO RBL TO 100NW RNO
MDT TO LCLY SVR TURBC BLO 140 DUE TO STG SWLY LOW LVL WIND FLO. TURBC MNLY VCNTY OF THE SIERRAS. CONDS CONTG THRU 08Z.

LCL MDT TURBC 2000-350 ACRSWA OR ASSOCD WITH STG JTSTR. CONT THRU 08Z.

SFOC FA 101940
SGFNT CLDS AND WX VALID UNTIL 110800...OTLK 110800-111400.

SAN FRANCISCO CLOUDS
AND WEATHER SFOC

IFR...WA OR CA
FROM YDC TO RDM TO MFR TO UKI TO 120W UKI TO 70 WSW TOU TO YDC OCNL CIGS BLO 10 OVC VSBYS OCNL BLO 3 IN FOG AND PCPN. CONDS CONTG THRU 08Z

MTN OBSCN...WA OR CA
FROM YDC TO RDM TO MFR TO UKI TO FOT TO TOU TO YDC
MTNUS TRRN OBSCD IN CLDS AND PCPN. CONDS CONTG THRU 08Z.

WA OR CASCDS WWD
20-30 BKN 40-60 OVC VSBYS 3-5 R-F. OCNL CIGS BLO 10 OVC VSBYS OCNLY BLO 3RF. WDLY SCT EMBDD TSTMS TIL 05Z. CB TOPS 300. MTNUS TRRN OBSCD. CLD TOPS 250. OTLK...MVFR FIG RW.

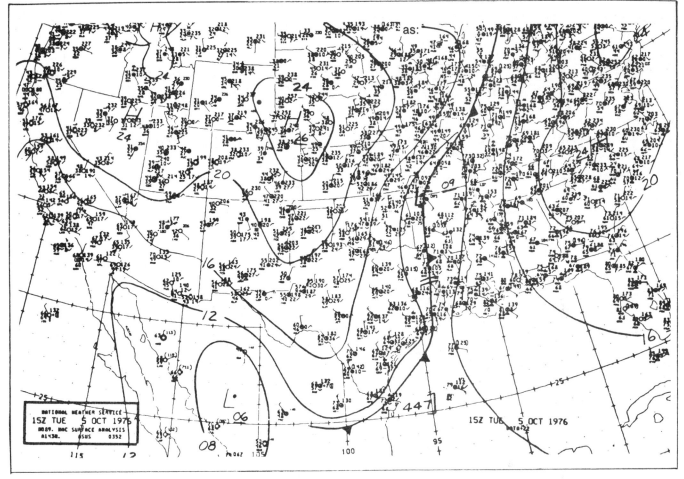

Figure 11-25. Surface Weather

ERN WA ERN OR
WRN PTN AREA 30-50 BKN 70-90 OVC. SCT RW-. ERN PTN AREA 100-120 BKN.
AFT 00Z BCMG 40-6- BKN 100-12- OVC. SCT R-. OTLK...VFR.

NRN CA
CSTL SXNS...20-30 OVC VSBYS 3-5R-F. OCNL CIGS BLOW 10 OVC VSBYS
OCNLY BLO 3RF. CSTL MTNS OBSCD. CLD TOPS 250. OTLK...IFR CIG R.

INTERIOR SXNS...40-60 SCT 120-140 BKN 240. 02Z-04Z BCMG 40-6- BKN 80-
100 OVC . VSBYS 3-5 IN SCT RW- XCP SC SW- OVR TRRN ABV 80. OTLK...IFR
CIG R.

This area forecast continues with predicted clouds and weather for small areas such as Northern California, Central California, coastal waters of Washington, Oregon and Northern California, etc. This format, broken down into a synopsis (SFOS), icing forecast (SFOI), turbulence forecast (SFOT), and a localized clouds and weather forecast (SFOC) allows the National Weather Service greater latitude in amending portions of the total area forecast (FA) without having to amend the entire forecast.

```
        FDUS2 KWBC 011644
DATA BASED ON 011200Z

VALID 020000Z    FOR USE 2100-0600Z. TEMPS NEG ABV 24000

FT  3000    6000    9000    12000   18000   24000   30000   34000   39000

ABI         2512+14 2519+09 2426+02 2438-14 2345-26 234840  234546  254152
ABQ                 3115+02 3125-04 2934-18 2944-31 285240  285145  295151
AMA         3013    3120+03 2823-03 2536-16 2447-30 245642  255447  265351
ATL 1510    1811+13 1909+08 2107+02 2708-12 2710-24 271339  271648  252057
BNA 1920    2220+13 2220+08 2319+02 2421-12 2426-24 243240  243449  243659
BRO 1811    1917+17 2015+11 2214+05 2517-09 2626-21 273937  274845  276155
DAL 2115    2322+15 2325+09 2328+02 2335-13 2342-25 234940  244946  254754
```

Figure 11-26. Winds Aloft Forecast

WINDS ALOFT FORECAST (FD)

These forecasts (figure 11-26) are issued twice daily and include a "valid time". Heights are above sea level, and no forecast is available within 1500' of the reporting station's elevation. Wind direction and velocity are read just as they are in an hourly sequence, except that no gusts are forecast. The last two digits are forecast temperature in degrees Centigrade. Above 24,000', all temperatures are negative, so no + or –signs are used.

Wind direction is in relation to true north, and velocity is forecast in knots. Look for rapid changes in wind direction or velocity with altitude as a warning of turbulence. The winds aloft forecast will be the first thing you check in choosing a cruising altitude for favorable winds. The code for calm is 0000, and for "light and variable" it is 9900. When wind velocities are forecast to exceed 100 knots, the weather service still codes the direction, velocity, and temperature using six digits. This is accomplished by adding 50 to the wind direction, and subtracting 100 from the wind velocity. 731624 means wind from 230° (23 + 50 = 73) at 116 knots, temperature –24°

INFLIGHT ADVISORIES

Weather information is available to the pilot in flight through listening to a Transcribed Weather Broadcast (TWEB) on selected NDBs and VORs (identified on charts by a rectangle in the corner of the frequency box). TWEBs contain forecasts for specific routes. If the taped information is not adequate, call Flight Watch on 122.0 MHz between 0600 and 2200 local time. Flight Watch stations are identified by triangles in the upper corners of the frequency boxes on aeronautical charts.

When weather hazardous to aircraft is forecast, a *SIGMET* or *AIRMET* will be issued and will be noted on the TWEB: "San Francisco AIRMET Charlie Two is current; contact the Flight Service Station for details." The Flight Watch specialist will have all applicable inflight warnings available when you call. An AIRMET concerns light aircraft only, and is issued when one or more of these conditions is forecast:

1. Moderate icing.
2. Moderate turbulence
3. Sustained winds of more than 30 knots at the surface.
4. Widespread areas of visibility less than 3 miles and/or ceilings less than 1000 feet.
5. Extensive mountain obscurement.

A SIGMET advises of weather potentially hazardous to *all* aircraft:

1. Severe icing.
2. Severe or extreme turbulence.
3. Widespread sand or dust storms lowering visibilities to less than 3 miles.

CONVECTIVE SIGMETs are issued in the continental United States when tornadoes, lines of thunderstorms, embedded thunderstorms, or hail ¾" or more in diameter are forecast. These SIGMETS are issued at 55 minutes past the hour and alerts will be broadcast on all FSS and ATC frequencies except 121.5 MHz.

The FAA has begun implementation of a HAZARDOUS IN-FLIGHT WEATHER ADVISORY SERVICE (HIWAS) which is a continuous broadcast of SIGMETs, CONVECTIVE SIGMETs, AIRMETs and urgent PIREPS on selected VORs. Where HIWAS has been implemented, all other broadcasts of hazardous weather have been eliminated. The publication CLASS II Notices to Airmen is your source of information on where HIWAS is in effect.

AUTOMATIC WEATHER OBSERVING SYSTEM (AWOS) is an un-manned station with weather sensors which detect ceiling, wind, and altimeter setting, and a voice synthesizer which broadcasts this information on a discrete frequency. The Airport/Facility Directory lists those airports with AWOS. Ceiling reported by the automatic sensor is the cloud cover immediately above the airport, and may not reflect cloud conditions only a mile or so away. If the AWOS says that conditions are close to VFR minimums, you should exercise extreme caution.

Your preflight weather briefing should equip you to make a go-no go decision, and while enroute you can re-evaluate that decision with the many in-flight weather services that are available. Because weather information is so readily available enroute, the FAA will not accept changed weather conditions as an excuse if you have a problem. On any flight away from the vicinity of an airport, you are required to have an alternative plan in mind in case you cannot carry out your planned flight.

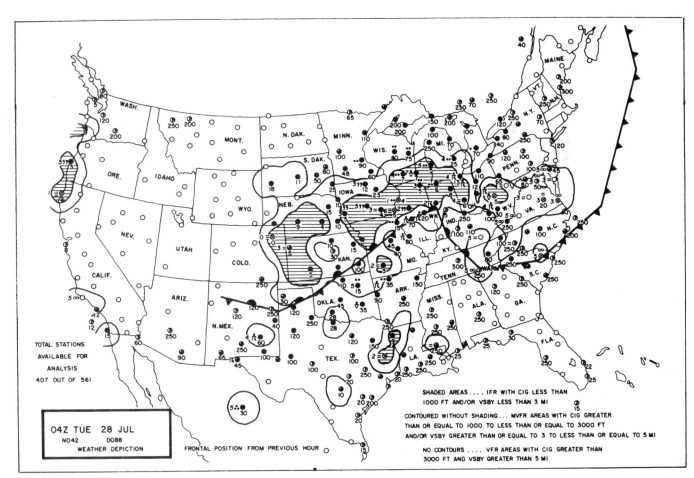

Figure 11-27. Weather Depiction Chart

WEATHER DEPICTION CHART

Figure 11-27 is a weather depiction chart which gives you a quick picture of where IFR and VFR weather was located at the valid time given on the chart. This is not forecast information but allows you to determine general weather conditions on which to base flight planning decisions. The legend is on the chart.

The numbers below the station symbols represent the lowest cloud layer in hundreds of feet where no ceiling exists (25,000' in Arkansas and Alabama, for example), and the ceiling in hundreds of feet where a ceiling is present (200' to 300' at the Oregon-California border). The numbers and symbols to the left of the station report visibility and the type of obstruction to visibility, if any (fog, in east Texas). Just as in a Terminal Forecast, visibilities are not given if they are more than 6 miles. Also shown on the weather depiction chart is the location of any frontal activity, using the same symbols as the surface analysis map.

RADAR SUMMARY CHART

Radar will show only precipitation, not clouds or fog. The radar summary chart (figure 11-28) shows the location of radar echoes from precipitation, and the direction and speed of movement of lines of cells and individual cells. The tops of precipitation as measured by radar are shown, as are any severe weather watch areas. The legend to decipher the chart is contained on the chart itself.

You can safely assume that turbulence will be associated with areas of heavy precipitation, and plan to avoid flight near those areas. Remember, weather radar does not indicate the presence of clouds or fog, only precipitation. Never rely on ground-based radar to steer you through an area of thunderstorms, and rely on airborne weather radar for storm avoidance only if you are trained in its interpretation.

LOW LEVEL SIGNIFICANT WEATHER PROGNOSTIC CHARTS

This panel of four charts (figure 11-29) is an important planning tool for all pilots. Using the forecast freezing level positions and cloud cover, instrument pilots can see where icing conditions might exist. VFR pilots can avoid turbulence and marginal ceilings and visibilities.

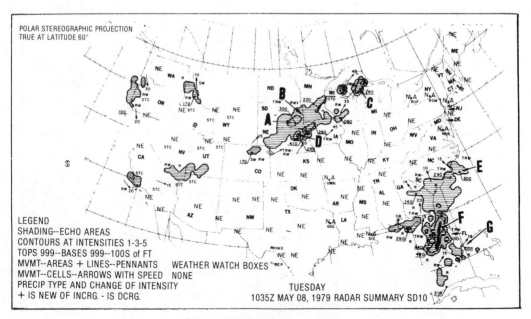

Figure 11-28. Radar Summary Chart

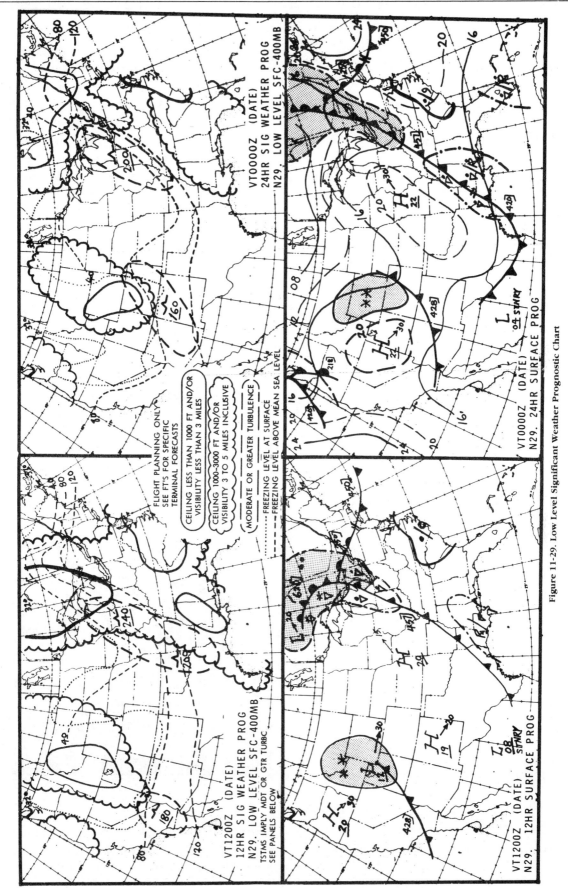

Figure 11-29. Low Level Significant Weather Prognostic Chart

The "low level" means that the data is for those altitudes between the surface and 24,000' MSL. "Prognostic" means that this is forecast information, not data based on actual observations, as is the case with the Radar Summary Chart, the Weather Depiction Chart, and the surface analysis map. The two panels on the left are a 12 hour forecast and the two right hand panels are a 24 hour forecast: the valid times are given on the charts. The top panels show the predicted position of the freezing level both at the surface (dotted line) and at altitude (identified by dashed lines), areas of forecast turbulence ("witches' hats"), and areas of IFR and MVFR weather. The bottom panels show predicted frontal positions, location of pressure systems, and type and extent of expected precipitation. The significant weather prognostic charts give you a larger view of tomorrow's weather than does the area forecast.

MISCELLANEOUS SOURCES

The Flight Service Station briefer (and the Flight Watch specialist) have satellite pictures of cloud cover available to supplement the printed weather data. National Weather Service meteorologists are stationed at FAA radar facilities to evaluate weather radar information and make it available to pilots on a current basis. Your local TV weather broadcaster is an excellent source of weather information, and will probably also have satellite pictures available. AM WEATHER is a televised early morning *aviation* weather broadcast on public television channels in many areas. Prepared specifically for pilots, it includes in graphic form all of the forecast information discussed in this chapter supplemented by time-lapse satellite photographs which allow you to see weather systems in motion.

The Voice Response System, presently (1985) undergoing evaluation, allows you to use your touch-tone telephone to ask a centrally located computer for weather reports and forecasts. A computer-generated voice responds to your requests for current and forecast weather for your selected route and altitude. When this system is fully implemented you will be able to call the computer in Kansas City using a local telephone number.

IN-FLIGHT WEATHER DETECTION DEVICES

As a VFR pilot you cannot fly into the clouds, but sometimes hazardous weather exists in or above a cloud mass that you are flying beneath. It is also possible to inadvertently encounter hazardous weather at night when it cannot be seen to be avoided. You can equip your airplane with devices to ensure that you are able to stay well clear of hazardous weather, day or night.

Airborne weather radar transmits pulses of radio frequency energy which reflect from precipitation. The reflected energy is amplified in the radar receiver and displayed on a cathode ray tube in the cockpit, providing information on the bearing and distance of the precipitation from the airplane. Both monochrome and color displays offer means of determining the relative strength of the reflected energy and therefore the intensity of the precipitation. Because heavy precipitation implies the presence of turbulence, you should use the radar information to stay well clear of any radar echoes. Because the return from a nearby heavy precipitation return may mask the existence of other echoes further away from your airplane, the interpretation of radar echoes requires training in the proper use of the equipment.

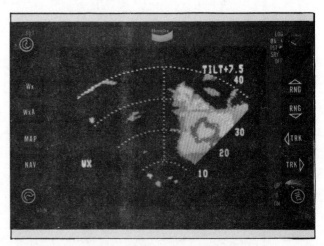

Figure 11-30. Airborne Weather Radar

A Stormscope Weather Mapping System is a passive receiver which detects and displays electrical discharges, instead of precipitation. Because lightning is a part of every thunderstorm, a StormScope's Weather Mapping System display can show you where the storms are so that you can avoid them.

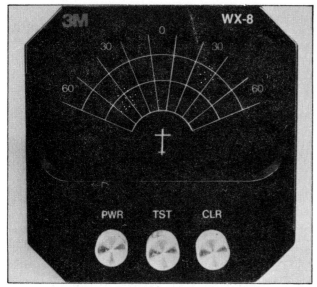

Figure 11-31. StormScope Weather Mapping System

You should not consider weather radar or a StormScope as a means of finding your way through a line of thunderstorms, since destructive turbulence that cannot be detected by either device may exist in an area where no echoes or returns are visible. Use these devices as weather avoidance aids.

STRUCTURAL ICING AND FROST

Structural icing and frost adversely affect airplane performance. For an airplane without deicing equipment, an encounter with inflight airframe icing is viewed as an emergency — to be avoided at all costs. As a VFR pilot (if you are following the rules), the only way you can encounter hazardous structural icing is to fly into an area of freezing rain. It takes both visible moisture and temperatures below freezing to produce ice on your airplane, and while you can comfortably fly in the rain and will enjoy flying in crisp, clear, cold air, you never want to mix the two. Freezing rain will coat your entire airplane (not just the leading edges of the wings and tail surfaces) with ice almost instantaneously, resulting in an immediate, unplanned descent.

The presence of ice pellets at the surface indicates that there is freezing rain at a higher altitude and you definitely should not be flying. The bright side of freezing rain is that conditions conducive to it are readily forecast (figure 11-32).

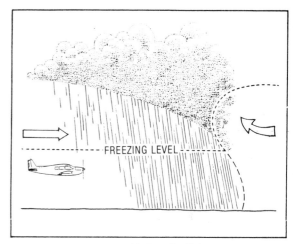

Figure 11-32. Freezing Rain

Frost presents more of a hazard to the VFR pilot than does freezing rain, because frost looks so harmless. When the surface temperature is below freezing, and the relative humidity is high, frost will form all over your airplane in a process called sublimation: the direct change from water vapor to solid form. Frost does not fall on your airplane, it forms on it. Frost does not weigh much, and it does not change the basic aerodynamic shape of the lifting surfaces; it does, however, create so much drag that it may be impossible to develop enough airspeed to become airborne. Airplanes that do manage to get airborne with a coat of frost find that stall speed has increased dramatically and/or they cannot climb.

Although it is time consuming and delays your flight, all frost must be removed from the airplane or at least polished smooth before flight is attempted. Do not attempt to remove frost (or snow, or ice) with water, either hot or cold. It can run back into control hinges, balanced control surfaces, or gear retraction mechanisms and freeze after takeoff. Use a de-icing fluid diluted as recommended by the manufacturer.

Frost can also be an in-flight hazard if the surface temperature of the airplane is below freezing and you fly into moist air. A layer of frost can form all over the airplane, including the windshield, and turn you into an unprepared, unsuspecting instrument pilot. The only answer is the defroster and/or a descent into warmer air.

Taxiing through puddles on a very cold day can also lead to complications — if you are flying a retractable gear airplane, cycle the gear once or twice after takeoff to be sure that water doesn't freeze the mechanism.

WEATHER
SECTION REVIEW

1. The conditions necessary for the formation of cumulonimbus clouds are a lifting action and

    1. Unstable air containing an excess of condensation nuclei.
    2. unstable, moist air.
    3. either stable or unstable air.
    4. stable, moist air.

2. In the Northern Hemisphere, what causes the wind to be deflected to the right?

    1. The pressure gradient force.
    2. Surface friction.
    3. Centrifugal force.
    4. Coriolis force.

3. Clouds, fog, or dew will always form when

    1. water vapor condenses.
    2. water vapor is present.
    3. relative humidity reaches or exceeds 100 percent.
    4. the temperature and dew point are equal.

4. Steady precipitation, in contrast to showery, preceding a front is an indication of

    1. cumuliform clouds with moderate turbulence.
    2. stratiform clouds with moderate turbulence.
    3. cumuliform clouds with little or no turbulence.
    4. stratiform clouds with little or no turbulence.

5. Frost which has not been removed from the lifting surfaces of an airplane before flight

    1. may prevent the airplane from becoming airborne.
    2. will change the camber (curvature of the wing) thereby increasing lift during the takeoff.
    3. may cause the airplane to become airborne with a lower angle of attack and at a lower indicated airspeed.
    4. would present no problems since frost will blow off when the airplane starts moving during takeoff.

6. What types of fog depend on a wind in order to exist?

    1. Radiation fog and ice fog.
    2. Steam fog and downslope fog.
    3. Precipitation-induced fog and ground fog.
    4. Advection fog and upslope fog.

7. What conditions are necessary for the formation of thunderstorms?

    1. Lifting force, high humidity, and unstable conditions.
    2. High humidity, high temperature, and cumulus clouds.
    3. Low pressure, high humidity, and cumulus clouds.
    4. Lifting force, high temperature, and unstable conditions.

8. If there is thunderstorm activity in the vicinity of an airport at which you plan to land, which hazardous and invisible atmospheric phenomenon might you expect to encounter on the landing approach?

    1. St. Elmo's fire.
    2. Wind shear turbulence.
    3. Tornadoes.
    4. Virga.

9. An almond or lens-shaped cloud hich appears stationary, but which may contain winds of 50 knots or more, is referred to as

    1. an inactive frontal cloud.
    2. a funnel cloud.
    3. a lenticular cloud.
    4. a stratus cloud.

10. Every physical process of weather is accompanied by or is the result of

    1. the movement of air.
    2. a pressure differential.
    3. a heat exchange.
    4. moisture.

11. What causes variations in altimeter settings between weather reporting points?

    1. Unequal heating of the Earth's surface.
    2. Variation in terrain elevation creating barriers to the movement of an air mass.
    3. Coriolis force reacting with friction.
    4. Friction of the air with the Earth's surface.

12. What are the standard pressure and temperature values for sea level?

    1. 15°C and 29.92' Hg.
    2. 59°C and 1013.2 millibars.
    3. 59°F and 29.92 millibars.
    4. 15°C and 1013.2' Hg.

13. Radar weather reports are of special interest to pilots because they report

    1. large areas of low ceilings and fog.
    2. location of precipitation along with type, intensity, and trend.
    3. location of broken to overcast clouds.
    4. icing conditions.

14. Ceiling, as used in aviation weather reports, is the height above the Earth's surface of the

    1. highest layer of clouds located above the reporting station.
    2. lowest layer of clouds or obscuration phenomena located above the reporting station.
    3. highest layer of clouds that is reported as overcast and not classified as thin or partial.
    4. lowest layer of clouds or obscuration phenomena that is reported as broken, overcast, or obscuration and not classified as thin or partial.

15. From which primary source should information be obtained regarding expected weather at your destination and estimated time of arrival?

    1. Low Level Prog Chart.
    2. Weather Depiction Chart.
    3. Terminal Forecast.
    4. Radar Summary and Weather Depiction Chart.

16. Upon encountering severe turbulence, which condition should the pilot attempt to maintain?

    1. Constant altitude.
    2. Constant airspeed (V_a).
    3. Level flight attitude.
    4. Constant altitude and constant airspeed.

17. Fog associated with a warm front is generally the
result of saturation due to

    1. evaporation of precipitation.
    2. adiabatic cooling.
    3. evaporation of surface moisture.
    4. nocturnal cooling.

As you progress with your pilot training, your instructor will give you what will seem to be a never-ending series of instructions, procedures, methods, restrictions, and advisories, and you will wonder how you will be able to remember it all. You don't have to. The Government Printing Office distributes hundreds of publications on aviation subjects and you should become familiar with what is available. All goverment publications are available from the Government Printing Office (GPO) in Washington, D. C. and GPO bookstores in major cities, but you will find that your local pilot supply store carries many of them. Private publishers have reprints which are more convenient to use and considerably less expensive than the government publication (but no less official). The ASA editions of the Federal Aviation Regulations and Airman's Information Manual are excellent examples.

AIRMAN'S INFORMATION MANUAL

This is the basic reference for procedures, although it contains invaluable information on a host of aviation subjects. This list of chapter headings will give you some idea of the extent of coverage:

1. Navigation Aids
2. Aeronautical Lighting and Airport Marking Aids
3. Airspace
4. Air Traffic Control
5. Emergency Procedures
6. Safety of Flight
7. Medical Facts for Pilots
8. Aeronautical Charts and Related Publications

Figure 12-1 is an example of the type of detailed information on procedures available in the Airman's Information Manual. The **AIM** also includes a Pilot/Controller Glossary, so that you will know exactly what the controller means when instructions are given, and it is reprinted in the Appendix for your convenience. The AIM is updated every 16 weeks and is available by subscription from the Government Printing Office. You will also find it for sale by itself or combined with the Federal Aviation Regulations by ASA at your pilot supply store. ASA provides free update sheets with each volume to keep pilots current on changes in regulations and procedures.

FEDERAL AVIATION REGULATIONS

Every pilot should have a copy of the **FAR**s, and you will find the ASA combination AIM/FAR books at the pilot supply store. The FAA does not change the regulations very often, and proposed changes are well publicized in aviation newspapers and magazines. The FARs are available from the Government Printing Office by subscription; subscribers are sent Notices of Proposed Rule Making when regulatory changes are being considered. In this book, the FARs will be discussed as they apply in discussing each subject. In Chapter 14 there is a discussion of FARs requiring explanation or illustration.

AIRPORT/FACILITY DIRECTORY

Before setting off on a cross-country flight, you are required to become familiar with all available information regarding the flight, and the Airport/Facility Directory is your source of information on the destination airport and any others along the route you may decide to visit. Aeronautical charts show the elevation, runway length, and limited radio frequency information for an airport, but only in the Airport/Facility Directory will you learn that the runway is gravel, 75 feet wide, with trees on the west, and that it slopes upward to the north. The legend for individual airport listings is provided here (figures 12-2 through 12-8). You will also find pertinent excerpts in Chapter 16 (Flight Planning). In addition to the individual airport listings, the A/FD contains:

Special notices in regard to airports listed

FSS and National Weather Service telephone numbers

Frequencies of Air Route Traffic Control Centers

FAA General Aviation District Office telephone numbers

VOR receiver check points

Parachute jumping areas

Aeronautical Chart Bulletin

Location of Enroute Flight Advisory Stations (Flight Watch)

The Airport/Facility Directory is published in seven volumes depending on geographic location and is revised every 56 days.

ADVISORY CIRCULARS

The Federal Aviation Regulations are brief and concise, written by and for lawyers, not pilots. There are many situations where a regulation or a procedure needs to be explained in detail so that the flying public can understand exactly what is required. This is the function of Advisory Circulars. ACs are non-regulatory in nature, serving only to explain the actual regulation or provide additional useful information to aid in compliance; however, the government expects every pilot to be aware of information published only in Advisory Circulars! Unfortunately, many pilots are unaware of their existence. Your instructor or flight school should have a copy of Advisory Circular 00, which is a complete listing of all current Advisory Circulars.

Advisory Circulars are numbered to correspond with the FARs — here are two examples: FAR Part 61 deals with airman and flight instructor certification, while Advisory Circular 61-65 explains flight instructor duties and responsibilities; FAR Part 91 is General Operating Rules, and Advisory Circular 91-23 is "the book" on weight and balance. Most pilots are only aware of those Advisory Circulars which are published in book form, such as AVIATION WEATHER or the FLIGHT TRAINING HANDBOOK, but you should investigate whether the FAA publishes an AC on any subject you may be curious about. You can order Advisory Circulars (most are free, but some are for sale) from the Superintendent of Documents at the Government Printing Office in Washington, D. C.

Section 3. AIRPORT OPERATIONS

220. GENERAL

Increased traffic congestion, aircraft in climb and descent attitudes, and pilots preoccupation with cockpit duties are some factors that increase the hazardous accident potential near the airport. The situation is further compounded when the weather is marginal — that is, just meeting VFR requirements. Pilots must be particularly alert when operating in the vicinity of an airport. This section defines some rules, practices and procedures that pilots should be familiar with, and adhere to, for safe airport operations.

221. TOWER CONTROLLED AIRPORTS

a. When operating at an airport where traffic control is being exercised by a control tower, pilots are required to maintain two-way radio contact with the tower while operating within the airport traffic area unless the tower authorizes otherwise. Initial call-up should be made about 15 miles from the airport. Unless there is a good reason to leave the tower frequency before exiting the airport traffic area it is a good operating practice to remain on the tower frequency for the purpose of receiving traffic information. In the interest of reducing tower frequency congestion, pilots are reminded that it is not necessary to request permission to leave the tower frequency once outside of the airport traffic area.

b. When necessary, the tower controller will issue clearances or other information for aircraft to generally follow the desired flight path (traffic patterns) when flying in the airport traffic area/control zone, and the proper taxi routes when operating on the ground. If not otherwise authorized or directed by the tower, pilots of fixed-wing aircraft approaching to land must circle the airport to the left. Pilots approaching to land in a helicopter must avoid the flow of fixed-wing traffic. However, in all instances, an appropriate clearance must be received from the tower before landing.

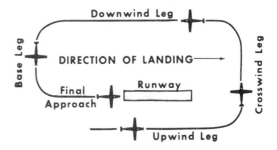

NOTE.— This diagram is intended only to illustrate terminology used in identifying various components of a traffic pattern. It should not be used as a reference or guide on how to enter a traffic pattern.

c. The following terminology for the various components of a traffic pattern has been adopted as standard for use by control towers and pilots:

(1) Upwind leg — A flight path parallel to the landing runway in the direction of landing.

(2) Crosswind leg — A flight path at right angles to the landing runway off its takeoff end.

(3) Downwind leg — A flight path parallel to the landing runway in the opposite direction of landing.

(4) Base leg — A flight path at right angles to the landing runway off its approach end and extending from the downwind leg to the intersection of the extended runway centerline.

(5) Final approach — A flight path in the direction of landing along the extended runway centerline from the base leg to the runway.

Figure 12-1. Example of Detailed Information on Procedures in AIM

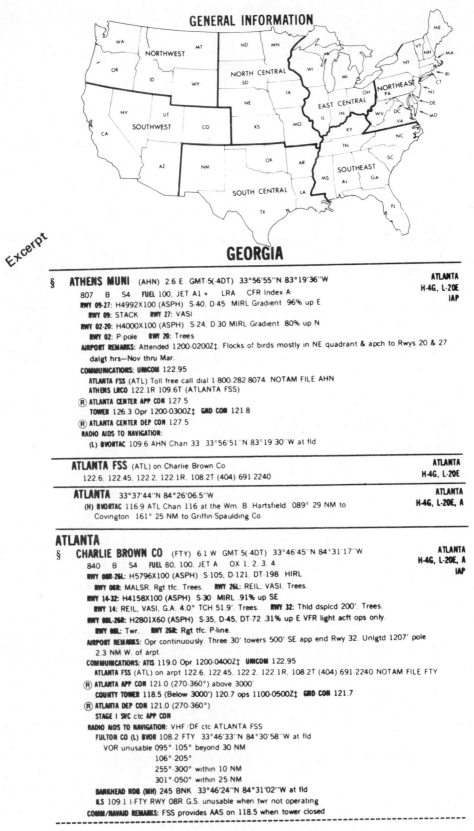

GENERAL INFORMATION

GEORGIA

§ **ATHENS MUNI** (AHN) 2.6 E GMT-5(-4DT) 33°56'55"N 83°19'36"W
    ATLANTA
    H-4G, L-20E
    IAP

  807 B S4 **FUEL** 100, JET A1 + LRA CFR Index A
  RWY 09-27: H4992X100 (ASPH) S-40, D-45 MIRL Gradient .96% up E
    RWY 09: STACK **RWY 27:** VASI
  RWY 02-20: H4000X100 (ASPH) S-24, D-30 MIRL Gradient .80% up N
    RWY 02: P-pole **RWY 20:** Trees
  AIRPORT REMARKS: Attended 1200-0200Z‡. Flocks of birds mostly in NE quadrant & apch to Rwys 20 & 27
    dalgt hrs—Nov thru Mar.
  COMMUNICATIONS: UNICOM 122.95
    ATLANTA FSS (ATL) Toll free call dial 1-800-282-8074. NOTAM FILE AHN
    ATHENS LRCO 122.1R 109.6T (ATLANTA FSS)
  Ⓡ **ATLANTA CENTER APP CON** 127.5
    TOWER 126.3 Opr 1200-0300Z‡ **GND CON** 121.8
  Ⓡ **ATLANTA CENTER DEP CON** 127.5
  RADIO AIDS TO NAVIGATION:
    (L) **BVORTAC** 109.6 AHN Chan 33 33°56'51"N 83°19'30"W at fld

ATLANTA FSS (ATL) on Charlie Brown Co
  122.6, 122.45, 122.2, 122.1R, 108.2T (404) 691-2240
    ATLANTA
    H-4G, L-20E

ATLANTA 33°37'44"N 84°26'06.5"W
  (H) **BVORTAC** 116.9 ATL Chan 116 at the Wm. B. Hartsfield 089° 29 NM to
    Covington 161° 25 NM to Griffin-Spaulding Co
    ATLANTA
    H-4G, L-20E, A

ATLANTA

§ **CHARLIE BROWN CO** (FTY) 6.1 W GMT-5(-4DT) 33°46'45"N 84°31'17"W
    ATLANTA
    H-4G, L-20E, A
    IAP

  840 B S4 **FUEL** 80, 100, JET A OX 1, 2, 3, 4
  RWY 08R-26L: H5796X100 (ASPH) S-105, D-121, DT-198 HIRL
    RWY 08R: MALSR. Rgt tfc. Trees. **RWY 26L:** REIL, VASI. Trees.
  RWY 14-32: H4158X100 (ASPH) S-30 MIRL .91% up SE
    RWY 14: REIL, VASI, G.A. 4.0° TCH 51.9'. Trees. **RWY 32:** Thld dsplcd 200'. Trees.
  RWY 08L-26R: H2801X60 (ASPH) S-35, D-45, DT-72 .31% up E VFR light acft ops only.
    RWY 08L: Twr. **RWY 26R:** Rgt tfc. P-line.
  AIRPORT REMARKS: Opr continuously. Three 30' towers 500' SE app end Rwy 32. Unlgtd 1207' pole
    2.3 NM W. of arpt.
  COMMUNICATIONS: ATIS 119.0 Opr 1200-0400Z‡ **UNICOM** 122.95
    ATLANTA FSS (ATL) on arpt 122.6, 122.45, 122.2, 122.1R, 108.2T (404) 691-2240 NOTAM FILE FTY
  Ⓡ **ATLANTA APP CON** 121.0 (270-360°) above 3000'
    COUNTY TOWER 118.5 (Below 3000') 120.7 ops 1100-0500Z‡ **GND CON** 121.7
  Ⓡ **ATLANTA DEP CON** 121.0 (270-360°)
  STAGE I SVC ctc **APP CON**
  RADIO AIDS TO NAVIGATION: VHF/DF ctc ATLANTA FSS
    FULTON CO (L) **BVOR** 108.2 FTY 33°46'33"N 84°30'58"W at fld
      VOR unusable 095°-105° beyond 30 NM
             106°-205°
             255°-300° within 10 NM
             301°-050° within 25 NM
    BANKHEAD NDB (MH) 245 BNK 33°46'24"N 84°31'02"W at fld
    ILS 109.1 I-FTY RWY 08R G.S. unusable when twr not operating
  COMM/NAVAID REMARKS: FSS provides AAS on 118.5 when tower closed

Figure 12-2. A/FD Excerpt

DIRECTORY LEGEND
SAMPLE

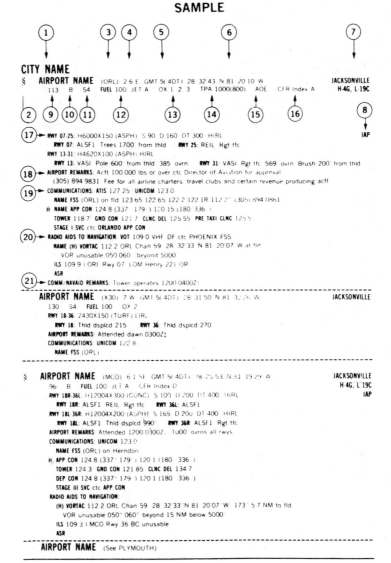

ABBREVIATIONS

The following abbreviations are those commonly used within this Directory. Other abbreviations may be found in the Legend and are not duplicated below.

acft	aircraft	med	medium
apch	approach	NFCT	non federal
arpt	airport		control tower
avbl	available	ngt	night
bcn	beacon	ntc	notice
blo	below	opr	operate
byd	beyond	ops	operates operation
ctc	contact	ovrn	overrun
dalgt	daylight	p-line	power line
dsplc	displace	req	request
dsplcd	displaced	rqr	requires
emerg	emergency	rgt tfc	right traffic
fld	field	rwy	runway
ints	intensity	svc	service
lgtd	lighted	tkf	take off
lgts	lights	tfc	traffic
ldg	landing	thld	threshold

Figure 12-3. A/FD Excerpt

DIRECTORY LEGEND
LEGEND

This Directory is an alphabetical listing of data on record with the FAA on all airports that are open to the public, associated terminal control facilities, air route traffic control centers and radio aids to navigation within the conterminous United States, Puerto Rico and the Virgin Islands. Airports are listed alphabetically by associated city name and cross referenced by airport name. Facilities associated with an airport, but with a different name, are listed individually under their own name, as well as under the airport with which they are associated.

The listing of an airport in this directory merely indicates the airport operator's willingness to accommodate transient aircraft, and does not represent that the facility conforms with any Federal or local standards, or that it has been approved for use on the part of the general public.

The information on obstructions is taken from reports submitted to the FAA. It has not been verified in all cases. Pilots are cautioned that objects not indicated in this tabulation (or on charts) may exist which can create a hazard to flight operation.

Detailed specifics concerning services and facilities tabulated within this directory are contained in Airman's Information Manual, Basic Flight Information and ATC Procedures.

The legend items that follow explain in detail the contents of this Directory and are keyed to the circled numbers on the sample on the preceding page.

① CITY/AIRPORT NAME

Airports and facilities in this directory are listed alphabetically by associated city and state. Where the city name is different from the airport name the city name will appear on the line above the airport name. Airports with the same associated city name will be listed alphabetically by airport name and will be separated by a dashed rule line. All others will be separated by a solid rule line.

② NOTAM SERVICE

§—NOTAM "D" (Distant teletype dissemination) and NOTAM "L" (Local dissemination) service is provided for airport. Absence of annotation § indicates NOTAM "L" (Local dissemination) only is provided for airport. See AIM, Basic Flight Information and ATC Procedures for detailed description of NOTAM.

③ LOCATION IDENTIFIER

A three or four character code assigned to airports. These identifiers are used by ATC in lieu of the airport name in flight plans, flight strips and other written records and computer operations.

④ AIRPORT LOCATION

Airport location is expressed as distance and direction from the center of the associated city in nautical miles and cardinal points, i.e., 3.5 NE.

⑤ TIME CONVERSION

Hours of operation of all facilities are expressed in Greenwich Mean Time (GMT) and shown as "Z" time. The directory indicates the number of hours to be subtracted from GMT to obtain local standard time and local daylight saving time GMT-5(-4DT). The symbol ‡ indicates that during periods of Daylight Saving Time effective hours will be one hour earlier than shown. In those areas where daylight saving time is not observed that (-4DT) and ‡ will not be shown. All states observe daylight savings time except Arizona and that portion of Indiana in the Eastern Time Zone and Puerto Rico and the Virgin Islands.

⑥ GEOGRAPHIC POSITION OF AIRPORT

⑦ CHARTS

The Sectional Chart and Low and High Altitude Enroute Chart and panel on which the airport or facility is located.

⑧ INSTRUMENT APPROACH PROCEDURES

IAP indicates an airport for which a prescribed (Public Use) FAA Instrument Approach Procedure has been published.

⑨ ELEVATION

Elevation is given in feet above mean sea level and is the highest point on the landing surface. When elevation is sea level it will be indicated as (00). When elevation is below sea level a minus (-) sign will precede the figure.

⑩ ROTATING LIGHT BEACON

B indicates rotating beacon is available. Rotating beacons operate dusk to dawn unless otherwise indicated in AIRPORT REMARKS.

⑪ SERVICING

S1: Minor airframe repairs.
S2: Minor airframe and minor powerplant repairs.
S3: Major airframe and minor powerplant repairs.
S4: Major airframe and major powerplant repairs.

Figure 12-4. A/FD Excerpt

(12) **FUEL**

FUEL

CODE   PRODUCT
80   Grade 80 gasoline (Red)
100   Grade 100 gasoline (Green)
100LL   Grade 100LL gasoline (low lead) (Blue)
115   Grade 115 gasoline
A   Jet A—Kerosene freeze point—40° C.
A1   Jet A-1—Kerosene, freeze point—50° C.
A1 +   Jet A-1—Kerosene with icing inhibitor, freeze point—50° C.
B   Jet B—Wide-cut turbine fuel, freeze point—50° C.
B +   Jet B—Wide-cut turbine fuel with icing inhibitor, freeze point—50° C.

(13) **OXYGEN**

OX 1   High Pressure
OX 2   Low Pressure
OX 3   High Pressure—Replacement Bottles
OX 4   Low Pressure—Replacement Bottles

(14) **TRAFFIC PATTERN ALTITUDE**

Traffic Pattern Altitude (TPA)—The first figure shown is TPA above mean sea level. The second figure in parentheses is TPA above airport elevation.

(15) **AIRPORT OF ENTRY AND LANDING RIGHTS AIRPORTS**

AOE—Airport of Entry-A customs Airport of Entry where permission from U.S. Customs is not required, however, at least one hour advance notice of arrival must be furnished.

LRA—Landing Rights Airport-Application for permission to land must be submitted in advance to U.S. Customs. At least one hour advance notice of arrival must be furnished.

NOTE: Advance notice of arrival at both an AOE and LRA airport may be included in the flight plan when filed in Canada or Mexico, if destination is an airport where flight notification service is available. This notice will also be treated as an application for permission to land in the case of an LRA. Although advance notice of arrival may be relayed to customs through Mexican, Canadian, and U.S. Communications facilities by flight plan, the aircraft operator is solely responsible for insuring that customs receives the notification. (See Customs, Immigration and Naturalization, Public Health and Agriculture Department requirements in the International Flight Information Manual for further details.)

(16) **CERTIFICATED AIRPORT (FAR 139) and FAA INSPECTION**

Airports serving Civil Aeronautics Board certified carriers and certified under FAR, Part 139, are indicated by the CFR index; i.e., CFR Index A, which relates to the availability of crash, fire, rescue equipment.

All airports not inspected by FAA will be identified by the note: Not insp. This indicates that the airport information has been provided by the owner or operator of the field.

FAR—PART 139 CERTIFICATED AIRPORTS
INDICES AND FIRE FIGHTING AND RESCUE EQUIPMENT REQUIREMENTS

Airport Index	Required No. Vehicles	Aircraft Length		Scheduled Departures	Agent + Water for Protein Foam
A	1	≤ 90'		≥ 1	500 # DC or 450 # DC + 50 gal H²0
		) 90',	≤ 126'	(5	300 # DC + 500 gal H²0
B	2	) 90',	≤ 126'	≥ 5	Index A + 1500 gal H²0
		) 126',	≤ 160'	(5	
C	3	) 126',	≤ 160'	≥ 5	Index A + 3000 gal H²0
		) 160',	≤ 200'	(5	
D	3	) 160',	≤ 200'	≥ 5	Index A + 4000 gal H²0
		) 200'		(5	
E	3	) 200'		≥ 5	Index A + 6000 gal H²0
Ltd.	Vehicle and capacity requirements for airports limited operating certificates are determined on a case by case basis.				

) Greater Than: (Less Than   ≥ Equal or Greater Than: ≤ Equal or Less Than; H²0—Water; DC—Dry Chemical.

NOTE: If AFFF (Aqueous Film Forming Foam) is used in lieu of Protein Foam, the water quantities listed for Indices A thru E can be reduced 33-1/3%.

(17) **RUNWAY DATA**

Runway information is shown on two lines. That information common to the entire runway is shown on the first line while information concerning the runway ends are shown on the second or following line. Lengthy information will be footnoted and placed in the Airport Remarks.

Runway direction, surface, length, width, weight bearing capacity, lighting, gradient (when gradient exceeds 0.3 percent) and appropriate remarks are shown for each runway. Direction, length, width, lighting and remarks are shown for sealanes.

Figure 12-5. A/FD Excerpt

RUNWAY SURFACE AND LENGTH

Runway lengths prefixed by the letter "H" indicate that the runways are hard surfaced (concrete, asphalt). If the runway length is not prefixed, the surface is sod, clay, etc. The runway surface composition is indicated in parentheses after runway length as follows:

(ASPH)–Asphalt   (GRVL)–Gravel, or cinders
(CONC)–Concrete   (TURF)–Sod
(DIRT)–Dirt

The full dimensions of helipads are shown, i.e., 50X50.

RUNWAY WEIGHT BEARING CAPACITY

Runway strength data shown in this publication is derived from available information and is a realistic estimate of capability at an average level of activity. It is not intended as a maximum allowable weight or as an operating limitation. Many airport pavements are capable of supporting limited operations with gross weights of 25-50% in excess of the published figures. Permissible operating weights, insofar as runway strengths are concerned, are a matter of agreement between the owner and user. When desiring to operate into any airport at weights in excess of those published in the publication, users should contact the airport management for permission. Add 000 to figure following S, D, DT, DDT and MAX for gross weight capacity.

    S–Runway weight bearing capacity for aircraft with single-wheel type landing gear, (DC-3), etc.
    D–Runway weight bearing capacity for aircraft with dual-wheel type landing gear, (DC-6),etc.
    DT–Runway weight bearing capacity for aircraft with dual-tandem type landing gear, (707), etc.
    DDT–Runway weight bearing capacity for aircraft with double dual-tandem type landing gear, (747), etc.

Quadricycle and dual-tandem are considered virtually equal for runway weight bearing consideration, as are single-tandem and dual-wheel.

Omission of weight bearing capacity indicates information unknown.

RUNWAY LIGHTING

Lights are in operation sunset to sunrise. Lighting available by prior arrangement only or operating part of the night only and or pilot controlled and with specific operating hours are indicated under airport remarks as footnotes. Since obstructions are usually lighted, obstruction lighting is not included in this code. Unlighted obstructions on or surrounding an airport will be noted in airport remarks.

Temporary, emergency or limited runway edge lighting such as flares, smudge pots, lanterns or portable runway lights will also be shown in airport remarks, instead of being designated by code numbers.

Types of lighting are shown with the runway or runway end they serve.

LIRL–Low intensity Runway Lights
MIRL–Medium Intensity Runway Lights
HIRL–High Intensity Runway Lights
REIL–Runway End Identifier Lights
CL–Centerline Lights
TDZ–Touchdown Zone Lights
ODALS–Omni Directional Approach Lighting System.
AF OVRN–Air Force Overrun 1000' Standard
        Approach Lighting System
LDIN–Lead-In Lighting System
MALS–Medium Intensity Approach Lighting System.
MALSF–Medium Intensity Approach Lighting System
    with Sequenced Flashing Lights.
MALSR–Medium Intensity Approach Lighting System
    with Runway Alignment Indicator Lights.

SALS–Short Approach Lighting System.
SALSF–Short Approach Lighting System with Sequenced
    Flashing Lights
SSALS–Simplified Short Approach Lighting System.
SSALF–Simplified Short Approach Lighting System with
    Sequenced Flashing Lights.
SSALR–Simplified Short Approach Lighting System with
    Runway Alignment Indicator Lights.
ALSF1–High Intensity Approach Lighting System with Se-
    quenced Flashing Lights. Category I, Configuration.
ALSF2–High Intensity Approach Lighting System with Se-
    quenced Flashing Lights, Category II, Configu-
    ration
VASI–Visual Approach Slope Indicator System.

VASI approach slope angle and TCH will be shown only when slope angle exceeds 3°.

RUNWAY GRADIENT

Runway gradient will be shown only when it is 0.3 percent or more. When available the direction of slope upward will be indicated, i.e., 0.5% up NW.

RUNWAY END DATA

Lighting systems such as VASI, MALSR, REIL, obstructions, displaced thresholds will be shown on the specific runway end. "Rgt tfc"-Right traffic indicates right turns should be made on landing and takeoff for specified runway end.

(18) AIRPORT REMARKS

"Landing Fee" indicates landing charges for private or non-revenue producing aircraft, in addition, fees may be charged for planes that remain over a couple of hours and buy no services, or at major airline terminals for all aircraft.

Obstructions—Because of space limitations only the more prominent obstacles are indicated. Natural obstruction, such as trees, clearly discernible for contact operations are not included. On the other hand, all obstructions within at least a 20:1 approach ratio are indicated.

Remarks—Data is confined to operational items affecting the status and usability of the airport.

(19) COMMUNICATIONS

Communications will be listed in sequence in the order shown below:

Automatic Terminal Information Service (ATIS) and Private Aeronautical Stations (UNICOM) along with their frequency is shown, where available, on the line following the heading "COMMUNICATIONS".

Flight Service Station (FSS) information. The associated FSS will be shown followed by the identifier and information concerning availability of telephone service. e.g. Direct Line (DL), Local Call (LC), etc. Where the airport NOTAM File identifier is different then the associated FSS it will be shown as "NOTAM FILE IAD." Where the FSS is located

Figure 12-6. A/FD Excerpt

on the field it will be indicated as "on arpt" following the identifier. Frequencies available will follow. The FSS telephone number will follow along with any significant operational information. FSS's whose name is not the same as the airport on which located will also be listed in the normal alphabetical name listing for the state in which located Limited Remote Communication Outlet (LRCO) or Remote Communications Outlet (RCO) providing service to the airport followed by the frequency and name of the Controlling FSS.

FSS's and CS Ts provide information on airport conditions, radio aids and other facilities, and process flight plans. Airport Advisory Service is provided at the pilot's request on 123.6 or 123.65 by FSS's located at non tower airports or when the tower is not in operation. (See AIM, ADVISORIES AT NON TOWER AIRPORTS.)

Aviation weather briefing service is provided by FSS's and CS T's however, CS T personnel are not certified weather briefers and therefore provide only factual data from weather reports and forecasts. Flight and weather briefing services are also available by calling the telephone numbers listed.

Limited Remote Communications Outlet (LRCO)—Unmanned satellite air ground communications facility, which may be associated with a VOR. These outlets effectively extend service range of the FSS and provide greater communications reliability.

Remote Communications Outlet (RCO)—An unmanned satellite air to ground communication stations remotely controlled and providing UHF and VHF communications capability to extend the service range of an FSS

Civil communications frequencies used in the FSS air ground system are now operated simplex on 122 0, 122.2, 122.3, 122.4, 122.6, 123.6; emergency 121.5; plus receive-only on 122.05, 122.1, 122.15 and 123.6.

    a.   122.0 is assigned as the Enroute Flight Advisory Service channel at selected FSS's.

    b.   122.2 is assigned to all FSS's as a common enroute simplex service.

    c.   123.6 is assigned as the airport advisory channel at non tower FSS locations, however, it is still in commission at some FSS's collocated with towers to provide part-time Airport Advisory Service.

    d.   122.1 is the primary receive-only frequency at VORs. 122.05, 122.15 and 123.6 are assigned at selected VORs meeting certain criteria.

    e.   Some FSS's are assigned 50kHz channels for simplex operation in the 122-123 MHz band (e.g. 122.35)

Pilots using the FSS A G system should refer to this directory or appropriate charts to determine frequencies available at the FSS or remoted facility through which they wish to communicate.

Part time FSS hours of operation are shown in remarks under facility name.

    Emergency frequency 121 5 is available at all Flight Service Stations, Towers, Approach Control and RADAR facilities, unless indicated as not available

Frequencies published followed by the letter "T" or "R", indicate that the facility will only transmit or receive respectively on that frequency. All radio aids to navigation frequencies are transmit only.

TERMINAL SERVICES

ATIS—A continuous broadcast of recorded non-control information in selected areas of high activity.

UNICOM—A non-government air ground radio communications facility utilized to provide general airport advisory service.

APP CON—Approach Control. The symbol Ⓡ indicates radar approach control.

TOWER—Control tower.

GND CON—Ground Control

DEP CON—Departure Control. The symbol Ⓡ indicates radar departure control.

CLNC DEL—Clearance Delivery.

PRE TAXI CLNC—Pre taxi clearance

VFR ADVSY SVC—VFR Advisory Service. Service provided by Non Radar Approach Control.

STAGE I SVC—Radar Advisory Service for VFR aircraft

STAGE II SVC—Radar Advisory and Sequencing Service for VFR aircraft

STAGE III SVC—Radar Sequencing and Separation Service for participating VFR Aircraft within a Terminal Radar Service Area (TRSA)

TCA—Radar Sequencing and Separation Service for all aircraft in a Terminal Control Area (TCA)

TOWER APP CON and DEP CON RADIO CALL will be the same as the airport name unless indicated otherwise

⑳ RADIO AIDS TO NAVIGATION

The Airport Facility Directory lists by facility name all Radio Aids to Navigation, except Military TACANS, that appear on National Ocean Survey Visual or IFR Aeronautical Charts and those upon which the FAA has approved an Instrument Approach Procedure.

All VOR, VORTAC and ILS equipment in the National Airspace System has an automatic monitoring and shutdown feature in the event of malfunction. Unmonitored as used in the publication means that FSS or tower personnel cannot observe the malfunction or shutdown signal.

NAVAID information is tabulated as indicated in the following sample

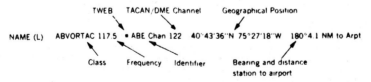

NAME (L) ABVORTAC 117.5 • ABE Chan 122 40°43'36"N 75°27'18"W 180°4.1 NM to Arpt

VOR unusable 020°-060° beyond 26 NM below 3500'

               Restrictions

ASR—indicates that civil radar instrument approach minimums are published.

VOT—VOR Test Facility. Will be shown on the same line as and following RADIO AIDS TO NAVIGATION, where available.

NAME () BVORTAC 300°/36 NM

Figure 12-7. A/FD Excerpt

DIRECTORY LEGEND

RADIO CLASS DESIGNATIONS

Identification of VOR VORTAC TACAN Stations by Class (Operational Limitations)

Normal Usable Altitudes and Radius Distances

Class	Altitudes	Distance (miles)
(T)	12.000' and below	25
(L)	Below 18.000'	40
(H)	Below 18.000'	40
(H)	Within the Conterminous 48 States only, between 14.500' and 17.999'	100
(H)	18.000' FL 450	130
(H)	Above FL 450	100

(H) = High   (L) = Low   (T) = Terminal

NOTE An (H) facility is capable of providing (L) and (T) service volume and an (L) facility additionally provides (T) service volume.

The term VOR is. operationally, a general term covering the VHF omnidirectional bearing type of facility without regard to the fact that the power. the frequency protected service volume, the equipment configuration, and operational requirements may vary between facilities at different locations.

AB _____ Automatic Weather Broadcast (also shown with ● following frequency.)
B _____ Scheduled Broadcast Station (broadcasts weather at 15 minutes after the hour.)
DF _____ Direction Finding Service.
DME _____ UHF standard (TACAN compatible) distance measuring equipment.
H _____ Non-directional radio beacon (homing), power 50 watts to less than 2.000 watts.
HH _____ Non-directional radio beacon (homing), power 2.000 watts or more.
H SAB _____ Non-directional radio beacons providing automatic transcribed weather service.
ILS _____ Instrument Landing System (voice, where available, on localizer channel).
LDA _____ Localizer Directional Aid.
LMM _____ Compass locator station when installed at middle marker site.
LOM _____ Compass locator station when installed at outer marker site.
MH _____ Non-directional radio beacon (homing) power less than 50 watts.
S _____ Simultaneous range homing signal and/or voice.
SABH _____ Non-directional radio beacon not authorized for IFR or ATC. Provides automatic weather broadcasts.
SDF _____ Simplified Direction Facility.
TACAN _____ UHF navigational facility omnidirectional course and distance information.
VOR _____ VHF navigational facility omnidirectional course only.
VOR DME _____ Collocated VOR navigational facility and UHF standard distance measuring equipment.
VORTAC _____ Collocated VOR and TACAN navigational facilities.
W _____ Without voice on radio facility frequency.
Z _____ VHF station on location marker at a LF radio facility.

㉑ COMM/NAVAID REMARKS:
Pertinent remarks concerning communications and NAVAIDS.

Figure 12-8. A/FD Excerpt

AC NO: 91-43
DATE: 6/26/75

ADVISORY CIRCULAR

DEPARTMENT OF TRANSPORTATION
FEDERAL AVIATION ADMINISTRATION

SUBJECT: UNRELIABLE AIRSPEED INDICATIONS

1. <u>PURPOSE</u>. The purpose of this Advisory Circular is to alert pilots to the possibility of erroneous airspeed/Mach indications that may be caused by blocking or freezing of the pitot system, and corrective action to be taken.

2. <u>BACKGROUND</u>. Unreliable airspeed/Mach indications may have contributed to one recent serious incident and a fatal accident. A frozen or blocked pitot system may have caused the unreliable indications. These erroneous readings can be so subtle, that a pilot may not detect the problem until it is too late for adequate corrective action. Many pilots may associate a frozen pitot head with symptoms of a rapidly decreasing or zero airspeed indication. This is not always the case, especially when operating high performance aircraft at high altitudes.

3. <u>DESCRIPTION</u>. When blocking or freezing of the pitot system occurs, two situations can develop as follows:

   a. If the ram air input to the pitot head is blocked, the indicated airspeed may drop to zero; and

   b. If the ram air input plus the drain hole is blocked, the pressure is trapped in the system and the airspeed indicator may react as an altimeter; e.g.:

      (1) During level flight, airspeed indication will not change even when actual airspeed is varied by large power changes;

      (2) During climb, airspeed indication will increase; and

      (3) During descent, airspeed indication will decrease.

4. <u>RECOMMENDATIONS</u>. Due to the critical nature of this in-flight problem, pilots should be aware of indications symptomatic of a frozen or blocked pitot system and take the following corrective action:

   a. Emphasis should be on attitude flying when these symptoms are recognized.

   b. Check position of pitot heat switches and associated circuit breakers.

   c. If conditions during or shortly after takeoff are conducive to pitot system icing, pitot heat should be on prior to flight.

R. P. SKULLY, Director
Flight Standards Service

Figure 12-9. Typical Advisory Circular

EXAM-O-GRAMS

The FAA keeps records on which questions seem to give written examination applicants the most trouble, assuming that if the majority of the applicants do not understand a subject then the FAA must be at fault for not making that subject clear. That is where Exam-o-Grams come in. The FAA publishes both VFR and IFR Exam-o-Grams on a wide variety of tricky subjects, explaining them in easy to understand language and graphics (figure 12-10). They are available from the **GPO** or the pilot supply store.

DEPARTMENT OF TRANSPORTATION
Federal Aviation Administration
VFR PILOT EXAM-O-GRAM° NO. 47

GROUND EFFECT

It is possible to fly an aircraft a few feet above the ground at an airspeed lower than that required to sustain level flight at an altitude only slightly higher. This is the result of a phenomenon called ground effect -- apparently better known than understood by many pilots. In terms as nontechnical as possible, we will here define and discuss the major problems associated with this rather complex subject.

WHAT IS GROUND EFFECT? It is not possible, nor would it serve our purpose, to attempt in the space available an indepth discussion of the precise aerodynamics of ground effect. Suffice it to say, that in simple terms, it is the result of interaction between wing airflow patterns and the surface of the earth. All airfoils such as wings, rotor blades, etc., produce tip vortices and exhibit distinct airstream downwash characteristics when developing lift. The vertical components of such tip vortices and downwash velocities are progressively reduced as the airfoil nears the surface, and at touchdown are almost completely canceled by surface interference. This alteration in airflow pattern decreases induced drag (the drag produced by lift). The closer the airfoil to the surface, the greater the reduction. Induced drag, at a height of approximately one-tenth of a wing span above the surface, may be 47% less than when the airplane is operating out of ground effect. It is this decrease in drag which explains basic airplane reactions when in ground effect.

HOW DOES A REDUCTION IN INDUCED DRAG AFFECT PERFORMANCE? To the pilot the reduction in drag means increased performance. That is, lift will increase with no increase in angle of attack, or the same lift can be obtained at a smaller angle of attack. This can be useful since it allows the pilot to either decrease angle of attack/power to maintain level flight, or as on

most landings, to maintain wing lift while reducing power. A word of caution is in order, however. A full stall landing will require several more degrees of up elevator deflection than would a full stall when done free of ground effect. This is true because ground effect usually changes horizontal tail effectiveness in airplanes of conventional configuration.

UP TO WHAT ALTITUDE CAN GROUND EFFECT BE DETECTED? A pilot is unlikely to detect ground effect if his height above the surface exceeds the airplane's wing span. In fact, there is appreciable ground effect only if height is less than half the wing span. At this or lower altitudes, ground effect is quite pronounced.

WHAT MAJOR PROBLEMS CAN BE CAUSED BY GROUND EFFECT? Floating during landing is, in part, a result of ground effect. An airplane will continue to remain airborne just above the surface at a speed which would have produced an immediate stall had the airplane been a bit higher. Therefore, a pilot may run out of both runway and options if he carries excess speed in the approach, or does not allow for at least a small margin of float after the flare from a normal approach.

Another and perhaps more serious problem, can develop during takeoff and climb out, especially when using a runway of marginal length. Deluded into believing that he has climb-out capability simply because he was able to get in the air, a pilot may raise the gear the instant he is airborne or initiate an immediate climb. For a few feet, all may go well but he may really have only marginal climb performance even in ground effect, and therefore, an acute need for added thrust as he begins to move out of ground effect. Moving out of ground effect, even if it only slightly increases the effectiveness of the elevators, the nose will usually tend to pitch up. At the resultant high angle of attack, the pilot finds he cannot climb, or even worse, may begin to sink. Desperately holding his nose-high attitude in a futile effort to gain altitude, he steadily mushes or stalls back to the runway or into obstructions if no excess power is available to correct the situation. Add high gross weight and density altitude and a bit of turbulence to this scene and an accident is even more likely.

Airspeed indicator unreliability in ground effect is another though less critical problem. Usually it will indicate slightly higher as you leave and slightly lower as you enter ground effect.

Just remember, ground effect is always there; it may prolong the glide or permit an aircraft to get airborne with insufficient power to sustain flight outside the area of ground effect. If this occurs the pilot must allow the airplane to accelerate while still in ground effect, before attempting to continue the climb. Panic attempts to force a climb can only make lift/climb problems worse.

VFR 47
1/74

* Exam-O-Grams are non-directive in nature and are issued solely as an information service to individuals interested in Airman Written Examinations.

FAA Aeronautical Center
Flight Standards Technical Division
Operations Branch
P. O. Box 25082
Oklahoma City, Oklahoma 73125
Exam-O-Grams available free of charge - single copy only per request. Permission is hereby granted to reproduce this material.

Figure 12-10. VFR Exam-o-Gram

NOTICES TO AIRMEN

Information that might affect the safety of a flight, such as a runway closure, navigational aid outage, lighting system change, etc., is available from your Flight Service Station briefer, who receives Notices to Airmen (NOTAMS) on the teletype circuit with the hourly weather sequences. Conditions which are not of a temporary nature are listed in a publication called Class II Notices to Airmen which is available at General Aviation District Offices and Flight Service stations. Ask your briefer for any NOTAMs, published or temporary, which might affect your flight, as it is your responsibility to have this information. You must request published NOTAMs — they will not be volunteered by the Flight Service Station specialist.

AVIATION MEDIA

All pilots are expected to stay abreast of changes in regulations and procedures, but advancing technology is teaching new ways of navigating and of solving some of the mysteries of weather, and pilots cannot expect today's methods to apply forever. The aviation press is the best source of information on the changing world of flight, and we recommend that you read aviation newspapers and magazines.

Figure 12-11. FAR/AIM Series

PUBLICATIONS
SECTION REVIEW

Refer to Notices to Airmen (figure Q12-1) for questions 1 and 2.

```
                            FLORIDA

      FT LAUDERDALE EXECUTIVE ARPT:  TPA   800   ft.
         TPA  for  jets  1300  ft. 4 Box VASI cmsnd
         left side Rwy 26. 2 Box  VASI  cmsnd   left
         side Rwy 13.  (3/81)
      FT LAUDERDALE-HOLLYWOOD INTL ARPT: TPA 1000
         ft.  Thr Rwy 27L dsplcd 401  ft.  Thr  Rwy
         09L dsplcd 609 ft.  Thr Rwy 27R dsplcd 599
         ft. (3/81)
      FT   MYERS  PAGE  FIELD  ARPT:  Unicom  Freq
         123.05. (3/81)
      MIAMI INTL ARPT: Wide Body & DC-8 acft  lndg
         Rwy  09L  & desiring to taxi west on Twy M
         are advised to use Twys M-8, M-9, M-10, M-
         11 or the end. Twys are numbered W  to  E.
         (3/81)  RVR Rwy 27L OTS UFN. (3/81)
      NEW  SMYRNA  BEACH  MUNI ARPT: Rwy 15/33 Rwy
         lgts oper dusk-dawn. Rwy  11/29  Rwy  lgts
         oper  dusk-2400.  For VASI and Rwy 11/29
         Rwy lgts after 2400 key 122.8 3 times  for
         low,  5  times  for  med,  and 7 times for
         high. (1/81)
```

Figure Q12-1. Notices to Airmen

1. What is the status of the runway lights for a landing at New Smyrna Beach Muni. on Rwy 15 after 2400?

   1. For runway lights, key the transmitter the proper number of times on 122.8 MHz.
   2. The lights on this runway are not operated at night.
   3. The runway lights operate from dark to dawn.

4. Runway lights are on request.

2. The traffic pattern for light airplanes and gyroplanes at Ft. Lauderdale-Hollywood International Airport is changed to

   1. 800 ft.
   2. 1,000 ft.
   3. 1,300 ft.
   4. and additional 1,000 ft.

3. FAA Advisory Circulars (some free, others at cost) are available to all pilots and are obtained by

   1. distribution from the nearest FAA district office.
   2. ordering those desired.
   3. subscribing to the Federal Register.
   4. subscribing to the FAR's.

4. Information concerning parachute jumping sites may be found in the

   1. Graphic Notices and Supplemental Data.
   2. legend of sectional aeronautical charts only.
   3. Airport/Facility Directory.
   4. NOTAMS.

MEDICAL FACTORS FOR PILOTS

Chapter 3 discussed how to determine the health of the engine, and Chapter 6 discussed airplane performance under different conditions. This chapter will discuss the human element: how the performance of the pilot is affected by health and environmental factors. Many physical conditions which have minimal

Figure 13-1. Self-grounding is Required When a Pilot is Feeling Ill

effect on the body's performance at ground level can have severe consequences "at altitude", which includes the upper limit operating levels of even small, single-engine airplanes. You should be aware of these conditions so that you can avoid problems with your

own physical state during flight, and help your passengers have a safe and comfortable experience.

DRUGS AND ALCOHOL

The effects of drugs and alcohol on performance are intensified by altitude, and pilots are prohibited from flying within 8 hours of ingesting *any* alcoholic beverage and from flying while under the influence of any drug or medication. Even over-the-counter medications as seemingly innocuous as cough suppressants can affect judgment, memory, and alertness at altitude; pilots should check with an Aviation Medical Examiner for advice if in doubt about any medication. Pilots are

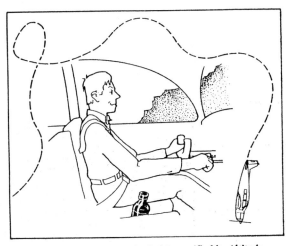

Figure 13-2. Effects of Alcohol Intensified by Altitude

required to ground themselves if they have any medical condition which affects their abilities as flight crewmembers.

HYPOXIA

Our bodies are acclimated to life on the ground, where the atmosphere contains approximately 21 percent oxygen, and they require that same *amount* of oxygen in order to operate efficiently at altitude, where the atmosphere is thinner. A small pressure differential is required in your lungs to allow oxygen to be transferred to your bloodstream. As you climb to altitudes where pressure is reduced, the exchange of oxygen is inhibited, and the symptoms of hypoxia (oxygen sickness) begin to occur unless *supplemental* oxygen is used. These symptoms usually do not affect healthy, non-smoking pilots at altitudes below 12,000 feet in the daytime; deterioration in night vision can occur as low as 5,000 feet. *The body has no built-in alarm system to warn of hypoxia!*. Symptoms of hypoxia include impaired judgment, memory, alertness, coordination, and the loss of ability to make calculations, and are followed by headache and drowsiness. The most insidious symptom is a state of euphoria or well-being: "I feel great! I just can't seem to figure out this VOR."

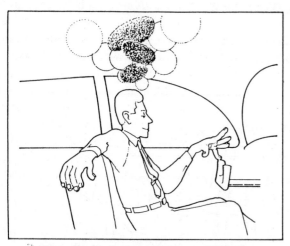

Figure 13-3. Euphoria is a Symptom of Hypoxia

The agent in the blood which absorbs oxygen is called hemoglobin, and the ability of the hemoglobin to utilize oxygen can be reduced by carbon monoxide from smoking or exhaust fumes. Heavy smokers may experience the symptoms of hypoxia at much lower altitudes than non-smokers.

You can experience the symptoms of hypoxia under controlled conditions in an altitude chamber at a military facility. The local office of the Federal Aviation Administration has details on how to apply for this valuable physiology training. You may say, "it can't happen to me", but when you find that you can't write your name or add a column of figures when deprived of oxygen in an altitude chamber, you will be convinced of the value of supplemental oxygen. The regulations governing use of oxygen are discussed in Chapter 15.

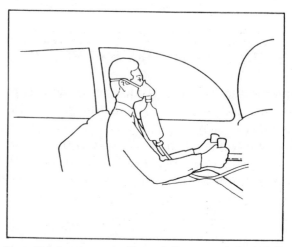

Figure 13-4. Supplementary Oxygen is Recommended at Altitudes Above 10,000' MSL

HYPERVENTILATION

Rapid breathing under stress can reduce the amount of carbon dioxide in the lungs, leading to lightheadedness, drowsiness, tingling in the fingers, and eventual unconsciousness. The body requires a certain level of carbon dioxide in order to trigger the breathing reflex.

Flight situations which seem quite normal to a pilot may create stress in passengers, and hyperventilation is usually a passenger problem. A conscious slowing of the breathing rate will relieve symptoms of hyperventilation, and breathing into cupped hands or a paper bag to increase intake of carbon dioxide will also help. It is usually difficult to get children to control their breathing rate, and the cupped hands or bag method is most effective with them.

Figure 13-5. Hyperventilation Causes Dizziness and May Lead to Loss of Consciousness

It is possible to experience the symptoms of hypoxia and hyperventilation simultaneously (if you are above 14,000 feet without oxygen you will surely be under stress!). If oxygen *is* available it should be set to deliver full flow immediately. As is the case in many other precarious flight situations, the best preventive is not getting into the situation in the first place.

CARBON MONOXIDE POISONING

Even small amounts of carbon monoxide in the lungs inhibit the ability of the blood's hemoglobin to use oxygen efficiently, and the most common source of carbon monoxide in flight is the airplane's heater system. Carbon monoxide is tasteless and odorless, and the smell of exhaust gas cannot be relied on to warn of its presence. Chemical detectors which darken in the presence of carbon monoxide are available at pilot supply stores. If the smell of exhaust *is* noticed, of course, the heater should be shut off, all air vents opened, and a landing made at the nearest airport. If carbon monoxide does get into your bloodstream, it may take several days to dissipate — you can't get the heater fixed and take off again the same day without the possibility of experiencing hypoxia.

FLYING AND DIVING

Many pilots enjoy both flying and scuba diving, and if you are in this group you should be aware that the two do not mix. Diving immediately after landing should cause no problems. Flying immediately after diving will cause problems, because the nitrogen forced into your joints while underwater may cause the "bends" in flight due to the reduced pressure at altitude. An extra day on the beach will probably eliminate that possibility.

EAR PROBLEMS

The changing pressures of flight can cause painful ear problems if the pilot or passenger is unable to equalize the pressure in the middle ear. When the airplane is climbing, air trapped in the middle ear expands and exits through the eustachian tubes into the mouth, causing no problems. During descent, however, the pilot or passenger must attempt to equalize the pressure in the middle ear by yawning, swallowing, or tensing the throat muscles. Chewing gum can help. Holding the nose and "blowing gently" with the head held back can open the eustachian tubes — this is called the "valsalva" maneuver. CAUTION: don't ever "valsalva" when you have a head cold, as serious sinus infection may result.

If a passenger is experiencing ear blockage during descent, it may be necessary to climb until the pain is relieved, and then descend at a reduced rate. Because the potential for ear problems is always present when flying, pilots should not fly with any upper respiratory infection, such as a cold or sore throat. Be very wary of accepting passenger's assurances that, although they have a cold, they will not be bothered by flying. Remember, the problem becomes apparent on the way *down*, after it is too late to avoid it!

VERTIGO

There are several illusions in flight which can lead to vertigo, which is best described as a disagreement between what your eyes and your body report to your brain. Almost everyone has had the experience of sitting in an automobile when an adjacent automobile begins to move slowly — the natural reaction is to step on your brakes, because for an instant your brain isn't sure which vehicle is moving. That is one form of vertigo, or spatial disorientation.

There are many situations which can lead to spatial disorientation in flight, but the most common is loss of visual reference to the horizon. Non-instrument rated pilots, or pilots who have not learned to use the flight instruments when visual reference is lost, react to bodily sensations and may lose control of the airplane. It is not possible to "fly by the seat of your pants".

Your middle ear contains three tubes filled with liquid, and the inner surfaces of these tubes are lined with thousands of tiny hairs which sense movement of the liquid. It is the message that these tiny hairs sends to your brain that provides your sense of balance. When a turn begins, your brain gets the correct message, but if the maneuver is protracted the liquid stops moving, and the information to the brain is that the turn has stopped. If you then actually stop the turn, the liquid begins to flow the other way, and your middle ear tells your brain that the turn has reversed! During your training for the private pilot certificate, you will be taught how to use the flight instruments to keep the airplane under control while returning to visual conditions.

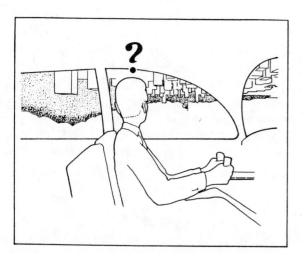

Figure 13-6. Disorientation Results When the Senses Disagree

The most valuable of the five senses in flight is vision: believe the instruments, and avoid head movement. Another source of illusion and the potential for vertigo is flight on a clear, starlit night with scattered lights on the ground. With no horizon to separate the lights on the ground from the stars, it is possible to become disoriented and lose control of the airplane. Again, training in the use of the flight instruments will keep you right side up.

NIGHT VISION AND SCANNING

Your eyes will adapt to dim light conditions, but only after a considerable period of time. It takes at least 30 minutes in total darkness for complete dark adaptation, and that adaptation can be lost by a few seconds exposure to a bright light. The use of red lights for cockpit lighting at night causes difficulty in reading aeronautical charts, and dim white lighting is standard. You should make every effort to become dark adapted, however, because other airplanes can only be detected at night by their lights and you want to detect them as far away as possible.

Scanning the sky for other aircraft is just as important as maintaining control of your airplane, and deserves equal attention. You should not limit your scan to those areas ahead of the airplane at your altitude, but should scan systematically from over your left shoulder to as far to the right as you can see, looking both below and above your altitude. A constant sweep of the eyes will not be effective, because your eyes need time to focus on objects, so momentarily stopping for at least a second will enhance your ability to detect other airplanes. At night, because of the way your eyes work, you will see only those objects which are slightly out of your direct line of sight, and your scan will have to be slower and more deliberate.

PHYSIOLOGICAL EFFECTS
SECTION REVIEW

1. A state of temporary confusion resulting from misleading information being sent to the brain by various sensory organs is defined as

    1. spatial disorientation.
    2. hyperventilation.
    3. hypoxia.
    4. motion sickness.

2. To preclude the effects of hypoxia, you should

    1. avoid flying above 10,000 ft. MSL for prolonged periods without breathing supplemental oxygen.
    2. rely on your body's built-in alarm system to warn when you are not getting enough oxygen.
    3. try swallowing, yawning, or holding the nose and mouth shut and forcibly try to exhale.
    4. avoid hyperventilation which is caused by rapid heavy breathing and results in excessive carbon dioxide in the bloodstream.

3. Hypoxia is caused by

    1. nitrogen bubbles forming in the blood at high altitudes.
    2. trapped gasses in the body.
    3. reduced atmospheric pressure.
    4. toxic substances in the blood.

4. What is the most effective way to use the eyes during night flight?

    1. Look only at far away, dim lights.
    2. Scan slowly to permit off center viewing.
    3. Blink the eyes rapidly when concentrating on an object.
    4. Concentrate directly on each object for a few seconds.

As you plan a cross-country flight, you know that the ability to maneuver in three dimensions makes you responsible for being aware at all times of your position, both geographic and vertical. You must insure that you are always in compliance with the airspace regulations of the FARs. These regulations are intended to keep airplanes safely separated and, in the case of VFR pilots, to provide minimum visibility and cloud clearance distances so that conflicting traffic can be seen in time for corrective action to be taken. "See and be seen" is the basis of safe operations in the National Airspace System.

CONTROLLED vs UNCONTROLLED AIRSPACE

You will encounter the terms controlled and uncontrolled airspace frequently, and you must not assume that flight in controlled airspace means that Big Brother will be watching you to detect violations, or that uncontrolled airspace is a no-man's land for flight. For your purposes as a VFR pilot, controlled and uncontrolled airspace refer to visibility and cloud clearance standards, nothing more. Controlled airspace is "controlled" to protect pilots flying under instrument flight rules from conflict with pilots flying under visual flight rules; when a pilot operating under IFR pops out of a cloud there should be enough visibility and cloud clearance to see and avoid a VFR flight. For that reason, you should accept the restrictions discussed in this chapter *as minimums* and allow more leeway whenever possible.

In any discussion of airspace, there are several terms that sound alike and tend to confuse pilots, and these will be defined before going further.

CONTROLLED AIRSPACE is a term that includes several airspace designations. Look at the Sectional chart excerpt and note the blue and magenta tint lines that seem to include virtually all of the chart — they represent the horizontal boundaries of the controlled airspace (figure 14-1). Note that just east of Mount Rainier, near the bottom of the chart, there is a triangular area not surrounded by a blue tint — that is uncontrolled airspace. Included in the tinted areas on the chart excerpt are Control Areas, Control Zones, Victor airways, a Terminal Control Area, a Terminal Radar Service Area, and Airport Traffic Areas; each will be discussed separately.

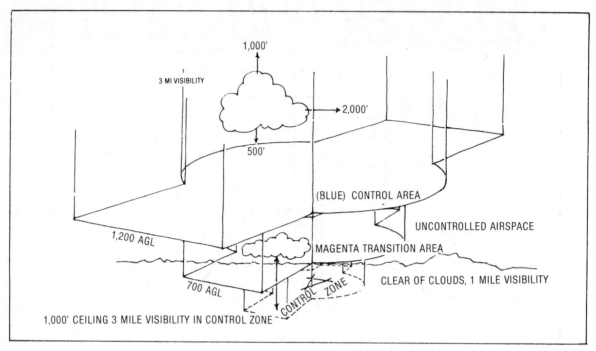

Figure 14-1. Color Control Areas

CONTROL ZONES are shown on the Sectional chart as dashed lines surrounding airport symbols (figure 14-2). Note on the chart excerpt the control zones at Olympia, Fort Lewis, McChord AFB, and Paine Field. There are three airports with control zones clustered in the Seattle metropolitan area.

They are Seattle-Tacoma, Boeing Field, and Renton. Seattle-Tacoma's control zone is outlined by T's, indicating that no fixed-wing Special VFR operations are allowed. You will have to look closely to find the boundaries of the Boeing Field and Renton control zones. In congested areas, chart details may make it difficult to see the boundaries, yet you must know what is required of you to operate in that airspace.

Whether or not you can fly into or out of a control zone without a clearance is entirely dependent on the weather. If the ground visibility is reported to be less than 3 statute miles, you cannot take off, land, or enter the traffic pattern under basic visual flight rules. If there is no weather observer to report ground visibility, flight visibility becomes the controlling factor and you are the judge. If you intend to operate beneath the ceiling in a control zone, as you would during takeoff or landing, the reported ceiling must be at least 1,000'

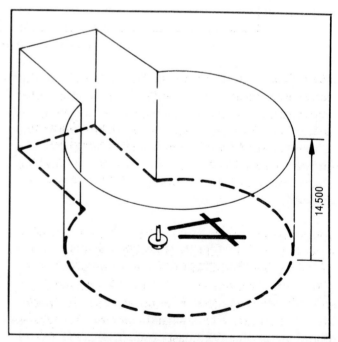

Figure 14-2. Control Zone

above ground level. If you are flying VFR above the clouds, and want to pass through the control zone, go ahead — the ceiling restriction has no effect on you. Either of these restrictions *will* affect you: visibility of less than 3 miles *or* a ceiling of less than 1,000' will

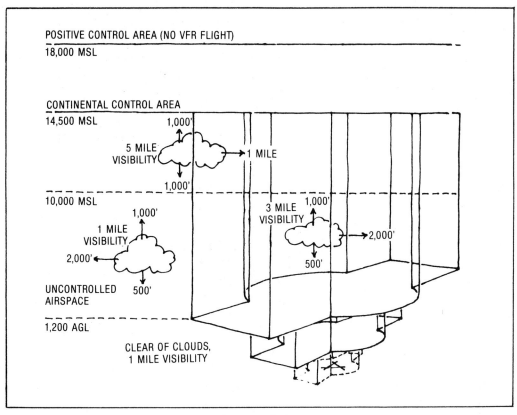

POSITIVE CONTROL AREA (NO VFR FLIGHT)
18,000 MSL

CONTINENTAL CONTROL AREA
14,500 MSL   1,000'
5 MILE
VISIBILITY   1 MILE
1,000'

10,000 MSL   1,000'
1,000'   3 MILE
1 MILE   VISIBILITY
VISIBILITY   2,000'
2,000'
500'
UNCONTROLLED   500'
AIRSPACE

1,200 AGL
CLEAR OF CLOUDS,
1 MILE VISIBILITY

Figure 14-3. Controlled Airspace

make that control zone IFR. When you hear the expression "basic VFR is a 1,000 foot ceiling and 3 miles visibility", that statement applies only within the dashed lines defining a control zone. In the continental U. S. and eastern Alaska, control zones extend from the surface to 14,500' MSL, the base of the Continental Control Area, and to infinity in western Alaska and Hawaii.

Controlled airspace begins at ground level in a control zone. In CONTROL AREAS, controlled airspace begins 700 feet above the ground in the magenta tinted areas, 1,200 feet above the ground in the blue tinted areas, and "where designated" in mountainous areas (figure 14-3). For an example of what that means, look at the mountainous area northeast of Seattle where the blue tint surrounds an area marked "9,500 MSL". In that location, instead of trying to figure whether you are within 1,200 feet of the terrain, you know that controlled airspace begins at 9,500' indicated altitude. All of these colored areas define CONTROL AREAS, but don't forget that except inside of those dashed lines defining

control zones, there is uncontrolled airspace *underneath* the control areas. Control areas extend up to 14,500' MSL, where they join the Continental Control Area.

Victor airways, the blue lines identified with VOR radials, are eight miles wide, centered on the airway. On an airway, controlled airspace begins at 1,200' above the ground and goes right up 18,000' MSL, which is the floor of Positive Control Airspace. That altitude is also the base of the high altitude route structure, where airways are "Jet Routes" — J5, J20, etc. Airways are control areas because they are tinted blue. If you are flying on an airway under Visual Flight Rules, you are expected to stay on the centerline except when you are climbing or descending. Move off to the right while climbing or descending, however, because IFR pilots will maintain the centerline at all times.

Now that you know where controlled airspace is, what does it mean? It means that you must fly 500' below the clouds or 1,000' above the clouds, stay 2,000' horizontally from all clouds, and have at least 3 miles flight visibility. These very reasonable *minimum* requirements guard against someone popping out of a cloud before you have time to react. The magenta areas, where controlled airspace extends within 700 feet of the ground, are called transition areas because they afford the instrument pilot a little more protection from itinerant VFR flights when descending on an instrument approach. These cloud clearance and visibility rules only apply up to 10,000' MSL. Above that altitude there is no speed limit, and jets can and do come roaring out of clouds at 400-500 knots. At those speeds, 3 miles visibility and 2,000' from clouds just isn't enough, so above 10,000' you must fly 1,000' above *or* below the clouds, 1 mile horizontally from all clouds, and have 5 miles flight visibility.

UNCONTROLLED AIRSPACE is what is left when all of the controlled airspace has been identified. In the airspace between the surface and 700' AGL in the magenta tinted areas, between the surface and 1,200' AGL in the blue tinted areas, between the terrain and "where designated" in the mountains, and in areas like the little triangle east of Mount Rainier you will find uncontrolled airspace (figure 14-4). In uncontrolled airspace less than 1,200' above the ground you need

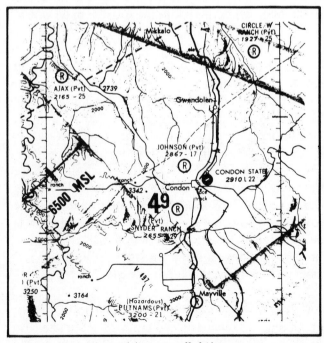

Figure 14-4. Uncontrolled Airspace

only 1 mile flight visibility and must remain clear of all clouds in order to fly VFR legally. In that little triangle east of the mountain you can get away with 1 mile visibility, but if you climb above 1,200' AGL you will have to have the same 500' below, 1,000' above, and 2,000' horizontally that you had to have in controlled airspace. One mile flight visibility is not a whole lot, even at 60 knots. Before you get excited about flying legally with only one mile visibility, go up with a qualified instrument pilot when visibility is down to one mile — you will be shocked to learn how little that is.

When you get up above 10,000' you will find that nothing has changed — the jets fly just as fast whether the airspace is controlled or uncontrolled, and you are still required to fly no less than 1,000' above, 1,000' below, and 1 mile laterally from clouds, with 5 miles flight visibility.

THE CONTINENTAL CONTROL AREA begins at 14,500' MSL; above that altitude virtually all airspace is controlled. The FAA makes exceptions to the visibility and cloud clearance requirements if you are inclined to fly over mountains which are more than 14,500 ft. tall — if you stay within 1,500' of the peak you are in uncontrolled airspace. No change in visibility or cloud clearance requirements occurs at 14,500' (except over mountain tops), and it is a distinction of interest only to instrument pilots. Below 14,500', when instrument pilots fly into uncontrolled airspace they are on their own insofar as the ATC system is concerned —the controllers have no authority or responsibility for air traffic in uncontrolled airspace.

POSITIVE CONTROL AIRSPACE begins at 18,000' MSL and is of major importance to VFR pilots of turbocharged airplanes: all operations above 18,000' MSL must be under Instrument Flight Rules, and the pilot and airplane must both be IFR current. Even if your pressurized, turbocharged airplane is capable of climbing to 24,000', it's "no go" until you have an instrument rating.

TERMINAL CONTROL AREAs are designated at major hub airports, and are intended to insure that air traffic controllers are aware of the position and intentions of all airplanes operating within TCA airspace under

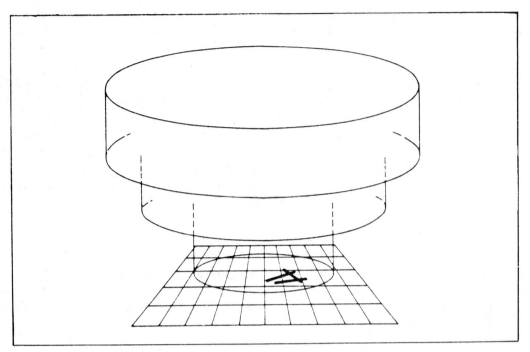

Figure 14-5. Terminal Control Area

either visual or instrument flight rules (figure 14-5). This is accomplished by requiring that all airplanes intending to operate in a TCA receive an ATC clearance *before* penetrating the TCA.

Under present (1985) regulations there are 23 Terminal Control Areas divided into Group I and Group II. To operate in either a Group I or Group II TCA you must have an ATC clearance, a two-way radio, a VOR or TACAN receiver and a 4096 code transponder (that is the only type of transponder there is). To operate in Group I TCAs, which are the very busiest, your transponder must also have altitude reporting capability (Mode C) and you must hold a Private Pilot certificate or better. An instrument rating or an instrument clearance is not required to operate in any TCA.

Seattle's Group II TCA is outlined in blue on the sectional chart excerpt. Note that it is divided into sectors, each identified with the upper limit of the TCA (7,000' MSL), and the base of the TCA for that sector, varying from 5,000' at the northern edge to the surface right at the airport.

AIRPORT TRAFFIC AREAs exist at airports with operating control towers. They are 5 statute miles in radius (centered on the airport), and extend from the surface of the airport up to but not including 3,000' AGL (figure 14-6). Because the tower controller needs to know the intentions of any pilot operating in the airport traffic area in order to safely coordinate arriving and departing flights, you must communicate with the tower for clearance to enter the ATA and for clearance to take off.

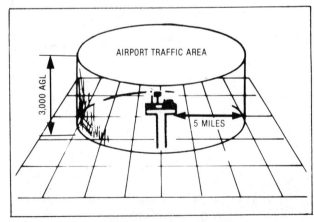

Figure 14-6. Airport Traffic Area

If you intend to pass through the airport traffic area at an altitude of less than 3,000' above the surface, you must receive permission to do so. Passing over an airport *higher* than 3,000' AGL requires no clearance at all. Airports with control towers have their airport symbols printed in blue on aeronautical charts. Many are not full-time towers, and when the tower is not operating there is no airport traffic area. There is no marking on a chart showing the boundaries of an airport traffic area — they are all the same.

SPECIAL VFR

When flying more than 1,200' above the ground in a control area or more than 700' above the ground in a transition area, you are complying with visual flight rules if you have 3 miles flight visibility, are 500' below, 1,000' above, and 2,000' horizontally from any clouds. Suppose you discover that the weather at your destination airport, which has a control zone, is reported as visibility 2½ miles, ceiling 900' broken; that is less than basic VFR minimums (ceiling 1,000' *and* visibility 3 miles). Is there any way you can legally enter the control zone and land? Or, if you are at the airport waiting for takeoff, and know that the weather outside the control zone is VFR and forecast to improve, can you leave?

The answer is yes, but in both situations you will need a Special VFR clearance from Air Traffic Control. You may request the clearance through the Flight Service Station or through the tower, but you must have a Special VFR clearance to operate in a control zone when the weather is less than basic VFR. Special VFR minimums are the same as in uncontrolled airspace: 1 mile visibility and clear of clouds. Because clouds are virtually invisible at night, Special VFR clearances at night will only be issued to instrument rated pilots.

Some large airports prohibit Special VFR operations by fixed wing aircraft within their control zones, and in these instances the control zone is outlined with "T"'s instead of dashes (see Seattle-Tacoma Airport on the Sectional chart excerpt). When the tower or Flight Service Station says, "The control zone is below basic VFR minimums, what are your intentions?", if the visibility is at least one mile and you can stay clear of the clouds say "I request a Special VFR clearance."

SPECIAL USE AIRSPACE

These airspace divisions are marked on your Sectional chart and you must be aware of their significance. With the exception of Prohibited and Restricted areas, all special use airspace is used on a "keep a sharp lookout" basis and no clearance of any kind is required.

PROHIBITED AREAS are just that (figure 14-7).

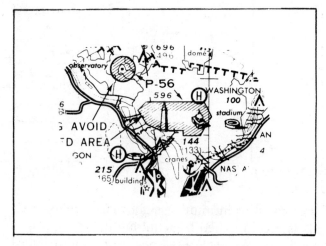

Figure 14-7. Prohibited Area

There are not very many, they are identified on aeronautical charts, and you simply cannot fly into one. You may be able to fly over one, however — the vertical extent of a Prohibited area is included in a tabulation of special use airspace on the chart.

RESTRICTED AREAS are far more prevalent. They are used by the military services and denote hazards to aircraft such as firing ranges, bombing ranges, guided missile ranges, etc. Each restricted area has a designation and there is a tabulation on the chart identifying the controlling agency, the hours of operation of the Restricted Area, and its vertical limits. You must receive a clearance from the controlling agency (or through the FSS) to enter a Restricted Area. You can always fly around the area, and possibly over it, but it is always worth a call to find out if a clearance straight through is available.

MILITARY OPERATING AREAS, or MOAs, require no clearance. You must use extreme caution while in a MOA — you are in the military's airspace and they are

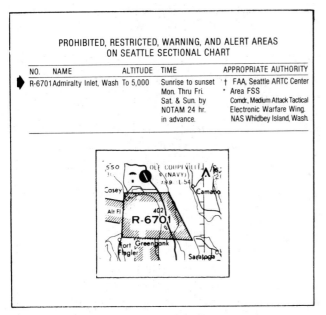

Figure 14-8. Restricted Area

exempt from restrictions on aerobatics. Information on military activities in a MOA can be obtained from a Flight Service Station within 100 miles of the MOA.

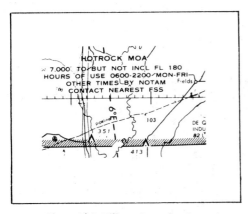

Figure 14-9. Military Operating Area

MILITARY TRAINING ROUTES are not airspace divisions but are shown on charts to warn pilots of their existence. These routes are designated below 10,000' MSL and aircraft speeds may be in excess of 250 knots. Note that on the sectional chart there are several grey lines identified as "VR" (visual rules) or "IR" (instrument rules) with a route number. Three digit route numbers indicate training activities more than 1,500' above ground level while four digit identifiers indicate military training activity less than 1,500' AGL. Look at

the sectional chart excerpt for the military training route crossing from north to south. You would expect to encounter military aircraft flying under Visual Flight Rules less than 1,500' above the ground at speeds of over 250 knots. Legally, you could be flying along in uncontrolled airspace less than 1,200' above the ground with 1 mile visibility, and staying clear of all clouds, and have a military aircraft approaching at 250 knots or more. Be especially alert when crossing a Military Training Route, and have much more than the minimum required visibility and cloud clearance.

The nearest Flight Service Station is your source of information on military training activities. Tell the FSS specialist your position, route, and destination when asking about military activity. Military fighters move far too fast for you to try to see and avoid them, and their pilots are occupied with mission duties. Military pilots do adhere to the published routes and altitudes, and the civilian pilot can easily acquire the information necessary to avoid the military flights.

ALERT AREAS warn pilots of a high volume of military training activity (figure 14-10). Again, no clearance is required but you must exercise extreme caution. Collision avoidance is every pilot's responsibility in an Alert Area — the FARs apply equally to civil and military pilots in Alert Areas.

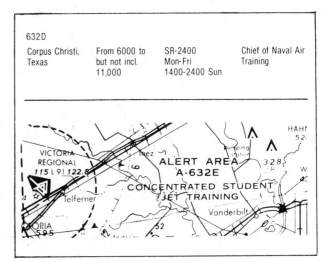

Figure 14-10. Alert Area

WARNING AREAS are similar to Restricted Areas but no clearance is required because Warning Areas are over international waters outside the 3 mile limit. The type of activities that take place in a Warning Area are just like those in a Restricted Area, so make your own decision on whether you want to venture into a Warning Area. You can check on periods of activity with the Flight Service Station.

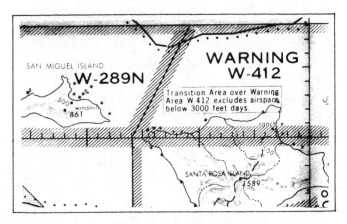

Figure 14-11. Warning Area

TERMINAL RADAR SERVICE AREAS are shown on Sectional charts with a magenta outline —there is one on your Seattle Sectional excerpt. Its vertical limits are identified in the same manner as those of Terminal Control Areas. Each TRSA has an associated radar facility which will provide you with limited radar vectoring and provide separation from all IFR and all *participating* VFR traffic. Not all VFR pilots participate, and you must not rely exclusively on the radar controller to warn you of traffic. That point cannot be emphasized too strongly: pilots who do not check in with the radar controller and/or who do not use their transponders will not be called out to you as traffic (and there are an alarming number of them). As a VFR pilot you cannot accept any headings or altitudes from the radar controller that will cause you to get closer to the clouds than VFR minimums permit. The controller cannot see the clouds on the radar.

Terminal Radar Service is voluntary — you can decline radar service if it is offered, but the use of this service is strongly recommended. If you are departing from an airport where Terminal Radar Service is available, you should request it from the ground controller; if you are in flight, call the appropriate approach control frequency shown on the sectional chart or in the Airport/Facility Directory. Use of radar service is an exellent method of transiting the airspace around busy airports or getting vectors to the traffic pattern at a strange airport.

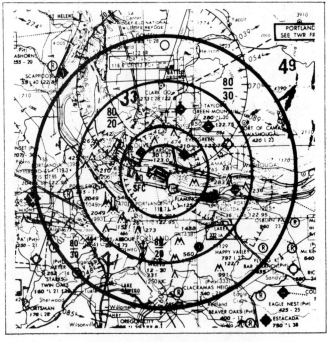

Figure 14-12. Terminal Radar Service Area

CONTROLLED AIRSPACE

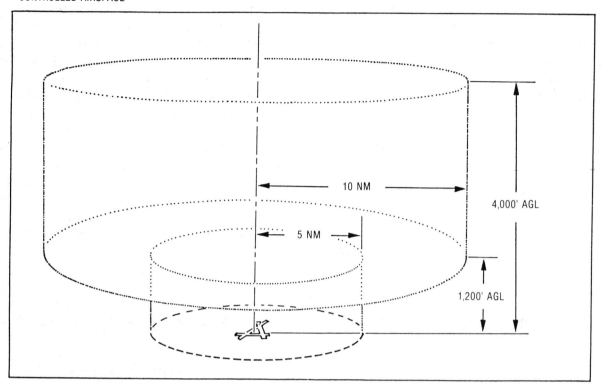

Figure 14-13. Airport Radar Service Area

AIRPORT RADAR SERVICE AREA

Terminal Radar Service Areas vary in shape and vertical dimensions, and the type of radar service offered varies. To standardize, the FAA is implementing Airport Radar Service Areas to replace TRSAs. All ARSAs will be the same size and shape (figure 14-13): at the surface they will be 5 miles in radius, coinciding with the Airport Traffic Area, and at 1,200' above the surface they will expand to 10 miles in radius. Each ARSA will have a top 4,000' above ground level. Pilots operating in the ARSA will be required to maintain two-way radio communication with ATC to depart, land, or pass through, although no formal clearance will be required.

There will be no special equipment or pilot certification requirements. Radar vectoring will continue to be available on a voluntary basis in the airspace surrounding the ARSA.

NATIONAL AIRSPACE SYSTEM
SECTION REVIEW

1. Under what conditions, if any, may civil pilots enter a restricted area?

    1. For takeoff and landing to take care of official business.
    2. With the controlling agency's authorization.
    3. On airways with ATC clearance.
    4. Under no condition.

2. What type airspace is designated as VOR Federal airways?

    1. Control areas.
    2. Positive control areas.
    3. Transition areas.
    4. Continental control areas.

3. What is the upper limit of a control zone in the conterminous United States?

    1. 2,000 ft. above the surface.
    2. Up to, but not including, 3,000 ft. AGL.
    3. The base of the continental control area.
    4. There is no upper limit.

4. What are the horizontal limits of an airport traffic area?

    1. 3 SM from the airport boundary.
    2. 5 SM from the airport boundary.
    3. 5 SM from the geographical center of the airport.
    4. 3 SM from the geographical center of the airport.

5. An airport traffic area is automatically in effect when

    1. its associated control tower is in operation.
    2. the weather is below VFR minimums.
    3. nighttime hours exist.
    4. radar service is available.

6. Unless otherwise specified, Federal airways extend from

    1. 1,200 ft. above the surface upward to 14,500 ft. MSL and are 16 NM wide.
    2. 700 ft. above the surface upward to the continental control area and are 10 NM wide.
    3. 1,200 ft. above the surface upward to 18,000 ft. MSL and are 8 NM wide.
    4. the surface upward to 18,000 ft. MSL and are 4 NM wide.

7. Control areas within the contiguous United States extend upward from either 700 ft. or 1,200 ft. above the surface to, but not including

    1. the base of the continental control area.
    2. 3,000 ft. MSL.
    3. 18,000 ft. MSL.
    4. 24,000 ft. MSL.

8. What is the purpose of an airport traffic area?

   1. To provide for the control of aircraft landing and taking off from an airport with an operating control tower.
   2. To provide for the control of all aircraft operating in the vicinity of an airport with an operating control tower.
   3. To provide for the control of air traffic within a control zone that has an operating control tower.
   4. To restrict aircraft without radios from operating in the vicinity of an airport with an operating control tower.

9. What is the minimum weather condition required for airplanes operating under special VFR in a control zone?

   1. 1-mi. flight visibility.
   2. 1-mi. flight visibility and 1,000 ft. ceiling.
   3. 3-mi. flight visibility and 1,000 ft. ceiling.
   4. 3-mi. flight visibility.

10. For VFR flight operations above 10,000 ft. MSL and more than 1,200 ft. AGL, the minimum horizontal distance from clouds required is

    1. 1,000 ft.
    2. 2,000 ft.
    3. 1 mile.
    4. 5 miles.

11. No person may operate an airplane within a control zone at night under special VFR unless

    1. the flight can be conducted 500 ft. below the clouds.
    2. an instructor is aboard.
    3. the airplane is equipped for instrument flight.
    4. the flight visibility is at least 3 mi.

12. The minimum ceiling and visibility to operate an airplane VFR in a control zone are

    1. 500 ft. and 1 mi.
    2. 1,000 ft. and 3 mi.
    3. 1,400 ft. and 2 mi.
    4. 2,000 ft. and 3 mi.

13. In which type of airspace are VFR flights prohibited?

    1. Terminal control area.
    2. Continental control area.
    3. Control zone.
    4. Positive control area.

14. What minimum pilot certification is required for operating in a Group I terminal control area?

    1. Student pilot certificate with appropriate logbook endorsements.
    2. Private pilot certificate.
    3. Private pilot certificate with an instrument rating.
    4. Commercial pilot certificate.

15. What minimum navigation equipment is required for operating in a Group I terminal control area?

    1. VOR or TACAN receiver.
    2. VOR or TACAN receiver and a 4096 code transponder.
    3. VOR or TACAN and a 4096 code transponder with Mode C capability.
    4. DME, VOR or TACAN, and a transponder.

16. What procedure is recommended when climbing or descending VFR on an airway?

    1. Offset 4 mi. or more from centerline of the airway before changing altitude.
    2. Squawk 1400 on the aircraft transponder with Mode C selected.
    3. Advise the nearest FSS of the desired altitude change.
    4. Climb or descend on the right side of the airway center line.

The FAA expects you to be familiar with all of the Federal Aviation Regulations which apply to your flight operations, but as you read through the FARs you should be able to distinguish between those that are nice to know but do not affect your day-to-day flying (carriage of candidates in Federal elections, for example), and those which you simply *must* know (basic visual flight rules or right-of-way rules). This chapter will discuss those regulations which require explanation or illustration for full understanding.

Part 61 — Certification:
Pilots and Flight Instructors

61.3: *Requirements for certificates, ratings, and authorizations.* If you are going to act as pilot in command or as a required flight crewmember you must have *in your possession* your pilot certificate and medical certificate. You must present these documents for inspection upon request by an official of the FAA, the NTSB, or any law enforcement officer.

61.5: *Certificates and ratings.* There are five pilot certificates: student, private, commercial, airline transport pilot, and flight instructor.

STUDENT PILOT: Limited to solo or dual (instructional) flights only.

PRIVATE PILOT: May carry passengers or cargo, day or night, as long as no charge is made. Is permitted to share expenses with passengers. May fly in conjunction with employment if flying is only incidental to the employment.

COMMERCIAL PILOT: may fly for compensation or hire. Must also meet requirements of FAR Part 135 to fly as air taxi pilot.

AIRLINE TRANSPORT PILOT: may fly as pilot-in-command on an airline flight or on a multiengine scheduled commuter flight.

Your certificate will carry a category and class rating such as Airplane: Single Engine Land (figure 15-1). You cannot carry passengers unless you hold the appropriate category and class ratings, and an instrument rating is required for IFR whether you are carrying passengers or not. Figure 15-1 shows the categories and the applicable class ratings.

CATEGORY/CLASS	TYPE
AIRPLANE	
single-engine land	ex. B-727
multi-engine land	
single-engine sea	
multi-engine sea	
ROTORCRAFT	
helicopter	ex. S-61
gyroplane	
LIGHTER-THAN-AIR	
airship	n.a.
free balloon	
GLIDER	
n.a.	

Figure 15-1. Categories and Class Ratings

61.19: *Duration of pilot certificates.* Your student pilot certificate expires at the end of the 24th calendar month after it was issued. *All other pilot certificates have no expiration date* and are kept active by having a current medical certificate and a current biennial flight review.

61.23: *Duration of medical certificates.* The type of medical certificate you hold determines the privileges you can exercise as a pilot, according to the certificate you hold. Figure 15-2 lists the classes of medical certificates, their durations, and the privileges authorized during the valid period. Medical certificates expire at the end of the *calendar* month; for example, a physical taken on the 15th of the month will expire at the *end* of the 6th, 12th, or 24th month, depending on the class of physical.

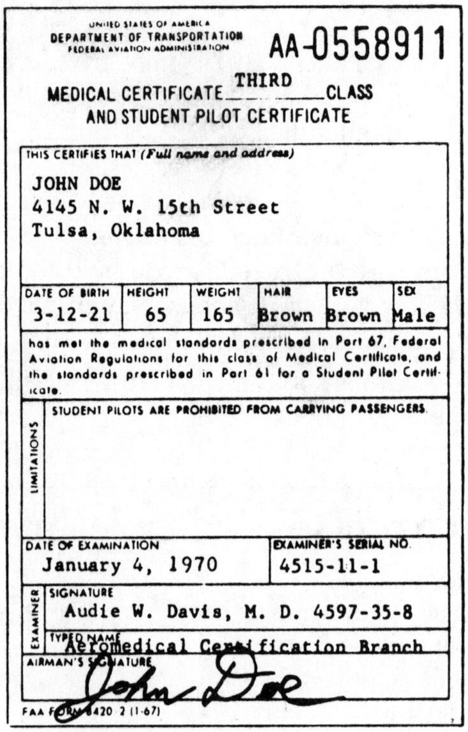
UNITED STATES OF AMERICA
DEPARTMENT OF TRANSPORTATION
FEDERAL AVIATION ADMINISTRATION
AA-0558911
MEDICAL CERTIFICATE THIRD CLASS
AND STUDENT PILOT CERTIFICATE

THIS CERTIFIES THAT *(Full name and address)*
JOHN DOE
4145 N. W. 15th Street
Tulsa, Oklahoma

DATE OF BIRTH	HEIGHT	WEIGHT	HAIR	EYES	SEX
3-12-21	65	165	Brown	Brown	Male

has met the medical standards prescribed in Part 67, Federal Aviation Regulations for this class of Medical Certificate, and the standards prescribed in Part 61 for a Student Pilot Certificate.

LIMITATIONS: STUDENT PILOTS ARE PROHIBITED FROM CARRYING PASSENGERS.

DATE OF EXAMINATION	EXAMINER'S SERIAL NO.
January 4, 1970	4515-11-1

EXAMINER SIGNATURE: Audie W. Davis, M. D. 4597-35-8
TYPED NAME: Aeromedical Certification Branch
AIRMAN'S SIGNATURE: John Doe
FAA FORM 8420 2 (1-67)

To Exercise Privileges	Valid Months
THIRD CLASS MEDICAL CERTIFICATE	
Private Pilot	24
SECOND CLASS MEDICAL CERTIFICATE	
Commercial Pilot	12
Private Pilot	24
FIRST CLASS MEDICAL CERTIFICATE	
Airline Transport Pilot	6
Commercial Pilot	12
Private Pilot	24

To exercise the privileges of their pilot certificates, ATPs must get new medicals every 6 months, commercial pilots every 12 months, and private pilots every 24 months.

Medical certificates expire the last day of the 6th, 12th, or 24th month after they are issued, depending on the class of certificate.

Figure 15-2. Medical Certificates

Memory aid: M&M — medicals and maintenance, good until the last day of the month.

61.31: *General limitations*: Type ratings are required for airplanes weighing over 12,500 pounds or those powered by turbojets. A commercial pilot cannot operate an aircraft for compensation or hire without holding an appropriate category and class rating for that aircraft. No person may operate an airplane with more than 200 horsepower, or one that has retractable landing gear, flaps, and a controllable propeller, without having received flight instruction in that airplane, with a logbook endorsement to that effect made by the instructor.

61.51: *Pilot logbooks.* As a student pilot, you can log only solo and dual instruction time. After you have your private pilot certificate, you can log pilot in command time, and you will be able to count your pre-certification solo time as PIC. You can log as second in command time only that flight time when you act as SIC of an airplane requiring more than one pilot, or when operating under regulations which require more than one pilot (turbojets and aircraft weighing more than 12,500 pounds). You can log as instrument flight time only that time during which you operate the airplane solely by reference to instruments, under actual or simulated instrument conditions. As a student pilot, you must carry your logbook on all solo cross-country flights as evidence of the required instructor clearances and endorsements.

61.57: *Recent flight experience; pilot in command.* You may not act as pilot in command of an aircraft unless within the preceding 24 months (*not* calendar months!) you have received a biennial flight review or have taken a checkride or proficiency check required by the FAA. Read that again. *Unless you have a current biennial flight review (or equivalent), you cannot even fly solo.* You may not carry passengers unless you have current experience, and that means 3 takeoffs and landings within the preceding 90 days in an aircraft of the same category and class as that in which you plan to carry passengers. You may fly solo to make those three takeoffs and landings, of course. If you are going to carry passengers in a tailwheel airplane, your 3 takeoffs and landings must have been in a taildragger, and to a full stop — no touch-and-goes permitted. Touch-and-goes are approved for tricycle gear airplanes. To carry passengers at night you must, within the preceding 90 days, have made 3 takeoffs and landings to a full stop *in an aircraft of the same category and class* during the period from one hour after sunset to one hour before sunrise. That means that if you are current at night in single engine landplanes, for instance, your night currency does not extend to multiengine landplanes, and you must do the 3 full-stop landings at night before carrying passengers in a twin at night.

A current pilot is one who meets the requirement for 3 takeoffs and landings within 90 days, and who also has accomplished a satisfactory current biennial flight review.

61.60: *Change of address.* If you change your permanent mailing address and do not advise the FAA within 30 days you cannot exercise the privileges of your pilot certificate. Just as soon as you have notified them you are back in the air again.

61.63: *Additional aircraft ratings.* If you want to add a category or class rating to your certificate (rotorcraft might be a new category, multiengine land a new class rating), you must take a checkride, but no written examination is required for powered aircraft. You must present a logbook record that you have received instruction and are competent in the category or class for which the addition is sought.

61.89-61.93: *Student pilot, general limitations; cross-country requirements.* Student pilots may not carry passengers, act as pilot-in-command on an international flight, fly for compensation or hire, or fly in furtherance of a business. A student pilot must have his or her solo endorsement renewed every 90 days by a flight instructor, and must be specifically signed off for each cross-country flight with very narrowly limited exceptions.

61.118: *Private pilot privileges and limitations; pilot in command.* Private pilots may not accept compensation for flying; they are allowed to share the operating expenses of the flight with their passengers, but the FARs do not go into detail on just what is allowable as expenses (your insurance might not cover a flight for which a charge is made). Private pilots are allowed to fly in connection with their employment, if they are not being paid solely for their piloting activities. For instance, you can fly some clients over some property they are considering as a part of your duties in real estate, but you cannot be asked by your employer to transport customers on flights unrelated to real estate if your employer reimburses you. You, as a private pilot, may carry paying passengers on a flight for a charitable organization if the passengers have contributed to the organization. Approved charities are very narrowly defined, and the airplane must meet commercial maintenance requirements. You may demonstrate airplanes as an airplane salesperson after you have logged 200 hours of flight time.

PART 91 — AIR TRAFFIC AND GENERAL OPERATING RULES

91.3: *Responsibility and authority, pilot in command.* You, as the pilot in command, are the final authority as to the operation of your aircraft. In an emergency, you can take any action required to meet the emergency, although that action might violate the FARs. If, however, you do deviate from the rules in an emergency you may be *requested* to send a written report to the FAA. This regulation is your authority to tell a controlling agency that you cannot follow a directive because in your estimation to do so would be unsafe.

91.5: *Preflight action.* Before beginning any flight, you are required to familiarize yourself with *all* information concerning the flight. You can't say "I didn't know."

The information must always include runway lengths at airports you intend to use, and the takeoff and landing performance figures for your airplane under the conditions to be expected. For flights not in the vicinity of an airport (cross country flights), you must also have an alternative plan of action in mind if your planned flight cannot be completed, know the fuel requirements for the flight, and get weather reports *and forecasts* for the time of flight.

91.7: *Flight crewmembers at stations.* During takeoff and landing, each required crewmember must be at his or her station with seatbelt and shoulder harness fastened (if shoulder harnesses are provided). The shoulder harness can be unfastened if you can show that you cannot perform required duties — tune radios or operate controls — with it fastened.

91.9: *Careless or reckless operation.* This is a catch-all regulation. If you have any type of accident or incident, the assumption is that you must have been either careless or reckless. Your responsibility is to leave nothing to chance: use written checklists rather than rely on memory. As pilot in command, do not let anyone interfere with your control of the airplane (see 91.11 below).

91.11: *Liquor and drugs.* You cannot act as a crewmember of a civil aircraft within 8 hours of consuming alcoholic beverages. This is the "bottle to throttle" rule. Also, you may not allow a passenger under the influence of alcohol or drugs on your aircraft unless that person is under the care of medical personnel.

91.13: *Dropping objects.* You may not drop or allow to be dropped from your aircraft any object that creates a hazard to persons or property. If reasonable precautions to avoid injury or damage are taken, dropping objects is authorized.

91.14: *Use of safety belts.* Your passengers must have seatbelts fastened during takeoff and landing. It is your responsibility to insure that they are fastened, and that passengers have been briefed on how to fasten and unfasten their seatbelts.

91.15: *Parachutes and parachuting.* Parachutes must be worn by all occupants of an aircraft if aerobatic maneuvers are to be performed, unless the maneuvers are being taught in preparation for a certificate or rating. The FAA defines aerobatic maneuvers as any bank angle that exceeds 60°, or any nose-up or nose-down attitude that exceeds 30° relative to the horizon.

Flight training maneuvers for the private pilot and commercial pilot certificates do not include any acrobatic maneuvers. Any parachute used must have been packed within the preceding 120 days by a rated parachute rigger.

91.19: *Portable electronic devices.* Some portable electronic devices interfere with the airplane's radio navigation systems, and may not be used on air carrier airplanes or when operating IFR. You, as pilot in command, should ensure that any such device in use in your airplane will not affect the operation of your radios.

91.22: *Fuel requirements for flight under VFR.* You must carry enough fuel to reach your destination plus 30 minutes reserve for day VFR and 45 minutes for night VFR. It should be apparent that if everyone followed this rule, there would be no fuel exhaustion incidents. Don't be the exception to this rule.

91.24: *ATC transponder equipment and use.* You must have a transponder to enter any Terminal Control Area (TCA), and to enter a *Group I* TCA your transponder must have altitude reporting capability (Mode C). You also need Mode C to fly in controlled airspace above 12,500' MSL.

91.27: *Certifications required.* You must have your aircraft registration certificate and the airplane's *Certificate of Airworthiness* (figure 15-3) on board at all times; weight and balance data and the FAA Approved Flight Manual must also be carried, although markings and placards can substitute for the Flight Manual.

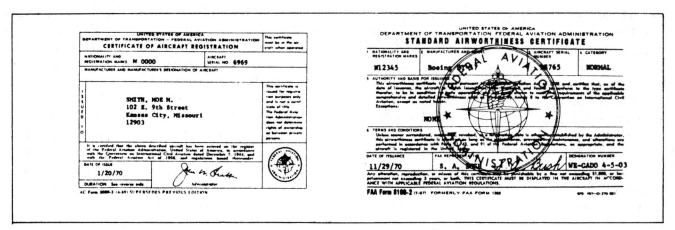

Figure 15-3. Certificate of Registration and Airworthiness Certificate

Airplane and engine logs are not required to be on board the airplane. Remember:

A   Aircraft registration.
R   Radio station license.
R   Registration.
O   Operating limitations (flight manual)
W   Weight and balance data.

The Certificate of Airworthiness must be displayed where it can be seen easily by passengers and crew.

91.32: *Supplemental oxygen.* If your flight will be above 12,500' MSL for more than 30 minutes, then you, the pilot, must use supplemental oxygen (either a portable tank or a fixed installation) for any time over 30 minutes. If the flight will be above 14,000' MSL, you must use oxygen at all times. At altitudes above 15,000' you must provide oxygen for your passengers. Be sure

they know how to use it before you leave the ground and NO SMOKING. Also, be sure that the oxygen system is serviced with *aviator's breathing oxygen!* Medical oxygen contains moisture (which may freeze) and welding oxygen contains impurities which may become health hazards.

91.42: *Experimental certificates; limitations.* You cannot fly an airplane with an EXPERIMENTAL certificate (such as a homebuilt airplane) over a densely populated area or on a congested airway.

91.67: *Right-of-way rules.* The right-of-way rules are first broken down on the basis of maneuverability, except that an aircraft in distress, regardless of category, has the right of way over all other aircraft (figure 15-4). Balloons, being least maneuverable, have the right of way over any other category. An aircraft towing another aircraft has priority over all other engine-driven aircraft.

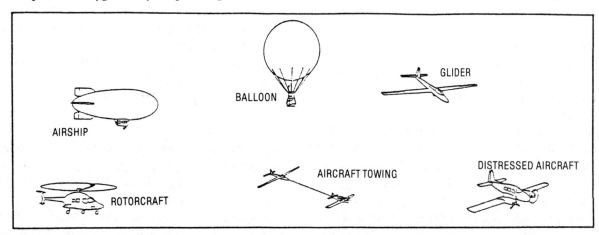

Figure 15-4. Right-of-Way Priority

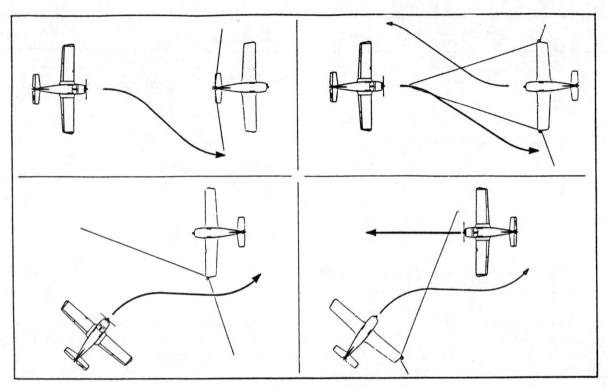

Figure 15-5. Rules of the Road

Gliders have the right of way over airships, airplanes, and rotorcraft. Airships have the right of way over airplanes and rotorcraft. When two aircraft of the same category converge, the one on the right has the right of way. Refer to figure 15-5 and 91.73 below for these situations: the pilot seeing a red light and an anticollision light must pass behind the other airplane (lower left), while the pilot who sees a green light and an anticollision light maintains course (lower right). In an overtaking situation, the white position light and the anticollision light are visible, and the overtaking airplane must give way to the right while the overtaken airplane maintains course (upper left). When you see both a red and a green light, you are head-on, and both pilots must change course to the right (upper right).

A provision of 91.67 that causes problems, usually at uncontrolled airports, is this: when two aircraft are approaching an airport to land, the lower of the two has the right of way — but it may not take advantage of this rule by cutting in front of the other aircraft.

91.70: *Aircraft speed.* There is no speed limit above 10,000' MSL. That is why the visibility and cloud clearance requirements are more stringent above that altitude (figure 15-6). Below 10,000' MSL the *general* speed limit is 250 knots. When flying on a jet you will experience what seems like a period of "coasting" as you approach the destination airport — your pilot is holding altitude and reducing speed to 250 knots before descending through 10,000'. That 250 knot speed limit extends to the ground in any terminal control area. When you fly beneath the horizontal limits of a TCA or in a VFR corridor through a TCA your speed is limited to 200 knots — very few student pilots have trouble complying! In an airport traffic area (operating control tower), propeller driven airplanes are limited to 156 knots and turbine powered aircraft are limited to 200 knots. If that airport traffic area coincides with a TAC, the 250 knot limit mentioned above applies.

91.71: *Acrobatic flight.* Acrobatics are prohibited over a congested area, over an open air assemblage of persons (air shows get waivers), within a control zone, below 1,500' AGL or when visibility is less than 3 miles.

91.73: *Aircraft lights.* During the period from sunset to sunrise (there are special rules for Alaska), you must

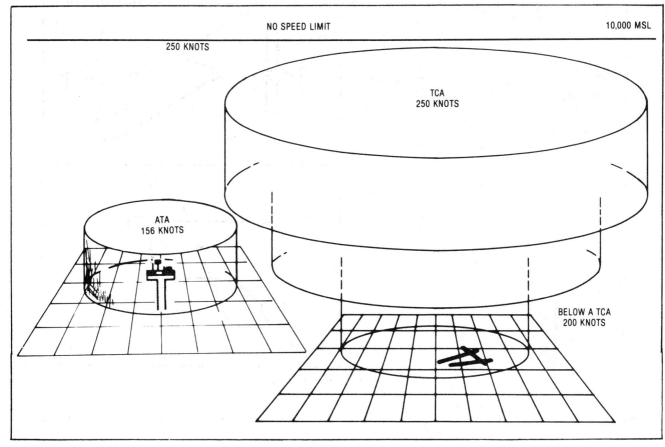

NO SPEED LIMIT   10,000 MSL

250 KNOTS

TCA
250 KNOTS

ATA
156 KNOTS

BELOW A TCA
200 KNOTS

Figure 15-6. Speed Limits

turn on your position lights: a red light on the left wingtip, a green light on the right wingtip, and a white light on the tail. Position lights allow a pilot who sees your lights at night to determine your direction of movement. You must also have a flashing anti-collision light system, either red or white. Many airplanes have both red rotating beacons and white strobe lights — if either system fails, the remaining system meets the requirements of the regulation. The anti-collision system cannot take the place of the position lights, however.

91.75: *Compliance with Air Traffic Control clearances and instructions.* An air traffic controller can only provide you with vectors and traffic information in controlled airspace — when you enter uncontrolled airspace you are on your own. When you receive a clearance from an air traffic controller you must comply EXCEPT when, in your opinion, to do so would be unsafe. Just tell the controller that you can't comply (due to weather, for example). You can always exercise your pilot's emergency authority. *If you are given priority* over other aircraft, even if no emergency is involved, you *MAY* be requested to make a written report within 48 hours to the Chief of the ATC facility that gave you the priority.

91.77 *ATC light signals.* Light signals are used by tower controllers when you have no radio or when your radio has failed (figure 15-7). The wisest course, in the event of radio failure, is to land at an uncontrolled airport and make arrangements with the tower controllers by telephone.

If this option is not available, you are allowed to join the controlled airport's traffic pattern (after determining the direction of traffic flow) and your actions will be directed with light signals.

Color and Type of Signal	On the Ground	In Flight
STEADY GREEN	Cleared for takeoff	Cleared to land
FLASHING GREEN	Cleared to taxi	Rreturn for landing (to be followed by steady green at proper time)
STEADY RED	Stop	Give way to other aircraft and continue circling
FLASHING RED	Taxi clear of landing area (runway) in use	Airport unsafe — do not land
FLASHING WHITE	Return to starting point on airport	
ALTERNATING RED & GREEN	General Warning Signal — Exercise Extreme Caution	

Figure 15-7. Light Signals

91.79: *Minimum safe altitudes; general.* Figure 15-8 illustrates minimum safe altitudes. *Except when necessary for take off or landing*, you must always fly high enough to be able to make a safe emergency landing without hazard to persons or property on the ground. Over a congested area, you must fly 1000' above the highest obstacle within 2000' horizontally.

Question: if you are only 1000' above the highest obstacle over downtown Houston or Chicago, for example, can you make a safe emergency landing?

Probably not. Considerably more altitude would be better. Over other than congested areas you must stay at least 500' above the surface, except that over sparsely settled areas and over water you must stay at least 500' horizontally from any person, vehicle, or structure on the surface. This means boats, barns, swimmers, etc.

91.81: *Altimeter settings.* If you can receive an altimeter setting by radio (or by visiting the Flight Service Station) you must adjust your altimeter setting window

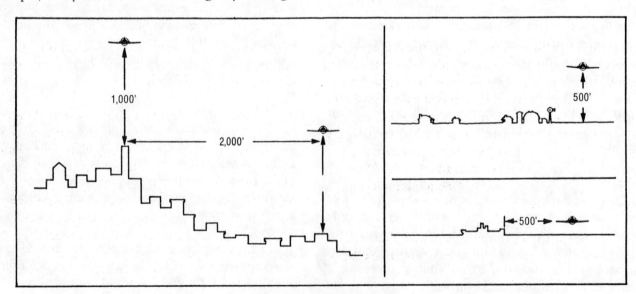

Figure 15-8. Minimum Safe Altitudes

Form Approved: OMB No. 2120-0026

U.S. DEPARTMENT OF TRANSPORTATION FEDERAL AVIATION ADMINISTRATION **FLIGHT PLAN**	(FAA USE ONLY) □ PILOT BRIEFING □ VNR □ STOPOVER					TIME STARTED	SPECIALIST INITIALS

1. TYPE	2. AIRCRAFT IDENTIFICATION	3. AIRCRAFT TYPE/ SPECIAL EQUIPMENT	4. TRUE AIRSPEED	5. DEPARTURE POINT	6. DEPARTURE TIME		7. CRUISING ALTITUDE
VFR					PROPOSED (Z)	ACTUAL (Z)	
IFR							
DVFR			KTS				

8. ROUTE OF FLIGHT

9. DESTINATION (Name of airport and city)	10. EST. TIME ENROUTE		11. REMARKS
	HOURS	MINUTES	

12. FUEL ON BOARD		13. ALTERNATE AIRPORT(S)	14. PILOT'S NAME, ADDRESS & TELEPHONE NUMBER & AIRCRAFT HOME BASE	15. NUMBER ABOARD
HOURS	MINUTES			
			17. DESTINATION CONTACT/TELEPHONE (OPTIONAL)	

16. COLOR OF AIRCRAFT	CIVIL AIRCRAFT PILOTS. FAR Part 91 requires you file an IFR flight plan to operate under instrument flight rules in controlled airspace. Failure to file could result in a civil penalty not to exceed $1,000 for each violation (Section 901 of the Federal Aviation Act of 1958, as amended). Filing of a VFR flight plan is recommended as a good operating practice. See also Part 99 for requirements concerning DVFR flight plans.

FAA Form 7233-1 (8-82)   **CLOSE VFR FLIGHT PLAN WITH_____ FSS ON ARRIVAL**

Figure 15-9. Flight Plan Form

accordingly. If you are enroute, you must update the altimeter setting by calling a FSS within 100 miles along your route of flight (every time you contact air traffic control or a Flight Service Station you will be given an altimeter setting). If you are on the ground, and no altimeter setting information is available, you should set your altimeter to read field elevation and then get a correction as soon as you can contact a Flight Service Station by radio. Above 18,000' MSL, all altimeters must be set to 29.92' Hg.

91.83: *Flight plan; information required.* Figure 15-9 includes all of the information called for by this section.

You should list as your destination airport the last airport at which you intend to land (you can include enroute airports in block 11).

Block 12 should reflect total fuel on board. VFR flight plans, although not mandatory, aid in search-and-rescue efforts if you do not complete your planned flight.

91.97: *Positive control areas.* As a VFR-rated private pilot you may not climb above 18,000 feet MSL without an instrument rating and an instrument clearance. This is Positive Controlled Airspace.

91.105: *Basic VFR weather minimums.* VFR visibility and cloud clearance requirements have been discussed earlier; this is the table from Part 91 (table 15-1):

ALTITUDE	FLIGHT VISIBILITY	DISTANCE FROM CLOUDS
1,200 feet or less above the surface (regardless of MSL altitude)		500 below 1000 above
Within controlled airspace.........	3 statute miles	2000 horizontal
Outside controlled airspace........	1 statute mile	Clear of clouds
More than 1,200 feet AGL, but less than MSL 10,000		
Within controlled airspace.........	3 statute miles	500 below 1000 above
Outside controlled airspace........	1 statute mile	2000 horizontal
More than 1,200 feet above the surface and at or above 10,000 MSL...........	5 statute miles	1000 below 1000 above 1 mile horizontal

Table 15-1. Weather Minimums

91.109: *VFR cruising altitudes or flight levels.* This is called the hemispherical rule. Based on magnetic *course*, not magnetic heading, and applicable only when you are more than 3,000' above the ground (figure 15-10).

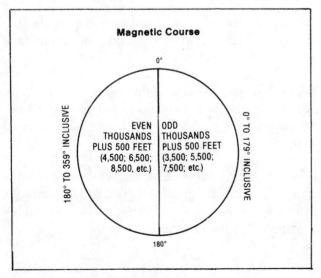

Figure 15-10. Hemispherical Cruising Rule

91.167: *Carrying persons other than crewmembers after repairs or alterations.* This section requires a test flight by a *private pilot* or better before passengers can be carried on an airplane that has had maintenance or repair that affected the flight characteristics.

91.169: *Inspections.* Annual maintenance inspections are required for all airplanes not on an approved progressive maintenance program. An annual inspection expires at the end of the twelfth month following the inspection. 100 hour inspections are required on all airplanes operated for hire.

An annual inspection may substitute for a 100 hour inspection. After a required inspection has been completed, the airplane is "returned to service" by an appropriate logbook entry by the inspector. *The aircraft's Certificate of Airworthiness never expires as long as the required inspections have been made.* An aircraft is "out of license" if an inspection is overdue, and it is the responsibility of the owner or operator to be sure that all required inspections have been performed.

Airworthiness Directives are FAA mandated repairs or inspections, and the aircraft and engine logs should show that all required ADs have been performed. It is the responsibility of the pilot in command to insure the airworthiness of the aircraft, and this is usually interpreted to mean that you should make a thorough preflight inspection. As a renter pilot, however, you should also check the aircraft and engine logs.

This section does not contain all of the FARs, only those which in our opinion warranted explanation or illustration. There are many more regulations in Parts 61 and 91 than are covered in this book, and we recommend that you get a copy of the ASA Federal Aviation Regulations or the combined FAR/AIM book published by ASA.

ACCIDENT REPORTING

National Transportation Safety Board Regulations, Part 830: These regulations govern accidents and accident reporting. *They are not Federal Aviation Regulations* but will be discussed in this chapter on regulations.

The first thing you should know about Part 830 is the difference between an accident and an incident. An accident is an occurrence during which any person suffers death or serious injury, or one in which the aircraft receives substantial damage. There are fine points on just what constitutes serious injury, of course. An incident is an occurrence, other than an accident, which affects the safety of operations.

The following *incidents* require that the NTSB be notified:

1.   Flight control malfunction or failure.

2.   Inability of a required flight crewmember to perform flight duties as a result of injury or illness.

3.   Failure of structural components of a turbine engine, *excluding* compressor and turbine blades and vanes.

4.   In-flight fire.

5.   Aircraft collide in flight.

The NTSB must also be notified when an aircraft is overdue and is believed to have been involved in an accident.

The following types of damage are exempt from being defined as "substantial damage":

> Engine failure, damage limited to an engine, bent fairings or cowling, dented skin, small puncture holes in the skin or fabric, ground damage to rotor or propeller blades, damage to landing gear, wheels, tires, flaps, engine accessories, brakes, or wingtips.

In practical terms, this means that a gear-up landing in which no one was seriously injured is not a reportable accident. A fire while taxiing is not a reportable accident. Running into a structure or another airplane on the ground is not reportable. Failure of flaps to extend (or failure of one flap to extend) is not reportable, because flaps are not flight controls.

When a reportable accident does occur, the NTSB is to be notified immediately (this is usually, but not always, done by the FAA). If a written report is required, it must be submitted within 10 days.

Memory aid: Notify immediately, report within 10 days.

REGULATION
SECTION REVIEW

1. What is the general direction of movement of the other aircraft during a night flight if you observe a steady red light and a flashing red light ahead and at the same altitude?

    1. The other aircraft is crossing to the left.
    2. The other aircraft is crossing to the right.
    3. The other aircraft is approaching head-on.
    4. The other aircraft is headed away from you.

2. If an aircraft is involved in an accident which resulted in substantial damage to the aircraft, the nearest NTSB field office should be notified
    1. immediately.
    2. within 5 days.
    3. within 7 days.
    4. within 10 days.

3. Of the following incidents, which would require an immediate notification to the nearest NTSB field office?

    1. An in-flight generator/alternator failure.
    2. An in-flight fire.
    3. An in-flight loss of VOR receiver capability.
    4. Ground damage to the propeller blades.

4. A private pilot acting as pilot in command, or in any other capacity as a required pilot flight crewmember, must have in their personal possession while aboard the aircraft

    1. a current logbook endorsement to show that a flight review has been satisfactorily accomplished.
    2. the current and appropriate pilot and medical certificates.

    3. a current endorsement on the pilot certificate to show that a flight review has been satisfactorily accomplished.
    4. the pilot logbook to show recent experience requirements to serve as pilot in command have been met.

5. What is the duration, if any, of a private pilot certificate?

    1. It expires 24 months after issuance.
    2. As long as the flight review and the medical certificate are current.
    3. It expires 90 days after the currency of the flight review has lapsed.
    4. Indefinite.

6. A third-class medical certificate was issued on May 3, this year. To exercise the privileges of a private pilot certificate, the medical certificate will be valid through

    1. May 31, 1 year later.
    2. May 31, 2 years later.
    3. May 3, 1 year later.
    4. May 3, 2 years later.

7. To act as pilot in command of an airplane that has more than 200 hp., a person is required to do which of the following?

    1. Make three solo takeoffs and landings in such an airplane.
    2. Receive flight instruction in an airplane that has more than 200 hp.
    3. Pass a flight test in such an airplane.
    4. Hold a 200 hp. class rating.

8. To act as pilot in command of an airplane with passengers aboard, the pilot must have made at least three takeoffs and landings in an aircraft of the same category and class within the preceding

1. 120 days.
2. 90 days.
3. 24 mo.
4. 12 mo.

9. If recency of experience requirements for night flight have not been met and official sunset is 1830, the latest time passengers may be carried is

1. 1730.
2. 1830.
3. 1900.
4. 1930.

10. To meet the recent flight experience requirements for acting as pilot in command carrying passengers at night, a pilot must have made, within the preceding 90 days and at night, at least

1. three takeoffs and landings to a full stop in the same category and class of aircraft to be used.
2. three takeoffs and landings in the same category and class of aircraft to be used.
3. three takeoffs and three landings, either full stop or touch-and-go, but must be accompanied by a certificated flight instructor who meets the recent experience requirement for night flight.
4. three takeoffs and landings to a full stop in the same category but not necessarily in the same class of aircraft to be used.

11. According to regulations pertaining to general privileges and limitations, a private pilot may

1. not be paid in any manner for the operating expenses of a flight.
2. be paid for the operating expenses of a flight if at least 3 takeoffs and landings were made by the pilot within the preceding 90 days.

3. share the operating expenses of a flight with the passengers.
4. charge a reasonable fee for acting as pilot in command.

12. What preflight action is required for every flight?

1. Check weather reports and forecasts.
2. Determine runway length at airports of intended use.
3. Determine alternatives if the flight cannot be completed.
4. Check for any known traffic delays.

13. In addition to other preflight actions for a VFR flight away from the vicinity of the departure airport, regulations require the pilot in command to

1. file a flight plan.
2. check each fuel tank visually to ensure that it is full.
3. check the accuracy of the omninavigation equipment and the emergency locator transmitter.
4. determine runway lengths at airports of intended use and the airplane's takeoff and landing distance data.

14. Under what condition may a person act as pilot in command of an aircraft after consuming alcohol which may affect that person's faculties?

1. Passengers may not be carried.
2. A waiver must be obtained.
3. Only after the expiration of 8 hours.
4. Only after release from a doctor.

15. What is the fuel requirement for flight under VFR at night?

1. Full fuel tanks.
2. Enough to complete the flight at normal cruising flight with adverse wind conditions.
3. Enough to fly to the first point of intended landing and to fly after that for 30 min. at normal cruising speed.

4. Enough to fly to the first point of intended landing and to fly after that for 45 minutes at normal cruising speed.

16. Where, in the 48 contiguous United States and the District of Columbia, is a radar beacon transponder equipped with a Mode 3/A 4096 code capability required?

1. In Group I TCA's only.
2. In all TCA's only.
3. In all TCA's and in controlled airspace above 12,500' MSL if more than 2,500' AGL.
4. In controlled airspace above 12,500' MSL if more than 2,500' AGL only.

CHAPTER SIXTEEN

FLIGHT PLANNING

This chapter will give you the opportunity to put together all of the information you have learned from the rest of the book in a practical form. With your knowledge of performance charts, weather, regulations, navigational charts, publications, and the airspace system, you should be able to plan a cross-country flight that is within the capability of your airplane, while complying with the regulations at all times.

FILING A FLIGHT PLAN

You will file this VFR flight plan as a round-robin (or round trip), noting in the remarks section that you will be landing at Ellensburg and at Paine Field. The basic purpose for filing a VFR flight plan is to aid Search and Rescue forces if you fail to complete the flight, and with that in mind filling out the flight plan form should be easy.

BLOCK 1:
> You will be filing a VFR flight plan.

BLOCK 2:
> Fill in the complete registration (or "N" number) of your airplane. Be sure that friends or relatives who may be waiting for you know the registration number of your airplane.

BLOCK 3:
> Fill in the manufacturer's name and the model of the airplane (Piper PA-28) and the letter designating the equipment on board. The Flight Service Station briefer will help you with this.

BLOCK 4:
> Enter your *computed* true airspeed at your chosen cruising altitude.

BLOCK 5:
> Enter the 3-letter identifier for the departure airport or the name of the airport if you don't know the identifier.

BLOCK 6:
> Fill in your proposed departure time in the Greenwich Mean Time (ZULU).

BLOCK 7:
> Enter your proposed cruising altitude or the letters VFR.

BLOCK 8:
> Define your route by navigational aids, by airways, or by freeways, but remember that if you do not arrive at your destination, searchers will rely on the information in this block to plan the initial search. If you decide to divert from your planned route *report the change to the FSS* so that searchers

will not be misdirected. This information is for your benefit, not the FAA's.

BLOCK 9:

Enter the identifier or name of the destination airport. If it is a round-robin (as is your exercise trip) the departure airport and the destination airport will be the same.

BLOCK 10:

Enter your total planned time enroute including any stops along the way. It is when this total time expires that the FAA becomes concerned for your safety.

BLOCK 11:

This block might include "sightseeing Mt. Rushmore" or "overflying Disney World" to explain planned diversions or, as in the case of your planned trip, to note that you will be on the ground at Ellensburg for 30 minutes and at Paine Field for one hour.

BLOCK 12:

This block should contain the total fuel on board, not how much you expect to use.

BLOCK 13:

As a VFR pilot you are not required to file an alternate airport, but it is an excellent idea if you think that you might not reach the destination airport due to weather, etc. The regulations require that you always have an alternative plan in mind if your original flight cannot be completed.

BLOCK 14:

Fill in your complete name and address, and supply sufficient information to identify the airplane's home base and/or operator. Provide a phone number which will reach someone who is aware of your plans — possibly the airport manager or the owner of the airplane. It is this number that the FAA will call first if you have not closed your flight plan, so don't use your home phone number unless someone there could provide information on your location or plans.

BLOCK 15:

Enter the total number of persons on board.

BLOCK 16:

Enter the predominant colors of the airplane.

Almost all overdue airplane searches end with the first telephone call (the pilot has failed to close the flight plan), or with the second call (the airplane is parked at an enroute airport).

PREPARING THE FLIGHT LOG

Remember that groundspeed and wind correction angle calculations require *true* course, *true* airspeed, wind direction in relation to *true* north, and wind velocity. Measure courses as accurately as possible using your flight plotter: this measurement is the only truly accurate element of flight planning. True airspeed figures from the airplane's performance chart were accurate when the airplane was new, but its condition may no longer allow it to match the book figures.

Winds aloft as received from the Flight Service Station briefer are only forecasts, and the winds you experience in flight may vary greatly from those forecast. That is why you *plan* the flight by dead reckoning but *fly* it by pilotage.

In the calculations below, the forecast wind at cruise altitude is used for figuring groundspeed and heading during climb: 90 knots is used as climb true airspeed, and time to cruise altitude is based on a climb rate of 500 feet per minute. During the climb, fuel consumption is 9 gallons per hour, while in cruising flight only 7 gallons per hour are consumed.

ROUTE:

Olympia — Ellensburg — Paine Field — Olympia

1st Leg:

Pilotage to V-2, then direct.

2nd Leg:

Direct using VOR navigation.

3rd Leg:

Pilotage.

AIRPLANE:

4 seats, fixed gear.
Gross weight 2,300 lbs., empty weight 1,364 lbs.,
150 HP., fixed pitch propeller.
Fuel capacity 38 gallons usable, 100LL.
Oil 8 qts. not included in empty weight.
2 navcomms, 360 channel comm,
200 channel nav. ADF, transponder.

Pilot:

190 lbs.

Passengers:

185 and 110 pounds.

Baggage:

25 pounds.

WEIGHT AND BALANCE CALCULATION

		MOMENT (from MFR)
Empty weight	1,364	51.7
Fuel (usable)	228	11.0
Baggage	25	2.0
Oil (2 gals.)	15	−0.2
Pilot and 110 lb. passenger	300	11.2
Rear passenger	185	13.5
Totals	2,117	89.2

See Page 16-13 at the end of this chapter for the Loading Graph and Center of Gravity Moment Envelope.

Loading is within limits with most adverse weight distribution; moving the 110 pound passenger to the rear seat and the 185 pound passenger to the front seat would move the center of gravity forward. With these passengers and this fuel load you cannot mis-load the airplane.

WEATHER BRIEFING

This is a telephone weather briefing from the Seattle FSS (local phone number from Olympia is found in the Airport/Facility Directory):

"No hazardous weather is forecast for your route and time of flight. The synopsis is for a southwesterly flow aloft over Washington, caused by a stationary low at the surface and aloft 250 miles offshore from Vancouver Island. The airmass is somewhat unstable. At the surface, there is weak high pressure west of the Cascades. Freezing level is 8 thousand along the coast, sloping to 13 thousand at the eastern border.

"The route forecast calls for mountains occasionally obscured in clouds, conditions continuing beyond 0000Z.

"Olympia is reporting 10,000' scattered and 15 miles at this time. Wenatchee and Yakima report 9,000' broken with 25 mile visibility. We have no weather from Ellensburg. Stampede Pass is reporting a ceiling of 6,000' broken now.

"The route forecast is calling for obscuration of mountain valleys by ground fog which is expected to burn off.

"The Yakima terminal forecast is calling for 10,000 broken until 1800Z then 7,000 scattered, wind 270° at 10 knots. Wenatchee is the same except the wind is forecast to be 320° at 10 knots. Olympia will remain essentially unchanged all day.

"The winds aloft for Seattle at 6,000' are forecast to be 220° at 13 knots, at 9,000' 210° at 21 knots.

"Restricted Area 6714 is active 13,000' and below. The threshold of runway 11 at Paine Field is displaced 1,100' eastward."

If you want to know the status of military Operating Areas or Military Training Routes, you will have to ask the briefer; this information will not be volunteered.

PLANNING THE FLIGHT

Your flight planning process will include fuel planning, preparing a flight log, and checking over the proposed route on your chart to be sure you haven't missed anything. In this text all of the details of planning the first leg will be examined, leaving the second and third legs for you to do.

An important part of pre-flight planning is reviewing your flight on the navigational chart to be sure that you are aware of any airspace restrictions, and that you know who to contact for any required clearances. You should also pick out easily identified groundspeed checkpoints, and establish visual "brackets" on either side of your course and at the destination to insure that you do not wander too far off course or overfly the destination.

PLANNING CONSIDERATIONS, FIRST LEG

Olympia direct Gray Radiobeacon to avoid R-6703A, past the northwest tip of Lake Tapps to intercept V-2 at Palmer, thence via V-2 to Ellensburg.

Overfly Nisqually Wildlife Refuge at least 2,000' AGL.

Use Tacoma terminal radar service for advisories (121.1 MHz, from Airport/Facility Directory)

Need clearance for Gray AAF or McChord AFB airport traffic areas or control zones? Not if in contact with Tacoma Approach Control or more than 3,000' above field elevation.

May need clearance to transit Seattle TCA, top of Seattle TCA is 7,000' MSL.

Military VFR route crosses V-2 near Lester State. Military flights will be below 1,500' AGL.

Hemispherical rule calls for odd 1,000 plus 500' eastbound when more than 3,000' AGL.

Highest terrain within 5 miles of route is 5,720' MSL.

Except for transition area at Ellensburg, entire leg will be in controlled airspace.

Groundspeed checkpoints: McChord AFB to northwest tip of Lake Tapps 13 NM; 13 NM to Palmer and V-2.

Hanson Reservoir dam to Lester State Airport 14 NM; 40 NM to Ellensburg.

Side brackets: Puget Sound, Cascade Mountains.

End bracket: I-90 freeway.

Frequencies: Gray radiobeacon, Olympia ground control and tower, Seattle Radio (open flight plan) Tacoma Approach Control (advisories), Seattle and Ellensburg VORs, Seattle Center (flight following).

Which cruise altitude would you choose for crossing the mountains eastbound?

1. 5,500' MSL.
2. 6,500' MSL.
3. 7,500' MSL.
4. 8,500' MSL.
5. 9,500' MSL.

The hemispherical rule requires that you fly eastbound at an odd-thousand plus 500 feet, so answer 4 is definitely wrong. The hemispherical rule does not apply within 3,000 feet of the surface, making 6,500' a possible choice, but that altitude is only 1,000' above the ridges, and there is a southwest wind which will create turbulence on the lee slopes. Answer 1 is too close to the terrain. A ceiling of 6,000' at Stampede Pass means a cloud layer at approximately 9,800', ruling out 9,500' as a cruise altitude. Choose 7,500' as your cruise altitude eastbound, and use 8,500' westbound.

In preparing your flight log, you should record the *results* of your calculations, and not the individual elements. That is, you need to know the magnetic heading, but you do not need to record the true course, the magnetic variation, or the wind for in-flight use. (See the FAA Flight Planner, figure 16-1). In addition (considering the built-in inaccuracy of the wind forecasts), computing and recording compass deviation and compass heading are unnecessary (although valuable for the written examination). If the heading indicator becomes inoperative, or of questionable accuracy, use your computed magnetic heading and the compass correction card to get compass course to steer. A compass correction card for the airplane you are using in this flight is provided here (figure 16-2).

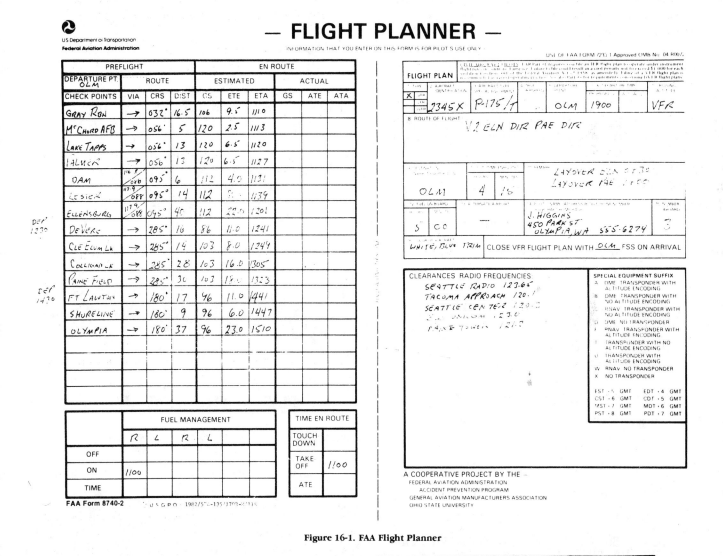

Figure 16-1. FAA Flight Planner

FOR	N	030	060	E	120	150	S	210	240	W	300	330
STEER	0	031	062	094	125	154	181	208	237	266	297	328

Figure 16-2. Compass Correction Card

OLYMPIA-ELLENSBURG

Begin by measuring the distance and true course for each leg, using your flight plotter. Here are the figures for the first leg, with variation and deviation applied to

derive a compass course. These are "no wind" *courses* — when wind is factored in, you have *headings* to follow.

	DIST	TC	VAR	MC	DEV	CC
Olympia-Gray Rbn.	16.5 NM	049°	−20.5° E.	028.5°	+1	029.5°
Gray Rbn-Palmer	31.0 NM	071°	−20.5° E.	050.5°	+1.5	052°
Palmer-Ellensburg	58.0 NM	105.5°	−20.5° E.	085°	+4.0	089°

Eastbound, interpolate the wind at 7,500' from the winds aloft given by the briefer: 220°, 13 knots at 6,000' and 210°, 21 knots at 9,000'. This is how the magnetic

heading and groundspeed for the first leg is calculated, rounding off fractional results:

	TC	WIND	TAS	WCA	TH	VAR	MH	GS
Olympia-Gray Rbn.	049°	215 @ 17	90	2.5°R	052°	20°	032°	106
Gray-V2 airway.	071°	215 @ 17	107	5.5°R	076°	20°	056°	120
V2-Ellensburg	106°	215 @ 17	107	9°R	115°	20°	095°	112

The wind will have a greater effect during the relatively slow climb than when at cruise. Only the distance, magnetic heading, and groundspeed figures from these calculations will appear in your flight log.

NOTE: Several flight computers, both manual and electronic, were used in making the heading and groundspeed calculations: your own answers may vary slightly.

FUEL PLANNING THE FIRST LEG

The climb from field elevation at Olympia (206' MSL) to the cruising altitude of 7,500' should take 15 minutes and consume 3 gallons of fuel (always round fuel consumption figures off to the next highest figure). Using the most conservative *groundspeed* of 90 knots, 'you will be 23 miles into the trip with 83 miles to go when you reach cruise altitude. If you plan to descend at cruise speed, maintaining a groundspeed of 112

knots, you will reach Ellensburg 44 minutes after levelling off, and will consume 6 gallons during that portion of the trip.

FLYING THE FIRST LEG

Follow along on the sectional chart excerpt.

Tune the ADF receiver to 216 KHz. After leaving the Olympia airport traffic area, climb as rapidly as possible to pass over wildlife refuge at least 2,000' AGL (Sectional chart legend). Home to Gray radiobeacon. Open VFR flight plan with Seattle Radio on 123.65.

Contact Tacoma Approach Control (frequency in A/FD) for traffic advisories. No clearance required for Gray AAF or McChord AFB Airport Traffic Areas if more than 3,000' AGL. After passing the radiobeacon (start time for groundspeed check) steer toward Lake Tapps;

if not above 7,000' when crossing McChord Air Force Base extended runway centerline, ask for clearance into Seattle TCA.

Check time at northwest tip of Lake Tapps and compute groundspeed. Estimate time of arrival at Palmer. Tune #1 VOR receiver to Seattle frequency and identify. Set omni bearing selector to 085°. Note railroad to right of course passes through Palmer. As VOR course deviation needle centers, turn to predetermined magnetic heading.

Start timing opposite dam at west end of reservoir. Maintain 7,500' MSL to comply with 91.105 (at least 500' below all clouds) and 91.109 (magnetic course 0° through 179° maintain odd thousand + 500') noting that during part of this leg a cruising altitude of 7,500' will be less than 3,000' above the ground and the odd-even rule does not apply. Check time opposite Lester State; compute groundspeed and estimate time of arrival at Ellensburg. Tune VOR receiver to Ellensburg frequency and identify. Be alert for military traffic beneath you just east of Lester State Airport (AIM 132). Contact Ellensburg UNICOM or broadcast intentions (AIM 157). Note freeway crosses flightpath 10 NM from airport and that airport is north of town. Report on the ground to Seattle Radio on 122.2.

FIRST LEG FLIGHT LOG

Dep OLM 1100   Cruise 7,500' MSL

CHECKPOINT	ROUTE		ESTIMATED				ACTUAL		
	VIA	CRS	DIST	GS	ETE	ETA	GS	ATE	ATA
Gray Rbn.	DIR	032°	16.5	106	9.5	1110			
McChord.	DIR	056°	5.0	120	2.5	1113			
Lake Tapps.	DIR	056°	13.0	120	6.5	1120		8.0	
Palmer.	DIR	056°	13.0	120	6.5	1127			
Dam.	V-2	095°	6.0	112	4.0	1131			
Lester State	V-2	095°	14.0	112	8.0	1139		10.0	
Ellensburg.	V-2	095°	40.0	112	22.0	1201			

The actual times enroute between groundspeed checkpoints have been provided; revise the ETA at Ellensburg based on the measured groundspeed.

Figure 16-3. Ellensburg

ELLENSBURG — PAINE FIELD

Since this is a direct flight, the easiest thing to do is to measure the magnetic course from the Ellensburg VORTAC to Paine Field, using the VORTAC's compass rose — 285° magnetic. For the wind problem, *add* 20° for magnetic variation to get the true course. The winds at 8,500' will not be appreciably different than those at 9,000' — use 220° at 21 knots for your heading and groundspeed calculations.

PLANNING CONSIDERATIONS, SECOND LEG

Ellensburg direct Paine Field via VOR.

Military training route crosses direct course just west of Kachess Lake.

Course crosses Alpine Lakes Wilderness Area.

Flight will enter controlled airspace 700' AGL departing Ellensburg.

Flight will be in uncontrolled airspace briefly while crossing corner of area with 9,500' MSL floor.

Maximum elevation figures show 9,800', 7,800' and 8,300', but highest terrain enroute is 6,680' MSL.

Groundspeed checkpoints: DeVere Airport to tip of Cle Elum Lake — 14 NM; lake to Paine Field 58 NM.

Side brackets: Mt. Stuart, Mt. Daniel. End bracket: Puget Sound.

Frequencies: Seattle Radio (position report), Seattle Center (flight following), Paine VOR, Paine ATIS, Paine tower and ground control.

FUEL PLANNING

The climb out of Ellensburg to 8,500' will take approximately 13 minutes and will consume 2 gallons of fuel. You will reach cruising altitude 19 miles from Ellensburg with 69 miles to go at a groundspeed of 101 knots, and during the 41 minutes between leveling off and arriving at Paine Field you will consume an additional 5 gallons.

FLYING THE SECOND LEG

With VOR receiver tuned to Ellensburg, set OBS on 285°. After takeoff, turn to intercept VOR radial and proceed on course. Contact Seattle Radio on 122.2 and report airborne. Keep freeway and CleElum airports on left until high enough to see lakes, and set course across north tips of lakes. Start timing for groundspeed check opposite paved DeVere Airport. First half of this leg will be less than 3,000' above terrain and hemispherical rule will not apply. At north tip of Kachess Lake, be alert for military aircraft; tune VOR receiver to Paine Field and identify, make groundspeed check and compute ETA at Paine Field. Note that between Snoqualmie Pass and Colligan Lake, controlled airspace floor is 9,500' MSL. Listen to Paine Field ATIS and call tower for clearance into airport traffic area. (The Paine Tower record of your takeoff and landing will serve as a position report if you get lost between Paine and Olympia).

Dep. ELN 1230 — Cruise altitude 8,500' MSL.

CHECKPOINT	VIA	CRS	DIST	GS	ETE	ETA	GS	ATE	ATA
DeVere Airport........	DIR	285°	16.0	86	11.0	1241			
Cle Elum Lake	DIR	285°	14.0	103	8.0	1249		7.0	
Colligan Lake.........	DIR	285°	28.0	103	16.0	1305			
Paine Field	DIR	285°	30.0	103	18.0	1322			

Are you computing a heading and a groundspeed during the climb to cruise altitude at 90 knots and 500' per minute, and also at 107 knots during cruise? This leg is flown using the ELN 285° radial and the PAE 102° radial as backup to ground reference navigation. If the wind forecast is valid, a magnetic heading of 274° should keep the VOR needle centered.

Figure 16-4. Paine Field

PAINE FIELD — OLYMPIA PLANNING CONSIDERATIONS, THIRD LEG

Paine Field direct Olympia via pilotage.

Entire flight is in controlled airspace.

Course line crosses point of land at Fort Lawton.

Floor of Seattle TCA is 3,000' MSL along route.

No conflict with Bremerton National or Tacoma Narrows airports.

Twin obstructions 1,000' MSL left of course line opposite long lake right of course line.

Use Tacoma Approach for traffic advisories into Olympia.

Groundspeed checkpoints: Fort Lawton to shoreline at Port Orchard — 9 miles; shoreline 37 miles to Olympia.

Side brackets: Seattle and Bremerton.

End bracket: Hills south of Olympia.

Frequencies: Paine ground and tower, Paine VOR, Seattle Center, Seattle Approach Control, Tacoma Approach Control, Olympia VOR, Olympia tower.

FUEL PLANNING

Using the winds for 6,000' (210° at 13 knots), the groundspeed works out to 96 knots. Only 3 minutes of climb are involved, so compute the leg at a true airspeed of 107 knots. Fuel consumption for 40 minutes at 7 gallons per hour is 5 gallons.

FLYING THE THIRD LEG

Set omni bearing selector to 180° (Paine VORTAC) as backup to pilotage. Set course just west of drivein theater with point of land off Fort Lawton straight ahead. Start timing for groundspeed check off Fort Lawton. Check time over shoreline east of Port Orchard and compute groundspeed and ETA at Olympia. Be alert for towers left of course passing long lake. Contact Tacoma Approach Control for traffic advisories and vectoring to Olympia traffic pattern.

Figure 16-5. Olympia

Dep Paine 1345 — Cruise 2,500' MSL.

CHECKPOINT	VIA	CRS	DIST	GS	ETE	ETA	GS	ATE	ATA
Fort Lawton	DIR	180°	17.0		11.0	1356			
Shoreline.............	DIR	180°	9.0	96	6.0	1402		9.0	
Olympia	DIR	180°	37.0	96	23.0	1426			

This leg is flown using the Paine and Olympia VORs as backups to visual navigation.

Fuel consumption for the trip is planned at 21 gallons. A 30 minute reserve (3.5 gallons) is required for day VFR, so you should have at least that much in the tanks upon landing at Olympia.

Did you close your flight plan with Seattle Radio?

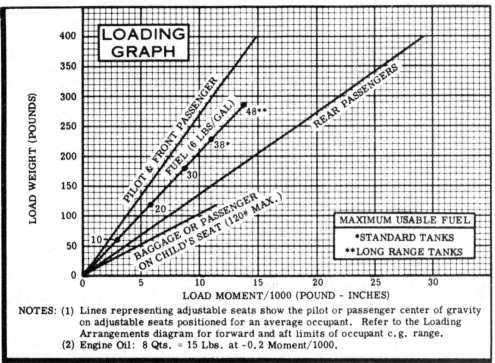

NOTES: (1) Lines representing adjustable seats show the pilot or passenger center of gravity on adjustable seats positioned for an average occupant. Refer to the Loading Arrangements diagram for forward and aft limits of occupant c.g. range.
(2) Engine Oil: 8 Qts. = 15 Lbs. at -0.2 Moment/1000.

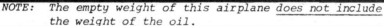

NOTE: The empty weight of this airplane *does not include* the weight of the oil.

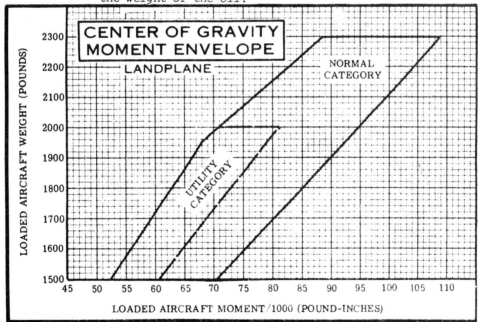

FLIGHT PLANNING
SECTION REVIEW

1. Refer to the sectional chart excerpt in the back of the book. Select the true statement regarding Restricted Area R-6703C near Olympia.

    1. The pilot must be instrument rated and file an IFR flight plan before penetrating this area.
    2. Flight within this Restricted Area is prohibited during hours of daylight.
    3. Before penetrating this Restricted Area, authorization must be obtained from the controlling agency.
    4. The aircraft must have an operable VOR receiver, two-way communications radio, and a radar beacon transponder.

2. While enroute between Olympia and Ellensburg, weather information is available by contacting

    1. Ellensburg UNICOM on 123.0 MHz.
    2. Seattle Radio (Flight Service Station) on 122.2 MHz.
    3. Seattle Flight Watch on 122.0 MHz.
    4. Wenatchee Tower on 122.3 MHz.

3. Assume that you are over the Cle Elum Airport (47°11'00"N 120°53'00"W) flying eastbound at 4,500' MSL. A westbound airplane passes at your altitude. Which statement is correct?

    1. The westbound airplane is legally at 4,500' MSL and you are at the wrong altitude for your direction of flight.
    2. The westbound airplane should be either 1,000' above or below you in controlled airspace.
    3. Both airplanes are being operated legally within 3,000' of the ground, where the hemispherical rule does not apply.
    4. You should be flying at an odd altitude plus 500 feet eastbound.

4. Your calls to Ellensburg UNICOM on 123.0 MHz are not answered. What action should you take?

    1. Attempt to contact Ellensburg UNICOM on the distress frequency, 121.5 MHz.
    2. Cancel your plans to land at Ellensburg because you cannot obtain a landing clearance.
    3. Attempt to obtain landing clearance from Seattle Radio by transmitting on 122.1 MHz and listening on 117.9 MHz.
    4. Enter the Ellensburg traffic pattern and land, announcing your position and intentions on 123.0 MHz.

5.   Assume that when you contact the Paine Field tower for landing clearance you are advised that the ceiling is 900' and the visibility is 2 miles. Which statement is correct?

      1.   You can proceed into the pattern and land, because you need only remain clear of all clouds if visibility is at least 1 mile.
      2.   You must remain clear of the Paine Field control zone and request a Special VFR clearance from the tower.
      3.   You cannot land at Paine Field unless there is at least a 1,000' ceiling and 3 miles visibility.
      4.   You can proceed into the pattern and land because Paine Field does not have a control zone.

6.   On the direct route from Ellensburg to Paine Field you cross the corner of an area marked "9,500 MSL." As you fly through this area at 8,500' MSL

      1.   you must have 3 miles visibility and remain clear of all clouds.

2.   you must stay at least 1,000' above, 500' below, and 2,000' horizontally from all clouds and have 3 miles flight visibility.
3.   you are in uncontrolled airspace more than 1,200' AGL and need only 1 mile visibility and must remain 500' below or 1,000' above all clouds.
4.   you can fly through thin clouds if you are in contact with a radar facility.

7.   Refer to the Airport/Facility Directory listings for Ellensburg and Olympia. Which one of the following statements is true?

      1.   There are no restrictions listed for approaching Olympia VORTAC from the north.
      2.   The Ellensburg VORTAC is unusable on the 145° radial at 7,500' beyond 25 NM.
      3.   The Olympia VORTAC is unusable on the 160° radial at 8,500'.
      4.   The Ellensburg VORTAC is usable on the 255° radial at 6,500' at a distance of 35 NM.

THE COMPLETE PRIVATE PILOT

Appendix A

PILOT/CONTROLLER GLOSSARY

This Glossary was compiled to promote a common understanding of the terms used in the Air Traffic Control system. It includes those terms which are intended for pilot/controller communications. Those terms most frequently used in pilot/controller communications are printed in **bold italics**. The definitions are primarily defined in an operational sense applicable to both users and operators of the National Airspace System. Use of the Glossary will preclude any misunderstandings concerning the system's design, function, and purpose.

Because of the international nature of flying, terms used in the "Lexicon", published by the International Civil Aviation Organization (ICAO), are included when they differ from FAA definitions. These terms are *italicized*. For the reader's convenience, there are also cross references to related terms in other parts of the Glossary and to other documents, such as the Federal Aviation Regulations (FARs) and the Airman's Information Manual (AIM).

This Glossary will be revised as necessary to maintain a common understanding of the system.

ABBREVIATED IFR FLIGHT PLANS— An authorization by ATC requiring pilots to submit only that information needed for the purpose of ATC. It includes only a small portion of the usual IFR flight plan information. In certain instances, this may be only aircraft identification, location, and pilot request. Other information may be requested if needed by ATC for separation/control purposes. It is frequently used by aircraft which are airborne, desire an instrument approach, or by aircraft on the ground which desire a climb to VFR on top. (See VFR-ON-TOP) (Refer to AIM)

ABEAM— An aircraft is "abeam" a fix, point or object when that fix, point or object is approximately 90 degrees to the right or left of the aircraft track. Abeam indicates a general position rather than a precise point.

ABORT— To terminate a preplanned aircraft maneuver; e.g., an aborted takeoff.

ACKNOWLEDGE— Let me know that you have received and understand my message.

ACROBATIC FLIGHT— An intentional maneuver involving an abrupt change in an aircraft's attitude, an abnormal attitude, or abnormal acceleration, not necessary for normal flight. (Refer to FAR Part 91)

ICAO—ACROBATIC FLIGHT— Maneuvers intentionally performed by an aircraft involving an abrupt change in its attitude, an abnormal attitude, or an abnormal variation in speed.

ADDITIONAL SERVICES— Advisory information provided by ATC which includes but is not limited to the following:
1. Traffic advisories.
2. Vectors, when requested by the pilot, to assist aircraft receiving traffic advisories to avoid observed traffic.

3. Altitude deviation information of 300 feet or more from an assigned altitude as observed on a verified (reading correctly) automatic altitude readout (Mode C).

4. Advisories that traffic is no longer a factor.

5. Weather and chaff information.

6. Weather assistance.

7. Bird activity information.

8. Holding pattern surveillance.

Additional services are provided to the extent possible contingent only upon the controller's capability to fit them into the performance of higher priority duties and on the basis of limitations of the radar, volume of traffic, frequency congestion and controller workload. The controller has complete discretion for determining if he is able to provide or continue to provide a service in a particular case. The controller's reason not to provide or continue to provide a service in a particular case is not subject to question by the pilot and need not be made known to him. (See Traffic Advisories) (Refer to AIM)

ADMINISTRATOR— The Federal Aviation Administrator or any person to whom he has delegated his authority in the matter concerned.

ADVISE INTENTIONS— Tell me what you plan to do.

ADVISORY— Advice and information provided to assist pilots in the safe conduct of flight and aircraft movement. (See Advisory Service)

ADVISORY FREQUENCY— The appropriate frequency to be used for Airport Advisory Service. (See Airport Advisory Service and UNICOM) (Refer to Advisory Circular No. 90-42 and AIM)

ADVISORY SERVICE— Advice and information provided by a facility to assist pilots in the safe conduct of flight and aircraft movement. (See Airport Advisory Service, Traffic Advisories, Safety Advisories, Additional Services, Radar Advisory, En Route Flight Advisory Service) (Refer to AIM)

AERIAL REFUELING/IN-FLIGHT REFUELING— A procedure used by the military to transfer fuel from one aircraft to another during flight. (Refer to VFR/IFR Wall Planning Charts).

AERODROME— A defined area on land or water (including any buildings, installations and equipment) intended to be used either wholly or in part for the arrival, departure and movement of aircraft.

AERONAUTICAL BEACON— A visual NAVAID displaying flashes of white and/or colored light to indicate the location of an airport, a heliport, a landmark, a certain point of a Federal airway in mountainous terrain, or an obstruction. (See Airport Rotating Beacon) (Refer to AIM)

AERONAUTICAL CHART— A map used in air navigation containing all or part of the following: Topographic features, hazards and obstructions, navigation aids, navigation routes, designated airspace, and airports. Commonly used aeronautical charts are:

1. Sectional Charts—1:500,000—Designed for visual navigation of slow or medium speed aircraft. Topographic information on these charts features the portrayal of relief, and a judicious selection of visual check points for VFR flight. Aeronautical information includes visual and radio aids to navigation, airports, controlled airspace, restricted areas, obstructions and related data.

2. VFR Terminal Area Charts—1:250,000—Depict Terminal Control Area (TCA) airspace which provides for the control or segregation of all the aircraft within the TCA. The chart depicts topographic information and aeronautical information which includes visual and radio aids to navigation, airports, controlled airspace, restricted areas, obstructions, and related data.

3. World Aeronautical Charts (WAC)—1:1,000,000—Provide a standard series of aeronautical charts covering land areas of the world at a size and scale convenient for navigation by moderate speed aircraft. Topographic information includes cities and towns, principal roads, railroads, distinctive landmarks, drainage, and relief. Aeronautical information includes visual and radio aids to navigation, airports, airways, restricted areas, obstructions and other pertinent data.

4. En Route Low Altitude Charts—Provide aeronautical information for en route instrument navigation (IFR) in the low altitude stratum. Information includes the portrayal of airways, limits of controlled airspace, position identification and frequencies of radio aids, selected airports, minimum en route and minimum obstruction clearance altitudes, airway distances, reporting points, restricted areas, and related data. Area charts which are a part of this series furnish terminal data at a larger scale in congested areas.

5. En Route High Altitude Charts—Provide aeronautical information for en route instrument navigation (IFR) in the high altitude stratum. Information includes the portrayal of jet routes, identification and frequencies of radio aids, selected airports, distances, time zones, special use airspace, and related information.

6. Instrument Approach Procedures (IAP) Charts—Portray the aeronautical data which is required to execute an instrument approach to an airport. These charts depict the procedures, including all related data, and the airport diagram. Each procedure is designated for use with a specific type of electronic navigation system including NDB, TACAN, VOR, ILS and RNAV. These

charts are identified by the type of navigational aid(s) which provide final approach guidance.

7. Standard Instrument Departure (SID) Charts—Designed to expedite clearance delivery and to facilitate transition between takeoff and en route operations. Each SID procedure is presented as a separate chart and may serve a single airport or more than one airport in a given geographical location.

8. Standard Terminal Arrival (STAR) Charts—Designed to expedite air traffic control arrival route procedures and to facilitate transition between en route and instrument approach operations. Each STAR procedure is presented as a separate chart and may serve a single airport or more than one airport in a given geographical location.

9. Airport Taxi Charts—Designed to expedite the efficient and safe flow of ground traffic at an airport. These charts are identified by the official airport name; e.g., Washington National Airport.

ICAO— AERONAUTICAL CHART—A representation of a portion of the earth, its culture and relief, specifically designated to meet the requirements of air navigation.

AFFIRMATIVE— Yes.

AIR CARRIER DISTRICT OFFICE/ACDO— An FAA field office serving an assigned geographical area, staffed with Flight Standards personnel serving the aviation industry and the general public on matters related to the certification and operation of scheduled air carriers and other large aircraft operations.

AIRCRAFT— Device/s that are used or intended to be used for flight in the air, and when used in air traffic control terminology, may include the flight crew.

ICAO-AIRCRAFT— Any machine that can derive support in the atmosphere from the reactions of the air other than the reactions of the air against the earth's surface.

AIRCRAFT APPROACH CATEGORY— A grouping of aircraft based on a speed of 1.3 times the stall speed in the landing configuration at maximum gross landing weight. An aircraft shall fit in only one category. If it is necessary to maneuver at speeds in excess of the upper limit of a speed range for a category, the minimums for the next higher category should be used. For example, an aircraft which falls in Category A, but is circling to land at a speed in excess of 91 kinots, should use the approach Category B minimums when circling to land. The categories are as follows:

1. Category A—Speed less than 91 knots.

2. Category B—Speed 91 knots or more but less than 121 knots.

3. Category C—Speed 121 knots or more but less than 141 knots.

4. Category D—Speed 141 knots or more but less than 166 knots.

5. Category E—Speed 166 knots or more.

(Refer to FAR Parts 1 and 97)

AIRCRAFT CLASSES— For the purposes of Wake Turbulence Separation Minima, ATC classifies aircraft as Heavy, Large, and Small as follows:

1. Heavy—Aircraft capable of takeoff weights of 300,000 pounds or more whether or not they are operating at this weight during a particular phase of flight.

2. Large—Aircraft of more than 12,500 pounds, maximum certificated takeoff weight, up to 300,000 pounds.

3. Small—Aircraft of 12,500 pounds or less maximum certificated takeoff weight. (Refer to AIM)

AIR DEFENSE EMERGENCY— A military emergency condition declared by a designated authority. This condition exists when an attack upon the continental U.S., Alaska, Canada, or U.S. installations in Greenland by hostile aircraft or missiles is considered probable, is imminent, or is taking place. (Refer to AIM)

AIR DEFENSE IDENTIFICATION ZONE/ADIZ— The area of airspace over land or water, extending upward from the surface, within which the ready identification, the location, and the control of aircraft are required in the interest of national security.

1. Domestic Air Defense Identification Zone— An ADIZ within the United States along an international boundary of the United States.

2. Coastal Air Defense Identification Zone— An ADIZ over the coastal waters of the United States.

3. Distant Early Warning Identification Zone (DEWIZ)— An ADIZ over the coastal waters of the State of Alaska.

ADIZ locations and operating and flight plan requirements for civil aircraft operations are specified in FAR Part 99. (Refer to AIM)

AIRMAN'S INFORMATION MANUAL/AIM— A publication containing Basic Flight Information and ATC Procedures designed primarily as a pilot's instructional manual for use in the National Airspace System of the United States.

ICAO-AERONAUTICAL INFORMATION PUBLICATION— A publication issued by or with the authority of a state and containing aeronautical information of a lasting character essential to air navigation.

AIRMET/WA/**AIRMAN'S METEOROLOGICAL INFORMATION—** In-flight weather advisories issued only to amend the area forecast concerning weather phenomena which are of operational interest to all aircraft and potentially hazardous to aircraft having limited capability because of lack of equipment, instrumentation, or pilot qualifications. AIRMET's concern weather of less severity than that covered by SIGMET's or Convective SIGMET's. AIRMET's cover moderate icing, moderate turbulence, sustained winds of 30 knots or more at the surface, widespread areas of ceilings less than 1,000 feet and/or visibility less than 3 miles, and extensive mountain obscurement. (See SIGMET and Convective SIGMET) (Refer to AIM)

AIR NAVIGATION FACILITY— Any facility used in, available for use in, or designed for use in, aid of air navigation, including landing areas, lights, any apparatus or equipment for disseminating weather information, for signaling, for radio-directional finding, or for radio or other electrical communication, and any other structure or mechanism having a similar purpose for guiding or controlling flight in the air or the landing and take-off of aircraft. (See Navigational Aid)

AIRPORT— An area on land or water that is used or intended to be used for the landing and takeoff of aircraft and includes its buildings and facilities, if any.

AIRPORT ADVISORY AREA— The area within ten miles of an airport without a control tower or where the tower is not in operation, and on which a Flight Service Station is located. (See Airport Advisory Service) (Refer to AIM)

AIRPORT ADVISORY SERVICE/AAS— A service provided by flight service stations located at airports not serviced by a control tower. This service consists of providing information to arriving and departing aircraft concerning wind direction and speed, favored runway, altimeter setting, pertinent known traffic, pertinent known field conditions, airport taxi routes and traffic patterns, and authorized instrument approach procedures. This information is advisory in nature and does not constitute an ATC clearance. (See Airport Advisory Area)

AIRPORT ELEVATION/FIELD ELEVATION— The highest point of an airport's usable runways measured in feet from mean sea level. (See Touchdown Zone Elevation)

ICAO-AERODROME ELEVATION— The elevation of the highest point of the landing area.

AIRPORT/FACILITY DIRECTORY— A publication designed primarily as a pilot's operational manual containing all airports, seaplane bases, and heliports open to the public including communications data, navigational facilities, and certain special notices and procedures. This publication is issued in seven volumes according to geographical area.

AIRPORT INFORMATION DESK/AID— An airport unmanned facility designed for pilot self-service briefing, flight planning, and filing of flight plans. (Refer to AIM)

AIRPORT LIGHTING— Various lighting aids that may be installed on an airport. Types of airport lighting include:

1. Approach Light System/ALS—An airport lighting facility which provides visual guidance to landing aircraft by radiating light beams in a directional pattern by which the pilot aligns the aircraft with the extended centerline of the runway on his final approach for landing.

   Condenser-Discharge Sequential Flashing Lights/Sequenced Flashing Lights may be installed in conjunction with the ALS at some airports. Types of Approach Light Systems are:

   a. ALSF-I—Approach Light System with Sequenced Flashing Lights in ILS Cat-I configuration.

   b. ALSF-II—Approach Light System with Sequenced Flashing Lights in ILS Cat-II configuration.

   c. SSALF—Simplified Short Approach Light System with Sequenced Flashing Lights.

   d. SSALR—Simplified Short Approach Light System with Runway Alignment Indicator Lights.

   e. MALSF—Medium Intensity Approach Light System with Sequenced Flashing Lights.

   f. MALSR—Medium Intensity Approach Light System with Runway Alignment Indicator Lights.

   g. LDIN—Sequenced Flashing Lead-in Lights.

   h. RAIL—Runway Alignment Indicator Lights (Sequenced Flashing Lights which are installed only in combination with other light systems).

   i. ODALS—Omnidirectional Approach Lighting System consists of seven omnidirectional flashing lights located in the approach area of a nonprecision runway. Five lights are located on the runway centerline extended with the first light located 300 feet from the threshold and extending at equal intervals up to 1,500 feet from the threshold. The other two lights are located, one on each side of the runway threshold, at a lateral distance of 40 feet from the runway edge, or 75 feet from the runway edge when installed on a runway equipped with a VASI. (Refer to Order 6850.2A)

2. Runway Lights/Runway Edge Lights—Lights having a prescribed angle of emission used to define the lateral limits of a runway. Runway lights are uniformly spaced at intervals of approximately 200 feet, and the intensity may be controlled or preset.

3. Touchdown Zone Lighting—Two rows of transverse light bars located symmetrically about the runway centerline normally at 100 foot intervals. The basic system extends 3,000 feet along the runway.

4. Runway Centerline Lighting—Flush centerline lights spaced at 50-foot intervals beginning 75 feet from the landing threshold and extending to within 75 feet of the opposite end of the runway.

5. Threshold Lights—Fixed green lights arranged symmetrically left and right of the runway centerline, identifying the runway threshold.

6. Runway End Identifier Lights/REIL—Two synchronized flashing lights, one on each side of the runway threshold, which provide rapid and positive identification of the approach end of a particular runway.

7. Visual Approach Slope Indicator/VASI— An airport lighting facility providing vertical visual approach slope guidance to aircraft during approach to landing by radiating a directional pattern of high intensity red and white focused light beams which indicate to the pilot that he is "on path" if he sees red/white, "above path" if white/white, and "below path" if red/red. Some airports serving large aircraft have three-bar VASIs which provide two visual glide paths to the same runway.

8. Boundary Lights—Lights defining the perimeter of an airport or landing area. (Refer to AIM)

AIRPORT MARKING AIDS— Markings used on runway and taxiway surfaces to identify a specific runway, a runway threshold, a centerline, a hold line, etc. A runway should be marked in accordance with its present usage such as:

1. Visual.

2. Nonprecision instrument.

3. Precision instrument. (Refer to AIM)

AIRPORT ROTATING BEACON— A visual NAVAID operated at many airports. At civil airports, alternating white and green flashes indicate the location of the airport. At military airports, the beacons flash alternately white and green, but are differentiated from civil beacons by dualpeaked (two quick) white flashes between the green flashes. (See Special VFR Operations, Instrument Flight Rules) (Refer to AIM, Rotating Beacons)

*ICAO-AERODROME BEACON—*Aeronautical beacon used to indicate the location of an aerodrome.

AIRPORT SURFACE DETECTION EQUIPMENT/ASDE— Radar equipment specifically designed to detect all principal features on the surface of an airport including aircraft and vehicular traffic and to present the entire image on a radar indicator console in the control tower. Used to augment visual observation by tower personnel of aircraft and/or vehicular movements on runways and taxiways.

AIRPORT SURVEILLANCE RADAR/ASR— Approach control radar used to detect and display an aircraft's position in the terminal area. ASR provides range and azimuth information but does not provide elevation data. Coverage of the ASR can extend up to 60 miles.

AIRPORT TRAFFIC AREA— Unless otherwise specifically designated in FAR Part 93, that airspace within a horizontal radius of 5 statute miles from the geographical center of any airport at which a control tower is operating, extending from the surface up to, but not including, an altitude of 3,000 feet above the elevation of an airport. Unless otherwise authorized or required by ATC, no person may operate an aircraft within an airport traffic area except for the purpose of landing at, or taking off from, an airport within that area. ATC authorizations may be given as individual approval of specific operations or may be contained in written agreements between airport users and the tower concerned. (Refer to FAR Parts 1 and 91).

AIRPORT TRAFFIC CONTROL SERVICE— A service provided by a control tower for aircraft operating on the movement area and in the vicinity of an airport. (See Movement Area, Tower.

*ICAO-AERODROME CONTROL SERVICE—*Air traffic control service for aerodrome traffic.

AIR ROUTE SURVEILLANCE RADAR/ARSR— Air route traffic control center (ARTCC) radar used primarily to detect and display an aircraft's position while en route between terminal areas. The ARSR enables controllers to provide radar air traffic control service when aircraft are within the ARSR coverage. In some instances, ARSR may enable an ARTCC to provide terminal radar services similar to but usually more limited than those provided by a radar approach control.

AIR ROUTE TRAFFIC CONTROL CENTER/ARTCC— A facility established to provide air traffic control service to aircraft operating on IFR flight plans within controlled airspace and principally during the en route phase of flight. When equipment capabilities and controller workload permit, certain advisory/assistance services may be provided to VFR aircraft. (See NAS Stage A, En Route Air Traffic Control Service) (Refer to AIM)

AIRSPEED— The apeed of an aircraft relative to its surrounding air mass. The unqualified term "airspeed" means one of the following:

1. Indicated Airspeed—The speed shown on the aircraft airspeed indicator. This is the speed used in pilot/controller communications under the general term "airspeed." (Refer to FAR Part 1)

2. True Airspeed—The airspeed of an aircraft relative to undisturbed air. Used primarily in flight planning and en route portion of flight. When used in pilot/controller communications, it is referred to as "true airspeed" and not shortened to "airspeed".

AIRSTART— The starting of an aircraft engine while the aircraft is airborne, preceded by engine shutdown during training flights or by actual engine failure.

AIR TAXI— Used to describe a helicopter/VTOL aircraft movement conducted above the surface but normally not above 100 feet AGL. The aircraft may proceed either via hover taxi or flight at speeds more than 20 knots. The pilot is solely responsible for selecting a safe airspeed/altitude for the operation being conducted. (See Hover Taxi) (Refer to AIM)

AIR TRAFFIC— Aircraft operating in the air or on an airport surface, exclusive of loading ramps and parking areas.

*ICAO—AIR TRAFFIC—*All aircraft in flight or operating on the maneuvering area of an aerodrome.

AIR TRAFFIC CLEARANCE/ATC CLEARANCE— An authorization by air traffic control, for the purpose of preventing collision between known aircraft, for an aircraft to proceed under specified traffic conditions within controlled airspace. (See ATC Instructions)

*ICAO—AIR TRAFFIC CONTROL CLEARANCE—*Authorization for an aircraft to proceed under conditions specified by an air traffic control unit.

AIR TRAFFIC CONTROL/ATC— A service operated by appropriate authority to promote the safe, orderly and expeditious flow of air traffic.

*ICAO—AIR TRAFFIC CONTROL SERVICE—*A service provided for the purpose of:
1. Preventing collisions:
   a. Between aircraft, and
   b. On the maneuvering area between aircraft and obstructions, and
2. Expediting and maintaining an orderly flow of air traffic.

AIR TRAFFIC CONTROL SERVICE— (See Air Traffic Control)

AIR TRAFFIC CONTROL SPECIALIST/CONTROLLER— A person authorized to provide air traffic control service. (See Air Traffic Control, Flight Service Station)

*ICAO—CONTROLLER—*A person authorized to provide air traffic control services.

AIR TRAFFIC CONTROL COMMAND CENTER/ATCCC— An air traffic service facility consisting of four operational units.

1. Central Flow Control Function/CFCF—Responsible for coordination and approval of all major intercenter flow control restrictions on a system basis in order to obtain maximum utilization of the airspace. (See Fuel Advisory Departure, Quota Flow Control)

2. Central Altitude Reservation Function/CARF—Responsible for coordinating, planning and approving special user requirements under the Altitude Reservation (ALTRV) concept. (See Altitude Reservation)

3. Airport Reservation Office/ARO—Responsible for approving IFR flights at designated high density traffic airports (John F. Kennedy, LaGuardia, O'Hare and Washington National) during specified hours. (Refer to FAR Part 93 and Airport/Facility Directory)

4. ATC Contingency Command Post—A facility which enables the FAA to manage the ATC system when significant portions of the system's capabilities have been lost or are threatened.

AIRWAY BEACON— Used to mark airway segments in remote mountain areas. The light flashes Morse Code to identify the beacon site. (Refer to AIM)

AIRWAY/FEDERAL AIRWAY— A control area or portion thereof established in the form of a corridor, the centerline of which is defined by radio navigational aids. (Refer to FAR Part 71, AIM)

*ICAO-AIRWAY—*A control area or portion thereof established in the form of corridor equipped with radio navigational aids.

ALERT AREA— (See Special Use Airspace)

ALERT NOTICE/ALNOT— A message sent by a Flight Service Station (FSS) or Air Route Traffic Control Center (ARTCC) that requests an extensive communication search for overdue, unreported, or missing aircraft.

ALPHANUMERIC DISPLAY/DATA BLOCK— Letters and numerals used to show identification, altitude, beacon code, and other information concerning a target on a radar display. (See Automated Radar Terminal Systems, NAS Stage A)

ALTERNATE AIRPORT— An airport at which an aircraft may land if a landing at the intended airport becomes inadvisable.

*ICAO-ALTERNATE AERODROME—*An aerodrome specified in the flight plan to which a flight may proceed when it becomes inadvisable to land at the aerodrome of intended landing.

ALTIMETER SETTING— The barometric pressure reading used to adjust a pressure altimeter for variations in existing atmospheric pressure or to the standard altimeter setting (29.92). Refer to FAR Part 91, AIM)

ALTITUDE— The height of a level, point, or object measured in feet Above Ground Level (AGL) or from Mean Sea Level (MSL). (See Flight Level)
1. MSL Altitude—Altitude expressed in feet measured from mean sea level.

2. AGL Altitude—Altitude expressed in feet measured above ground level.

3. Indicated Altitude—The altitude as shown by an altimeter. On a pressure or barometric altimeter it is altitude as shown uncorrected for instrument error and uncompensated for variation from standard atmospheric conditions.

ICAO-ALTITUDE— The vertical distance of a level, a point or an object considered as a point, measured from mean sea level.

ALTITUDE READOUT/AUTOMATIC ALTITUDE REPORT— An aircraft's altitude, transmitted via the Mode C transponder feature, that is visually displayed in 100-foot increments on a radar scope having read-out capability. (See Automated Radar Terminal Systems, NAS Stage A, Alphanumeric Display) (Refer to AIM)

ALTITUDE RESERVATION/ALTRV— Airspace utilization under prescribed conditions normally employed for the mass movement of aircraft or other special user requirements which cannot otherwise be accomplished. ALTRVs are approved by the appropriate FAA facility. (See Air Traffic Control Command Center)

ALTITUDE RESTRICTION— An altitude or altitudes stated in the order flown, which are to be maintained until reaching a specific point or time. Altitude restrictions may be issued by ATC due to traffic, terrain or other airspace considerations.

ALTITUDE RESTRICTIONS ARE CANCELLED— Adherence to previously imposed altitude restrictions is no longer required during a climb or descent.

APPROACH CLEARANCE— Authorization by ATC for a pilot to conduct an instrument approach. The type of instrument approach for which clearance and other pertinent information is provided in the approach clearance when required. (See Instrument Approach Procedure, Cleared for Approach) (Refer to AIM and FAR Part 91)

APPROACH CONTROL FACILITY— A terminal ATC facility that provides approach control service in a terminal area. (See Approach Control Service, Radar Approach Control Facility)

APPROACH CONTROL SERVICE— Air traffic control service provided by an approach control facility for arriving and departing VFR/IFR aircraft and, on occasion, en route aircraft. At some airports not served by an approach control facility, the ARTCC provides limited approach control service. (Refer to AIM)

*ICAO—APPROACH CONTROL SERVICE—*Air traffic service for arriving or departing controlled flights.

APPROACH GATE— The point on the final approach course which is 1 mile from the final approach fix on the side away from the airport or 5 miles from landing threshold, whichever is farther from the landing threshold. This is an imaginary point used within ATC as a basis for final approach course interception for aircraft being vectored to the final approach course.

APPROACH LIGHT SYSTEM— (See Airport Lighting)

APPROACH SEQUENCE— The order in which aircraft are positioned while on approach or awaiting approach clearance. (See Landing Sequence)

*ICAO—APPROACH SEQUENCE—*The order in which two or more aircraft are cleared to approach to land at the aerodrome.

APPROACH SPEED— The recommended speed contained in aircraft manuals used by pilots when making an approach to landing. This speed will vary for different segments of an approach as well as for aircraft weight and configuration.

APRON/RAMP— A defined area on an airport or heliport intended to accommodate aircraft for purposes of loading or unloading passengers or cargo, refueling, parking, or maintenance. With regard to seaplanes, a ramp is used for access to the apron from the water.

*ICAO—APRON—*A defined area, on a land aerodrome, intended to accommodate aircraft for purposes of loading or unloading passengers or cargo, refueling, parking or maintenance.

ARC— The track over the ground of an aircraft flying at a constant distance from a navigational aid by reference to distance measuring equipment (DME).

AREA NAVIGATION/RNAV— A method of navigation that permits aircraft operations on any desired course within the coverage of station-referenced navigation signals or within the limits of self-contained system capability. (Refer to AIM, FAR Part 71)

1. Area Navigation Low Route—An area navigation route within the airspace extending upward from 1,200 feet above the surface of the earth to, but not including 18,000 feet MSL.

2. Area Navigation High Route—An area navigation route within the airspace extending upward from and including 18,000 feet MSL to flight level 450.

3. Random Area Navigation Routes/Random RNAV Routes —Direct routes, based on area navigation capability, between waypoints defined in terms of latitude/longitude coordinates, degree/distance fixes, or offset from published or established routes/airways at a specified distance and direction.

4. RNAV Waypoint/W/P—A predetermined geographical position used for route or instrument approach definition or progress reporting purposes that is defined relative to a VORTAC station position/or in terms of latitude/longitude coordinates.

ICAO—AREA NAVIGATION/RNAV— A method of navigation which permits aircraft operation on any desired flight path within the coverage of station-referenced navigation aids or within the limits of the capability of self-contained aids or a combination of these.

ARMY AVIATION FLIGHT INFORMATION BULLETIN/ USAFIB— A bulletin that provides air operation data covering Army, National Guard, and Army Reserve aviation activities.

ARRESTING SYSTEM— A safety device consisting of two major components, namely, engaging or catching devices, and energy absorption devices for the purpose of arresting both tail hook and/or non-tail hook equipped aircraft. It is used to prevent aircraft from overrunning runways when the aircraft cannot be stopped after landing or during aborted takeoff. Arresting systems have various names; e.g., arresting gear, hook, device, wire barrier cable. (See Abort) (Refer to AIM)

ARRIVAL TIME— The time an aircraft touches down on arrival.

ARTCC— (See Air Route Traffic Control Center)

ASR APPROACH— (See Surveillance Approach)

ATC ADVISES— Used to prefix a message of noncontrol information when it is relayed to an aircraft by other than an air traffic controller. (See Advisory)

ATC ASSIGNED AIRSPACE/ATCAA— Airspace of defined vertical/lateral limits, assigned by ATC, for the purpose of providing air traffic segregation between the specified activities being conducted within the assigned airspace and other IFR air traffic. (See Military Operations Area, Alert Area)

ATC CLEARANCE— (See Air Traffic Clearance)

ATC CLEARS— Used to prefix an ATC clearance when it is relayed to an aircraft by other than an air traffic controller.

ATC INSTRUCTIONS— Directives issued by air traffic control for the purpose of requiring a pilot to take specific actions; e.g., "Turn left heading two five zero," "Go around," "Clear the runway." (Refer to FAR Part 91)

ATCRBS— (See Radar)

ATC REQUESTS— Used to prefix an ATC request when it is relayed to an aircraft by other than an air traffic controller.

AUTOMATED RADAR TERMINAL SYSTEMS/ARTS— The generic term for the ultimate in functional capability afforded by several automation systems. Each differs in functional capabilities and equipment. ARTS plus a suffix roman numeral denotes a specific system. A following letter indicates a major modification to that system. In general, an ARTS displays for the terminal controller aircraft identification, flight plan data, other flight associated information, e.g., altitude and speed, and aircraft position symbols in conjunction with his radar presentation. Normal radar co-exists with the alphanumeric display. In addition to enhancing visualization of the air traffic situation, ARTS facilitate intra/inter-facility transfer and coordination of flight information. These capabilities are enabled by specially designed computers and subsystems tailored to the radar and communications equipments and operational requirements of each automated facility. Modular design permits adoption of improvements in computer software and electronic technologies as they become available while retaining the characteristics unique to each system.

1. ARTS II—A programmable non-tracking, computer aided display subsystem capable of modular expansion. ARTS II systems provide a level of automated air traffic control capability at terminals having low to medium activity. Flight identification and altitude may be associated with the display of secondary radar targets. Also, flight plan information may be exchanged between the terminal and ARTCC.

2. ARTS III—The Beacon Tracking Level (BTL) of the modular programmable automated radar terminal system in use at medium to high activity terminals. ARTS III detects, tracks and predicts secondary radar derived aircraft targets. These are displayed by means of computer-generated symbols and alphanumeric characters depicting flight identification, aircraft altitude, ground speed and flight plan data. Although it does not track primary targets, they are displayed coincident with the secondary radar as well as the symbols and alphanumerics. The system has the capability of communicating with ARTCCs and other ARTS III facilities.

3. ARTS IIIA—The Radar Tracking and Beacon Tracking Level (RT&BTL) of the modular, programmable automated radar terminal system. ARTS IIIA detects, tracks and predicts primary as well as secondary radar-derived aircraft targets. This more sophisticated computer-driven system upgrades the existing ARTS III system by providing improved tracking, continuous data recording and fail-soft capabilities.

AUTOMATIC ALTITUDE REPORTING— That function of a transponder which responds to Mode C interrogations by transmitting the aircraft's altitude in 100-foot increments.

AUTOMATIC CARRIER LANDING SYSTEM/ACLS— U.S. Navy final approach equipment consisting of precision tracking radar coupled to a computer data link to provide continuous information to the aircraft, monitoring capability to the pilot and a backup approach system.

AUTOMATIC DIRECTION FINDER/ADF— An aircraft radio navigation system which senses and indicates the direction to a L/MF nondirectional radio beacon (NDB) ground transmitter. Direction is indicated to the pilot as a magnetic bearing or as a relative bearing to the longitudinal axis of the aircraft depending on the type of indicator installed in the aircraft. In certain applications, such as military, ADF operations may be based on airborne and ground transmitters in the VHF/UHF frequency spectrum. (See Bearing, Nondirectional Beacon)

AUTOMATIC TERMINAL INFORMATION SERVICE/ ATIS— The continuous broadcast of recorded noncontrol information in selected terminal areas. Its puspose is to improve controller effectiveness and to relieve frequency congestion by automating the repetitive transmission of essential but routine information, e.g., "Los Angeles information Alfa. One three zero zero Greenwich. Weather, measured ceiling two thousand overcast, visibility three, haze, smoke, temperature seven one, dew point five seven, wind two five zero at five, altimeter two niner niner six. I-L-S Runway Two Five Left approach in use, Runway Two Five Right closed, advise you have Alfa." (Refer to AIM)

ICAO—AUTOMATIC TERMINAL INFORMATION SERVICE— The provision of current, routine information to arriving and departing aircraft by means of continuous and repetitive broadcasts throughout the day or a specified portion of the day.

AUTOROTATION— A rotorcraft flight condition in which the lifting rotor is driven entirely by action of the air when the rotorcraft is in motion.

1. Autorotative Landing/Touchdown Autorotation—Used by a pilot to indicate that he will be landing without applying power to the rotor.

2. Low Level Autorotation—Commences at an altitude well below the traffic pattern, usually below 100 feet AGL and is used primarily for tactical military training.

3. 180 degrees Autorotation—Initiated from a downwind heading and is commenced well inside the normal traffic pattern. "Go around" may not be possible during the latter part of this maneuver.

AVIATION WEATHER SERVICE— A service provided by the National Weather Service (NWS) and FAA which collects and disseminates pertinent weather information for pilots, aircraft operators, and ATC. Available aviation weather reports and forecasts are displayed at each NWS office and FAA FSS. (See En Route Flight Advisory Service, Transcribed Weather Broadcast, Weather Ad-

visory Service, Transcribed Weather Broadcast, Weather Advisory, Pilots Automatic Telephone Weather Answering Service) (Refer to AIM)

BASE LEG— (See Traffic Pattern)

BEACON— (See Radar, Nondirectional Beacon, Marker Beacon, Airport Rotating Beacon, Aeronautical Beacon, Airway Beacon)

BEARING— The horizontal direction to or from any point, usually measured clockwise from true north, magnetic north, or some other reference point, through 360 degrees. (See Nondirectional Beacon)

BELOW MINIMUMS— Weather conditions below the minimums prescribed by regulation for the particular action involved; e.g., landing minimums, takeoff minimums.

BLAST FENCE— A barrier that is used to divert or dissipate jet or propeller blast.

BLIND SPEED— The rate of departure or closing of a target relative to the radar antenna at which cancellation of the primary radar target by moving target indicator (MTI) circuits in the radar equipment causes a reduction or complete loss of signal.

ICAO—BLIND VELOCITY— The radial velocity of a moving target such that the target is not seen on primary radars fitted with certain forms of fixed echo suppression.

BLIND SPOT/BLIND ZONE— An area from which radio transmissions and/or radar echos cannot be received. The term is also used to describe portions of the airport not visible from the control tower.

BOUNDARY LIGHTS— (See Airport Lighting)

BRAKING ACTION (GOOD, FAIR, POOR, OR NIL)— A report of conditions on the airport movement area providing a pilot with a degree/quality of braking that he might expect. Braking action is reported in terms of good, fair, poor, or nil. (See Runway Condition Reading)

BRAKING ACTION ADVISORIES— When tower controllers have received runway braking action reports which include the terms "poor" or "nil," or whenever weather conditions are conducive to deteriorating or rapidly changing runway braking conditions, the tower will include on the ATIS broadcast the statement, "BRAKING ACTION ADVISORIES ARE IN EFFECT." During the time Braking Action Advisories are in effect, ATC will issue the latest braking action report for the runway in use to each arriving and departing aircraft. Pilots should be prepared for deteriorating braking conditions and should request current runway condition information if not volunteered by controllers. Pilots should also be prepared to provide a descriptive runway condition report to controllers after landing.

— Transmission of information for which an acknowledgement is not expected.

ICAO—BROADCAST— transmission of information relating to air navigation that is not addressed to a specific station or stations.

CALL UP— Initial voice contact between a facility and an aircraft, using the identification of the unit being called and the unit initiating the call. (Refer to AIM)

CARDINAL ALTITUDES OR FLIGHT LEVELS— "Odd" or "Even" thousand-foot altitudes or flight levels; e.g., 5,000, 6,000, 7,000, FL 250, FL260, FL270. (See Altitude, Flight Levels)

CEILING— The heights above the earth's surface of the lowest layer of clouds or obscuring phenomena that is reported as "broken," "overcast," or "obscuration," and not classified as "thin" or "partial".

ICAO—CEILING— The height above the ground or water of the base of the lowest layer of cloud below 6,000 meters (20,000 feet) covering more than half the sky.

CELESTIAL NAVIGATION— The determination of geographical position by reference to celestial bodies. Normally used in aviation as a secondary means of position determination.

CENTER— (See Air Route Traffic Control Center)

CENTER'S AREA— The specified airspace within which an air route traffic control center (ARTCC) provides air traffic control and advisory service. (See Air Route Traffic Control Center) (Refer to AIM)

CENTER WEATHER ADVISORY/CWA— An unscheduled weather advisory issued by Center Weather Service Unit meteorologists for ATC use to alert pilots of existing or anticipated adverse weather conditions within the next 2 hours. A CWA may modify or redefine a SIGMET.

CHAFF— Thin, narrow metallic reflectors of various lengths and frequency responses, used to reflect radar energy. These reflectors when dropped from aircraft and allowed to drift downward result in large targets on the radar display.

CHARTED VISUAL FLIGHT PROCEDURE (CVFP) APPROACH— An approach wherein a radar-controlled aircraft on an IFR flight plan, operating in VFR conditions and having an ATC authorization, may proceed to the airport of intended landing via visual landmarks and altitudes depicted on a charted visual flight procedure.

CHASE/CHASE AIRCRAFT— An aircraft flown in proximity to another aircraft normally to observe its performance during training or testing.

CIRCLE-TO-LAND MANEUVER/CIRCLING MANEUVER— A maneuver initiated by the pilot to align the aircraft with a runway for landing when a straight-in landing from an instrument approach is not possible or is not desirable. This maneuver is made only after ATC authorization has been obtained and the pilot has established required visual reference to the airport (See Circle to Runway. Landing Minimums) (Refer to AIM)

CIRCLE TO RUNWAY (RUNWAY NUMBERED)— Used by ATC to inform the pilot that he must circle to land because the runway in use is other than the runway aligned with the instrument approach procedure. When the direction of the circling maneuver in relation to the airport/runway is required, the controller will state the direction (eight cardinal compass points) and specify a left or right downwind or base leg as appropriate; e.g., "Cleared VOR Runway Three Six Approach circle to Runway Two Two," or "Circle northwest of the airport for a right downwind to Runway Two Two." (See Circle-to-Land Maneuver, Landing Minimums) (Refer to AIM)

CIRCLING APPROACH— (See Circle-to-Land Maneuver)

CIRCLING MINIMA— (See Landing Minimums)

CLEAR-AIR·TURBULENCE/CAT— Turbulence encountered in air where no clouds are present. This term is commonly applied to high-level turbulence associated with wind shear. CAT is often encountered in the vicinity of the jet stream. (See Wind Shear, Jet Stream)

CLEARANCE— (See Air Traffic Clearance)

CLEARANCE LIMIT— The fix, point, or location to which an aircraft is cleared when issued an air traffic clearance.

ICAO—CLEARANCE LIMIT— The point of which an aircraft is granted an air traffic control clearance.

CLEARANCE VOID IF NOT OFF BY (TIME)— Used by ATC to advise an aircraft that the departure clearance is automatically cancelled if takeoff is not made prior to a specified time. The pilot must obtain a new clearance or cancel his IFR flight plan if not off by the specified time.

ICAO—CLEARANCE VOID TIME— A time specified by an air traffic control unit at which a clearance ceases to be valid unless the aircraft concerned has already taken action to comply therewith.

CLEARED AS FILED— Means the aircraft is cleared to proceed in accordance with the route of flight filed in the flight plan. This clearance does not include the altitude, SID, or SID Transition. (See Request Full Route Clearance) (Refer to AIM)

CLEARED FOR (Type Of) APPROACH— ATC authorization for an aircraft to execute a specific instrument approach procedure to an airport; e.g., "Cleared for ILS Runway Three Six Approach." (See Instrument Approach Procedure, Approach Clearance) (Refer to AIM, FAR Part 91)

CLEARED FOR APPROACH— ATC authorization for an aircraft to execute any standard or special instrument approach procedure for that airport. Normally, an aircraft will be cleared for a specific instrument approach procedure. (See Instrument Approach Procedure, Cleared for (Type of) Approach) (Refer to AIM, FAR Part 91)

CLEARED FOR TAKEOFF— ATC authorization for an aircraft to depart. It is predicated on known traffic and known physical airport conditions.

CLEARED FOR THE OPTION— ATC authorization for an aircraft to make a touch-and-go, low approach, missed approach, stop and go, or full stop landing at the discretion of the pilot. It is normally used in training so that an instructor can evaluate a student's performance under changing situations. (See Option Approach (Refer to AIM)

CLEARED THROUGH— ATC authorization for an aircraft to make intermediate stops at specified airports without refiling a flight plan while en route to the clearance limit.

CLEARED TO LAND— ATC authorization for an aircraft to land. It is predicated on known traffic and known physical airport conditions.

CLEARWAY— An area beyond the takeoff runway under the control of airport authorities within which terrain or fixed obstacles may not extend above specified limits. These areas may be required for certain turbine-powered operations and the size and upward slope of the clearway will differ depending on when the aircraft was certificated. (Refer to FAR Part 1)

CLIMBOUT— That portion of flight operation between takeoff and the initial cruising altitude.

CLIMB TO VFR— ATC authorization for an aircraft to climb to VFR conditions within a control zone when the only weather limitation is restricted visibility. The aircraft must remain clear of clouds while climbing to VFR. (See Special VFR) (Refer to AIM)

CLOSED RUNWAY— A runway that is unusable for aircraft operations. Only the airport management/military operations office can close a runway.

CLOSED TRAFFIC— Successive operations involving take-offs and landings or low approaches where the aircraft does not exit the traffic pattern.

CLUTTER— In radar operations, clutter refers to the reception and visual display of radar returns caused by precipitation, chaff, terrain, numerous aircraft targets, or other phenomena. Such returns may limit or preclude ATC from providing services based on radar. (See Ground Clutter, Chaff, Precipitation, Target)

ICAO—Radar Clutter—The visual indication on a display of unwanted signals.

COASTAL FIX— A navigation aid or intersection where aircraft transitions between the domestic route struct and the oceanic route structure.

CODES/TRANSPONDER CODES— The number assign to a particular multiple pulse reply signal transmitted by transponder. (See Discrete Code)

COMBINED CENTER-RAPCON/CERAP— An air traffic facility which combines the functions of an ARTCC and a radar approach control facility. (See Air Route Traffic Control Center/ARTCC, Radar Approach Control Facility)

COMMON ROUTE/COMMON PORTION— That segment of a North American Route between the inland navigation facility and the coastal fix.

COMMON TRAFFIC ADVISORY FREQUENCY/CTAF— A frequency designed for the purpose of carrying out airport advisory practices while operating to or from an uncontrolled airport. The CTAF may be a UNICOM, Multicom, FSS, or tower frequency and is identified in appropriate aeronautical publications. (Refer to AC—90-42C)

COMPASS LOCATOR— A low power, low or medium frequency (L/MF) radio beacon installed at the site of the outer or middle marker of an instrument landing system (ILS). It can be used for navigation at distances of approximately 15 miles or as authorized in the approach procedure.

1. Outer Compass Locator/LOM—A compass locator installed at the site of the outer marker of an instrument landing system. (See Outer Marker)

2. Middle Compass Locator/LMM—A compass locator installed at the site of the middle marker of an instrument landing system. (See Middle Marker)

ICAO—LOCATOR—An LM/MF NDB used as an aid to final approach.

COMPASS ROSE— A circle, graduated in degrees, printed on some charts or marked on the ground at an airport. It is used as a reference to either true or magnetic direction.

COMPOSITE FLIGHT PLAN— A flight plan which specifies VFR operation for one portion of flight and IFR for another portion. It is used primarily in military operations. (Refer to AIM)

COMPOSITE ROUTE SYSTEM— An organized oceanic route structure, incorporating reduced lateral spacing between routes, in which composite separation is authorized.

COMPOSITE SEPARATION— A method of separating aircraft in a composite route system where, by management of route and altitude assignments, a combination of half the lateral minimum specified for the area concerned and half the vertical minimum is applied.

REPORTING POINTS— Reporting points ___ reported to ATC. They are designated on ___ harts by solid triangles or filed in a flight plan ___ted to define direct routes. These points are ___ l locations which are defined by navigation ___ Pilots should discontinue position reporting over ___ ory reporting points when informed by ATC that ___ craft is in "radar contact."

___LICT ALERT— A function of certain air traffic control ___ated systems designed to alert radar controllers to ___ing or pending situations recognized by the program ___ameters that require his immediate attention/action.

___ONSOLAN— A low frequency, long-distance NAVAID ___ased principally for transoceanic navigations.

CONTACT—

1. Establish communication with (followed by the name of the facility and, if appropriate, the frequency to be used).

2. A flight condition wherein the pilot ascertains the attitude of his aircraft and navigates by visual reference to the surface. (See Contact Approach, Radar Contact)

CONTACT APPROACH— An approach wherein an aircraft on an IFR flight plan, having an air traffic control authorization, operating clear of clouds with at least 1 mile flight visibility and a reasonable expectation of continuing to the destination airport in those conditions, may deviate from the instrument approach procedure and proceed to the destination airport by visual reference to the surface. This approach will only be authorized when requested by the pilot and the **reported ground visibility** at the destination airport is at least 1 statute mile. (Refer to AIM)

CONTERMINOUS U.S.— The forty-eight adjoining states and the District of Columbia.

CONTINENTAL CONTROL AREA— (See Controlled Airspace)

CONTINENTAL UNITED STATES— The 49 states located on the continent of North America and the District of Columbia.

CONTROL AREA— (See Controlled Airspace)

CONTROLLED AIRSPACE— Airspace designated as a continental control area, control area, control zone, terminal control area, transition area, or positive control area within which some or all aircraft may be subject to air traffic control. (Refer to AIM, FAR Part 71)

*ICAO—CONTROLLED AIRSPACE—*Airspace of defined dimensions within which air traffic control service is provided to controlled flights.

Types of U.S. Controlled Airspace:

1. Continental Control Area—The airspace of the 48 contiguous states, the District of Columbia and Alaska, excluding the Alaska peninsula west of Long. 160° 00' 00"W, at and above 14,500 feet MSL, but does not include:

   a. The airspace less than 1,500 feet above the surface of the earth or,

   b. Prohibited and restricted areas, other than the restricted areas listed in FAR Part 71.

2. Control Area—Airspace designated as Colored Federal Airways, VOR Federal Airways, control areas associated with jet routes outside the continental control area (FAR 71.161), additional control areas (FAR 71.163), control area extensions (FAR 71.165), and area low routes. Control areas do not include the continental control area, but unless otherwise designated, they do include the airspace between a segment of a main VOR Federal Airway and its associated alternate segments with the vertical extent of the area corresponding to the vertical extent of the related segment of the main airway. The vertical extent of the various categories of airspace contained in control areas is defined in FAR Part 71.

*ICAO—Control Area—*A controlled airspace extending upward from a specified limit above the earth.

3. Control Zone—Controlled airspace which extends upward from the surface and terminates at the base of the continental control area. Control zones that do not underlie the continental control area have no upper limit. A control zone may include one or more airports and is normally a circular area within a radius of 5 statute miles and any extensions necessary to include instrument approach and departure paths.

*ICAO—Control Zone—*A controlled airspace extending upwards from the surface of the earth to a specified upper limit.

4. Terminal Control Area/TCA—Controlled airspace extending upward from the surface or higher to specified altitudes, within which all aircraft are subject to operating rules and pilot and equipment requirements specified in FAR Part 91. TCA's are depicted on Sectional, World Aeronautical, En Route Low Altitude, DOD FLIP and TCA charts. (Refer to FAR Part 91, AIM)

*ICAO—Terminal Control Area—*A control area normally established at the confluence of ATS routes in the vicinity of one or more major aerodromes.

5. Transition Area—Controlled airspace extending upward from 700 feet or more above the surface of the earth when designated in conjunction with an airport for which an approved instrument approach procedure

has been prescribed, or from 1,200 feet or more above the surface of the earth when designated in conjunction with airway route structures or segments. Unless otherwise limited, transition areas terminate at the base of the overlying controlled airspace. Transition areas are designed to contain IFR operations in controlled airspace during portions of the terminal operation and while transiting between the terminal and en route environment.

6. Positive Control Area/PCA—Airspace designated in FAR Part 71 within which there is positive control of aircraft. Flight in PCA is normally conducted under instrument flight rules. PCA is designated throughout most of the conterminous United States and its vertical extent is from 18,000 feet MSL to and including flight level 600. In Alaska PCA does not include the airspace less than 1,500 feet above the surface of the earth, nor the airspace over the Alaska Peninsula west of longitude 160 degrees West. Rules for operating in PCA are found in FARs 91.97 and 91.24.

CONTROLLER— (See Air Traffic Control Specialist)

CONTROL SECTOR— An airspace area of defined horizontal and vertical dimensions for which a controller, or group of controllers, has air traffic control responsibility, normally within an air route traffic control center or an approach control facility. Sectors are established based on predominant traffic flows, altitude strata, and controller workload. Pilot-communications during operations within a sector are normally maintained on discrete frequencies assigned to the sector. (See Discrete Frequency)

CONTROL SLASH— A radar beacon slash representing the actual position of the associated aircraft. Normally, the control slash is the one closest to the interrogating radar beacon site. When ARTCC radar is operating in narrowband (digitized) mode, the control slash is converted to a target symbol.

CONTROL ZONE— (See Controlled Airspace)

CONVECTIVE SIGMET/WST/CONVECTIVE SIGNIFICANT METEOROLOGICAL INFORMATION—

A weather advisory concerning convective weather significant to the safety of all aircraft. Convective SIGMET's are issued for tornadoes, lines of thunderstorms, embedded thunderstorms of any intensity level, areas of thunderstorms greater than or equal to VIP level 4 with an areal coverage of 4/10 (40%) or more, and hail 3/4 inch or greater. (See SIGMET, AIRMET) (Refer to AIM)

COORDINATES— The intersection of lines of reference, usually expressed in degrees/minutes/seconds of latitude and longitude, used to determine position or location.

COORDINATION FIX— The fix in relation to which facilities will handoff, transfer control of an aircraft, or coordinate flight progress data. For terminal facilities, it may also serve as a clearance for arriving aircraft.

CORRECTION— An error has been made in the transmission and the correct version follows.

COURSE—

1. The intended direction of flight in the horizontal plane measured in degrees from north.
2. The ILS localizer signal pattern usually specified as front course or back course.

(See Bearing, Radial, Instrument Landing Systems)

CRITICAL ENGINE— The engine which, upon failure, would most adversely affect the performance or handling qualities of an aircraft.

CROSS (FIX) AT (ALTITUDE)— Used by ATC when a specific altitude restriction at a specified fix is required.

CROSS (FIX) AT OR ABOVE (ALTITUDE)— Used by ATC when an altitude restriction at a specified fix is required. It does not prohibit the aircraft from crossing the fix at a higher altitude than specified; however, the higher altitude may not be one that will violate a succeeding altitude restriction or altitude assignment. (See Altitude Assignment, Altitude Restriction.) (Refer to AIM)

CROSS (FIX) AT OR BELOW (ALTITUDE)— Used by ATC when a maximum crossing altitude at a specific fix is required. It does not prohibit the aircraft from crossing the fix at a lower altitude; however, it must be at or above the minimum IFR altitude. (See Minimum IFR altitude, Altitude Restriction) (Refer to FAR Part 91)

CROSSWIND—

1. When used concerning the traffic pattern, the word means "crosswind leg." (See Traffic Pattern)
2. When used concerning wind conditions, the word means a wind not parallel to the runway or the path of an aircraft. (See Crosswind Component)

CROSSWIND COMPONENT— The wind component measured in knots at 90 degrees to the longitudinal axis of the runway.

CRUISE— Used in an ATC clearance to authorize a pilot to conduct flight at any altitude from the minimum IFR altitude up to and including the altitude specified in the clearance. The pilot may level off at any intermediate altitude within this block of airspace. Climb/descent within the block is to be made at the discretion of the pilot. However, once the pilot starts descent and verbally reports leaving an altitude in the block he may not return to that altitude without additional ATC clearance. Further, it is approval for the pilot to proceed to and make an approach at destination airport and can be used in conjunction with:

1. An airport clearance limit at locations with a standard/-special instrument approach procedure. The FARs require that if an instrument letdown to an airport is necessary the pilot shall make the letdown in accordance with a standard/special instrument approach procedure for that airport, or

2. An airport clearance limit at locations that are within/-below/outside controlled airspace and without a standard/special instrument approach procedure. Such a clearance is NOT AUTHORIZATION for the pilot to descend under IFR conditions below the applicable minimum IFR altitude nor does it imply that ATC is exercising control over aircraft in uncontrolled airspace; however, it provides a means for the aircraft to proceed to destination airport, descend and land in accordance with applicable FARs governing VFR flight operations. Also, this provides search and rescue protection until such time as the IFR flight plan is closed. (See Instrument Approach Procedure)

CRUISING ALTITUDE/LEVEL— An altitude or flight level maintained during en route level flight. This is a constant altitude and should not be confused with a cruise clearance. (See Altitude)

*ICAO—CRUISING LEVEL—*A level maintained during a significant portion of a flight.

DECISION HEIGHT/DH— With respect to the operation of aircraft, means the height at which a decision must be made during an ILS or PAR instrument approach to either continue the approach or to execute a missed approach.

*ICAO—DECISION HEIGHT—*A specified height at which a missed approach must be initiated if the required visual reference to continue the approach to land has not been established.

DECODER— The device used to decipher signals received from ATCRBS transponders to effect their display as select codes. (See Codes, Radar)

DEFENSE VISUAL FLIGHT RULES/DVFR— Rules applicable to flights within an ADIZ conducted under the visual flight rules in FAR Part 91. (See Air Defense Identification Zone) (Refer to FAR Part 99)

DELAY INDEFINITE (REASON IF KNOWN) EXPECT FURTHER CLEARANCE (TIME)— Used by ATC to inform a pilot when an accurate estimate of the delay time and the reason for the delay cannot immediately be determined; e.g., a disabled aircraft on the runway, terminal or center area saturation, weather below landing minimums, etc. (See Expect Further Clearance)

DEPARTURE CONTROL— A function of an approach control facility providing air traffic control service for departing IFR and, under certain condition, VFR aircraft. (See Approach Control) (Refer to AIM)

DEPARTURE TIME— The time an aircraft becomes airborne.

DEVIATIONS—

1. A departure from a current clearance, such as an off course maneuver to avoid weather or turbulence.

2. Where specifically authorized in the FAR's and requested by the pilot, ATC may permit pilots to deviate from certain regulations. (Refer to AIM)

DF APPROACH PROCEDURE— Used under emergency conditions where another instrument approach procedure cannot be executed. DF guidance for an instrument approach is given by ATC facilities with DF capability. (See DF Guidance, Direction Finder) (Refer to AIM)

DF FIX— The geographical location of an aircraft obtained by one or more direction finders. (See Direction Finder)

DF GUIDANCE/DF STEER— Headings provided to aircraft by facilities equipped with direction finding equipment. These headings, if followed, will lead the aircraft to a predetermined point such as the DF station or an airport. DF guidance is given to aircraft in distress or to other aircraft which request the service. Practice DF guidance is provided when workload permits. (See Direction Finder, DF Fix) (Refer to AIM)

DIRECT— Straight line flight between two navigational aids, fixes, points or any combination thereof. When used by pilots in describing off-airway routes, points defining direct route segments become compulsory reporting points unless the aircraft is under radar contact.

DIRECTION ALTITUDE AND IDENTITY READOUT/-DAIR— The DAIR System is a modification to the AN/TPX-42 Interrogator System. The Navy has two adaptations of the DAIR System, Carrier Air Traffic Control Direct Altitude and Identification Readout System for Aircraft Carriers and Radar Air Traffic Control Facility Direct Altitude and Identity Readout System for land based terminal operations. The DAIR detects, tracks, and predicts secondary radar aircraft targets. Targets are displayed by means of computer generated symbols and alphanumeric characters depicting flight identification, altitude, ground speed, and flight plan data. The DAIR System is capable of interfacing with ARTCC's.

DIRECTION FINDER/DF/UDF/VDF/UVDF— A radio receiver equipped with a directional sensing antenna used to take bearings on a radio transmitter. Specialized radio direction finders are used in aircraft as air navigation aids.

Others are ground based primarily to obtain a "fix" on a pilot requesting orientation assistance, or to locate downed aircraft. A location "fix" is established by the intersection of two or more bearing lines plotted on a navigational chart using either two separately located Direction Finders to obtain a fix on an aircraft or by a pilot plotting the bearing indications of his DF on two separately located ground based transmitters, both of which can be identified on his chart. UDFs receive signals in the ultra high frequency radio broadcast band; VDF's in the very high frequency band; and UVDFs in both bands. ATC provides DF service at those air traffic control towers and flight service stations listed in the Airport/Facility Directory, and DOD FLIP IFR En Route Supplement. (See DF Guidance, DF Fix)

DISCRETE CODE/DISCRETE BEACON CODE— As used in the Air Traffic Control Radar Beacon System (ATCRBS), any one of the 4096 selectable Mode 3/A aircraft transponder codes except those ending in zero zero; e.g., discrete codes: 0010, 1201, 2317, 7777; non-discrete codes: 0100, 1200, 7700. Non-discrete codes are normally reserved for radar facilities that are not equipped with discrete decoding capability and for other purposes such as emergencies (7700), VFR aircraft (1200), etc. (See Radar) (Refer to AIM)

DISCRETE FREQUENCY— A separate radio frequency for use in direct pilot-controller communications in air traffic control which reduces frequency congestion by controlling the number of aircraft operating on a particular frequency at one time. Discrete frequencies are normally designated for each control sector in en route/terminal ATC facilities. Discrete frequencies are listed in the Airport/Facility Directory, and DOD FLIP IFR En Route Supplement. (See Control Sector)

DISPLACED THRESHOLD— A threshold that is located at a point on the runway other than the designated beginning of the runway. (See Threshold) (Refer to AIM)

DISTANCE MEASURING EQUIPMENT/DMS— Equipment (airborne and ground) used to measure, in nautical miles, the slant range distance of an aircraft from the DME navigational aid. (See TACAN, VORTAC)

DISTRESS— A condition of being threatened by serious and/or imminent danger, and of requiring immediate assistance.

DME FIX— A geographical position determined by reference to a navigational aid which provides distance and azimuth information. It is defined by a specific distance in nautical miles and a radial or course (i.e., localizer) in degrees magnetic from that aid. (See Distance Measuring Equipment/-DME, Fix)

DME SEPARATION— Spacing of aircraft in terms of distances (Nautical miles) determined by reference to distance measuring equipment (DME) (See Distance Measuring Equipment)

DOD FLIP— Department of Defense Flight Information Publications used for flight planning, en route, and terminal operations. FLIP is produced by the Defense Mapping Agency for world-wide use. United States Government Flight Information Publications (en route charts and instrument approach procedure charts) are incorporated in DOD FLIP for use in the National Airspace System (NAS)

DOWNWIND LEG— (See Traffic Pattern)

DRAG CHUTE— A parachute device installed on certain aircraft which is deployed on landing roll to assist in deceleration of the aircraft.

***EMERGENCY—* A DISTRESS or URGENCY** condition.

EMERGENCY LOCATOR TRANSMITTER/ELT— A radio transmitter attached to the aircraft structure which operates from its own power source on 121.5 MHz and 243.0MHz. It aids in locating downed aircraft by radiating a downward sweeping audio tone, 2-4 times per second. It is designed to function without human action after an accident. (Refer to FAR Part 91, AIM)

EMERGENCY SAFE ALTITUDE— (See Minimum Safe Altitude)

E-MSAW— (See En Route Minimum Safe Altitude Warning)

EN ROUTE AIR TRAFFIC CONTROL SERVICES— Air traffic control service provided aircraft on IFR flight plans generally by centers, when these aircraft are operating between departure and destination terminal areas. When equipment capabilities and controller workload permit, certain advisory/assistance services may be provided to VFR aircraft. (See NAS Stage A, Air Route Traffic Control Center) (Refer to AIM)

EN ROUTE AUTOMATED RADAR TRACKING SYSTEM/-EARTS— An automated radar and radar beacon tracking system. Its functional capabilities and design are essentially the same as the terminal ARTS IIIA system except for the EARTS capability of employing both short-range (ASR) and long-range (ARSR) radars, use of full digital radar displays, and fail-safe design. (See Automated Radar Terminal Systems/-ARTS)

EN ROUTE CHARTS— (See Aeronautical Charts)

EN ROUTE DESCENT— Descent from the en route cruising altitude which takes place along the route of flight.

EN ROUTE FLIGHT ADVISORY SERVICE/FLIGHT WATCH— A service specifically designed to provide, upon pilot request, timely weather information pertinent to his type of flight, intended route of flight and altitude. The FSSs providing this service are listed in The Airport/Facility Directory. (Refer to AIM)

EN ROUTE MINIMUM SAFE ALTITUDE WARNING/E-MSAW— A function of the NAS Stage A en route computer that aids the controller by alerting him when a tracked aircraft is below or predicted by the computer to go below a predetermined minimum IFR altitude (MIA)

EXECUTE MISSED APPROACH— Instructions issued to a pilot making an instrument approach which means continue inbound to the missed approach point and execute the missed approach procedure as described on the Instrument Approach Procedure Chart, or as previously assigned by ATC. The pilot may climb immediately to the altitude specified in the missed approach procedure upon making a missed approach. No turns should be initiated prior to reaching the missed approach point. When conducting an ASR or PAR approach, execute the assigned missed approach procedure immediately upon receiving instructions to "execute missed approach." (Refer to AIM)

EXPECT (ALTITUDE) AT (TIME) or (FIX)— Used under certain conditions in a departure clearance to provide a pilot with an altitude to be used in the event of two-way communication failure. (Refer to AIM)

EXPECT DEPARTURE CLEARANCE (TIME)/-EDCT— Used in Fuel Advisory Departure (FAD) program. The time the operator can expect a gate release. Excluding long distance flights, an EDCT will always be assigned even though it may be the same as the Estimated Time of Departure (ETD). The EDCT is calculated by adding the ground delay factor. (See Fuel Advisory Departure)

EXPECT FURTHER CLEARANCE (TIME)/EFC— The time a pilot can expect to receive clearance beyond a clearance limit.

EXPECT FURTHER CLEARANCE VIA (AIRWAYS, ROUTES OR FIXES)— Used to inform a pilot of the routing he can expect if any part of the route beyond a short range clearance limit differs from that filed.

EXPEDITE— Used by ATC when prompt compliance is required to avoid the development of an imminent situation.

FAST FILE— A system whereby a pilot files a flight plan via telephone that is tape recorded and then transcribed for transmission to the appropriate air traffic facility. Locations having a fast file capability are contained in the Airport/Facility Directory. (Refer to AIM)

FEATHERED PROPELLER— A propeller whose blades have been rotated so that the leading and trailing edges are nearly parallel with the aircraft flight path to stop or minimize drag and engine rotation. Normally used to

indicate shutdown of a reciprocating or turboprop engine due to malfunction.

FEEDER ROUTE— A route depicted on instrument approach procedure charts to designate routes for aircraft to proceed from the en route structure to the initial approach fix (IAF). (See Instrument Approach Procedure)

FERRY FLIGHT— A flight for the purpose of:

1. Returning an aircraft to base,
2. Delivering an aircraft from one location to another.
3. Moving an aircraft to and from a maintenance base.

Ferry flights, under certain conditions may be conducted under terms of a special flight permit.

FILED— Normally used in conjunction with flight plans, meaning a flight plan has been submitted to ATC.

FILED EN ROUTE DELAY— Any of the following preplanned delays at points/areas along the route of flight which require special flight plan filing and handling techniques.

1. Terminal Area Delay—A delay within a terminal area for touch-and-go, low approach, or other terminal area activity.

2. Special Use Airspace Delay—A delay within a Military Operating Area, Restricted Area, Warning Area, or ATC Assigned Airspace.

3. Aerial Refueling Delay—A delay within an Aerial Refueling Track or Anchor.

FINAL— Commonly used to mean that an aircraft is on the final approach course or is aligned with a landing area. (See Final Approach Course, Final Approach—IFR, Traffic Pattern, Segments of an Instrument Approach Procedure)

FINAL APPROACH COURSE— A straight line extension of a localizer, a final approach radial/bearing, or a runway centerline, all without regard to distance. (See Final Approach—IFR, Traffic Pattern)

FINAL APPROACH FIX/FAF— The designated fix from or over which the final approach (IFR) to an airport is executed. The FAF identifies the beginning of the final approach segment of the instrument approach. (See Final Approach Point, Segments of an Instrument Approach Procedure, Glide Slope Intercept Altitude)

FINAL APPROACH—IFR— The flight path of an aircraft which is inbound to an airport on a final instrument approach course, beginning at the final approach fix or point and extending to the airport or the point where a circle to land maneuver or a missed approach is executed. (See Segments of an Instrument Approach Procedure, Final Approach Fix, Final Approach Course, Final Approach Point)

ICAO—FINAL APPROACH—That part of an instrument approach procedure from the time the aircraft has:

1. Completed the last procedure turn or base turn, where one is specified, or
2. Crossed a specified fix, or
3. Intercepted the last track specified for the procedures until it has crossed a point in the vicinity of an aerodrome from which:
   a. A landing can be made, or
   b. A missed approach procedure is initiated.

FINAL APPROACH POINT— The point, within prescribed limits of an instrument approach procedure, where the aircraft is established on the final approach course and final approach descent may be commenced. A final approach point is applicable only in nonprecision approaches where a final approach fix has not been established. In such instances, the point identifies the beginning of the final approach segment of the instrument approach. (See Final Approach Fix, Segments of an Instrument Approach Procedure, Glide Slope Intercept Altitude)

FINAL APPROACH SEGMENT— (See Segments of an Instrument Approach Procedure)

FINAL APPROACH—VFR— (See Traffic Pattern)

FINAL CONTROLLER— The controller providing information and final approach guidance during PAR and ASR approaches utilizing radar equipment. (See Radar Approach)

FIX— A geographical position determined by visual reference to the surface, by reference to one or more radio NAVAIDs, by celestial plotting, or by another navigational device.

FLAG/FLAG ALARM— A warning device incorporated in certain airborne navigation and flight instruments indicating that:

1. Instruments are inoperative or otherwise not operating satisfactorily, or
2. Signal strength or quality of the received signal falls below acceptable values.

FLAMEOUT— Unintended loss of combustion in turbine engines resulting in the loss of engine power.

FLIGHT CHECK— A call-sign prefix used by FAA aircraft engaged in flight inspection/certification of navigational aids and flight procedures. The word "recorded" may be added as a suffix; e.g., "Flight Check 320 recorded" to indicate that an automated flight inspection is in progress in terminal areas. (See Flight Inspection/Flight Check) (Refer to AIM)

FLIGHT INFORMATION REGION/FIR— An airspace of defined dimensions within which Flight Information Service and Alerting Service are provided.

1. Flight Information Service—A service provided for the purpose of giving advice and information useful for the safe and efficient conduct of flights.
2. Alerting Service—A service provided to notify appropriate organizations regarding aircraft in need of search and rescue aid, and assist such organizations as required.

FLIGHT INSPECTION/FLIGHT CHECK— Inflight investigation and evaluation of a navigational aid to determine whether it meets established tolerances. (See Navigational Aid)

FLIGHT LEVEL— A level of constant atmospheric pressure related to a reference datum of 29.92 inches of mercury. Each is stated in three digits that represent hundreds of feet. For example, flight level 250 represents a barometric altimeter indication of 25,000 feet; flight level 255, an indication of 25,500 feet.

*ICAO—FLIGHT LEVELS→*Surfaces of constant atmospheric pressure which are related to a specific pressure datum, 1013.2 mb (29.92 inches) and are separated by specific pressure intervals.

FLIGHT LINE— A term used to describe the precise movement of a civil photogrammetric aircraft along a predetermined course(s), at a predetermined altitude, during the actual photographic run.

FLIGHT PATH— A line, course, or track along which an aircraft is flying or intended to be flown. (See Track, Course)

FLIGHT PLAN— Specified information relating to the intended flight of an aircraft that is filed orally or in writing with an FSS or an ATC facility. (See Fast File, Filed) (Refer to AIM)

FLIGHT RECORDER— A general term applied to any instrument or device that records information about the performance of an aircraft in flight or about conditions encountered in flight. Flight recorders may make records of airspeed, outside air temperature, vertical acceleration, engine RPM, manifold pressure, and other pertinent variables for a given flight.

*ICAO—FLIGHT RECORDER—*Any type of recorder installed in the aircraft for the purpose of complementing accident/-incident investigation.

FLIGHT SERVICE STATION/FSS— Air traffic facilities which provide pilot briefing, en route communications and VFR search and rescue services, assist lost aircraft and aircraft in emergency situations, relay ATC clearances, originate Notices to Airmen, broadcast aviation weather and NAS information, receive and process IFR flight plans and monitor NAVAIDS. In addition, at selected locations FSSs provide Enroute Flight Advisory Service (Flight Watch), take weather observations, issue airport advisories, and advise Customs and Immigration of transborder flights. (Refer to AIM)

FLIGHT STANDARDS DISTRICT OFFICE/FSDO— An FAA field office serving an assigned geographical area, staffed with Flight Standards personnel who serve the aviation industry and the general public on matters relating to the certification and operation of air carrier and general aviation aircraft. Activities include general surveillance of operational safety, certification of airmen and aircraft, accident prevention, investigation, enforcement, etc.

FLIGHT TEST— A flight for the purpose of:

1. Investigating the operation/flight characteristics of an aircraft or aircraft component.
2. Evaluating an applicant for a pilot certificate or rating.

FLIGHT VISIBILITY— (See Visibility)

FLIGHT WATCH— A shortened term for use in air-ground contacts on frequency 122.0 MHz to identify the flight service station providing En Route Flight Advisory Service; e.g., "Oakland Flight Watch." (See En Route Flight Advisory Service)

FLIP— (See DOD FLIP)

FLOW CONTROL— Measures designed to adjust the flow of traffic into a given airspace, along a given route, or bound for a given aerodrome (airport) so as to ensure the most effective utilization of the airspace. (See Quota Flow Control) (Refer to Airport/Facility Directory)

FLY HEADING (DEGREES)— Informs the pilot of the heading he should fly. The pilot may have to turn to, or continue on, a specific compass direction in order to comply with the instructions. The pilot is expected to turn in the shorter direction to the heading, unless otherwise instructed by ATC.

FORMATION FLIGHT— More than one aircraft which, by prior arrangement between the pilots, operate as a single aircraft with regard to navigation and position reporting. Separation between aircraft within the formation is the responsibility of the flight leader and the pilots of the other aircraft in the flight. This includes transition periods when aircraft within the formation are maneuvering to attain separation from each other to effect individual control and during join-up and breakaway.

1. A standard formation is one in which a proximity of no more than 1 mile laterally or longitudinally and within 100 feet vertically from the flight leader is maintained by each wingman.
2. Nonstandard formations are those operating under any of the following conditions:

a. When the Flight leader has requested and ATC has approved other than standard formation dimensions.
b. When operating within an authorized altitude reservation (ALTRV) or under the provisions of a letter of agreement.
c. When the operations are conducted in airspace specifically designed for a special activity. (See Altitude Reservation) (Refer to FAR Part 91)

FSS— (See Flight Service Station)

FUEL ADVISORY DEPARTURE/FAD— Procedures to minimize engine running time for aircraft destined for an airport experiencing prolonged arrival delays. (Refer to AIM)

FUEL DUMPING— Airborne release of usable fuel. This does not include the dropping of fuel tanks. (See Jettisoning of External Stores)

FUEL SIPHONING/FUEL VENTING— Unintentional release of fuel caused by overflow, puncture, loose cap, etc.

GATE HOLD PROCEDURES— Procedures at selected airports to hold aircraft at the gate or other ground location whenever departure delays exceed or are anticipated to exceed 5 minutes. The sequence for departure will be maintained in accordance with initial call up unless modified by Flow Control restrictions. Pilots should monitor the ground control/clearance delivery frequency for engine startup advisories or new proposed start time if the delay changes. (See Flow Control)

GENERAL AVIATION— That portion of civil aviation which encompasses all facets of aviation except air carriers holding a certificate of public convenience and necessity from the Civil Aeronautics Board and large aircraft commercial operators.

*ICAO—GENERAL AVIATION—*All civil aviation operations other than scheduled air services and non-scheduled air transport operations for remuneration or hire.

GENERAL AVIATION DISTRICT OFFICE/GADO— An FAA field office serving a designated geographical area, staffed with Flight Standards personnel, who have responsibility for serving the aviation industry and the general public on all matters relating to the certification and operation of general aviation aircraft.

GLIDE PATH, (ON/ABOVE/BELOW)— Used by ATC to inform an aircraft making a PAR approach of its vertical position (elevation) relative to the descent profile. The terms "slightly" and "well" are used to describe the degree of deviation; e.g., "slightly above glidepath." Trent information is also issued with respect to the elevation of the aircraft and may be modified by the terms "rapidly" and "slowly," e.g., "well above glidepath", coming down rapidly." (See PAR Approach)

GLIDE SLOPE/GS— Provides vertical guidance for aircraft during approach and landing. The glide slope consists of the following:

1. Electronic components emitting signals which provide vertical guidance by reference to airborne instruments during instrument approaches such as ILS, or

2. Visual ground aids, such as VASI, which provide vertical guidance for VFR approach or for the visual portion of an instrument approach and landing.

*ICAO—GLIDE PATH—*A descent profile determined for vertical guidance during a final approach.

GLIDE SLOPE INTERCEPT ALTITUDE— The minimum altitude of the intermediate approach segment prescribed for a precision approach which assures required obstacle clearance. It is depicted on instrument approach procedure charts. (See Segments of an Instrument Approach Procedure, Instrument Landing System)

GO AHEAD— Proceed with your message. Not to be used for any other purpose.

GO AROUND— Instructions for a pilot to abandon his approach to landing. Additional instructions may follow. Unless otherwise advised by ATC, a VFR aircraft or an aircraft conducting visual approach should overfly the runway while climbing to traffic pattern altitude and enter the traffic pattern via the crosswind leg. A pilot on an IFR flight plan making an instrument approach should execute the published missed approach procedure or proceed as instructed by ATC, e.g., "Go around" (additional instructions, if required). (See Low Approach, Missed Approach)

GROUND CLUTTER— A pattern produced on the radar scope by ground returns which may degrade other radar returns in the affected area. The effect of ground clutter is minimized by the use of moving target indicator (MTI) circuits in the radar equipment resulting in a radar presentation which displays only targets which are in motion. (See Clutter)

GROUND CONTROLLED APPROACH/GCA— A radar approach system operated from the ground by air traffic control personnel transmitting instructions to the pilot by radio. The approach may be conducted with surveillance radar (ASR) only or with both surveillance and precision approach radar (PAR). Usage of the term "GCA" by pilots is discouraged except when referring to a GCA facility. Pilots should specifically reques a "PAR" approach when a precision radar approach is desired or request an "ASR" or "surveillance" approach when a nonprecision radar approach is desired. (See Radar Approach)

GROUND SPEED— The speed of an aircraft relative to the surface of the earth.

GROUND VISIBILITY— (See Visibility)

HANDOFF— An action taken to transfer the radar identification of an aircraft from one controller to another if the aircraft will enter the receiving controller's airspace and radio communications with the aircraft will be transferred.

HAVE NUMBERS— Used by pilots to inform ATC that they have received runway, wind, and altimeter information only.

HEAVY (AIRCRAFT)— (See Aircraft Classes)

HEIGHT ABOVE AIRPORT/HAA— The height of the Minimum Descent Altitude above the published airport elevation. This is published in conjunction with circling minimums. (See Minimum Descent Altitude)

HEIGHT ABOVE LANDING/HAL The height above a designated helicopter landing area used for helicopter instrument approach procedures. (Refer to FAR Part 97)

HEIGHT ABOVE TOUCHDOWN/HAT— The height of the Decision Height or Minimum Descent Altitude above the highest runway elevation in the touchdown zone (first 3,000 feet of the runway). HAT is published on instrument approach charts in conjunction with all straight-in minimums. (See Decision Height, Minimum Descent Altitude)

HELICOPTER/COPTER— Rotorcraft that, for its horizontal motion, depends principally on its engine-driven rotors.

*ICAO—HELICOPTER—*A heavier-than-air aircraft supported in flight by the reactions of the air on one or more power-driven rotors on substantially vertical axes.

HELIPAD— A small, designated area, usually with a prepared surface, on a heliport, airport, landing/take-off area, apron/ramp, or movement area used for takeoff, landing, or parking of helicopters.

HELIPORT— An area of land, water, or structure used or intended to be used for the landing and takeoff of helicopters and includes its buildings and facilities, if any.

HERTZ/Hz— The standard radio equivalent of frequency in cycles per second of an electromagnetic wave. Kilohertz (kHz) is a frequency of one thousand cycles per second. Megahertz (MHz) is a frequency of one million cycles per second.

HIGH FREQUENCY COMMUNICATIONS/HF COMMUNICATIONS— High radio frequencies (HF) between 3 and 30 MHz used for air-to-ground voice communication in overseas operations.

HIGH FREQUENCY/HF— The frequency band between 3 and 30 MHz. (See High Frequency Communications)

HIGH SPEED TAXIWAY/EXIT/TURNOFF— A long radius taxiway designed and provided with lighting or marking to define the path of aircraft, traveling at high speed (up to 60 knots), from the runway center to a apoint on the center of a taxiway. Also referred to as long radius exit or turn-off taxiway. The high speed taxiway is designed to expedite aircraft turning off the runway after landing, thus reducing runway occupancy time.

HOLD/HOLDING PROCEDURE— A predetermined maneuver which keeps aircraft within a specified airspace while awaiting further clearance from air traffic control. Also used during ground operations to keep aircraft within a specified area or at a specified point while awaiting further clearance from air traffic control. (See Holding Fix) (Refer to AIM)

HOLDING FIX— A specified fix identifiable to a pilot by NAVAIDS or visual reference to the ground used as a reference point in establishing and maintaining the position of an aircraft while holding. (See Fix, Hold, Visual Holding) (Refer to AIM)

ICAO—HOLDING POINT— A specified location, identified by visual or other means, in the vicinity of which the position of an aircraft in flight is maintained with air traffic control clearances.

HOMING— Flight toward a NAVAID, without correcting for wind, by adjusting the aircraft heading to maintain a relative bearing of zero degrees. (See Bearing)

ICAO—HOMING— The procedure of using the direction-finding equipment of one radio station with the emission of another radio station, where at least one of the stations is mobile, and whereby the mobile station proceeds continuously towards the other station.

HOVER CHECK— Used to describe when a helicopter/VTOL aircraft required a stabilized hover to conduct a performance/power check prior to hover taxi, air taxi, or takeoff. Altitude of the hover will vary based on the purpose of the check.

HOVER TAXI— Used to describe a helicopter/VTOL aircraft movement conducted above the surface and in ground effect at airspeeds less than approximately 20 knots. The actual height may vary and some helicopters may require hover taxi above 25 feet AGL to reduce ground effect turbulence or provide clearance for cargo slingloads. (See Air Taxi, Hover Check) (Refer to AIM)

HOW DO YOU HEAR ME?— A question relating to the quality of the transmission or to determine how well the transmission is being received.

IDENT— A request for a pilot to activate the aircraft transponder identification feature. This will help the controller to confirm an aircraft identity or to identify an aircraft. (Refer to AIM)

IDENT FEATURE— The special feature in the Air Traffic Control Radar Beacon System (ATCRBS) equipment. It is used to immediately distinguish one displayed beacon target from other beacon targets. (See IDENT)

IF FEASIBLE, REDUCE SPEED TO (SPEED)— (See Speed Adjustment)

IF NO TRANSMISSION RECEIVED FOR (TIME)— Used by ATC in radar approaches to prefix procedures which should be followed by the pilot in event of lost communications. (See Lost Communications)

IFR AIRCRAFT/IFR FLIGHT— An aircraft conducting flight in accordance with instrument flight rules.

IFR CONDITIONS— Weather conditions below the minimum for flight under visual flight rules. (See Instrument Meteorological Conditions)

IFR DEPARTURE PROCEDURE— (See IFR Takeoff Minimums and Departure Procedures) (Refer to AIM)

IFR MILITARY TRAINING ROUTES (IR)— Routes used by the Department of Defense and associated Reserve and Air Guard units for the purpose of conducting low-altitude navigation and tactical training in both IFR and VFR weather conditions below 10,000 feet MSL at airspeeds in excess of 250 knots IAS.

IFR TAKEOFF MINIMUMS AND DEPARTURE PROCEDURES— FAR, Part 91, prescribes standard takeoff rules for certain civil users. At some airports, obstructions or other factors require the establishment of nonstandard takeoff minimums, departure procedures, or both, to assist pilots in avoiding obstacles during climb to the minimum en route altitude. Those airports are listed in NOS/DOD Instrument Approach Charts (IAPs) under a section entitled "IFR Takeoff Minimums and Departure Procedures." The NOS/DOD IAP chart legend illustrates the symbol used to alert the pilot to nonstandard takeoff minimums and departure procedures. When departing IFR from such airports, or from any airports where there are no departure procedures, SIDs, or ATC facilities available, pilots should advise ATC of any departure limitations. Controllers may query a pilot to determine acceptable departure directions, turns, or headings after takeoff. Pilots should be familiar with the departure procedures and must assure that their aircraft can meet or exceed any specified climb gradients.

ILS CATEGORIES—

1. ILS Category I—An ILS approach procedure which provides for approach to a height above touchdown of not less than 200 feet and with runway visual range of not less than 1,800 feet.

2. ILS Category II—An ILS approach procedure which provides for approach to a height above touchdown of not less than 100 feet and with runway visual range of not less than 1,200 feet.

3. ILS Category III.

    a. IIIA—An ILS approach procedure which provides for approach without a decision height minimum and with runway visual range of not less than 700 feet.

    b. IIIB—An ILS approach procedure which provides for approach without a decision height minimum and with runway visual range of not less than 150 feet.

    c. IIIC—An ILS approach procedure which provides for approach without a decision height minimum and without runway visual range minimum.

IMMEDIATELY— Used by ATC when such action compliance is required to avoid an imminent situation.

INCREASE SPEED TO (SPEED)— (See Speed Adjustment

INFORMATION REQUEST/INREQ— A request originated by an FSS for information concerning an overdue VFR aircraft.

INITIAL APPROACH FIX/IAF— The fixes depicted on instrument approach procedure charts that identify the beginning of the initial approach segment(s). (See Fix, Segments of an Instrument Approach Procedure)

INITIAL APPROACH SEGMENT— (See Segments of an Instrument Approach Procedure)

INNER MARKER/IM/INNER MARKER BEACON— A marker beacon used with an ILS (CAT II) precision approach located between the middle marker and the end of the ILS runway, transmitting a radiation pattern keyed at six dots per second and indicating to the pilot, both aurally and visually, that he is at the designated decision height (DH), normally 100 feet above the touchdown zone elevation, on the ILS CAT II approach. It also marks progress during a CAT III approach. (See Instrument Landing System) (Refer to AIM)

INSTRUMENT APPROACH PROCEDURE/IAP/INSTRUMENT APPROACH— A series of predetermined maneuvers for the orderly transfer of an aircraft under instrument flight conditions from the beginning of the initial approach to a landing, or to a point from which a landing may be made visually. It is prescribed and approved for a specific airport by competent authority. (See Segments of an Instrument Approach Procedure) (Refer to FAR Part 91, AIM)

1. U.S. civil standard instrument approach procedures are approved by the FAA as prescribed under FAR, Part 97, and are available for public use.

2. U.S. military standard instrument approach procedures are approved and published by the Department of Defense.

3. Special instrument approach procedures are approved by the FAA for individual operators, but are not published in FAR, Part 97, for public use.

*ICAO—INSTRUMENT APPROACH PROCEDURE—*A series of predetermined maneuvers for the orderly transfer of an aircraft under instrument flight conditions from the beginning of the initial approach to a landing, or to a point from which a landing may be made visually.

INSTRUMENT FLIGHT RULES/IFR— Rules governing the procedures for conducting instrument flight. Also a term used by pilots and controllers to indicate type of flight plan. (See Visual Flight Rules, Instrument Meteorological Conditions, Visual Meteorological Conditions) (Refer to AIM)

*ICAO—INSTRUMENT FLIGHT RULES—*A set of rules governing the conduct of flight under instrument meteorological conditions.

INSTRUMENT LANDING SYSTEM/ILS— A precision instrument approach system which normally consists of the following electronic components and visual aids:

1. Localizer (See Localizer)

2. Glide Slope (See Glide Slope)

3. Outer Marker (See Outer Marker)

4. Middle Marker (See Middle Marker)

5. Approach Lights (See Airport Lighting)
    (Refer to FAR Part 91, AIM)

INSTRUMENT METEOROLOGICAL CONDITIONS/IMC— Meteorological conditions expressed in terms of visibility, distance from cloud, and ceiling less than the minima specified for visual meteorological conditions. (See Visual Meteorological Conditions, Instrument Flight Rules, Visual Flight Rules)

INSTRUMENT RUNWAY— A runway equipped with electronic and visual navigation aids for which a precision or nonprecision approach procedure having straight-in landing minimums has been approved.

*ICAO—INSTRUMENT RUNWAY—*A runway intended for the operation of aircraft using nonvisual aids and comprising:

1. Instrument Approach Runway—An instrument runway served by a nonvisual aid providing at least directional guidance adequate for a straight-in approach.

2. Precision Approach Runway, Category I—An instrument runway served by ILS or GCA approach aids and visual aids intended for operations down to 60 metres (200 feet) decision height and down to an RVR of the order of 800 metres (2,600 feet.)

3. Precision Approach Runway, Category II—An instrument runway served by ILS and visual aids intended for operations down to 30 metres (100 feet) decision

height and down to an RVR of the order of 400 metres (1,200 feet.)

4. Precision Approach Runway, Category III—An instrument runway served by ILS (no decision height being applicable) and:

a. By visual aids intended for operations down to an RVR of the order of 200 metres (700 feet);

b. By visual aids intended for operations down to an RVR of the order of 50 metres (150 feet);

c. Intended for operations without reliance on external visual reference.

INTERMEDIATE APPROACH SEGMENT— (See Segments of an Instrument Approach Procedure)

INTERMEDIATE FIX/IF— The fix that identifies the beginning of the intermediate approach segment of an instrument approach procedure. The fix is not normally identified on the instrument approach chart as an intermediate fix (IF). (See Segments of an Instrument Approach Procedure)

INTERNATIONAL AIRPORT— Relating to international flight, it means:

1. An airport of entry which has been designated by the Secretary of Treasury or Commissioner of Customs as an international airport for customs service.

2. A landing rights airport at which specific permission to land must be obtained from customs authorities in advance of contemplated use.

3. Airports designated under the Convention on International Civil Aviation as an airport for use by international commercial air transport and/or international general aviation. (Refer to Airport/Facility Directory and IFIM).

*ICAO—INTERNATIONAL AIRPORT—*Any airport designated by the Contracting State in whose territory it is situated as an airport of entry and departure for international air traffic, where the formalities incident to customs, immigration, public health, animal and plant quarantine, and similar procedures are carried out.

INTERNATIONAL CIVIL AVIATION ORGANIZATION/ ICAO— A specialized agency of the United Nations whose objective is to develop the principles and techniques of international air navigation and to foster planning and development of international civil air transport.

INTERNATIONAL FLIGHT INFORMATION MANUAL/ IFIM— A publication designed primarily as a pilot's preflight planning guide for flights into foreign airspace and for flights returning to the U.S. from foreign locations.

INTERROGATOR— The ground-based surveillance radar beacon transmitter-receiver, which normally scans in synchronism with a primary radar, transmitting discrete radio signals which repetitively request all transponders, on the mode being used, to reply. The replies received are mixed with the primary radar returns and displayed on the same plan position indicator (radar scope). Also applied to the airborne element of the TACAN/DME system. (See Transponder) (Refer to AIM)

INTERSECTING RUNWAYS— Two or more runways which cross or meet within their lengths. (See Intersection)

INTERSECTION—

1. A point defined by any combination of courses, radials or bearings of two or more navigational aids.

2. Used to describe the point where two runways, a runway and a taxiway, or two taxiways cross or meet.

INTERSECTION DEPARTURE/INTERSECTION TAKE-OFF— A takeoff or proposed takeoff on a runway from an intersection. (See Intersection)

I SAY AGAIN— The message will be repeated.

JAMMING— Electronic or mechanical interference which may disrupt the display of aircraft on radar or the transmission/ reception of radio communications/navigation.

JET BLAST— Jet engine exhaust (thrust stream turbulence). (See Wake Turbulence)

JET ROUTE— A route designed to serve aircraft operations from 18,000 feet MSL up to and including flight level 450. The routes are referred to as "J" routes with numbering to identify the designated route; e.g., J105. (See Route) (Refer to FAR Part 71)

JET STREAM— A migrating stream of high-speed winds present at high altitudes.

JETTISONING OF EXTERNAL STORES— Airborne release of external stores; e.g., tiptanks, ordinances (See Fuel Dumping) (Refer to FAR Part 91)

JOINT USE RESTRICTED AREA— (See Restricted Area)

KNOWN TRAFFIC— With respect to ATC clearances, means aircraft whose altitude, position and intentions are known to ATC.

LANDING/TAKEOFF AREA— Any locality either on land, water, or structures, including airports/heliports and intermediate landing fields, which is used, or intended to be used, for the landing and takeoff of aircraft whether or not facilities are provided for the shelter, servicing, or for receiving or discharging passengers or cargo.

*ICAO—LANDING AREA—*That part of the movement area intended for the landing and takeoff of aircraft.

LANDING DIRECTION INDICATOR— A device which visually indicates the direction in which landings and takeoffs should be made. (See Tetrahedron) (Refer to AIM)

LANDING MINIMUMS/IFR LANDING MINIMUMS— The minimum visibility prescribed for landing a civil aircraft while using an instrument approach procedure. The minimum applies with other limitations set forth in FAR Part 91 with respect to the Minimum Descent Altitude (MDA) or Decision Height (DH) prescribed in the instrument approach procedures as follows:

1. Straight-in landing minimums—A statement of MDA and visibility, or DH and visibility, required for straight-in landing on a specified runway, or
2. Circling minimums—A statement of MDA and visibility required for the circle-to-land maneuver.

Descent below the established MDA or DH is not authorized during an approach unless the aircraft is in a position from which a normal approach to the runway of intended landing can be made and adequate visual reference to required visual cues is maintained. (See Straight-in Landing, Circle-to-Land Maneuver, Decision Height, Minimum Descent Altitude, Visibility, Instrument Approach Procedure) (Refer to FAR Part 91)

LANDING ROLL— The distance from the point of touchdown to the point where the aircraft can be brought to a stop or exit the runway.

LANDING SEQUENCE— The order in which aircraft are positioned for landing. (See Approach Sequence)

LAST ASSIGNED ALTITUDE— The last altitude/flight level assigned by ATC and acknowledged by the pilot. (See Maintain) (Refer to FAR Part 91)

LATERAL SEPARATION— The lateral spacing of aircraft at the same altitude by requiring operation on different routes or in different geographical locations. (See Separation)

LIGHTED AIRPORT— An airport where runway and obstruction lighting is available. (See Airport Lighting) (Refer to AIM)

LIGHT GUN— A handheld directional light signaling device which emits a brilliant narrow beam of white, green, or red light as selected by the tower controller. The color and type of light transmitted can be used to approve or disapprove anticipated pilot actions where radio communication is not available. The light gun is used for controlling traffic operating in the vicinity of the airport and on the airport movement area. (Refer to AIM)

LOCALIZER— The component of an ILS which provides course guidance to the runway. (See Instrument Landing System) (Refer to AIM)

ICAO—LOCALIZER COURSE (ILS)— The locus of points, in any given horizontal plane, at which the DDM (Difference in depth of modulation) is zero.

LOCALIZER TYPE DIRECTIONAL AID/LDA— A NAVAID used for nonprecision instrument approaches with utility and accuracy comparable to a localizer but which is not a part of a complete ILS and is not aligned with the runway. (Refer to AIM)

LOCALIZER USABLE DISTANCE— The maximum distance from the localizer transmitter at a specified altitude, as verified by flight inspection, at which reliable course information is continuously received. (Refer to AIM)

LOCAL TRAFFIC— Aircraft operating in the traffic pattern or within sight of the tower, or aircraft known to be departing or arriving from flight in local practice areas, or aircraft executing practice instrument approaches at the airport. (See Traffic Pattern)

LONGITUDINAL SEPARATION— The longitudinal spacing of aircraft at the same altitude by a minimum distance expressed in units of time or miles. (See Separation) (Refer to AIM)

LORAN/LONG RANGE NAVIGATION— An electronic navigational system by which hyperbolic lines of position are determined by measuring the difference in the time of reception of synchronized pulse signals from two fixed transmitters. Loran A operates in the 1750—1950 kHz frequency band. Loran C and D operate in the 100—110 kHz frequency band. (Refer to AIM)

LOST COMMUNICATIONS/TWO-WAY RADIO COMMUNICATIONS FAILURE— Loss of the ability to communicate by radio. Aircraft are sometimes referred to as NORDO (No Radio). Standard pilot procedures are specified in FAR Part 91. Radar controllers issue procedures for pilots to follow in the event of lost communications during a radar approach when weather reports indicate that an aircraft will likely encounter IFR weather conditions during the approach. (Refer to FAR Part 91, AIM)

LOW ALTITUDE AIRWAY STRUCTURE/FEDERAL AIRWAYS— The network of airways serving aircraft operations up to but not including 18,000 feet MSL. (See Airway) (Refer to AIM)

LOW ALTITUDE ALERT, CHECK YOUR ALTITUDE IMMEDIATELY— (See Safety Advisory)

LOW ALTITUDE ALERT SYSTEM/LAAS— An automated function of the TPX-42 that alerts the controller when a Mode C transponder-equipped aircraft on an IFR flight plan is below a predetermined minimum safe altitude. If requested by the pilot, LAAS monitoring is also available to VFR Mode C transponder-equipped aircraft.

LOW APPROACH— An approach over an airport or runway following an instrument approach or a VFR approach including the go-around maneuver where the pilot intentionally does not make contact with the runway. (Refer to AIM)

LOW FREQUENCY/LF— The frequency band between 30 and 300 kHz. (Refer to AIM)

MACH NUMBER— The ratio of true airspeed to the speed of sound; e.g., MACH .82, MACH 1.6 (See Airspeed)

MAINTAIN—

1. Concerning altitude/flight level, the term means to remain at the altitude/flight level specified. The phrase "climb and" or "descend and" normally precedes "maintain" and the altitude assignment; e.g., "descend and maintain 5,000."

2. Concerning other ATC instructions, the term is used in its literal sense; e.g., maintain VFR.

MAKE SHORT APPROACH— Used by ATC to inform a pilot to alter his traffic pattern so as to make a short final approach. (See Traffic Pattern)

MANDATORY ALTITUDE— An altitude depicted on an instrument Approach Procedure Chart requiring the aircraft to maintain altitude at the depicted value.

MARKER BEACON— An electronic navigation facility transmitting a 75 MHz vertical fan or boneshaped radiation pattern. Marker beacons are identified by their modulation frequency and keying code, and when received by compatible airborne equipment, indicate to the pilot, both aurally and visually, that he is passing over the facility. (See Outer Marker, Middle Marker, Inner Marker) (Refer to AIM)

MAXIMUM AUTHORIZED ALTITUDE/MAA— A published altitude representing the maximum usable altitude or flight level for an airspace structure or route segment. It is the highest altitude on a Federal airway, Jet route, area navigation low or high route, or other direct route for which an MEA is designated in FAR Part 95 at which adequate reception of navigation and signals is assured.

MAYDAY— The international radiotelephony distress signal. When repeated three times, it indicates imminent and grave danger and that immediate assistance is requested. (See PAN) (Refer to AIM)

METEOROLOGICAL IMPACT STATEMENT/MIS— An unscheduled planning forecast describing conditions expected to begin within 4 to 12 hours which may impact the flow of air traffic in a specific center's (ARTCC) area.

METERING— A method of time-regulating arrival traffic flow into a terminal area so as not to exceed a predetermined terminal acceptance rate.

METERING FIX— A fix along an established route from over which aircraft will be metered prior to entering terminal airspace. Normally, this fix should be established at a distance from the airport which will facilitate a profile descent 10,000 feet above airport elevation (AAE) or above.

MIA— (See Minimum IFR Altitudes)

MICROWAVE LANDING SYSTEM/MLS— An instrument landing system operating in the microwave spectrum which provides lateral and vertical guidance to aircraft having compatible avionics equipment. (See Instrument Landing System) (Refer to AIM)

MIDDLE COMPASS LOCATOR— (See Compass Locator)

MIDDLE MARKER/MM— A marker beacon that defines a point along the glide slope of an ILS normally located at or near the point of decision height (ILS Category). It is keyed to transmit alternate dots and dashes, with the alternate dots and dashes keyed at the rate of 95 dot/dash combinations per minute, on a 1300 Hz tone, which is received aurally and visually by compatible airborne equipment. (See Marker Beacon, Instrument Landing System) (Refer to AIM)

MID RVR— (See Visibility)

MILITARY AUTHORITY ASSUMES RESPONSIBILITY FOR SEPARATION OF AIRCRAFT/MARSA— A condition whereby the military services involved assume responsibility for separation between participating military aircraft in the ATC system. It is used only for required IFR operations which are specified in letters of agreement or other appropriate FAA or military documents.

MILITARY OPERATIONS AREA/MOA— (See Special Use Airspace)

MILITARY TRAINING ROUTES/MTR— Airspace of defined vertical and lateral dimensions established for the conduct of military flight training at airspeeds in excess of 250 knots IAS. (See IFR (IR) and VFR (VR) Military Training Routes)

MINIMUM CROSSING ALTITUDE/MCA— The lowest altitude at certain fixes at which an aircraft must cross when proceeding in the direction of a higher minimum en route IFR altitude (MEA). See Minimum En Route IFR Altitude)

MINIMUM DESCENT ALTITUDE/MDA— The lowest altitude, expressed in feet above mean sea level, to which descent is authorized on final approach or during circle-to-land maneuvering in execution of a standard instrument approach procedure where no electronic glide slope is provided. (See Nonprecision Approach Procedure)

MINIMUM EN ROUTE IFR ALTITUDE/MEA— The lowest published altitude between radio fixes which assures acceptable navigational signal coverage and meets obstacle clearance requirements between those fixes. The MEA prescribed for a Federal airway or segment thereof, area navigation low or high route or other direct route applies to the entire width of the airway, segment or route between the radio fixes defining the airway, segment, or route. (Refer to FAR Parts 91 and 95; AIM)

MINIMUM FUEL— Indicates that an aircraft's fuel supply has reached a state where, upon reaching the destination, it can accept little or no delay. This is not an emergency situation but merely indicates an emergency situation is possible should any undue delay occur. (Refer to AIM)

MINIMUM HOLDING ALTITUDE/MHA— The lowest altitude prescribed for a holding pattern which assures navigational signal coverage, communications, and meets obstacle clearance requirements.

MINIMUM IFR ALTITUDES/MIA— Minimum altitudes for IFR operations as prescribed in FAR Part 91. These altitudes are published on aeronautical charts and prescribed in FAR Part 95 for airways and routes, and in FAR Part 97 for standard instrument approach procedures. If no applicable minimum altitude is prescribed in FAR Parts 95 or 97, the following minimum IFR altitude applies:

1. In designated mountainous areas, 2,000 feet above the highest obstacle within a horizontal distance of 5 statute miles from the course to be flown; or

2. Other than mountainous areas, 1,000 feet above the highest obstacle within a horizontal distance of 5 statute miles from the course to be flown; or

3. As otherwise authorized by the Administrator or assigned by ATC. (See Minimum En Route IFR Altitude, Minimum Obstruction Clearance Altitude, Minimum Crossing Altitude, Minimum Safe Altitude, Minimum Vectoring Altitude) (Refer to FAR Part 91)

MINIMUM OBSTRUCTION CLEARANCE ALTITUDE/ MOCA— The lowest published altitude in effect between radio fixes on VOR airways, off-airway routes, or route segments which meets obstacle clearance requirements for the entire route segment and which assures acceptable navigational signal coverage only within 25 statute (22 nautical) miles of a VOR. (Refer to FAR Part 91 and 95)

MINIMUM RECEPTION ALTITUDE/MRA— The lowest altitude at which an intersection can be determined. (Refer to FAR Part 95)

MINIMUM SAFE ALTITUDE/MSA—

1. The minimum altitude specified in FAR Part 91 for various aircraft operations.

2. Altitudes depicted on approach charts which provide at least 1,000 feet of obstacle clearance for emergency use within a specified distance from the navigation facility upon which a procedure is predicated. These altitudes will be identified as MINIMUM SECTOR ALTITUDES or EMERGENCY SAFE ALTITUDES and are established as follows:

a. Minimum Sector Altitudes—Altitudes depicted on approach charts which provide at least 1,000 feet of obstacle clearance within a 25-mile radius of the navigation facility upon which the procedure is predicated. Sectors depicted on approach charts must be at least 90 degrees in scope. These altitudes are for emergency use only and do not necessarily assure acceptable navigational signal coverage.

ICAO—MINIMUM SECTOR ALTITUDE— The lowest altitude which may be used under emergency conditions which will provide a minimum clearance of 300 meters (1,000 feet) above all obstacles located in an area contained within a sector of a circle of 25 nautical mile radius centered on a radio aid to navigation.

b. Emergency Safe Altitudes—Altitudes depicted on approach charts which provide at least 1,000 feet of obstacle clearance in nonmountainous areas and 2,000 feet of obstacle clearance in designated mountainous areas with a 100-mile radius of the navigation facility upon which the procedure is predicated and normally used only in military procedures. These altitudes are identified on published procedures as "Emergency Safe Altitudes."

MINIMUM SAFE ALTITUDE WARNING (MSAW)— A function of the ARTS III computer that aids the controller by alerting him when a tracked Mode C equipped aircraft is below or is predicted by the computer to go below a predetermined minimum safe altitude. (Refer to AIM)

MINIMUMS/MINIMA— Weather condition requirements established for a particular operation or type of operation; e.g., IFR takeoff or landing, alternate airport for IFR flight plans, VFR flight, etc. (See Landing Minimums, IFR takeoff Minimums, VFR Conditions, IFR Conditions) Refer to FAR Part 91, AIM)

MINIMUM VECTORING ALTITUDE/MVA— The lowest MSL altitude at which an IFR aircraft will be vectored by a radar controller, except as otherwise authorized for radar approaches, departures and missed approaches. The altitude meets IFR obstacle clearance criteria. It may be lower than the published MEA along an airway or J-route segment. It may be utilized for radar vectoring only upon the controller's determination that an adequate radar return is being received from the aircraft being controlled. Charts depicting minimum vectoring altitudes are normally available only to the controllers and not to pilots. (Refer to AIM)

MISSED APPROACH—

1. A maneuver conducted by a pilot when an instrument approach cannot be completed to a landing. The route of flight and altitude are shown on instrument approach procedure charts. A pilot executing a missed approach prior to the Missed Approach Point (MAP) must continue along the final approach to the MAP. The pilot may climb immediately to the altitude specified in the missed approach procedure.

2. A term used by the pilot to inform ATC that he is executing the missed approach.

3. At locations where ATC radar service is provided, the pilot should conform to radar vectors, when provided by ATC, in lieu of the published missed approach procedure. (See Missed Approach Point) (Refer to AIM)

ICAO—MISSED APPROACH PROCEDURE— The procedure to be followed if, after an instrument approach, a landing is not effected, and occuring normally:

1. When the aircraft has descended to the decision height and has not established visual contact, or

2. When directed by airtraffic control to pull up or to go around again.

MISSED APPROACH POINT/MAP— A point prescribed in each instrument approach procedure at which a missed approach procedure shall be executed if the required visual reference does not exist. (See Missed Approach, Segments of an Instrument Approach Procedure)

MISSED APPROACH SEGMENT— (See Segments of an Instrument Approach Procedure)

MODE— The letter or number assigned to a specific pulse spacing of radio signals transmitted or received by ground interrogator or airborne transponder components of the Air Traffic Control Radar Beacon System (ATCRBS). Mode A (military Mode 3) and Mode C (altitude reporting) are used in air traffic control. (See Transponder, Interrogator, Radar) (Refer to AIM)

ICAO—MODE (SSR MODE)— The letter or number assigned to a specific pulse spacing of the interrogation signals transmitted by an interrogator. There are 4 modes, A,B,C, and D corresponding to four different interrogation pulse spacings.

MOVEMENT AREA— The runways, taxiways, and other areas of an airport/heliport which are utilized for taxiing/hover taxiing, air taxiing, takeoff, and landing of aircraft, exclusive of loading ramps and parking areas. At those airports/heliports with a tower, specific approval for entry onto the movement area must be obtained from ATC.

ICAO—MOVEMENT AREA— That part of an aerodrome intended for the surface movement of aircraft, including the maneuvering area and aprons.

MOVING TARGET INDICATOR/MTI— An electronic device which will permit radar scope presentation only from targets which are in motion. A partial remedy for ground clutter.

MSAW— (See Minimum Safe Altitude Warning)

NAS STAGE A— The en route ATC system's radar, computers and computer programs, controller plan view displays (PVDs/RadarScopes), input/output devices, and the related communications equipment which are integrated to form the heart of the automated IFR air traffic control system. This equipment performs Flight Data Processing (FDP) and Radar Data Processing (RDP). It interfaces with automated terminal systems and is used in the control of en route IFR aircraft. (Refer to AIM)

NATIONAL AIRSPACE SYSTEM/NAS— The common network of U.S. airspace; air navigation facilities, equipment and services, airports or landing areas; aeronautical charts, information and services; rules, regulations and procedures, technical information, and manpower and material. Included are system components shared jointly with the military.

NATIONAL BEACON CODE ALLOCATION PLAN AIR-SPACE/NBCAP AIRSPACE— Airspace over United States territory located within the North American continent between Canada and Mexico, including adjacent territorial waters outward to about boundaries of oceanic control areas (CTA)/Flight Information Regions (FIR). (See Flight Information Region)

NATIONAL FLIGHT DATA CENTER/NFDC— A facility in Washington D.C., established by FAA to operate a central aeronautical information service for the collection, validation, and dissemination of aeronautical data in support of the activities of government, industry, and the aviation community. The information is published in the National Flight Data Digest. (See National Flight Data Digest)

NATIONAL FLIGHT DATA DIGEST/NFDD— A daily (except weekends and federal holidays) publication of flight information appropriate to aeronautical charts, aeronautical publications, Notices to Airmen or other media serving the purpose of providing operational flight data essential to safe and efficient aircraft operations.

NATIONAL SEARCH AND RESCUE PLAN— An inter-agency agreement which provides for the effective utilization of all available facilities in all types of search and rescue missions.

NAVAID CLASSES— VOR, VORTAC, and TACAN aids are classed according to their operational use. The Three classes of NAVAIDS are:

    T—Terminal

    L—Low altitude

    H—High altitude

The normal service range for T, L, and H class aids is found in the AIM. Certain operational requirements make it necessary to use some of these aids at greater service ranges than specified. Extended range is made possible through flight inspection determinations. Some aids also have lesser service range due to location, terrain, frequency protection, etc. Restrictions to service range are listed in Airport/Facility Directory.

NAVIGABLE AIRSPACE— Airspace at and above the minimum flight altitudes prescribed in the FARs including airspace needed for safe takeoff and landing. (Refer to FAR Part 91)

NAVIGATIONAL AIR/NAVAID— Any visual or electronic device airborne or on the surface which provides point to point guidance information or position data to aircraft in flight. (See Air Navigation Facility)

NDB— (See Nondirectional beacon)

NEGATIVE— "No" or "permission not granted" or "that is not correct."

NEGATIVE CONTACT— Used by pilots to inform ATC that:

1. Previously issued traffic is not in sight. It may be followed by the pilot's request for the controller to provide assistance in avoiding the traffic.
2. They were unable to contact ATC on a particular frequency.

NIGHT— The time between the end of evening civil twilight and the beginning of morning civil twilight, as published in the American Air Almanac, converted to local time.

ICAO—NIGHT—The hours between the end of evening civil twilight and the beginning of morning civil twilight or such other period between sunset and sunrise as may be specified by the appropriate authority.

NO GYRO APPROACH/VECTOR— A radar approach/vector provided in case of a malfunctioning gyro-compass or directional gyro. Instead of providing the pilot with headings to be flown, the controller observes the radar track and issues control instructions "turn right/left" or "stop turn" as appropriate. (Refer to AIM)

NONAPPROACH CONTROL TOWER— Authorizes aircraft to land or takeoff at the airport controlled by the tower, or to transit the airport traffic area. The primary function of a nonapproach control tower is the sequencing of aircraft in the traffic pattern and on the landing area. Nonapproach control towers also separate aircraft operating under instrument flight rules clearances from approach controls and centers. They provide ground control services to aircraft, vehicles, personnel, and equipment on the airport movement area.

NONCOMPOSITE SEPARATION— Separation in accordance with minima other than the composite separation minimum specified for the area concerned.

NONDIRECTIONAL BEACON/RADIO BEACON/NDB— An L/MF or UHF radio beacon transmitting nondirectional signals whereby the pilot of an aircraft equipped with direction finding equipment can determine his bearing to or from the radio beacon and "home" on or track to or from the station. When the radio beacon is installed in conjunction with the Instrument Landing System marker, it is normally called a Compass Locator. (See Compass Locator, Automatic Direction Finder)

NONPRECISION APPROACH PROCEDURE/NONPRECISION APPROACH— A standard instrument approach procedure in which no electronic glide slope is provided; e.g., VOR, TACAN, NDB, LOC, ASR, LDA, or SDF approaches.

NONRADAR— Precedes other terms and generally means without the use of radar, such as:

1. Nonradar Route—A flight path or route over which the pilot is performing his own navigation. The pilot may be receiving radar separation, radar monitoring or other ATC services while on a nonradar route. (See Radar Route)
2. Nonradar Approach—Used to describe instrument approaches for which course guidance on final approach is not provided by ground based precision or surveillance radar. Radar vectors to the final approach course may or may not be provided by ATC. Examples of nonradar approaches are VOR, ADF, TACAN, and ILS, approaches. (See Final Approach—IFR, Final Approach Course, Radar Approach, Instrument Approach Procedure)
3. Nonradar Separation—The spacing of aircraft in accordance with established minima without the use of radar; e.g., vertical, lateral, or longitudinal separation. (See Radar Separation)

ICAO—NonRadar Separation—The separation used when aircraft position information is derived from sources other than radar.

4. Nonradar Arrival—An arriving aircraft that is not being vectored to the final approach course for an instrument approach or towards the airport for a visual approach. The aircraft may or may not be in a radar environment and may or may not be receiving radar separation, radar monitoring or other services provided by ATC. (See Radar Arrival, Radar Environment)

NONRADAR APPROACH CONTROL— An ATC facility providing approach control service without the use of radar. (See Approach Control, Approach Control Service)

NORDO— (See Lost Communications)

NORTH AMERICAN ROUTE— A numerically coded route preplanned over existing airway and route systems to and from specific coastal fixes serving the North Atlantic. North American Routes consist of the following:

1. Common Route/Portion—That segment of a North American route between the inland navigation facility and the coastal fix.

2. Non-Common Route/Portion—That segment of a North American route between the inland navigation facility and a designated North American terminal

3. Inland Navigation Facility—A navigation aid on a North American route at which the common route and/or the non-common route begins or ends.

4. Coastal Fix—A navigation aid or intersection where an aircraft transitions between the domestic route structure and the oceanic route structure.

NOTICES TO AIRMEN PUBLICATION— A publication designed primarily as a pilot's operational manual containing current NOTAM information considered essential to the safety of flight as well as supplemental data to other aeronautical publications. (See Notice to Airmen/NOTAM)

NOTICE TO AIRMEN/NOTAM— A notice containing information (not known sufficiently in advance to publicize by other means) concerning the establishment, condition or change in any component (facility, service, or procedure of, or hazard in the National Airspace System) the timely knowledge of which is essential to personnel concerned with flight operations.

1. NOTAM(D)—A NOTAM given (in addition to local dissemination) distant dissemination via teletypewriter beyond the area of responsibility of the Flight Service Station. These NOTAMS will be stored and repeated hourly until cancelled.

2. NOTAM(L)—A NOTAM given local dissemination by voice, (teletypewriter where applicable), and a wide variety of means such as: teleautograph, teleprinter, facsimile reproduction, hot line, telecopier, telegraph, and telephone to satisfy local user requirements.

3. FDC NOTAM—A notice to airmen, regulatory in nature, transmitted by NFDC and given all-circuit dissemination.

*ICAO—NOTAM—*A notice, containing information concerning the establishment, condition or change in any aeronautical facility, service, procedure or hazard, the timely knowledge of which is essential to personnel concerned with flight operations.

NUMEROUS TARGETS VICINITY (LOCATION)—A traffic advisory issued by ATC to advise pilots that targets on the radar scope are too numerous to issue individually. (See Traffic Advisories)

obstacle— An existing object, object of natural growth, or terrain at a fixed geographical location, or which may be expected at a fixed location within a prescribed area, with reference to which vertical clearance is or must be provided during flight operation.

OBSTRUCTION— Any object/obstacle exceeding the obstruction standards specified by FAR Part 77, Sub-part C.

OBSTRUCTION LIGHT— A light, or one of a group of lights, usually red or white, frequently mounted on a surface structure or natural terrain to warn pilots of the presence of an obstruction.

OFF-ROUTE VECTOR— A vector by ATC which takes an aircraft off a previously assigned route. Altitudes assigned by ATC during such vectors provide required obstacle clearance.

OFFSET PARALLEL RUNWAYS— Staggered runways having centerlines which are parallel.

ON COURSE—

1. Used to indicate that an aircraft is established on the route centerline.

2. Used by ATC to advise a pilot making a radar approach that his aircraft is lined up on the final approach course. (See On-Course Indication)

ON-COURSE INDICATION— An indication on an instrument which provides the pilot a visual means of determining that the aircraft is located on the centerline of a given navigational track; or an indication on a radar scope that an aircraft is on a given track.

OPTION APPROACH— An approach requested and conducted by a pilot which will result in either a touch-and-go, missed approach, low approach, stop-and-go or full stop landing. (See Cleared for the option) (Refer to AIM)

ORGANIZED TRACK SYSTEM— A moveable system of oceanic tracks that traverses the North Atlantic between Europe and North America the physical position of which is determined twice daily taking the best advantage of the winds aloft.

OUT— The conversation is ended and no response is expected.

OUTER COMPASS LOCATOR— (See Compass Locator)

OUTER FIX— A general term used within ATC to describe fixes in the terminal area, other than the final approach fix. Aircraft are normally cleared to these fixes by an Air Route Traffic Control Center or an Approach Control Facility. Aircraft are normally cleared from these fixes to the final approach fix or final approach course.

OUTER MARKER/OM— A marker beacon at or near the glide slope intercept altitude of an ILS approach. It is keyed to transmit two dashes per second on a 400 Hz tone which is received aurally and visually by compatible airborne equipment. The OM is normally located four to seven miles from the runway threshold on the extended centerline of the runway. (See Marker Beacon, Instrument Landing System) (Refer to AIM)

OVER— My transmission is ended; I expect a response.

OVERHEAD APPROACH/360 OVERHEAD— A series of predetermined maneuvers prescribed for VFR arrival of military aircraft (often in formation) for entry into the VFR traffic pattern and to proceed to a landing. The pattern usually specifies the following:

1. The radio contact required of the pilot.
2. The speed to be maintained.
3. An initial approach 3 to 5 miles in length.
4. An elliptical pattern consisting of two 180 degree turns.
5. A break point at which the first 180 degree turn is started.
6. The direction of turns.
7. Altitude (at least 500 feet above the conventional pattern).
8. A "Roll-out" on final approach not less than ¼ mile from the landing threshold and not less than 300 feet above the ground.

PAN— The international radio-telephony urgency signal. When repeated three times indicates uncertainty or alert, followed by nature of urgency. (See MAYDAY) (Refer to AIM)

PARALLEL ILS APPROACHES— ILS approaches to parallel runways by IFR aircraft which, when established inbound toward the airport on the adjacent localizer courses, are radar-separated by at least 2 miles. (See Simultaneous ILS Approaches).

PARALLEL OFFSET ROUTE— A parallel track to the left or right of the designated or established airway/route. Normally associated with Area Navigation (RNAV) operations. (See Area Navigation)

PARALLEL RUNWAYS— Two or more runways at the same airport whose centerlines are parallel. In addition to runway number, parallel runways are designated as L (left) and R (right) or, if three parallel runways exist, L (left), C (center), and R (right).

PERMANENT ECHO— Radar signals reflected from fixed objects on the earth's surface; e.g., buildings, towers, terrain. Permanent echoes are distinguished from "ground clutter" by being definable locations rather than large areas. Under certain conditions they may be used to check radar alignment.

PHOTO RECONNAISSANCE (PR)— Military activity that requires locating individual photo targets and navigating to the targets at a preplanned angle and altitude. The activity normally requires a lateral route width of 16NM and altitude range of 1,500 feet to 10,000 feet AGL.

PILOT BRIEFING/PRE-FLIGHT PILOT BRIEFING— A service provided by the FSS to assist pilots in flight planning. Briefing items may include weather information, NOTAMS, military activities, flow control information and other items as requested. (Refer to AIM)

PILOT IN COMMAND— The pilot responsible for the operation and safety of an aircraft during flight time. (Refer to FAR Part 91)

PILOTS AUTOMATIC TELEPHONE WEATHER ANSWERING SERVICE/PATWAS— A continuous telephone recording containing current and forecast weather information for pilots. (See Flight Service Station) (Refer to AIM)

PILOT'S DISCRETION— When used in conjunction with altitude assignments, means that ATC has offered the pilot the option of starting climb or descent whenever he wishes and conducting the climb or descent at any rate he wishes. He may temporarily level off at any intermediate altitude. However, once he has vacated an altitude he may not return to that altitude.

PILOT WEATHER REPORT/PIREP— A report of meteorological phenomena encountered by aircraft in flight. (Refer to AIM)

POSITION REPORT/PROGRESS REPORT— A report over a known location as transmitted by an aircraft to ATC. (Refer to AIM)

POSITION SYMBOL— A computer generated indication shown on a radar display to indicate the mode of tracking.

POSITIVE CONTROL— The separation of all air traffic, within designated airspace, by air traffic control. (See Positive Control Area)

POSITIVE CONTROL AREA/PCA— (See Controlled Airspace

PRACTICE INSTRUMENT APPROACH— An instrument approach procedure conducted by a VFR or IFR aircraft for the purpose of pilot training or proficiency demonstrations.

PRECIPITATION— Any of all forms of water particles (rain, sleet, hail, or snow), that fall from the atmosphere and reach the surface.

PRECISION APPROACH PROCEDURE/PRECISION APPROACH— A standard instrument approach procedure in which an electronic glide slope is provided, e.g., ILS and PAR. (See Instrument Landing System, Precision Approach Radar)

PRECISION APPROACH RADAR/PAR— Radar equipment in some ATC facilities operated by the FAA, and/or the military services at joint-use civil/military locations and separate military installations, to detect and display azimuth, elevation, and range of aircraft on the final approach course to a runway. This equipment may be used to monitor certain non-radar approaches, but is primarily used to conduct a precision instrument approach (PAR) wherein the controller issues guidance instructions to the pilot based on the aircraft's position in relation to the final approach course (azimuth), the glide path (elevation), and the distance (range) from the touchdown point on the runway as displayed on the radar scope. (See Glide Path) (Refer to AIM)

The abbreviation "PAR" is also used to denote preferential arrival routes in ARTCC computers. (See Preferential Routes)

*ICAO—PRECISION APPROACH RADAR/PAR—*Primary radar equipment used to determine the position of an aircraft during final approach, in terms of lateral and vertical deviations relative to a nominal approach path, and in range relative to touchdown.

PREFERENTIAL ROUTES— Preferential routes (PDRs, PARs, and PDARs) are adapted in ARTCC computers to accomplish inter/intra-facility controller coordination and to assure that flight data is posted at the proper control positions. Locations having a need for these specific inbound and outbound routes normally publish such routes in local facility bulletins and their use by pilots minimizes flight plan route amendments. When the workload or traffic situation permits, controllers normally provide radar vectors or assign requested routes to minimize circuitous routing. Preferential routes are usually confined to one ARTCC's area and are referred to by the following names or acronyms:

1. Preferential Departure Route/PDR—A specific departure route from an airport or terminal area to an en route point where there is no further need for flow control. It may be included in a Standard Instrument Departure (SID) or a Preferred IFR Route.

2. Preferential Arrival Route/PAR—A specific arrival route from an appropriate en route point to an airport or terminal area. It may be included in a Standard Terminal Arrival Route (STAR) or a Preferred IFR Route. The abbreviation "PAR" is used primarily within the ARTCC and should not be confused with the abbreviation for Precision Approach Radar.

3. Preferential Departure and Arrival Route/PDAR—A route between two terminals which are within or immediately adjacent to one ARTCC's area. PDARs are not synonomous with Preferred IFR Routes but may be listed as such as they do accomplish essentially the same purpose. (See Preferred IFR Routes, NAS Stage A)

PREFERRED IFR ROUTES— Routes established between busier airports to increase system efficiency and capacity. They normally extend through one or more ARTCC areas and are designed to achieve balanced traffic flows among high density terminals. IFR clearances are issued on the basis of these routes except when severe weather avoidance procedures or other factors dictate otherwise. Preferred IFR Routes are listed in the Airport/Facility Directory. If a flight is planned to or from an area having such routes but the departure or arrival point is not listed in the Airport/Facility Directory, pilots may use that part of a Preferred IFR Route which is appropriate for the departure or arrival point that is listed. Preferred IFR Routes are correlated with SIDs and STARs and may be defined by airways, jet routes, direct routes between NAVAIDs, Waypoints, NAVAID radials/DME, or any combinations thereof. (See Standard Instrument Departure, Standard Terminal Arrival Route, Preferential Routes, Center's Area) (Refer to Airport/Facility Directory and Notices to Airmen Publication)

PREVAILING VISIBILITY— (See Visibility)

PROCEDURE TURN INBOUND— That point of a procedure turn maneuver where course reversal has been completed and an aircraft is established inbound on the intermediate approach segment or final approach course. A report of "procedure turn inbound" is normally used by ATC as a position report for separation purposes. (See Final Approach Course, Procedure Turn, Segments of an Instrument Approach Procedure)

PROCEDURE TURN/PT— The maneuver prescribed when it is necessary to reverse direction to establish an aircraft on the intermediate approach segment or final approach course. The outbound course, direction of turn, distance within which the turn must be completed, and minimum altitude are specified in the procedure. However, unless otherwise restricted, the point at which the turn may be commenced, and the type and rate of turn, are left to the discretion of the pilot

*ICAO—PROCEDURE TURN—*A maneuver in which a turn is made away from a designated track followed by a turn in the opposite direction, both turns being executed so as to permit the aircraft to intercept and proceed along the reciprocal of the designated track.

PROFILE DESCENT— An uninterrupted descent (except where level flight is required for speed adjustment; e.g., 250 knots at 10,000 feet MSL) from cruising altitude/level to interception of a glide slope or to a minimum altitude specified for the initial or intermediate approach segment of a nonprecision instrument approach. The profile descent normally terminates at the approach gate or where the glide slope or other appropriate minimum altitude is intercepted.

PROGRAMMABLE INDICATOR DATA PROCESSOR/-PIDP— The PIDP is a modification to the AN/TPX-42 interrogator system currently installed in fixed RAPCONs. The PIDP detects, tracks, and predicts secondary radar aircraft targets. These are displayed by means of computer-generated symbols and alphanumeric characters depicting flight identification, aircraft altitude, ground speed, and flight plan data. Although primary radar targets are not tracked, they are displayed coincident with the secondary radar targets as well as with the other symbols and alphanumerics. The system has the capability of interfacing with ARTCCs.

PROHIBITED AREA— (See Special Use Airspace).

*ICAO—PROHIBITED AREA—*An airspace of defined dimensions, above the land areas or territorial waters of a State, within which the flight of aircraft is prohibited.

PROPOSED BOUNDARY CROSSING TIME/PBCT— Each center has a PBCT parameter for each internal airport. Proposed internal flight plans are transmitted to the adjacent center if the flight time along the proposed route from the departure airport to the center boundary is less than or equal to the value of PBCT or if airport adaptation specifies transmission regardless of PBCT.

PUBLISHED ROUTE— A route for which an IFR altitude has been established, and published, e.g., Federal Airways, Jet Routes, Area Navigation Routes, Specified Direct Routes.

QUADRANT— A quarter part of a circle, centered on a NAVAID, oriented clockwise from magnetic north as follows: NE quadrant 000-089, SE quadrant 090-179, SW quadrant 180-269, NW quadrant 270-359.

QUICK LOOK— A feature of NAS Stage A and ARTS which provides the controller the capability to display full data blocks of tracked aircraft from other control positions.

QUOTA FLOW CONTROL/QFLOW— A flow control procedure by which the Central Flow Control Function (CFCF) restricts traffic to the ARTC Center area having an impacted airport thereby avoiding sector/area saturation. (See Air Traffic Control Systems Command Center) (Refer to Airport/-Facility Directory)

RADAR/RADIO DETECTION AND RANGING— A device which, by measuring the time interval between transmission and reception of radio pulses and correlating the angular orientation of the radiated antenna beam or beams in azimuth and/or elevation, provides information on range, azimuth, and/or elevation of objects in the path of the transmitted pulses.

1. Primary Radar—A radar system in which a minute portion of a radio pulse transmitted from a site is reflected by an object and then received back at that site for processing and display at an air traffic control facility.
2. Secondary Radar/Radar Beacon/ATCRBS—A radar system in which the object to be detected is fitted with cooperative equipment in the form of a radio receiver/-

transmitter (transponder). Radar pulses transmitted from the searching transmitter/receiver (interrogator) site are received in the cooperative equipment and used to trigger a distinctive transmission from the transponder. This reply transmission rather than a reflected signal, is then received back at the transmitter/-receiver site for processing and display at an air traffic control facility. (See Transponder, Interrogator) (Refer to AIM)

*ICAO—RADAR—*A radio detection device which provides information on range, azimuth, and/or elevation of objects.

1. Primary Radar—A radar system which uses reflected radio signals.
2. Secondary Radar—A radar system wherein a radio signal transmitted from a radar station initiates the transmission of a radio signal from another station.

RADAR ADVISORY— The provision of advice and information based on radar observations. (See Advisory Service)

RADAR APPROACH— An instrument approach procedure which utilizes Precision Approach Radar (PAR) or Airport Surveillance Radar (ASR). (See PAR Approach, Surveillance Approach, Airport Surveillance Radar, Precision Approach Radar, Instrument Approach Procedure) (Refer to AIM)

*ICAO—RADAR APPROACH—*An approach, executed by an aircraft, under the direction of a radar controller.

RADAR APPROACH CONTROL FACILITY— A terminal ATC facility that uses radar and nonradar capabilities to provide approach control services to aircraft arriving, departing, or transiting airspace controlled by the facility (see Approach Control Service). Provides radar ATC services to aircraft operating in the vicinity of one or more civil and/or military airports in a terminal area. The facility may provide services of a ground controlled approach (GCA); i.e., ASR and PAR approaches. A radar approach control facility may be operated by FAA, USAF, US Army, USN, USMC, or jointly by FAA and a military service. Specific facility nomenclatures are used for administrative purposes only and are related to the physical location of the facility and the operating service generally as follows:

Army Radar Approach Control/ARAC (Army).
Radar Air Traffic Control Facility/RATCF (Navy/FAA).
Radar Approach Control/RAPCON (Air Force/FAA).
Terminal Radar Approach Control/TRACON (FAA).
Tower/Airport Traffic Control Tower/ATCT (FAA). (Only those towers delegated approach control authority.)

RADAR ARRIVAL— An arriving aircraft which is being vectored to the final approach course for an instrument approach or toward the airport for a visual approach. (See Radar Approach, Visual Approach)

RADAR BEACON— (See Radar)

RADAR CONTACT—

1. Used by ATC to inform an aircraft that it is identified on the radar display and radar flight following will be provided until radar identification is terminated. Radar service may also be provided within the limits of necessity and capability. When a pilot is informed of "radar contact" he automatically discontinues reporting over compulsory reporting points. (See Radar Flight Following, Radar Contact Lost, Radar Service, Radar Service Terminated). (Refer to AIM)

2. The term used to inform the controller that the aircraft is identified and approval is granted for the aircraft to enter the receiving controller's airspace.

*ICAO—RADAR CONTACT—*The situation which exists when the radar blip of a particular aircraft is seen and identified on a radar display.

RADAR CONTACT LOST— Used by ATC to inform a pilot that radar identification of his aircraft has been lost. The loss may be attributed to several things including the aircraft merging with weather or ground clutter, the aircraft flying below radar line of sight, the aircraft entering an area of poor radar return or a failure of the aircraft transponder or ground radar equipment. (See Clutter, Radar Contact)

RADAR ENVIRONMENT— An area in which radar service may be provided. (See Radar Contact, Radar Service, Additional Services, Traffic Advisories)

RADAR FLIGHT FOLLOWING— The observation of the progress of radar identified aircraft, whose primary navigation is being provided by the pilot, wherein the controller retains and correlates the aircraft identity with the appropriate target or target symbol displayed on the radar scope. (See Radar Contact, Radar Service) (Refer to AIM)

RADAR IDENTIFICATION— The process of ascertaining that an observed radar target is the radar return from a particular aircraft. (See Radar Contact, Radar Service)

*ICAO—RADAR IDENTIFICATION—*The process of correlating a particular radar blip with a specific aircraft.

RADAR IDENTIFIED AIRCRAFT— An aircraft, the position of which has been correlated with an observed target or symbol on the radar display. (See Radar Contact, Radar Contact Lost.

RADAR MONITORING— (See Radar Service)

RADAR NAVIGATIONAL GUIDANCE— (See Radar Service)

RADAR POINT OUT/POINT OUT— Used between controllers to indicate radar handoff action where the initiating controller plans to retain communications with an aircraft penetrating the other controller's airspace and additional coordination is required.

RADAR ROUTE— A flight path or route over which an aircraft is vectored. Navigational guidance and altitude assignments are provided by ATC. (See Flight Path, Route)

RADAR SEPARATION— (See Radar Service)

RADAR SERVICE— A term which encompasses one or more of the following services based on the use of radar which can be provided by a controller to a pilot of a radar identified aircraft.

1. Radar Separation.—Radar spacing of aircraft in accordance with established minima.

*ICAO—RADAR SEPARATION—*The separation used when aircraft position information is derived from radar sources.

2. Radar Navigational Guidance.—Vectoring aircraft to provide course guidance.

3. Radar Monitoring.—The radar flight following of aircraft, whose primary navigation is being performed by the pilot, to observe and note deviations from its authorized flight path, airway, or route. When being applied specifically to radar monitoring of instrument approaches, i.e., with precision approach radar (PAR) or radar monitoring of simultaneous ILS approaches, it includes advice and instructions whenever an aircraft nears or exceeds the prescribed PAR safety limit or simultaneous ILS no transgression zone. (See Additional Services, Traffic Advisories)

*ICAO—RADAR MONITORING—*The use of radar for the purpose of providing aircraft with information and advice relative to significant deviations from nominal flight path.

*ICAO—RADAR SERVICE—*Term used to indicate a service provided directly by means of radar.

RADAR SERVICE TERMINATED— Used by ATC to inform a pilot that he will no longer be provided any of the services that could be received while under radar contact. Radar service is automatically terminated, and the pilot is not advised in the following cases:

1. An aircraft cancels its IFR flight plan, except within a TCA, TRSA, or where Stage II service is provided.

2. At the completion of a radar approach.

3. When an arriving VFR aircraft receiving radar services is advised to contact the tower.

4. When an aircraft conducting a visual approach or contact approach is advised to contact the tower.

5. When an aircraft making an instrument approach has landed or the tower has the aircraft in sight, whichever occurs first.

RADAR SURVEILLANCE— The radar observation of a given geographical area for the purpose of performing some radar function.

RADAR TRAFFIC ADVISORIES— (See Traffic Advisories)

RADAR TRAFFIC INFORMATION SERVICE— (See Traffic Advisories)

RADAR WEATHER ECHO INTENSITY LEVELS— Existing radar systems cannot detect turbulence. However, there is a direct correlation between the degree of turbulence and other weather features associated with thunderstorms and the radar weather echo intensity. The National Weather Service has categorized six (6) levels of radar weather echo intensity. The following list gives the weather features likely to be associated with these levels during thunderstorm weather situations:

1. Level 1 (WEAK) and Level 2 (MODERATE). Light to moderate turbulance is possible with lightning.
2. Level 3 (STRONG). Severe turbulence possible, lightning.
3. Level 4 (VERY STRONG). Severe turbulence likely, lightning.
4. Level 5 (INTENSE). Severe turbulence, lightning, organized wind gusts. Hail likely.
5. Level 7 (EXTREME). Severe turbulence, large hail, lightning, extensive wind gusts, and turbulence.

RADIAL— A magnetic bearing extending from a VOR/VORTAC/TACAN navigation facility.

RADIO—

1. A device used for communication.
2. Used to refer to a flight service station; e.g., "Seattle Radio" is used to call Seattle FSS.

RADIO ALTIMETER/RADAR ALTIMETER— Aircraft equipment which makes use of the reflection of radio waves from the ground to determine the height of the aircraft above the surface.

RADIO BEACON— (See Nondirectional Beacon)

RADIO MAGNETIC INDICATOR/RMI— An aircraft navigational instrument coupled with a gyro compass or similar compass that indicates the direction of a selected NAVAID and indicates bearing with respect to the heading of the aircraft.

RAMP— (See Apron)

READ BACK— Repeat my message back to me.

RECEIVING CONTROLLER/FACILITY— A controller/facility receiving control of an aircraft from another controller/facility.

REDUCE SPEED TO (SPEED)— (See Speed Adjustment)

RELEASE TIME— A departure time restriction issued to a pilot by ATC when necessary to separate a departing aircraft from other traffic.

*ICAO—RELEASE TIME—*Time prior to which an aircraft should be given further clearance or prior to which it should not proceed in case of radio failure.

REMOTE COMMUNICATIONS AIR/GROUND FACILITY/RCAG— An unmanned VHF/UHF transmitter/receiver facility which is used to expand ARTCC air/ground communications coverage and to facilitate direct contact between pilots and controllers. RCAG facilities are sometimes not equipped with emergency frequencies 121.5 MHz and 243.0 MHz. ((Refer to AIM)

REMOTE COMMUNICATIONS OUTLET/RCO AND REMOTE TRANSMITTER/RECEIVER/RTR— An unmanned communications facility remotely controlled by air traffic personnel. RCO's serve FSS's. RTR's serve terminal ATC facilities. An RCO or RTR may be UHF or VHF and will extend the communication range of the air traffic facility. There are several classes of RCO's and RTR's. The class is determined by the number of transmitters or receivers. Classes A through G are used primarily for air/ground purposes. RCO and RTR class O facilities are nonprotected outlets subject to undetected and prolonged outages. RCO ((')'s and RTR(O)'s were established for the express purpose of providing ground-to-ground communications between air traffic control specialists and pilots located at a satellite airport for delivering en route clearances, issuing departure authorizations, and acknowledging instrument flight rules cancellations or departure/landing times. As a secondary function, they may be used for advisory purposes whenever the aircraft is below the coverage of the primary air/ground frequency.

REMOTE TRANSMITTER/RECEIVER/RTR— (See Remote Communications Outlet)

REPORT— Used to instruct pilots to advise ATC of specified information; e.g., "Report passing Hamilton VOR."

REPORTING POINT— A geographical location in relation to which the position of an aircraft is reported. (See Compulsory Reporting Point) (Refer to AIM)

*ICAO—REPORTING POINT—*A specified geographical location in relation to which the position of an aircraft can be reported.

REQUEST FULL ROUTE CLEARANCE/FRC— Used by pilots to request that the entire route of flight be read verbatim in an ATC clearance. Such request should be made to preclude receiving an ATC clearance based on the original filed flight plan when a filed IFR flight plan has been revised by the pilot, company, or operations prior to departure.

RESCUE COORDINATION CENTER/RCC— A search and rescue (SAR) facility equipped and manned to coordinate and control SAR operations in an area designated by the SAR plan. The U.S. Coast Guard and the U.S. Air Force have responsibility for the operation of RCCs.

*ICAO—RESCUE CO-ORDINATION CENTRE—*A unit responsible for promoting efficient organization of search and rescue service and for co-ordinating the conduct of search and rescue region.

RESTRICTED AREA— (See Special Use Airspace).

*ICAO—RESTRICTED AREA—*Airspace of defined dimensions, above the land areas or territorial waters of a State, within which the flight of aircraft is restricted in accordance with certain specified conditions.

RESUME OWN NAVIGATION— Used by ATC to advise a pilot to resume his own navigational responsibility. It is issued after completion of a radar vector or when radar contact is lost while the aircraft is being radar vectored. (See Radar Contact Lost, Radar Service Terminated)

RNAV— (See Area Navigation)

RNAV APPROACH— An instrument approach procedure which relies on aircraft area navigation equipment for navigational guidance. (See Instrument Approach Procedure, Area Navigation)

ROAD RECONNAISSANCE (RC)— Military activity requiring navigation along roads, railroads and rivers. Reconnaissance route/route segments are seldom along a straight line and normally require a lateral route width of 10NM to 30 NM and altitude range of 500 feet to 10,000 feet AGL.

ROGER— I have received all of your last transmission. It should not be used to answer a question requiring a yes or no answer. (See Affirmative, Negative)

ROLLOUT RVR— (See Visibility)

ROUTE— A defined path, consisting of one or more courses in a horizontal plane, which aircraft traverse over the surface of the earth. (See Airway, Jet Route, Published Route, Unpublished Route)

ROUTE SEGMENT— As used in Air Traffic Control, a part of a route that can be defined by two navigational fixes, two NAVAIDs, or a fix and a NAVAID. (See Fix, Route)

*ICAO—ROUTE SEGMENT—*A portion of a route to be flown, as defined by two consecutive significant points specified in a flight plan.

RUNWAY— A defined rectangular area, on a land airport prepared for the landing and takeoff run of aircraft along its length. Runways are normally numbered in relation to their magnetic direction rounded off to the nearest 10 degrees. e.g., Runway 01, Runway 25. (See Parallel Runways)

*ICAO—RUNWAY—*A defined rectangular area, on a land aerodrome prepared for the landing and takeoff run of aircraft along its length.

RUNWAY CENTERLINE LIGHTING— (See Airport Lighting)

RUNWAY CONDITION READING/RCR— Numerical decelerometer readings relayed by air traffic controllers at USAF and certain civil bases for use by the pilot in determining runway braking action. These readings are routinely relayed only to USAF and Air National Guard Aircraft. (See Braking Action)

RUNWAY END IDENTIFIER LIGHTS— (See Airport Lighting)

RUNWAY GRADIENT— The average slope, measured in percent, between two ends or points on a runway. Runway gradient is depicted on Government aerodrome sketches when total runway gradient exceeds 0.3%.

RUNWAY HEADING— The magnetic direction indicated by the runway number. When cleared to "fly/maintain runway heading," pilots are expected to comply with the ATC clearance by flying the heading indicated by the runway number without applying any drift correction; e.g., Runway 4, 040° magnetic heading; Runway 20, 200° magnetic heading.

RUNWAY IN USE/ACTIVE RUNWAY/DUTY RUNWAY— Any runway or runways currently being used for takeoff or landing. When multiple runways are used, they are all considered active runways.

RUNWAY LIGHTS— (See Airport Lighting)

RUNWAY MARKINGS— (See Airport Marking Aids.)

RUNWAY PROFILE DESCENT— An instrument flight rules (IFR) air traffic control arrival procedure to a runway published for pilot use in graphic and/or textual form and may be associated with a STAR. Runway Profile Descents provide routing, and may depict crossing altitudes, speed restrictions, and headings to be flown from the en route structure to the point where the pilot will receive clearance for and execute an instrument approach procedure. A Runway Profile Descent may apply to more than one runway if so stated on the chart. (Refer to AIM)

RUNWAY USE PROGRAM— A noise abatement runway selection plan designed to enhance noise abatement efforts with regard to airport communities for arriving and departing aircraft. These plans are developed into runway use programs and apply to all turbojet aircraft 12,500 pounds or heavier; turbojet aircraft less than 12,500 pounds are included only if the airport proprietor determines that the aircraft creates a noise problem. Runway use programs are coordinated with FAA offices, and safety criteria used in these programs are developed by the Office of Flight Operations. Runway use programs are administered by the Air Traffic Service as "Formal" or "Informal" programs.

1. Formal Runway Use Program—An approved noise abatement program which is defined and acknowledged in a Letter of Understanding between Flight Operations, Air Traffic Service, the airport proprietor, and the users. Once established, participation in the program is mandatory for aircraft operators and pilots as provided for in FAR:91.87.

2. Informal Runway Use Program—An approved noise abatement program which does not require a Letter of Understanding, and participation in the program is voluntary for aircraft operators/pilots.

RUNWAY VISIBILITY VALUE— (See Visibility)

RUNWAY VISUAL RANGE— (See Visibility)

SAFETY ADVISORY— A safety advisory issued by ATC to aircraft under their control if ATC is aware the aircraft is at an altitude which, in the controller's judgment, places the aircraft in unsafe proximity to terrain, obstructions, or other aircraft. The controller may discontinue the issuance of further advisories if the pilot advises he is taking action to correct the situation or has the other aircraft in sight.

1. Terrain/Obstruction Advisory—A safety advisory issued by ATC to aircraft under their control if ATC is aware the aircraft is at an altitude which, in the controller's judgment, places the aircraft in unsafe proximity to terrain/obstruction, e.g., "Low Altitude Alert, check your altitude immediately."

2. Aircraft Conflict Advisory—A safety advisory issued by ATC to aircraft under their control if ATC is aware of an aircraft that is not under their control at an altitude which, in the controller's judgment, places both aircraft in unsafe proximity to each other. With the alert, ATC will offer the pilot an alternate course of action when feasible, e.g., "Traffic Alert, advise you turn right heading zero niner zero or climb to eight thousand immediately."

The issuance of a safety advisory is contingent upon the capability of the controller to have an awareness of an unsafe condition. The course of action provided will be predicated on other traffic under ATC control. Once the advisory is issued, it is solely the pilot's prerogative to determine what course of action, if any, he will take.

SAIL BACK— A maneuver during high wind conditions (usually with power off) where float plane movement is controlled by water rudders/opening and closing cabin doors.

SAY AGAIN— Used to request a repeat of the last transmission. Usually specifies transmission or portion thereof not understood or received, e.g., "Say again all after ABRAM VOR."

SAY ALTITUDE— Used by AC to ascertain an aircraft's specific altitude/flight level. When the aircraft is climbing or descending, the pilot should state the indicated altitude rounded to the nearest 100 feet.

SAY HEADING— Used by ATC to request an aircraft heading. The pilot should state the actual heading of the aircraft.

SEA LANE— A designated portion of water outlined by visual surface markers for and intended to be used by aircraft designed to operate on water.

SEARCH AND RESCUE FACILITY— A facility responsible for maintaining and operating a search and rescue (SAR) service to render aid to persons and property in distress. It is any SAR unit, station, NET or other operational activity which can be usefully employed during an SAR Mission, e.g., a Civil Air Patrol Wing or a Coast Guard Station. (See Search and Rescue)

SEARCH AND RESCUE/SAR— A service which seeks missing aircraft and assists those found to be in need of assistance. It is a cooperative effort using the facilities and services of available Federal, state and local agencies. The U.S. Coast Guard is responsible for coordination of search and rescue for the Maritime Region and the U.S. Air Force is responsible for search and rescue for the Inland Region. Information pertinent to search and rescue should be passed through any air traffic facility or be transmitted directly to the Rescue Coordination Center by telephone. (See Flight Service Station, Rescue Coordination Center) (Refer to AIM)

SEE AND AVOID— A visual procedure wherein pilots of aircraft flying in visual meteorological conditions (VMC), regardless of type of flight plan, are charged with the responsibility to observe the presence of other aircraft and to maneuver their aircraft as required to avoid the other aircraft. Right-of-way rules are contained in FAR, Part 91. (See Instrument Flight Rules, Visual Flight Rules, Visual Meteorological Conditions, Instrument Meteorological Conditions)

SEGMENTED CIRCLE— A system of visual indicators designed to provide traffic pattern information at airports without operating control towers. (Refer to AIM)

SEGMENTS OF AN INSTRUMENT APPROACH PROCEDURE— An instrument approach procedure may have as many as four separate segments depending on how the approach procedure is structured.

1. Initial Approach—The segment between the initial approach fix and the intermediate fix or the point

where the aircraft is established on the intermediate course or final approach course.

2. Intermediate Approach—The segment between the intermediate fix or point and the final approach fix.

3. Final Approach—The segment between the final approach fix or point and the runway, airport, or missed approach point.

4. Missed Approach—The segment between the missed approach point, or point of arrival at decision height, and the missed approach fix at the prescribed altitude. (Refer to FAR Part 97)

ICAO

1. *Initial Approach*—That part of an instrument approach procedure consisting of the first approach to the first navigational facility associated with the procedure, or to a predetermined fix.

2. *Intermediate Approach*—That part of an instrument approach procedure from the first arrival at the first navigational facility or predetermined fix, to the beginning of the final approach.

3. *Final Approach*—That part of an instrument approach procedure from the time the aircraft has:

   a. Completed the last procedure turn or base turn where one is specified, or

   b. Crossed a specified fix, or

   c. Intercepted the last track specified for the procedures until it has crossed a point in the vicinity of an aerodrome from which:

      (1)A landing can be made, or

      (2)A missed approach procedure is initiated.

4. *Missed Approach Procedure*— The procedure to be followed if, after an instrument approach, a landing is not effected and occurring normally:

   a. When the aircraft has descended to the decision height and has not established visual contact, or

   b. When directed by air traffic control to pull up or to go around again.

SEPARATION— In air traffic control, the spacing of aircraft to achieve their safe and orderly movement in flight and while landing and taking off. (See Separation Minima)

ICAO—SEPARATION— Spacing between aircraft, levels or tracks.

SEPARATION MINIMA— The minimum longitudinal, lateral, or vertical distances by which aircraft are spaced through the application of air traffic control procedures. (See Separation)

SEVERE WEATHER AVOIDANCE PLAN/SWAP— An approved plan to minize the affect of severe weather on traffic flows in impacted terminal and/or ARTCC areas. SWAP is normally implemented to provide the least disruption to the ATC system when flight through portions of airspace is difficult or impossible due to severe weather.

SHORT RANGE CLEARANCE— A clearance issued to a departing IFR flight which authorizes IFR flight to a specific fix short of the destination while air traffic control facilities are coordinating and obtaining the complete clearance.

SHORT TAKEOFF AND LANDING AIRCRAFT/STOL AIRCRAFT— An aircraft which, at some weight within its approved operating weight, is capable of operating from a STOL runway in compliance with the applicable STOL characteristics, airworthiness, operations, noise, and pollution standards. (See Vertical Takeoff and Landing Aircraft)

SIDESTEP MANEUVER— A visual maneuver accomplished by a pilot at the completion of an instrument approach to permit a straight-in landing on a parallel runway not more than 1200 feet to either side of the runway to which the instrument approach was conducted. (Refer to AIM)

***SIGMET*/WS/SIGNIFICANT METEOROLOGICAL INFORMATION—** A weather advisory issued concerning weather significant to the safety of all aircraft. SIGMET advisories cover severe and extreme turbulence, severe icing, and widespread dust or sandstorms that reduce visibility to less than 3 miles. (See AIRMET and Convective SIGMET) (Refer to AIM)

*ICAO—SIGMET INFORMATION—*Information prepared by a meteorological watch office regarding the occurrence or expected occurrence of one or more of the following phenomena:

1. At subsonic cruising levels:

   Active thunderstorm area.
   Tropical revolving storm.
   Severe line squall.
   Heavy hail.
   Severe turbulence.
   Severe icing.
   Marked mountain waves.
   Widespread sandstorm/duststorm.

2. At transonic levels and supersonic cruising levels:

   Moderate or severe turbulence.
   Cumulonimbus clouds.
   Hail

SIMPLIFIED DIRECTIONAL FACILITY/SDF— A NAVAID used for nonprecision instrument approaches. The final approach course is similar to that of an ILS localizer except that the SDF course may be offset from the runway, generally not more than 3 degrees, and the course may be wider than the localizer, resulting in a lower degree of accuracy. (Refer to AIM)

SIMULATED FLAMEOUT/SFO— A practice approach by a jet aircraft (normally military) at idle thrust to a runway. The approach may start at a relatively high altitude over a runway (high key) and may continue on a realtively high and wide downwind leg with a high rate of descent and a continuous turn to final. It terminates in a landing or low approach. The purpose of this approach is to simulate a flameout. (See Flameout)

SIMULTANEOUS ILS APPROACHES— An approach system permitting simultaneous ILS approaches to airports having parallel runways separated by at least 4,300 feet between centerlines. Integral parts of a total system are ILS, radar, communications, ATC procedures, and appropriate airborne equipment. (See Parallel Runways) (Refer to AIM)

SINGLE DIRECTION ROUTES— Preferred IFR Routes which are sometimes depicted on high altitude en route charts and which are normally flown in one direction only. (See Preferred IFR Route) (Refer to Airport/Facility Directory)

SINGLE FREQUENCY APPROACH/SFA— A service provided under a letter of agreement to military single-piloted turbojet aircraft which permits use of a single UHF frequency during approach for landing. Pilots will not normally be required to change frequency from the beginning of the approach to touchdown except that pilots conducting an en route descent are required to change frequency when control is transferred from the air route traffic control center to the terminal facility. The abbreviation "SFA" in the DOD FLIP IFR Supplement under "Communications" indicates this service is available at an aerodrome.

SINGLE-PILOTED AIRCRAFT— A military turbojet aircraft possessing one set of flight controls, tandem cockpits or two sets of flight controls but operated by one pilot is considered single-piloted by ATC when determining the appropriate air traffic service to be applied. (See Single Frequency Approach)

SLASH— A radar beacon reply displayed as an elongated target.

SLOW TAXI— To taxi a float plane at low power or low RPM.

SPEAK SLOWER— Used in verbal communications as a request to reduce speech rate.

SPECIAL EMERGENCY— A condition of air piracy, or other hostile act by a person(s) aboard an aircraft, which threatens the safety of the aircraft or its passengers.

SPECIAL IFR— (See Fixed-Wing Special IFR)

SPECIAL INSTRUMENT APPROACH PROCEDURE— (See Instrument Approach Procedure)

SPECIAL USE AIRSPACE— Airspace of defined dimensions identified by an area on the surface of the earth wherein activities must be confined because of their nature and/or wherein limitations may be imposed upon aircraft operations that are not a part of those activities. TYPES OF SPECIAL USE AIRSPACE:

1. Alert Area—Airspace which may contain a high volume of pilot training activities or an unusual type of aerial activity, neither of which is hazardous to aircraft. Alert Areas are depicted on aeronautical charts for the information of nonparticipating pilots. All activities within an Alert Area are conducted in accordance with Federal Aviation Regulations and pilots of participating aircraft as well as pilots transiting the area are equally responsible for collision avoidance.

2. Controlled Firing Area—Airspace wherein activities are conducted under conditions so controlled as to eliminate hazards to nonparticipating aircraft and to ensure the safety of persons and property on the ground.

3. Military Operations Area(MOA)—An MOA is an airspace assignment of defined vertical and lateral dimensions established outside positive control areas to separate/-segregate certain military activities from IFR traffic and to identify for VFR traffic where these activities are conducted. (Refer to AIM)

4. Prohibited Area—Designated airspace within which the flight of aircraft is prohibited. (Refer to En Route Charts, AIM).

5. Restricted Area—Airspace designated under FAR, Part 73, within which the flight of aircraft, while not wholly prohibited, is subject to restriction. Most restricted areas are designated joint use and IFR/VFR operations in the area may be authorized by the controlling ATC facility when it is not being utilized by the using agency. Restricted areas are depicted on en route charts. Where joint use is authorized, the name of the ATC controlling facility is also shown. (Refer to FAR, Part 73 and AIM)

6. Warning Area—Airspace which may contain hazards to nonparticipating aircraft in international airspace.

SPECIAL VFR CONDITIONS— Weather conditions in a control zone which are less than basic VFR and in which some aircraft are permitted flight under Visual Flight Rules. (See Special VFR Operations) (Refer to FAR Part 91)

SPECIAL VFR OPERATIONS— Aircraft operating in accordance with clearances within control zones in weather conditions less than the basic VFR weather minima. Such operations must be requested by the pilot and approved by ATC. (See Special VFR Conditions)

*ICAO—SPECIAL VFR FLIGHT—*A controlled VFR flight authorized by air traffic control to operate within a control zone under meteorological conditions below the visual meteorological conditions.

SPEED— (See Airspeed, Groundspeed)

SPEED ADJUSTMENT— An ATC procedure used to request pilots to adjust aircraft speed to a specific value for the purpose of providing desired spacing. Pilots are expected to maintain a speed of plus or minus 10 knots or 0.02 mach number of the specified speed.

Examples of speed adjustments are:

1. "Increase/reduce speed to mach point (number)."
2. "Increase/reduce speed to (speed in knots)" or "Increase/reduce speed (number of knots) knots."
3. "If practical, reduce speed to (speed);" or "If practical, reduce speed (number of) knots."

SPEED BRAKES/DIVE BRAKES— Moveable aerodynamic devices on aircraft that reduce airspeed during descent and landing.

SQUAWK (Mode, Code, Function)— Activate specific modes/codes/functions on the aircraft transponder, e.g., "Squawk three/alpha, two one zero five, low." (See Transponder)

STAGE I/II/III SERVICE— (See Terminal Radar Program)

STANDARD INSTRUMENT APPROACH PROCEDURE— (See Instrument Approach Procedure)

STANDARD INSTRUMENT DEPARTURE/SID— A preplanned instrument flight rule (IFR) air traffic control departure procedure printed for pilot use in graphic and/or textual form. SIDs provide transition from the terminal to the appropriate en route structure. (See IFR Takeoff Minima and Departure Procedures) (Refer to AIM)

STANDARD RATE TURN— A turn of three degrees per second.

STANDARD TERMINAL ARRIVAL/STAR— A preplanned instrument flight rule (IFR) air traffic control arrival procedure published for pilot use in graphic and/or textual form. STARs provide transition from the en route structure to an outer fix or an instrument approach fix/arrival waypoint in the terminal area.

STAND BY— Means the controller or pilot must pause for a few seconds, usually to attend to other duties of a higher priority. Also means to wait as in "stand by for clearance." If a delay is lengthy, the caller should reestablish contact.

STATIONARY RESERVATIONS— Altitude reservations which encompass activities in a fixed area. Stationary reservations may include activities such as special test of weapons systems or equipment, certain U.S. Navy carrier, fleet, and anti-submarine operations, rocket, missile and drone operations, and certain aerial refueling or similar operations.

STEPDOWN FIX— A fix permitting additional descent within a segment of an instrument approach procedure by identifying a point at which a controlling obstacle has been safely overflown.

STEP TAXI— To taxi a float plane at full power or high RPM.

STEP TURN— A maneuver used to put a float plane in a planing configuration prior to entering an active sea lane for takeoff. The STEP TURN maneuver should only be used upon pilot request.

STEREO ROUTE— A routinely used route of flight established by users and ARTCCs identified by a coded name, e.g., ALPHA 2. These routes minimize flight plan handling and communications.

STOP ALTITUDE SQUAWK— Used by ATC to inform an aircraft to turn-off the automatic altitude reporting feature of its transponder. It is issued when the verbally reported altitude varies 300 feet or more from the automatic altitude report. (See Altitude Readout, Transponder)

STOP AND GO— A procedure wherein an aircraft will land, make a complete stop on the runway, and then commence a takeoff from that point. (See Low Approach, Option Approach)

STOPOVER FLIGHT PLAN— A flight plan format which permits, in a single submission, the filing of a sequence of flight plans through interim full-stop destinations to a final destination.

STOP SQUAWK (Mode or Code)— Used by ATC to tell the pilot to turn specified functions of the aircraft transponder off. (See Stop Altitude Squawk, Transponder)

STOP STREAM/BURST/BUZZER— Used by ATC to request a pilot to suspend electronic countermeasure activity. (See Jamming)

STOPWAY— An area beyond the takeoff runway designated by the airport authorities as able to support an airplane during an aborted takeoff. (Refer to FAR Part 1)

STRAIGHT-IN APPROACH—IFR— An instrument approach wherein final approach is begun without first having executed a procedure turn, not necessarily completed with a straight-in landing or made to straight-in landing minimums. (See Straight-in Landing, Landing Minimums, Straight-in Approach-VFR)

STRAIGHT-IN APPROACH—VFR— Entry into the traffic pattern by interception of the extended runway centerline (final approach course) without executing any other portion of the traffic pattern. (See Traffic Pattern)

STRAIGHT-IN LANDING— A landing made on a runway aligned within 30° of the final approach course following completion of an instrument approach. (See Straight-in Approach-IFR)

STRAIGHT-IN LANDING MINIMUMS/STRAIGHT-IN MINIMUMS— (See Landing Minimums)

SUBSTITUTE ROUTE— A route assigned to pilots when any part of an airway or route is unusable because of NAVAID status. These routes consist of:

1. Substitute routes which are shown on U.S. Government Charts.

2. Routes defined by ATC as specific NAVAID radials or courses.

3. Routes defined by ATC as direct to or between NAVAIDs.

SUNSET AND SUNRISE— The mean solar times of sunset and sunrise as published in the Nautical Almanac, converted to local standard time for the locality concerned. Within Alaska, the end of evening civil twilight and the beginning of morning civil twilight, as defined for each locality.

SURVEILLANCE APPROACH— An instrument approach wherein the air traffic controller issues instructions, for pilot compliance, based on aircraft position in relation to the final approach course (azimuth), and the distance (range) from the end of the runway as displayed on the controller's radar scope. The controller will provide recommended altitudes on final approach if requested by the pilot. (See PAR Approach) (Refer to AIM)

SYSTEM STRATEGIC NAVIGATION (SN)— Military activity accomplished by navigating along a preplanned route using internal aircraft systems to maintain a desired track. This activity normally requires a lateral route width of 10NM and altitude range of 1,000 feet to 6,000 feet AGL with some route segments that permit terrain following.

TACAN-ONLY AIRCRAFT— An aircraft, normally military, possessing TACAN with DME but no VOR navigational system capability. Clearances must specify TACAN or VORTAC fixes and approaches.

TACTICAL AIR NAVIGATION/TACAN— An ultra-high frequency electronic rho-theta air navigation aid which provides suitably equipped aircraft a continuous indication of bearing and distance to the TACAN station. (See VORTAC) (Refer to AIM)

TARGET— The indication shown on a radar display resulting from a primary radar return or a radar beacon reply. (See Radar, Target Symbol)

ICAO—TARGET— In radar:

1. Generally, any discrete object which reflects or retransmits energy back to the radar equipment.

2. Specifically, an object of radar search or surveillance.

TARGET SYMBOL— A computer-generated indication shown on a radar display resulting from a primary radar return or a radar beacon reply.

TAXI— The movement of an airplane under its own power on the surface of an airport (FAR Part 135.100-Note). Also, it describes the surface movement of helicopters equipped with wheels. (See Air Taxi, Hover Taxi) (Refer to AIM)

TAXI INTO POSITION AND HOLD— Used by ATC to inform a pilot to taxi onto the departure runway in takeoff position and hold. It is not authorization for takeoff. It is used when takeoff clearance cannot immediately be issued because of traffic or other reasons. (See HOLD, CLEARED FOR TAKEOFF).

TAXI PATTERNS— Patterns established to illustrate the desired flow of ground traffic for the different runways or airport areas available for use.

TERMINAL AREA— A general term used to describe airspace in which approach control service or airport traffic control service is provided.

TERMINAL AREA FACILITY— A facility providing air traffic control service for arriving and departing IFR, VFR, Special VFR, Special IFR aircraft and on occasion, en route aircraft. (See Approach Control, Tower)

TERMINAL CONTROL AREA— (See Controlled Airspace)

TERMINAL RADAR PROGRAM— A national program instituted to extend the terminal radar services, provided IFR aircraft, to VFR aircraft. Pilot participation in the program is urged but is not mandatory. The program is divided into two parts and referred to as Stage II and Stage III. The Stage service provided at a particular location is contained in the Airport/Facility Directory.

1. Stage I originally comprised two basic radar services (traffic advisories and limited vectoring to VFR aircraft). These services are provided by all commissioned terminal radar facilities, but the term "Stage I" has been deleted from use.

2. Stage II/Radar Advisory and Sequencing for VFR Aircraft—Provides, in addition to the basic radar services, vectoring and sequencing on a full-time basis to arriving VFR aircraft. The purpose is to adjust the flow of arriving IFR and VFR aircraft into the traffic pattern in a safe and orderly manner and to provide traffic advisories to departing VFR aircraft.

3. Stage III/Radar Sequencing and Separation Service for VFR Aircraft—Provides, in addition to the basic radar

services and State II, separation between all participating VFR aircraft. The purpose is to provide separation between all participating VFR aircraft and all IFR aircraft operating within the airspace defined as a Terminal Radar Service Area (TRSA) or Terminal Control Area (TCA). (See Controlled Airspace, Terminal Radar Service Area) (Refer to AIM, Airport/Facility Directory)

TERMINAL RADAR SERVICE AREA/TRSA— Airspace surrounding designated airports wherein ATC provides radar vectoring, sequencing and separation on a full-time basis for all IFR and participating VFR aircraft. Service provided in a TRSA is called Stage III Service. AIM contains an explanation of TRSA. TRSAs are depicted on VFR aeronautical charts. Pilot participation is urged but is not mandatory. (See Terminal Radar Program) (Refer to AIM, Airport/Facility Directory)

TERRAIN FOLLOWING/TF— The flight of a military aircraft maintaining a constant AGL altitude above the terrain or the highest obstruction. The altitude of the aircraft will constantly change with the varying terrain and/or obstruction.

TETRAHEDRON— A device normally located on uncontrolled airports and used as a landing direction indicator. The small end of a tetrahedron points in the direction of landing. At controlled airports, the tetrahedron, if installed, should be disregarded because tower instructions supersede the indicator. (See Segmented Circle) (Refer to AIM)

THAT IS CORRECT— The understanding you have is right.

THRESHOLD— The beginning of that portion of the runway usable for landing. (See Airport Lighting, Displaced Threshold)

THRESHOLD CROSSING HEIGHT/TCH— The theoretical height above the runway threshold at which the aircraft's glide slope antenna would be if the aircraft maintains the trajectory establshed by the mean ILS glidepath. (See Glide Slope, Threshold)

THRESHOLD LIGHTS— (See Airport Lighting)

TIME GROUP— Four digits representing the hour and minutes from the 24-hour clock. Time groups without time zone indicators are understood to be GMT (Greenwich Mean Time); e.g., "0205." A time zone designator is used to indicate local time; e.g., "0205M." The end and beginning of the day are shown by "2400" and "0000", respectively.

TORCHING— The burning of fuel at the end of an exhaust pipe or stack of a reciprocating aircraft engine, the result of an excessive richness in the fuel air mixture.

TOUCH-AND-GO/TOUCH-AND-GO LANDING— An operation by an aircraft that lands and departs on a runway without stopping or exiting the runway.

TOUCHDOWN—

1. The point at which an aircraft first makes contact with the landing surface.
2. Concerning a precision radar approach (PAR), it is the point where the glide path intercepts the landing surface.

ICAO—TOUCHDOWN— The point where the nominal glide path intercepts the runway.

TOUCHDOWN RVR— (See Visibility)

TOUCHDOWN ZONE— The first 3,000 feet of the runway beginning at the threshold. The area is used for determination of Touchdown Zone Elevation in the deveopment of straight-in landing minimums for instrument approaches.

TOUCHDOWN ZONE ELEVATION/TDZE— The highest elevation in the first 3,000 feet of the landing surface. TDZE is indicated on the instrument approach procedure chart when straight-in landing minimums are authorized. (See Touchdown Zone)

TOUCHDOWN ZONE LIGHTING— (See Airport Lighting)

TOWER/AIRPORT TRAFFIC CONTROL TOWER— A terminal facility that uses air/ground communications, visual signaling, and other devices to provide ATC services to aircraft operating in the vicinity of an airport or on the movement area. Authorizes aircraft to land or takeoff at the airport controlled by the tower or to transit the airport traffic area regardless of flight plan or weather conditions (IFR or VFR). A tower may also provide approach control services (radar or nonradar). (See Airport Traffic Area, Airport Traffic Control Service, Approach Control/Approach Control Facility, Approach Control Service, Movement Area, Tower En Route Control Service/Tower to Tower) (Refer to AIM)

ICAO—AERODROME CONTROL TOWER— A unit established to provide air traffic control service to aerodrome traffic.

TOWER EN ROUTE CONTROL SERVICE/TOWER TO TOWER— The control of IFR en route traffic within delegated airspace between two or more adjacent approach control facilities. This service is designed to expedite traffic and reduce control and pilot communication requirements.

TPX 42— A numeric beacon decoder equipment/system. It is designed to be added to terminal radar systems for beacon decoding. It provides rapid target identification, reinforcement of the primary radar target, and altitude information from Mode C. (See Automated Radar Terminal Systems, Transponder)

TRACK— The actual flight path of an aircraft over the surface of the earth. (See Course, Route, Flight Path)

ICAO—TRACK— The projection on the earth's surface of the path of an aircraft, the direction of which path at any point is usually expressed in degrees from north (true, magnetic, or grid).

TRAFFIC—

1. A term used by a controller to transfer radar identification of an aircraft to another controller for the purpose of coordinating separation action. Traffic is normally issued (a) in response to a handoff or point out, (b) in anticipation of a handoff or point out, or (c) in conjunction with a request for control of an aircraft.

2. A term used by ATC to refer to one or more aircraft.

(Identification), TRAFFIC ALERT. ADVISE YOU TURN LEFT/RIGHT (specific heading if appropriate), AND/OR CLIMB/DESCEND (specific altitude if appropriate) IMMEDIATELY. (See Safety Advisory)

TRAFFIC ADVISORIES— Advisories issued to alert pilots to other known or observed air traffic which may be in such proximity to the position or intended route of flight of their aircraft to warrant his attention. Such advisories may be based on:

1. Visual observation.

2. Observation of radar identified and nonidentified aircraft targets on an ATC radar display, or

3. Verbal reports from pilots or other facilities.

The word "traffic" followed by additional information, if known, is used to provide such advisories; e.g., "Traffic, 2 o'clock, one zero miles, southbound, eight thousand."

Traffic advisory service will be provided to the extent possible depending on higher priority duties of the controller or other limitations, e.g., radar limitations, volume of traffic, frequency congestion or controller workload. Radar/nonradar traffic advisories do not relieve the pilot of his responsibility to see and avoid other aircraft. Pilots are cautioned that there are many times when the controller is not able to give traffic advisories concerning all traffic in the aircraft's proximity; in other words, when a pilot requests or is receiving traffic advisories, he should not assume that all traffic will be issued. (Refer to AIM, Radar Traffic Information Service)

TRAFFIC INFORMATION— (See Traffic Advisories)

TRAFFIC IN SIGHT— Used by pilots to inform a controller that previously issued traffic is in sight. (See Negative Contact, Traffic Advisories)

TRAFFIC NO LONGER A FACTOR— Indicates that the traffic described in a previously issued traffic advisory is no longer a factor.

TRAFFIC PATTERN— The traffic flow that is prescribed for aircraft landing at, taxiing on, or taking off from an airport. The components of a typical traffic pattern are upwind leg, crosswind leg, downwind leg, base leg and final approach.

1. Upwind Leg—A flight path parallel to the landing runway in the direction of landing.

2. Crosswind Leg—A flight path at right angles to the landing runway off its upwind end.

3. Downwind Leg—A flight path parallel to the landing runway in the direction opposite to landing. The downwind leg normally extends between the crosswind leg and the base leg.

4. Base Leg—A flight path at right angles to the landing runway off its approach end. The base leg normally extends from the downwind leg to the intersection of the extended runway centerline.

5. Final Approach—A flight path in the direction of landing along the extended runway centerline. The final approach normally extends from the base leg to the runway. An aircraft making a straight-in approach VFR is also considered to be on final approach.

(See Straight-In Approach-VFR, Taxi Patterns) (Refer to AIM, FAR Part 91)

ICAO—AERODROME TRAFFIC CIRCUIT— The specified path to be flown by aircraft operating in the vicinity of an aerodrome.

TRANSCRIBED WEATHER BROADCAST/TWEB— A continuous recording of meteorological and aeronautical information that is broadcast on L/MF and VOR facilities for pilots. (Refer to AIM)

TRANSFER OF CONTROL— That action whereby the responsibility for the separation of an aircraft is transferred from one controller to another.

ICAO—TRANSFER OF CONTROL— Transfer of responsibility for providing air traffic control service.

TRANSFERRING CONTROLLER/FACILITY— A controller/facility transferring control of an aircraft to another controller/facility.

ICAO—TRANSFERRING UNIT/CONTROLLER— Air Traffic Control Unit/Air Traffic Controller in the process of transferring the responsibility for providing air traffic control service to an aircraft to the next air traffic control unit/air traffic controller along the route of flight.

TRANSITION—

1. The general term that describes the change from one phase of flight or flight condition to another, e.g., transition from en route flight to the approach or transition from instrument flight to visual flight.

2. A published procedure (SID Transition) used to connect the basic SID to one of several en route airways/jet routes, or a published procedure (STAR Transition) used to connect one of several en route airways/jet routes to the basic STAR. (Refer to SID/STAR Charts)

TRANSITION AREA— (See Controlled Airspace)

TRANSMISSOMETER— An apparatus used to determine visibility by measuring the transmission of light through the atmosphere. It is the measurement source for determining runway visual range (RVR) and runway visibility value (RVV). (See Visibility)

TRANSMITTING IN THE BLIND/BLIND TRANS-MISSION— A transmission from one station to other stations in circumstances where two-way communication cannot be established, but where it is believed that the called stations may be able to receive the transmission.

TRANSPONDER— The airborne radar beacon receiver/-transmitter portion of the Air Traffic Control Radar Beacon System (ATCRBS) which automatically receives radio signals from interrogators on the ground, and selectively replies with a specific reply pulse or pulse group only to those interrogations being received on the mode to which it is set to respond. (See Interrogator) (Refer to AIM)

*ICAO—TRANSPONDER—*A receiver/transmitter which will generate a reply signal upon proper interrogation; the interrogation and reply being on different frequencies.

TURBOJET AIRCRAFT— An aircraft having a jet engine in which the energy of the jet operates a turbine which in turn operates the air compressor.

TURBOPROP AIRCRAFt— An aircraft having a jet engine in which the energy of the jet operates a turbine which drives the propeller.

T-VOR/TERMINAL-VERY HIGH FREQUENCY OMNI-DIRECTIONAL RANGE STATION— A very high frequency terminal omnirange station located on or near an airport and used as an approach aid. (See Navigational Aid, VOR)

TWO WAY RADIO COMMUNICATIONS FAILURE— (See Lost Communications)

ULTRAHIGH FREQUENCY/UHF— The frequency band between 300 and 3,000 MHz. The bank of radio frequencies used for military air/ground voice communications. In some instances this may go as low as 225 MHz and still be referred to as UHF.

UNABLE— Indicates inability to comply with a specific instruction, request, or clearance.

UNCONTROLLED AIRSPACE— Uncontrolled airspace is that portion of the airspace that has not been designated as continental control area, control area, control zone, terminal control area, or transition area and within which ATC has neither the authority nor the responsibility for exercising control over air traffic. (See Controlled Airspace)

UNDER THE HOOD— Indicates that the pilot is using a hood to restrict visibility outside the cockpit while simulating instrument flight. An appropriately rated pilot is required in the other control seat while this operation is being conducted. (Refer to FAR Part 91)

UNICOM— A nongovernment communication facility which may provide airport information at certain airports. Locations and frequencies of UNICOMs are shown on aeronautical charts and publications. (Refer to AIM, Airport/Facility Directory.

UNPUBLISHED ROUTE— A route for which no minimum altitude is published or charted for pilot use. It may include a direct route between NAVAIDS, a radial, a radar vector, or a final approach course beyond the segments of an instrument approach procedure. (See Published Route, Route)

UPWIND LEG— (See Traffic Pattern)

URGENCY— A condition of being concerned about safety, and of requiring timely but not immediate assistance; a potential Distress condition.

*ICAO—URGENCY—*A condition concerning the safety of an aircraft or other vehicle, or of person on board or in sight, but which does not require immediate assistance.

VECTOR— A heading issued to an aircraft to provide navigational guidance by radar.

*ICAO—RADAR VECTORING—*Provision of navigational guidance to aircraft in the form of specific headings, based on the use of radar.

VERIFY— Request confirmation of information; e.g., "verify assigned altitude."

VERIFY SPECIFIC DIRECTION OF TAKEOFF (OR TURNS AFTER TAKEOFF)— Used by ATC to ascertain an aircraft's direction of takeoff and/or direction of turn after takeoff. It is normally used for IFR departures from an airport not having a control tower. When direct communication with the pilot is not possible, the request and information may be relayed through an FSS, dispatcher, or by other means. (See IFR Takeoff Minimums and Departure Procedures.)

VERTICAL SEPARATION— Separation established by assignment of different altitudes or flight levels. (See Separation)

ICAO—VERTICAL SEPARATION—Separation between aircraft expressed in units of vertical distance.

VERTICAL TAKEOFF AND LANDING AIRCRAFT/VTOL AIRCRAFT— Aircraft capable of vertical climbs and/or descents and of using very short runways or small areas for takeoff and landings. These aircraft include, but are not limited to, helicopters. (See Short Takeoff and Landing Aircraft)

VERY HIGH FREQUENCY/VHF— The frequency band between 30 and 300 MHz. Portions of this band, 108 to 118 MHz, are used for certain NAVAIDS; 118 to 136 MHz are used for civil air/ground voice communications. Other frequencies in this band are used for purposes not related to air traffic control.

VERY LOW FREQUENCY/VLF— The frequency band between 3 and 30 kHz.

VFR AIRCRAFT/VFR FLIGHT— An aircraft conducting flight in accordance with visual flight rules. (See Visual Flight Rules)

VFR CONDITIONS— Weather conditions equal to or better than the minimum for flight under visual flight rules. The term may be used as an ATC clearance/instruction only when:

1. An IFR aircraft requests a climb/descent in VFR conditions.
2. The clearance will result in noise abatement benefits where part of the IFR departure route does not conform to an FAA approved noise abatement route or altitude.
3. A pilot has requested a practice instrument approach and is not on an IFR flight plan.

All pilots receiving this authorization must comply with the VFR visibility and distance from cloud criteria in FAR Part 91. Use of the term does not relieve controllers of their responsibility to separate aircraft in TCAs/TRSAs as required by FAA Handbook 7110.65. When used as an ATC clearance/instruction, the term may be abbreviated "VFR;" e.g., "MAINTAIN VFR," "CLIMB/DESCEND VFR," etc.

VFR-ON-TOP— ATC authorization for an IFR aircraft to operate in VFR conditions at any appropriate VFR altitude (as specified in FAR and as restricted by ATC). A pilot receiving this authorization must comply with the VFR visibility, distance from cloud criteria, and the minimum IFR altitudes specified in FAR Part 91. The use of this term does not relieve controllers of their responsibility to separate aircraft in TCAs/TRSAs as required by FAA Handbook 7110.65.

VFR MILITARY TRAINING ROUTES (VR)— Routes used by the Department of Defense and associated Reserve and Air Guard units for the purpose of conducting low-altitude navigation and tactical training under VFR below 10,000 feet MSL at airspeeds in excess of 250 knots IAS.

VFR NOT RECOMMENDED— An advisory provided by a flight service station to a pilot during a preflight or inflight weather briefing that flight under visual flight rules is not recommended. To be given when the current and/or forecasted weather conditions are at or below VFR minimums. It does not abrogate the pilot's authority to make his own decision.

VIDEO MAP— An electronically displayed map on the radar display that may depict data such as airports, heliports, runway centerline extensions, hospital emergency landing areas, NAVAIDS and fixes, reporting points, airway/route centerlines, boundaries, handoff points, special use tracks, obstructions, prominent geographic features, map alignment indicators, range accuracy marks, minimum vectoring altitudes.

VISIBILITY— The ability, as determined by atmospheric conditions and expressed in units of distance, to see and identify prominent unlighted objects by day and prominent lighted objects by night. Visibility is reported as statute miles, hundreds of feet or meters. (Refer to FAR Part 91, AIM)

1. Flight Visibility—The average forward horizontal distance, from the cockpit of an aircraft in flight, at which prominent unlighted objects may be seen and identified by day and prominent lighted objects may be seen and identified by night.

ICAO—Flight Visibility—The visibility forward from the cockpit of an aircraft in flight.

2. Ground Visibility—Prevailing horizontal visibility near the earth's surface as reported by the United States National Weather Service or an accredited observer.

ICAO—Ground Visibility—The visibility at an aerodrome as reported by an accredited observer.

3. Prevailing Visibility—The greatest horizontal visibility equaled or exceeded throughout at least half the horizon circle which need not necessarily be continuous.

4. Runway Visibility Value/RVV—The visibility determined for a particular runway by a transmissometer. A meter provides a continuous indication of the visibility (reported in miles or fractions of miles) for the runway. RVV is used in lieu of prevailing visibility in determining minimums for a particular runway.

5. Runway Visual Range/RVR—An instrumentally derived value, based on standard calibrations, that represents the horizontal distance a pilot will see down the runway from the approach end. It is based on the sighting of either high intensity runway lights or on the visual contrast of other targets whichever yields the greater visual range. RVR, in contrast to prevailing or

runway visibility, is based on what a pilot in a moving aircraft should see looking down the runway. RVR is horizontal visual range, not slant visual range. It is based on the measurement of a transmissometer made near the touchdown point of the instrument runway and is reported in hundred of feet. RVR is used in lieu of RVV and/or prevailing visibility in determining minimums for a particular runway.

a. Touchdown RVR—The RVR visibility readout values obtained from RVR equipment serving the runway touchdown zone.

b. MID RVR—The RVR readout values obtained from RVR equipment located midfield of the runway.

c. Rollout RVR—The RVR readout values obtained from RVR equipment located nearest the rollout end of the runway.

ICAO—Runway Visual Range—The maximum distance in the direction of takeoff or landing at which the runway or the specified lights or markers delineating it can be seen from a position above a specified point on its centerline at a height corresponding to the average eye-level of pilots at touchdown.

VISUAL APPROACH— An approach wherein an aircraft on an IFR flight plan, operating in VFR conditions under the control of an air traffic control facility and having an air traffic control authorization, may proceed to the airport of destination in VFR conditions.

ICAO—VISUAL APPROACH—An approach by an IFR flight when either part of all of an instrument approach procedure is not completed and the approach is executed in visual reference to terrain.

VISUAL APPROACH SLOPE INDICATOR— (See Airport Lighting)

VISUAL DESCENT POINT/VDP— A defined point on the final approach course of a nonprecision straight-in approach procedure from which normal descent from the MDA to the runway touchdown point may be commenced, provided the approach threshold of that runway, or approach lights, or other markings identifiable with the approach end of that runway are clearly visible to the pilot.

VISUAL FLIGHT RULES/VFR— Rules that govern the procedures for conducting flight under visual conditions. The term "VFR" is also used in the United States to indicate weather conditions that are equal to or greater than minimum VFR requirements. In addition, it is used by pilots and controllers to indicate type of flight plan. (See Instrument Flight Rules, Instrument Meteorological Conditions, Visual Meteorological Conditions) (Refer to FAR Part 91, AIM)

VISUAL HOLDING— The holding of aircraft at selected, prominent, geographical fixes which can be easily recognized from the air. (See Hold, Holding Fixes)

VISUAL METEOROLOGICAL CONDITIONS/VMC— Meteorological conditions expressed in terms of visibility, distance from cloud, and ceiling equal to or better than specified minima. (See Instrument Flight Rules, Instrument Meteorological Conditions, Visual Flight Rules)

VISUAL SEPARATION— A means employed by ATC to separate aircraft in terminal areas. There are two ways to effect this separation:

1. The tower controller sees the aircraft involved and issues instructions, as necessary, to ensure that the aircraft avoid each other.

2. A pilot sees the other aircraft involved and upon instructions from the controller provides his own separation by maneuvering his aircraft as necessary to avoid it. This may involve following another aircraft or keeping it in sight until it is no longer a factor. (See See and Avoid) (Refer to FAR Part 91)

VORTAC/VHF OMNIDIRECTIONAL RANGE/TACTICAL AIR NAVIGATION— A navigation aid providing VOR azimuth, TACAN azimuth, and TACAN distance measuring equipment (DME) at one site. (See Distance Measuring Equipment, Navigational Aid TACAN, VOR) (Refer to AIM)

VORTICES/WING TIP VORTICES— Circular patterns of air created by the movement of an airfoil through the air when generating lift. As an airfoil moves through the atmosphere in sustained flight, an area of low pressure is created above it. The air flowing from the high pressure area to the low pressure area around and about the tips of the airfoil tends to roll up into two rapidly rotating vortices, cylindrical in shape. These vortices are the most predominant parts of aircraft wake turbulence and their rotational force is dependent upon the wing loading, gross weight, and speed of the generating aircraft. The vortices from medium to heavy aircraft can be of extremely high velocity and hazardous to smaller aircraft. (See Aircraft Classes Wake Turbulence) (Refer to AIM)

VOR/VERY HIGH FREQUENCY OMNIDIRECTIONAL RANGE STATION— A ground-based electronic navigation aid transmitting very high frequency navigation signals, 360 degrees in azimuth, oriented from magnetic north. Used as the basis for navigation in the National Airspace System. The VOR periodically identifies itself by Morse Code and may have an additional voice identification feature. Voice features may be used by ATC or FSS for transmitting instructions/information to pilots. (See Navigational Aid) (Refer to AIM)

VOT/VOR TEST SIGNAL— A ground facility which emits a test signal to check VOR receiver accuracy. Some VOT's are available to the user while airborne, and others are limited to ground use only. (Refer to FAR Part 91, AIM, Airport/Facility Directory)

WAKE TURBULENCE— Phenomena resulting from the passage of an aircraft through the atmosphere. The term includes vortices, thrust stream turbulence, jet blast, jet wash, propeller wash and rotor wash, both on the ground and in the air. (See Aircraft Classes, Jet Blast, Vortices) (Refer to AIM)

WARNING AREA— (See Special Use Airspace)

WAYPOINT— (See Area Navigation)

WEATHER ADVISORY/INFLIGHT WEATHER AD-VISORY— (See SIGMET, AIRMET)

WEATHER ADVISORY/WS/WST/WA/CWA— In aviation weather forecast practice, an expression of hazardous weather conditions not predicted in the area forecast, as they affect the operation of air traffic and as prepared by the NWS.

WHEN ABLE— When used in conjunction with ATC instructions, gives the pilot the latitude to delay compliance until a condition or event has been reconciled. Unlike "pilot discretion," when instructions are prefaced "when able," the pilot is expected to seek the first opportunity to comply. Once a maneuver has been initiated, the pilot is expected to continue until the specifications of the instructions have been met. "When able," should not be used when expeditious compliance is required.

WILCO— I have received your message, understand it, and will comply with it.

WIND SHEAR— A change in wind speed and/or wind direction in a short distance resulting in a tearing or shearing effect. It can exist in a horizontal or vertical direction and occasionally in both.

WORDS TWICE—

1. As a request: "Communication is difficult, Please say every phrase twice."
2. As information: "Since communications are difficult, every phrase in this message will be spoken twice."

THE COMPLETE PRIVATE PILOT

Appendix B

THE COMPLETE PRIVATE PILOT
GLOSSARY

Pronounceable acronyms will be in **bold italic**: all others are spoken as individual letters (e.g. FAA).

ADF: automatic direction finder; a receiver with an associated indicator which points to the transmitting station.

aerodynamics: the study of the forces acting on bodies moving through the air.

advection: horizontal movement of air.

A/FD: Airport/Facility Directory.

AGL: above ground level.

agonic line: the line of zero magnetic variation.

ailerons: movable control surfaces at the outer trailing edge of each wing. They control the airplane in rolling around the longitudinal axis of the airplane.

AIM: Airman's Information Manual.

airfoil: a shape designed to develop lift by accelerating airflow over its surface.

AIRMET: a broadcast of weather hazardous to light aircraft.

Airport Advisory Area: an area within 10 miles of an airport with a Flight Service Station.

Airport/Facility Directory (A/FD): a government publication containing information on all airports, including radio frequencies and navigational aids available.

Airport Traffic Area — a cylinder of airspace 5 statute miles in radius and 3,000' high centered on an airport with an *operating* control tower.

airspeed indicator: an instrument which measures the pressure difference between the pitot and static inputs and is calibrated in speed units.

altimeter: an instrument which indicates altitude by measuring changes in atmospheric pressure.

altimeter setting: a value received from a ground station to which the altimeter setting window must be adjusted to correct for pressure variations.

ammeter: a meter which indicates the output of the generator or alternator in amperes, the unit of electric current.

amphibian: an airplane able to land and takeoff on both land and water. Airplanes with boat hulls (and retractable wheels) and float planes (with retractable wheels) are amphibians.

angle of attack: the angle between the chord line and the relative wind; the pilot's best means of controlling lift development.

Angle of incidence: the fixed angle at which the wing is attached to the fuselage; the angle between the chord line and the longitudinal axis.

arm: the distance a weight is located from a fulcrum or datum point.

ARSA: Airport Radar Service Area: an area where pilots must maintain two-way communication with the controlling agency, and where radar service is available to VFR pilots.

ATA: Actual time of arrival. To be filled in on your flight log and compared with your estimates to determine how the actual flight is progressing.

ATC: Air Traffic Control.

ATE: actual time enroute.

ATIS: Automatic Terminal Information Service. A recorded broadcast of non-control information at busy airports.

attitude: the position of the airplane's nose or wings in relation to the natural horizon.

axis of control: an imaginary line around which the pilot controls the airplane.

bleed air: compressed air "bled" from the turbocharger to operate pressurization, cabin heating, and de-icing systems.

calibrated airspeed: the reading of the airspeed indicator, corrected for installation or position error.

camber: the convexity or curvature of an airfoil from its chord.

carburetor: a device which mixes a metered amount of fuel with airflow, atomizing it for combustion.

CDI: course deviation indicator. The "needle" on a VOR display that tells you if you are on the desired radial.

center of gravity: that part of a body (an airplane, in this case) about which all forces are balanced.

center of lift: the single point on the wing where all lifting forces are resolved (concentrated).

Certificate of Airworthiness: a certificate awarded at the time of manufacture which is kept current by compliance with maintenance and inspection requirements.

chord line: an imaginary line from the leading edge to the trailing edge of an airfoil.

coefficient of lift: a complex element of the lift formula which includes angle of attack as one component.

Compressor Discharge Temperature gauge: an instrument which monitors the temperature of the air being discharged from the compressor into the intake manifold of a turbocharged engine.

controllable pitch propeller: a propeller with two (or more) blades, joined at the hub and capable of having the blade angle changed in flight by a governor to maintain a constant engine speed.

controlled airport: an airport with an operating control tower.

control yoke: the control the pilot uses to pitch and roll the airplane; older airplanes used a "stick," and this term continues in use today.

convection: vertical movement of air.

Coriolis Force: a force generated by the rotation of the earth that deflects the gradient wind to the right in the Northern Hemisphere.

course: a line connecting two points on a planned flight.

cowling: the smooth metal or fiberglass enclosure surrounding the engine. The cowling streamlines the engine compartment and directs cooling air over the engine.

crosswind component — that portion of the total wind which tends to drift the airplane sideways.

CTAF: Common Traffic Advisory Frequency. A frequency used at uncontrolled airports by all airplanes operating at that airport; also, a frequency to be used at a controlled airport when the tower is not in operation.

cylinder head temperature gauge: an instrument which monitors the temperature of the cylinder head itself. It is a better guide to general engine overheating than is the oil temperature gauge.

density: weight per unit volume. A cubic foot of air that weighs two pounds is more dense than a cubic foot of air that weighs one pound.

detonation: the explosive burning of the fuel/air mixture in the cylinder, as opposed to smooth burning. Detonation can result in destructive forces in a matter of seconds.

deviation: a compass error caused by magnetic influences within the airplane which varies with magnetic heading.

dewpoint: the temperature at which an air mass becomes saturated with moisture.

displaced threshold — a threshold moved down the runway so that landing aircraft will clear obstructions in the approach path.

DME: Distance Measuring Equipment. DME operates in the UHF range and is limited to line-of-sight. It measures slant range between an airplane and a VORTAC or VOR-DME.

duplex: transmitting on one frequency while receiving on another.

EFAS: enroute flight advisory service (Flight Watch); a weather-only position at a flight service station.

elevator: a hinged surface at the rear of the horizontal stabilizer with which the pilot controls the airplane around the lateral (pitch) axis.

ELT: Emergency Locator Transmitter. A VHF/UHF transmitter designed to be turned on by impact and to transmit a signal to searchers.

empennage: the horizontal stabilizer, elevator, rudder, and vertical fin, or any combination thereof to control the airplane in pitch and bank.

ETA: estimated time of arrival.

ETE: estimated time enroute.

exhaust gas temperature gauge: an instrument used for proper leaning of the mixture. If the mixture contains too much fuel or too much air, the exhaust gas temperature will be lower than peak. (Use the manufacturer's recommended EGT setting.)

FA: an area weather forecast.

FAR: Federal Aviation Regulations.

FD: a winds-and-temperatures aloft forecast.

fixed-pitch propeller: a propeller which is forged from one solid piece of metal or laminated from several plies of wood, with a fixed "pitch" or blade angle.

flaps: hinged surfaces at the trailing edge of the wing which are deflected symmetrically to lower the stalling speed and allow for a steeper angle of descent while on a landing approach.

flight following: a workload-permitting service which ATC radar facilities provide to VFR pilots.

Flight Service Station (FSS): air traffic facilities which provide pilot briefing, enroute communications, and many other services to pilots.

Flight Watch: another name of Enroute Flight Advisory Service, a weather-information-only service of the Flight Service Station.

front: where two air masses with different properties meet.

FT: a terminal weather forecast.

fuel injection: an induction system which delivers a metered amount of fuel to each cylinder.

fuselage: the main body of the airplane to which the wings and empennage are attached. Passenger and crew seating is in the fuselage.

G: the force of gravity: one times the weight of an object.

GPO: Government Printing Office.

gradient wind, gradient force: the wind (and the force that drives it) caused solely by pressure differences.

Great Circle: an imaginary circle on the face of the earth cut by a plane which passes through the center of the earth. All meridians are Great Circles, and the Equator is a Great Circle.

ground controller: an air traffic control specialist in a control tower who controls operations on the ramps and taxiways of a controlled airport.

ground effect: a reduction in induced drag experienced when the wing is within one-half the wing span of the ground.

gyroscopic precession: a slow movement of the axis of a spinning body. Noticeable in gyroscopic heading indicators as a drift away from agreement with the magnetic compass.

heading: the direction in which the airplane is pointing. When correcting for wind drift, the heading will differ from the course by several degrees.

headwind component — that portion of the reported wind which opposes the forward motion of the airplane.

homing: navigating to a non-directional beacon by simply keeping the ADF needle pointed directly to the nose of the airplane.

Horizontal Situation Indicator (HSI): an instrument which incorporates a heading indicator and an omni indicator to show the pilot the airplane's position in relation to a VOR radial as seen from a point above the airplane.

horizontal stabilizer: an airfoil-shaped surface at the rear of the airplane which develops a negative lift force to balance (stabilize) the airplane's pitch attitude.

indicated airspeed: what the airspeed indicator reads, uncorrected for position and installation error. See calibrated airspeed.

induced drag: drag which is the inevitable result of lift generation. Induced drag increases with increased angle of attack, and is greatest at the low speeds which require large angles of attack.

International Standard Atmosphere (ISA): see standard day.

inversion: when warm air overlies cold air. The reverse of a stable condition.

isobars: lines of equal barometric pressure on a weather map.

isogonic lines: lines of equal magnetic variation.

KHz: Kilohertz (thousands of cycles per second); a measure of radio frequency.

knot: one nautical mile per hour. It is redundant to say "90 knots per hour."

Kollsman window: the altimeter setting window.

landing gear: the two main wheels and the nose-wheel (or tailwheel).

loadmeter: an ammeter which is calibrated to indicate the electrical load on the alternator in amperes.

longitudinal axis: an imaginary line from the nose to the tail of the airplane.

lateral axis: a line drawn from wingtip to wingtip.

Loran-C: a long-range navigation system using very low frequency transmissions.

magnetic bearing: the direction to or from a transmitting station measured in relation to magnetic north.

magnetic compass: a direction-indicating device that reacts to the earth's magnetic field.

Magnetic North: the direction to the magnetic North Pole, located in Northern Canada.

magneto: a self-powered source of ignition using fixed magnets.

manifold: a pipe with several lateral outlets. In an airplane, the intake manifold delivers the fuel/air mixture to the cylinders, and the exhaust manifold collects the exhaust from the cylinders and pipes it overboard or through a turbocharger.

manifold pressure: an indirect measure of power output, obtained by measuring the pressure of the air in the intake manifold. The higher the pressure, the greater the power output of the engine.

MAYDAY: the voice equivalent of SOS. Used to declare an emergency.

meridians: lines of longitude. They run from pole to pole and are all the same length; each degree of latitude measured along a line of longitude equals 60 nautical miles.

MHz: Megahertz (millions of cycles per second); a measure of radio frequency.

Mode A: the "location only" mode of a transponder.

Mode C: the "ALT" position on the transponder function switch. If an encoding altimeter is installed, Mode C will transmit your altitude to the ground radar facility.

moment: the product of a distance times a weight, used in loading calculations.

nautical mile: one minute of latitude; 6,080 feet (rounded off to 6,000 feet for convenience).

navaid: short for navigational aid.

NDB: non-directional beacon, used for navigation with an automatic direction finder.

northerly turning error: an error in the magnetic compass induced by the vertical component of the earth's magnetic field.

NTSB: National Transportation Safety Board.

NWS: National Weather Service, the source of all government weather information.

OBS: omni-bearing selector; used in VOR navigation to select radials.

occlusion: a type of weather front formed when a cold front overtakes a warm front.

omnidirectional: visible or usable in all directions.

orographic: induced by the presence of mountains.

overrun — a stabilized area of pavement, not used for normal operations, at the end of a runway.

P-factor: a force which causes a left-turning tendency at low speed and high power in airplanes with propellers which turn clockwise.

parallels: lines of latitude, which are parallel from the Equator to the poles.

parasite drag: drag that does not contribute to lift generation; drag caused by landing gear, struts, cooling intakes, antennas, rivet heads, etc.

pilotage: navigation from point to point by ground reference.

PIREPS: pilot reports of inflight weather.

pitch axis: an imaginary line drawn from wingtip to wingtip; also, lateral axis.

pitot-static system: a pressure-measuring system that provides input to the airspeed indicator, altimeter, and vertical speed indicator.

pitot tube: a forward facing tube or aperture that measures ram air pressure and delivers that pressure to the airspeed indicator.

position lights: the red, green, and white lights required for night flight.

radial: a line FROM a VOR station. Radials used as airways are printed in blue on sectional charts.

region of reversed command: that area in the power/airspeed relationship where it takes more power to go more slowly, and less power to increase speed.

relative bearing: the direction to a transmitting station measured clockwise from the nose of the airplane.

relative wind: wind caused by motion. A moving body experiences relative wind in calm air.

rich mixture: one with more than one part of fuel to fifteen of air.

RMI: radio magnetic indicator; a combination heading indicator, VOR indicator, and ADF indicator.

RNAV: area navigation; a random-route method of navigation using VORTACs and VOR-DMEs.

roll axis: an imaginary line from nose to tail; also, longitudinal axis.

rudder: a hinged surface at the rear of the vertical fin with which the pilot controls the airplane around the yaw axis.

SA: an hourly weather sequence report.

SIGMET: a broadcast of weather hazardous to all aircraft.

simplexing: communication where one person must complete a transmission before the other person can begin; transmitting and receiving on the same frequency.

stall: loss of lift caused by exceeding the critical angle of attack and destroying the smooth flow of air over an airfoil.

standard day: sea level altitude, a temperature of 15°C or 59°F and a barometric pressure of 29.92" Hg. (1013.2 mb).

static: at rest or in equilibrium; not dynamic or moving.

static source: a point on the airplane where no air pressure is exerted as a result of movement through the air; a reference input for the airspeed indicator; the source of air pressure change information for the altimeter and vertical speed indicator.

statute mile: a 5,280 foot mile.

struts: supports. The main landing gear and nosewheel have struts to absorb the shock of landing. Wing struts are braced to the fuselage to support the wing and help absorb any wing movement in relation to the fuselage when landing or in turbulence. Low wing airplanes and some high wing airplanes have no external bracing.

tachometer: an instrument which reads revolutions per minute: used on bicycles and automobiles as well as airplanes.

TCA: Terminal Control Area. An airspace division which requires a clearance from Air Traffic Control for entry.

threshold — the beginning of the landing surface at the approach end of a runway.

TO-FROM indicator: used in VOR navigation to tell the pilot whether the selected radial is the direction TO or FROM the transmitter; also, ambiguity indicator.

torque: a twisting force. Used as a term of convenience in flight instruction to incorporate several forces which combine to create a left-turning tendency.

tower controller: an air traffic control specialist in a control tower who controls operations on the active runway and in the airport traffic area. (Also "local controller.")

track: the actual path over the ground followed by an airplane.

trailing edge: the sharp edge of the wing; flaps and ailerons are hinged at the trailing edge of the wing.

transponder: a UHF transmitter which replies to coded inquiries from ground radar stations, giving your position and possibly your altitude for identification and traffic separation purposes.

trim tabs: small adjustable tabs on control surfaces (elevator, rudder, and ailerons) used by the pilot to relieve control forces. Typically, the tab moves opposite to desired control surface movement; deflecting the elevator trim tab downward causes the elevator to move upward.

TRSA: Radar Service Area: an area where radar service is available to VFR pilots on a voluntary basis; outlined in magenta on sectional charts.

true airspeed: indicated airspeed corrected for temperature and pressure altitude.

true airspeed indicator: an airspeed indicator which allows the pilot to set temperature and altitude values and read true airspeed directly.

True North Pole: the northern extremity of the earth's axis; where all of the lines of longitude meet.

true wind: the actual movement of air over the earth's surface.

turbocharged: an engine with intake air compressed by a turbine-driven compressor.

TWEB: a transcribed weather broadcast.

uncontrolled airport: an airport without a control tower, or an airport with a tower outside of the tower's hours of operation.

UNICOM: an acronym for Universal Communications. Also, Aeronautical Advisory Service, a radio service operated by individuals at airports to provide services to pilots. Not used for air traffic control purposes.

UHF: Ultra-high Frequency range, 300 MHz to 3,000 MHz. Used for DME and some radar equipment.

variation: the angular difference between measurements in relation to true north and magnetic north. Variation is independent of aircraft heading.

VASI: Visual approach slope indicator. A means of providing approach slope guidance to VFR pilots.

vector: a heading to steer, received from a controller.

venturi: a tube with a restriction which accelerates air and reduces pressure; venturis are used in carburetors and are used on older airplanes to deliver vacuum to power flight instruments.

vertical axis: an imaginary line through the center of gravity which intersects the lateral and longitudinal axes; also, yaw axis.

vertical fin: a fixed vertical airfoil at the rear of the airplane which stabilizes the airplane in the vertical axis.

vertical speed indicator: an instrument which indicates rate of change in altitude by measuring rate of change of air pressure.

VFR: Visual Flight Rules.

VHF: Very High Frequency range. 30 MHz to 300 MHz. Range limited to line-of-sight.

VHF/DF: Very High Frequency Direction Finding; a service available at some Flight Service Stations to orient lost pilots. No equipment other than a transmitter and a receiver is required in order to use this service.

vortex: a mass of air having a whirling or circular motion. Plural: vortices.

VOR: VHF omni-directional range. The basis for the airways system.

VOR-DME: the civilian equivalent of a VORTAC, with both navigation and distance measuring signals under the control of the FAA.

VORTAC: A VOR co-located with a military TACAN (tactical aid to navigations) station. Civilians use the navigational signal from the VOR and the distance information from the TACAN.

VOT: a special transmitter located at major airports to test VOR receivers for accuracy.

wind correction angle: the angular difference between course and heading.

wind drift: the sideways motion over the ground caused by a crosswind.

wind triangle: a graphic means of computing wind correction angle and groundspeed.

yaw axis: a vertical line through the center of gravity; the pilot uses rudder to control the airplane around the yaw axis.

yaw axis: a vertical line through the center of gravity which intersects the longitudinal and lateral axes.

ZULU time: time in relation to the time at Greenwich, England, or Greenwich Mean Time.

THE COMPLETE

PRIVATE PILOT

Appendix C

INDEX
for
THE COMPLETE PRIVATE PILOT TEXT BOOK